THE
ORGANIZATIONAL
WEAPON

THE ORGANIZATIONAL WEAPON

A Study of Bolshevik Strategy and Tactics

by

PHILIP SELZNICK

with 2014 Foreword by Martin Krygier

qp

Classics of the Social Sciences

QUID PRO BOOKS
New Orleans, Louisiana

Previously published in 1952 by McGraw-Hill (RAND series), New York, and in 1960 by the Free Press, Glencoe, Illinois.

Published in 2014 by Quid Pro Books.

ISBN 978-1-61027-272-8 (pbk)
ISBN 978-1-61027-275-9 (ebk)

QUID PRO, LLC
5860 Citrus Blvd., Suite D-101
New Orleans, Louisiana 70123
www.quidprobooks.com

This new presentation of Philip Selznick's *The Organizational Weapon* is part of a series, *Classics of the Social Sciences*, which includes several of his early works, with new introductions. Proceeds from his books in the Series benefit the Jurisprudence & Social Policy Program, University of California at Berkeley. This is an authorized and unabridged republication of the original work.

Publisher's Cataloging-in-Publication

Selznick, Philip, 1919–2010

    The organizational weapon : a study of Bolshevik strategy and tactics / Philip Selznick.

        p. cm. — (Classics of the social sciences)

    Includes bibliographical references and index.

    ISBN 978-1-61027-272-8 (pbk)

1. Communism. 2. Political organizations. 3. Bolshevism. I. Title. II. Series.

HX56 .S45 2014   2014238455

Cover image based on artwork "Old Communism Poster" copyright © by the Shutterstock contributor FourB, used by permission.

For

MARTIN D. and HERBERT G.

Affectionately

CONTENTS

Foreword • 2014

Philip Selznick published *The Organizational Weapon: A Study of Bolshevik Strategy and Tactics*, in 1952. It was republished in 1960. On this, its second republication, an obvious question occurs: why now? Why should anyone reissue an old book, about a movement which—after a lively presence, to be sure—was scuppered some thirty years ago? The question is worth asking and there are several compelling answers to it. I suggest four: the world-historical significance of the movement the book analyzes; the particular combination of political understanding and engagement with theoretical sophistication which Selznick brought to his subject; the distinctive focus and character of the analysis; and its continuing significance, in relation both to enduring social problems and to the *oeuvre* of a distinguished and distinctive thinker. On each of these levels, this book is exemplary. I will take them in turn.

I

In a felicitous phrase, Eric Hobsbawm dubbed the period 1914-1991 (others choose 1989) 'the short twentieth century'.[1] As the start of that century, of course, they had in mind the First World War and the literally shocking transformations it unleashed. For it was like nothing that preceded it. The scale of carnage, with its sixteen million killed and twenty million more casualties, buried the optimism of the nineteenth century—and, for many, even the possibility of optimism. It shredded the map of Europe, stripping it of much that had been around, as if natural and irremovable, for centuries. New players arose as a direct result of the war, none more consequential than Soviet Russia. Among other things, without July 1914 no October 1917.

Though the Revolution was catalyzed by the War, however, victory came to a revolutionary party organized, willing and able to exploit the circumstances the War generated. Other groups fell away or were destroyed. And whatever the complex sources of the Communist Revolution, it quickly took on a life of its own. Compare the reflection of the French philosopher, Joseph de Maistre, shortly after the French Revolution, which he had lived through: 'for a long time we did not fully understand the revolution of which we were witnesses; for a long time we took it to be an event. We were mistaken; it was an epoch.' So too, perhaps even more so, the Russian Revolution. The end of communism in central Europe (1989) and the Soviet Union (1991), and with them even the already faded dream of world communism, were in turn more than mere events. They ended the epoch.

---

[1] *The Age of Extremes: The Short Twentieth Century 1914-1991*, Michael Joseph, London, 1994.

i

For all but the first three years of the short century, then, the 'conceptual geography'[2] of the globe was indelibly shaped by communism and responses to it, and in a totally new way. No other great state had ever before been destroyed and reconstructed with the manifest intent of realising the secular, intellectual, and revolutionary project of one thinker. The Soviet Union, under the leadership of its Communist Party, began as just such a state.

Certainly the European neighbours and opponents of the Russian Soviet Federative Socialist Republic in 1917 were nothing like that: no one invented them, and while there were texts and ideologies, most came well after, at any rate during, the events and few were canonical. In many ways there are parallels with a slightly later invention, Nazism, also the thought of one man, also an unprecedented and defining part of the epoch, also a response to many of its dislocations, especially the War, also revolutionary and totalitarian in its ambitions, also led by a party like no other, and also responsible for almost unimaginable levels and kinds of 'violence, hubris, ruthlessness and human sacrifices.'[3] There were of course many differences between Communism and Fascism, but both were regimes constructed in service to an ideology and, as François Furet has stressed,[4] we don't have many of those in human history. Arguably, and he does so argue, these two were the first.

Nazism was defeated and destroyed in 1945. From then only one of these novel ideocratic constructions remained. Its influence, as actor, model, and counter-model, was profound. The post-War world was framed by the bipolar contest—over ideas as much as territories—between the liberal-democratic-capitalist West—the United States, its allies, subalterns, vassals and dependents—on the one hand, and the Communist East, first Russian, then Soviet, then Soviet and Chinese—with their attendants, acolytes, prospective emulators, and numerous victims, on the other. The rest of the world was a place of competition, between countries of course but more distinctively between two 'systems', frames and views of life, including political, economic and social life, that were diametrically different from each other, hostile and intensely rivalrous. Hobsbawm has noted that:

> The world that went to pieces at the end of the 1980s was the world shaped by the Russian Revolution of 1917. We have all been marked by it, for instance, inasmuch as we got used to thinking of the modern industrial economy in terms of binary opposites, 'capitalism' and 'socialism' as alternatives mutually excluding one another, the one being identified with economies organized on the model of the USSR, the other with all the rest.[5]

That's one—Marxist—way of putting it, with economics as the core. Another—political—way is to contrast ideological one party dictatorship versus pluralist liberal

---

[2]   Tony Judt, 'The Rediscovery of Central Europe,' 119, 1 (Winter 1990), *Daedalus*, 25.

[3]   Vladimir Tismaneanu, *The Devil in History*, University of California Press, Berkeley, 2012, i.

[4]   *The Passing of an Illusion, The Idea of Communism in the Twentieth Century*, University of Chicago Press, Chicago, 1999.

[5]   *The Age of Extremes: The Short Twentieth Century 1914-1991*, Michael Joseph, London, 1994, 4.

democracy. Either way the geopolitical map of the short century turns out the same, and radically different from what it was and what it has become.

Much of the century was dominated, then, by a stark and at times dramatic ideological, political, economic and often military contest between exemplars of antithetical and contending social/economic/political systems. Their conflicts were holistically conceived as between incompatible modes of social, political and economic life; not—as traditionally—as occurring from time to time between entities of more or less the same sort, even if differently adorned and even if hostile.

Countries became communist because communist parties won power in them, some internally by revolutions or coups, others by force of external power. Pervasive systemic features were imposed on and in them all, central among them rule by parties of a distinctive kind, whose leaders had all gone to the same school for power-seekers, that which took its ultimate professed ideals from Marx but its strategy for gaining power from Lenin. And so Marxism-Leninism. *The Organizational Weapon* is a study of Marxist-Leninist parties in pursuit of state power.

And that is an extraordinary subject. For while Marx's thought appealed to small groups of European revolutionaries in the nineteenth and early twentieth centuries, and while there were important reasons for that—intellectual, moral, spiritual, economic, political[6]—his followers were for a long time few. However, everything changed after Lenin's revolution of 1917.

For what becomes truly remarkable about October 1917 is not so much the animating thought—there have been other smart thinkers; nor even the event—there had already been revolutions in Russia in 1905 and in February 1917. Rather, the extraordinary thing, as Furet also observes, is that this 'successful putsch by a Communist sect, directed by an audacious leader in the most backward country of Europe, was transformed by circumstance into an exemplary event, destined to influence the direction of universal history as 1789 had done'.[7] Very soon Russia came to be seen by many to be universal in authority, its leaders infallible in judgement, and its practices exemplary for the world. How so?

Some of the explanation, as already suggested, has to do with the context in which the Communist Party of the Soviet Union emerged and took power, and there is much more to be said about that,[8] but much had to do with the nature of the Party itself. The latter is the subject of this book. Quite distinctive, and the source of much else, was the reification and idealisation of 'the Party', and its transformative historical mission. The Polish philosopher and former communist, Leszek Kołakowski, has observed that Lenin thought of himself as 'an organ of the Party, and not an individual. He talked as the Party and not as a person.'[9] And all those communists who endured torture and faced death, often from other com-

---

[6] See Leszek Kołakowski, *Main Currents of Marxism*, Oxford University Press, Oxford, 3 volumes, 1978.

[7] Furet, *op. cit.*, 21.

[8] I discuss some of these reasons in 'Intellectuals and Communism. A Peculiar Obsession,' in Gwenda Tavan, ed., *State of the Nation: Essays for Robert Manne*, Black Inc., Melbourne, 2013, 261-76.

[9] In *Czas ciekawy, czas niespokojny, [Interesting time, unquiet time]*, Wydawnictwo Znak, Cracow, 2007, vol. 1, 178.

munists, were not doing it for fun or money. For many Party loyalists, there came to be no truth, indeed no life, outside the Party.

This 'Party of a new type' contrived, as *The Organizational Weapon* shows, to transform recruits into 'deployable agents'. That is a rare ambition and an even rarer achievement, in significant part due to Lenin's organizational genius: to develop a machine and strategy for gaining and holding power. And it is that, quite specifically the *organizational* component of Communist strategy, which is the subject of this book.

II

Philip Selznick was born shortly after the start of the short century, in January 1919, and he saw it out. He died in 2010. His life and thought, particularly in his early years, were intertwined with some of the century's most important moments, particularly the Depression, the rise of communism and World War II.

In his youth he was actively involved, along with a remarkable collection of clever and politically engaged student intellectuals, in a dissident branch of communism, the New York Trotskyist movement. He found them first in Alcove 1, one of several alcoves adjoining the cafeteria of City College, New York, and now the subject of numerous memoirs,[10] as well as endless writings on the intellectual origins of neoconservatism,[11] and more generally on the 'New York intellectuals,'[12] of which Selznick's cohort was the second generation. They began their intellectual lives in that period and often in that small place.[13] Seymour Martin Lipset, one of them, evokes the scene well:

> The alcoves were the heart of radical politics at City College, a venue for a steady stream of debate and invective between Stalinists and anti-Stalinists. . . . The Stalinist or Communist alcove was known as the Kremlin, and the one next door, inhabited by a variety of anti-Stalinist radicals—Trotskyists, Socialists, anarchists, socialist Zionists, members of assorted splinter groups—was called Mexico City in honor of Leon Trotsky's exile home. Proximity, of course, led to shouting matches, even though the Communists forbade their members to converse with any Trotskyists, whom they de-

---

[10] See Seymour Martin Lipset, 'Steady Work,' and Lipset, 'Out of the Alcoves,' (1999) 23 *Wilson Quarterly* 84; Nathan Glazer, Irving Kristol, 'Memoirs of a Trotskyist'; Irving Howe, *A Margin of Hope: An Intellectual Autobiography*, Harcourt Brace Jovanovich, New York, 1982.

[11] E.g., Peter Steinfels, *The Neoconservatives: The Men who are Changing America's Politics,* Somon and Schuster, New York, 1979; Jacob Heilbrunn, *They Knew They Were Right: The Rise of the Neocons,* Doubleday, New York, 2008.

[12] Alexander Bloom, *Prodigal Sons: The New York Intellectuals and Their World,* New York, Oxford University Press, 1986; Alan M. Wald, *The New York Intellectuals,* University of North Carolina Press, Chapel Hill, 1987.

[13] See Joseph Dorman, *Arguing the World: The New York Intellectuals in Their Own Words,* University of Chicago Press, Chicago, 2001, 47. This is the text of a PBS film of that title, directed by Joseph Dorman, and exploring the early careers of Daniel Bell, Nathan Glazer, Irving Howe, and Irving Kristol. Selznick appears in the film.

fined as fascist agents. My recollection is that students, occasionally joined by some junior faculty, were there all day, talking, reading, arguing, and eating.[14]

The German sociologist Wolf Lepenies reports some recollections of Daniel Bell, another distinguished denizen of Alcove 1 and a long-time friend of Selznick's, that also catches the tone of those times:

> Bell's description of himself as a socialist makes him smile. He remembers a time when there were socialists everywhere at City College; many Stalinists were so argumentative that New York at the time was known as the most interesting city in the Soviet Union. The socialists at City College were abundantly self-conscious, returning manuscripts with the comment: 'Tolstoy did it better.' And in the midst of a political debate, one might hear someone say, entirely in earnest: 'I know what Trotsky should do, and so do you. But does *Trotsky* know?'[15]

The engagements and disputes that began in the Alcoves had an enormous impact on Selznick. It was not only a tumultuous but also an intellectually fertile association, at the same time his political and intellectual awakening. He joined the Trotskyist youth movement, the Young People's Socialist League (Fourth International) (YPSIL), adopting as his Party name, Philip Sherman.[16] He was an active member. He became organizer of its 'Joe Hill Unit' in the Washington Heights section of Manhattan, and in 1938, became a member of several executive committees, including the group's national executive.[17] He remained a Trotskyist for three years, and for some years after that an unaligned socialist. For the whole of his life, he recalled what began in Alcove 1 as the most intense intellectual experience of his life.

However, it didn't last. The Trotskyists were internally riven, particularly over Trotsky's insistence that however evil Stalin was and however much he had betrayed the Revolution, it was still a Bolshevik revolutionary's duty to support the Soviet Union against its 'imperialist' enemies. When World War II broke out and the Soviet Union revealied its alliance with Nazi Germany, the New York Trotsky-

---

[14] 'Out of the Alcoves,' 85.

[15] Dialogue between Daniel Bell and Wolf Lepenies, 'On society & sociology past & present,' *Daedalus,* Winter 2006, 121-22.

[16] Lipset recalls that 'If you joined the Trotskyist Yipsels, you were supposed to have a party name and mine was Lewis. The party name tradition went back to Russia, the Bolsheviks hiding from the Secret Police, confusing them. So the Communists all had party names, the Trotskyists all had party names, the Socialists didn't. Peter Rossi, the only guy I ever recruited for the movement, was Italian and came from Corona in Queens. He chose the party name Rosen. Well here we had one real gentile, a real *goy*, and he wanted to be called Rosen! So Howe [Hornstein] took it on himself to tell him that he should use another name, not a Jewish name.' In Dorfman, *Arguing the World*, 55-56.

[17] Douglas G. Webb, 'Philip Selznick and the New York Sociologists,' paper presented at the Annual Convention of the Canadian Historical Association, Ottawa, Ontario, June 9-11, 1982, 9.

ists split. An erstwhile leader, Max Shachtman, formed a new Marxist party, the Workers Party, taking with him the party journal, and many of the most talented young intellectuals in the movement.[18] Selznick followed Shachtman and stayed for a time in the Workers Party, but he was not destined to remain a Shachtmanite for long. He set up his own fraction of the Shachtmanite faction of the Trotskyite (heretical) wing of the Bolsheviks, with a bevy of other talented young intellectuals. They were known as the Shermanites, led by 'Philip Sherman.'

The group was small but smart. It was composed of a vivid collection of people later prominent both in academic and public life. They included Selznick's first wife, Gertrude Jaeger, whom he had met in 1938 and married in 1939; the historian and polemicist Gertrude Himmelfarb and her husband Irving Kristol (under the Party name, William Ferry),[19] public intellectuals and later parents of neoconservatism (both directly and metaphorically and, through their son William, indirectly and literally);[20] the sociologist Peter Rossi; political scientists Martin Diamond and Herbert Garfinkel; the historian, Marvin Meyers; the founder of the Free Press, Jeremiah Kaplan. Outside but friends with the group were Daniel Bell, Seymour Martin Lipset, Nathan Glazer, and other later luminaries of American academic life and public culture.

The Shermanites described themselves as 'revolutionary anti-Bolshevik.' In 1941 they left the Workers' Party and joined the youth movement of Norman Thomas's Socialist Party, the Young People's Socialist League (YPSL). Though they had already resigned, the Shachtmanites proceeded to expel them with the special delicacy typical of such movements:

Under Shachtman's direction, the Political Committee of the Workers Party issued 'Bolshevism and Democracy: On the Capitulation of the Sherman Group,' which accused Selznick of various crimes: organizing a secret group during a time in which he claimed to have no differences with the Workers Party leadership; indoctrinating the group's members without the benefit of a full and democratic discussion in the Workers Party; and carrying on secret discussions with both the Socialist Party and with James Burnham. Although the Shermanites by then had already departed to join the Socialist Party, the Workers Party Political Committee nonetheless declared that its anti-Bolshevik views rendered them ipso facto 'incompatible with party membership' and denounced them as 'weaklings taking one pretext or another to escape the discipline of the revolutionary party in time of hardship.' Shachtman, who had personally debated Selznick during one of the

---

[18] 'Shachtman took out with him 40 percent of the membership, but this included 80 percent of the Trotskyist youth.' Constance Ashton Myers, 'American Trotskyists: The First Years' (Spring/Summer 1977) X, 1 & 2, *Studies in Comparative Communism*, 144-45.

[19] 'Kristol became Ferry, his friend Earl Raab was Perry. Why? James P. Cannon, who was the leader of the Trotskyists, used to pronounce periphery, "perryferry." He'd talk about the "perryferry" of the movement. Kristol and Raab didn't join for a long time, but they were hanging around so they were on the periphery. They were the "perryferry." And when they joined they took the names Perry and Ferry!', Lipset in Dorman, *Arguing the World*, 56.

[20] Though I mention that biographical fact, I do not mean to endorse the claim made by self-styled 'paleoconservatives' that neoconservatism is a child of Trotskyism. That claim can withstand no serious scrutiny. See William F. King, 'Neoconservatives and Trotskyism' (2004) 3, 2 *American Communist History*, 247-66.

Workers Party discussions, mocked the decision of these organizational purists to join the social democrats as 'a very unappetizing ending—to join the 'party' of Norman Thomas and company. If there is one labor organization in the U.S. outside of the Communist Party which has a thoroughly undemocratic totalitarian-Fuehrer regime, it is the Thomas organization.' . . . Ten years later, after a revolutionary anti-Bolshevik period and then a return [sic] to liberalism Selznick found an academic use for the ideas that germinated in his debate with Shachtman. At the height of the Cold War, the Rand Corporation published Selznick's *The Organizational Weapon: A Study of Bolshevik Strategy and Tactics* [1952], dedicated to two former Shermanites, Diamond and Garfinkel.[21]

Shortly thereafter, Selznick/Sherman and his friend, indeed comrade at the time, Irving Kristol/Ferry began a small magazine, *Enquiry: A Journal of Independent Radical Thought.* Selznick edited it until he was drafted into the army in 1943, and then his wife, Gertrude Jaeger, and Kristol took over, until Kristol in turn was drafted. Nine issues appeared fitfully between 1942 and 1945. Selznick wrote still interesting pieces on politics, on the war, on organization and on the fate of ideals. By this time, he had learnt a great deal about communism, and ultimately came to reject it in all its forms.

During this period, Selznick had moved from City College to Columbia, wrote and published a master's thesis on the theory of bureaucracy[22] and, under the supervision of Robert Merton, ultimately wrote a doctoral thesis on the Tennessee Valley Authority. This became one of the most celebrated works of organizational theory, *TVA and the Grass Roots,* which he completed and published when he returned from war service. *TVA* explored how a well-meaning and intelligent leadership of an innovative organization had failed to understand the effects of its measures on the *character* of the organization it purported to lead. So much so, that in endeavouring to 'co-opt' potential opponents of its operations by bringing them in, it effectively lost control of the character and direction of the organization to them. The book operates at many levels, from close-grained analysis to philosophical reflection on the fate of ideals amidst the difficult, indeed intransigent, realities of practical affairs. It is, and was widely hailed as, a *tour de force.*[23]

Selznick was not the only ex-socialist sociologist to be interested in bureaucracy, indeed a bunch of brilliant students of Merton had overlapping interests, but he is distinctive in a way well captured by Webb:

> [W]hat is especially interesting about his career is the way he has used the burning issues of his radical past as the basis for his work as a professional sociologist. As a Trotskyist and Socialist, Selznick had been fascinated by the problems of bureaucracy and oligarchy and the dilemmas of organizational life. As an academic in the 1940s and 1950s, he turned these concerns

[21] Wald, *op. cit.,* 282-83.

[22] 'Approach to a Theory of Bureaucracy' (1943), 8 *American Sociological Review,* 49.

[23] *TVA and the Grass Roots: A Study in the Sociology of Formal Organization* (first published 1949), republished with a 2011 Foreword by Jonathan Simon, Quid Pro Books, New Orleans, Louisiana, 2011.

into the cool language of scientific analysis and became in the process one of the most important organizational theorists of his generation.[24]

In 1946-47 Selznick took his first academic appointment, as an instructor in sociology at the University of Minnesota, Minneapolis. Politically, he was no longer a socialist but a Truman liberal, and particularly an anti-communist liberal. While in Minnesota, a group of the liberal anti-communist Americans for Democratic Action, one of whose founders was Reinhold Niebuhr, was led by then mayor of Minneapolis, Hubert Humphrey. Selznick joined and was active.

In 1947, he left to join UCLA, where he stayed until 1952. When he arrived in Los Angeles, he got in contact with ADA people, and in particular made friends with a journalist Paul Jacobs freshly arrived from Chicago, and Frank Mankiewicz, also a journalist and political activist (and son of Herman Mankiewicz, the screenwriter who co-wrote *Citizen Kane*): 'About 1950 we were sitting around and talking and we said, we need some sort of education about liberalism and communism and so on, and we started a school: it had brochures, and several courses, went on for about two years, and was called "the liberal center." Its main mission was to reach liberals in the LA area who had been overly influenced by the communists. I think one felt there was a lot of that. . . . A lot of communist fellow-travelling was going on in those days.'[25] According to Jacobs, they ended the school when it became too successful for them to manage:

> While Phil was working on his book [*The Organizational Weapon*], a small group of us decided to start a school where we could try to discuss our views of the Communist problem with Los Angeles liberals. Unfortunately the School was so successful that we had to close it down: it took up more time than we could give. Every session was jammed with people who were active liberals in the community, genuinely concerned about California's future.[26]

At UCLA, Selznick also became close friends with the pragmatist philosopher, Abraham Kaplan, with whom he taught a course on 'ethical problems of social organization.' The course was important for Selznick, as those themes came to be central concerns of his writings. Kaplan also introduced him to members of the social sciences division of the RAND Corporation, and between 1948 and 1952, Selznick became a part-time research associate in that division. In that capacity he wrote a book on communist organization strategy, which became *The Organizational Weapon*, first published by RAND in 1952.

---

[24] Douglas G. Webb, 'Philip Selznick and the New York Sociologists,' 18.

[25] Martin Krygier, videotaped interview with Philip Selznick, 7 January 2002, available at http://law.berkeley.edu/selznick.htm. And see Paul Jacobs, *Is Curly Jewish? A Political Self-Portrait Illuminating Three Turbulent Decades of Social Revolt 1935-1965*, Athaneum, New York, 1965.

[26] Paul Jacobs, *Is Curly Jewish?*, 195.

III[27]

The Organizational Weapon is a study of the Marxist-Leninist 'combat party' seeking to gain power in non-communist states,[28] though not a study of any particular party but of a *type*. It was an attempt to develop, drawing upon a large array of sources from around the world:

> a model that will effectively expose a *central* pattern of motivation and action, applicable in its basic features to the bolshevik movement in all countries and throughout its history. We have therefore emphasized what the record shows to be *general*, recognizing that there can be and are deviations in detail from one country or period to another, but that there *is* a persistent underlying pattern.[29]

The model focused on a particular but crucial part of communist strategy: its organizational component. It was common observation that communist parties were organized and led in ways different from most organizations, indeed from most political parties. Not only outsiders noticed it, but ' "Our Party," the bolshevik leaders tell their ranks, "is not like other parties." '[30] Selznick agreed. Conventional democratic political parties, formed to contest other parties of different commitments but similar type, are 'committed to electoral victory in the short run, decentralized, capable of absorbing new ideas and social forces, incapable of making many demands upon a weakly involved party membership.'[31] Communist parties differed in ways Selznick considered to be systematic, and he sought to theorize those ways by explaining their systemic sources.

He discusses many elements characteristic and distinctive of communist organizational arrangements, but central to his concerns is what he calls 'the operational code' of communist parties. This, Selznick argued, consists of:

> distinctive modes of group membership and distinctive modes of social control. A system is created capable of making very large demands upon totally involved members. It is a system marked by *a distinctive competence to turn members of a voluntary association into disciplined and deployable political agents.*[32]

It is this *distinctive competence* that Selznick seeks to understand. An organiza-

---

[27] This section is largely drawn and adapted from my *Philip Selznick: Ideals in the World*, Stanford University Press, Stanford, Calif., 2012, 55-65, all rights reserved.

[28] The book is not concerned, except incidentally, with the *exercise* of power by communist parties, but with strategies for gaining it.

[29] *The Organizational Weapon*, 12. [Page references are to the previous editions' pagination, which in this edition's body is embedded into the text, for purposes of continuity.]

[30] *Ibid.*, 17.

[31] *Leadership in Administration*, Harper & Row, New York, 1957, reissued with a new preface by University of California Press, Berkeley, 1984, 48.

[32] *The Organizational Weapon*, Preface, xii.

tion of this sort 'could be built only over a long period and with great effort'.[33] It required the transformation of a voluntary organization into a 'managerial structure' by which *adherents* are converted into *cadres* of 'deployable personnel'.[34] That in turn depended upon an organization developing a specific competence (not found, for example, in the average post office or supermarket) to effect such transformations, since they do not occur naturally or even commonly, but have to be formed. Selznick's interest was in how that competence was established and sustained, often over long periods of time, in circumstances which were rarely welcoming or easy, indeed *because* circumstances were neither welcoming nor easy.

For Communist parties were a species of 'combat party'. As such, they were not fashioned to compete routinely in open elections within constitutionally established constraints and rules of the game, in the hope of winning control of government for a limited period of time. Rather they were forged as weapons in an in-principle unrestrained struggle for total hold on power. And the struggle is not merely played out in those areas of life conventionally thought of as 'political.' *All* areas are fair game in the struggle to establish the party's dominance; 'Bolshevism calls for the *continuous* conquest of power through full use of the potentialities of organization. These conquests are not restricted to the normal political arena and do not use conventional political tools.'[35]

One common way of seeking to understand revolutionary movements is to focus on their professed ideals and goals, and notwithstanding its allegedly scientific status Marxism is full of such ideals and goals. However, apart from the commonplace that the distance between ideals and practices is often huge, Selznick had another reason for not focusing there. As he had learnt from the American pragmatists, particularly John Dewey, and as all his work in the study of organizations had revealed, to understand a social movement, still more its likelihood of success, ideals are never enough. To have the distinctive competence for these and allied activities, such competence must be built into the apparatus itself, into its *means,* not merely its ends. Ends are alluring but means are crucial, though also commonly overlooked; that is a deep mistake. For as Selznick explains in his classic examination of a quite different organization, the TVA: 'the crucial question for democracy is not what to strive for, but by what means to strive. And the question of means is one of what to do now and what to do next—and these are basic questions in politics.'[36]

If you want to understand what is distinctive about the character and operations of an army, say, the professed ideals of its leaders will not take you very far. An organizational weapon is in many ways reminiscent of an army. However, it is unlike a regular army which typically has the backing of the state and law, and commonly keeps its troops in considerable isolation from non-military communities for long periods of time. Until they succeed, domestic communist parties never

---

[33] *Ibid.,* 22.

[34] *Ibid.,* 20.

[35] *Ibid.,* 17 (emphasis in original).

[36] *TVA and the Grass Roots,* 7.

have the backing of their own state (though they often were backed by external communist states); indeed they commonly started as ideologically suspect groups, often illegal, hiding their activities, in whole or in part, from hostile police and security services. Moreover, communist organizational strategies were intended to combat such attention and, often, persecution, not simply in order to survive and/or propagate the faith (as might be true of, say, the Falun Gong or Baha'i) but to gain power. This combination of aims led to an 'inherent tension':

> The combat party must continuously guard against certain characteristic dangers: excessive isolation on the one hand and liquidation on the other. To build and sustain the system requires a heavy emphasis on the withdrawal of members from society and upon ultimate doctrinal purity; at the same time the members must be deployed in the political arena. The first carries the risk that the party will be transformed into an isolated sect, the second that members will place the interests of target groups, such as trade unions, above those of the party itself. The working out of this inner conflict not only summarizes a considerable portion of communist history but also helps us to identify what the necessities of the system are, what has to be done in order to maintain its peculiar integrity.[37]

Party cadres have at the same time to be steeled against a world of temptations and ready to infiltrate it, but without losing their primary characters as party operatives. They have to become *insulated* from outside loyalties, ways of thought, and temptations and *absorbed* into the party and its work to an extent that is uncommon; '[t]hese are reciprocal, since insulation frees the individual for fuller absorption and the process of absorption aids insulation.'[38] They have to be trained for conspiratorial activity, and nerved for it, in 'the continuous and systematic search for 'pieces of power.''[39] They need to neutralize opponents, and for much of the time even more, rivals;[40] they need *access* to target groups and institutions in order to do what is required of them, they need to seek legitimacy, they need to mobilize support, but they must maintain at all times their identity and integrity as Party operatives, independent of the groups and institutions they seek to penetrate. With regard to these latter, they are required to reverse Kant's

---

[37] *The Organizational Weapon*, xiii.

[38] *Ibid.*, 26.

[39] *Ibid.*, 54.

[40] 'What is really urgent is that the other left-wing movements *compete for the same social base* as do the communists. . . . A political movement seeks out sources of power that can give it an indispensable leverage and thus permit it to intervene in the arena where great events are decided. To protect its relation to this social lever, to find a hold and tighten its grasp upon it, becomes for the communists a primary task. It is here that the part is most vulnerable, for without its base it is nothing. He who can expose the party before the *relevant* public—the labor movement and liberal opinion—is therefore its main and intolerable enemy.
'This is not a matter of emotional response but of the hard coin of politics. Programatically, the communists may declare that the "bankers and bosses" or the "imperialists" are the enemy. But these forces do not challenge the communists at the source of power.' *Ibid.*, 227.

categorical imperative: non-Party groups and institutions must at all times be treated merely as means and not as ends in themselves.[41] If not everyone meets these stringent requirements, well, like Kant's original imperative itself, they were regulative ideals, not universal behavioral predictions, and anyway there are highly elaborated organizational means of dealing with 'betrayal'.[42]

In all this, the party must sustain and communicate to the faithful a clear understanding of the distinctive *character* of the party that they serve. Otherwise they might dissolve into the waters in which they are supposed to swim purposefully and to feed. Indeed, understanding is only part of it. Members must come to embody that character, and that involves a lot more than talk:

> For Lenin, organization was an indispensable adjunct to ideology. He did not believe that he could win power by propaganda alone. . . . For him, the task was not so much to spread the 'truth' as to raise to power a select group of communicants. . . . Many costly errors in appraising communist activities have been made because too little attention was paid to the hidden organizational meaning of seemingly straight-forward propaganda activities.

The most general of such implications is the subordination of propaganda to the needs of organizational strategy.[43]

Not only must a party of the right sort of character be forged by the leadership, but it must constantly be guarded against myriad sources of corruption, to sustain and guard the kinds of commitments that enable the leadership 'to mobilize and "hurl" the organization against strategic targets in the struggle for power.'[44]

None of this comes easily or quickly. On the contrary, such transformations cannot 'simply be *resolved* into existence: a long process of indoctrination and action is required to inculcate methods of organization and work so deeply that they select and create congenial personality traits,'[45] '[t]he reorientation . . . is not simply one of technical organization, but of restructuring the *attitudes and actions* of the membership.'[46]

Selznick constantly probed the 'hidden organizational meaning'[47] of activities, such as propaganda, whose ostensible targets seemed to lie outside the organization, but whose real importance may be 'not to spread communist symbols, but simply to create an atmosphere conducive to the free use of the combat party and

---

[41] Cf. *ibid.*, 163: 'The communist attitude toward peripheral organizations is entirely secular, bare of all sentimental attachments. Only the party—and not even the name of the external form of the party, but its aims, basic methods, and leadership—is the object of idealization. Other organizations may be freely created or dissolved, depending on the exigencies of the political struggle. This is in keeping with their status as tools, whereas the power of the party is an end in itself.'

[42] See, e.g., *ibid.*, 64.

[43] *Ibid.*, 8.

[44] *Ibid.*, 65.

[45] *Ibid.*, 57.

[46] *Ibid.*, 59.

[47] *Ibid.*, 8.

its agencies. Similarly, we speak of the organizational relevance of ideology when it performs internally oriented morale functions.'[48] Again, 'Communist "theory" cannot be understood solely as a guide to action. It is partly that, but doubtless of equal significance is the managerial function Marxist-Leninist doctrine fulfills.'[49] The 'cults of personality' that typically develop in Communist states are also not simply due to the peculiar vanity of communist leaders. Rather they are part of a much more widespread endeavor of communist parties, in power and striving for it, to convert loyalty to the party to 'loyalty to the party *organization*. A halo is raised over party leaders, party organs, party decisions.'[50] In all this, Lenin appeared to have recognised those more general truths about organizations of all sorts, outlined in Selznick's first book on the TVA, and not always observed by its leaders: 'that proximate, operational goals are more important in the struggle for power than abstract, ultimate goals';[51] '[i]nstitutional loyalties are fostered as a way to give abstract ideals a content that can effectively summon psychological energies.'[52]

Much of *The Organizational Weapon* focuses on how to develop the 'vanguard'. But, of course, there is 'the mass'. Communist parties are not, as the naive might imagine, transparent tribunes of the masses; nor, however, are they *putschists* or saboteurs, for whom the people are mere by-standers. Bolshevik writings and actions embody a highly differentiated and complex analysis of the masses, who are key for 'they are the font of power.'[53] So they are indispensable, though in a curious way not central, and the party's relationship to them is of a special sort. For the Leninist party is a kind of caricature or logical reduction of Michels's 'iron law of oligarchy', which had much influenced, though not completely persuaded, Selznick:[54]

> Thousands of words have been written by bolshevik leaders to hammer home the thesis that the thoughts of the workers are sources of power for the party *if* manipulative control is established. Least of all are the thoughts of the workers to be taken as guideposts for the party. . . . It is the party,

---

[48]   *Ibid.*, 244. Cf.: 'I'll give you something I heard recently about the Mormons. Somebody was saying about the young Mormons who were sent out as missionaries, the important influence is not so much the converts that they get, but the way this activity influences the missionaries themselves. These young people, having been involved for two years in this kind of activity, are now, themselves, ineradicably fixed as Mormons. So there is that dynamic that all organizations have to take into account—what I called at one point the internal relevance of apparently external activity.' 'An Oral History with Philip Selznick,' conducted by Roger Cotterrell, 2002, Regional Oral History Office, Bancroft Library, University of California Berkeley, 2010, http://digitalassets.lib.berkeley.edu/roho/ucb/text/selznick_philip.pdf, 46.

[49]   *The Organizational Weapon*, 39.

[50]   *Ibid.*, 44.

[51]   *Ibid.*, 47.

[52]   *Ibid.*

[53]   *Ibid.*, 81.

[54]   See Krygier, *Philip Selznick: Ideals in the World*, esp. chapters 1 and 2.

not the workers, which is the arbiter of these historical interests. The workers are continually susceptible to 'reactionary prejudices', to being misled, deceived, betrayed, corrupted. The party is the great stabilizer which holds the class to the course fixed by history. It is the cleanser and the purifier, the teacher, the judge, and, at the inevitable hour, the jailer.[55]

Communist parties must *lead*, and ensuring such leadership is the primary goal of communist organizational work:

Communist organizational tactics are always qualified by a keen awareness of leadership as a political process. In a way that is foreign to the ordinary political machine, the communists display a high sensitivity to the role of the mass in society as a whole and in specialized organizations. Although they are quite prepared to assume the classic bureaucratic role when that seems expedient—as in minimizing participation in decisions—the bolsheviks are equally prepared to mobilize mass participation when that can be effectively controlled. Like other machine bosses, the communists depend on apathy. But they are also willing to appeal to the membership for support. A narrow machine hesitates to assume mass leadership and restricts itself to clique maneuvers.[56]

In relation to the masses, there is a panoply of organizational stratagems and tactics as well. As we have seen, the party seeks 'access' to the masses, 'legitimation' before them, targeted 'mobilization' of some of them, elimination or at least 'neutralization' of rivals and opponents. That requires mastery of tactics of penetration and infiltration, which Selznick discusses with remarkable perceptiveness and in great detail. They all were 'primarily means of creating power for the leaders.'[57] Communists are particularly good at such activities, for:

The tactical advantage which the communists gain in the course of unity maneuvers is not based on episodic or 'clever' manipulation. It derives from the fundamental increment of power offered by the combat party. The latter creates a corps of disciplined cadres dedicated to the ubiquitous pursuit of power. In this sense the basis of communist influence is real and not illusory. The ability to deploy forces in a controlled and systematic way makes possible minority control in large organizations, especially in an environment of general apathy and in the absence of competing power centers.[58]

The Organizational Weapon doubtless had an activist, or 'awakening' component. Written by a man blooded by earlier and intense membership of the

---

[55] *The Organizational Weapon*, 88-89.

[56] *Ibid.*, 215.

[57] *Ibid.*, 178.

[58] *Ibid.*, 164.

American Trotskyist movement,[59] confident he 'knew the score' about Bolshevism, it was conceived in part as an exposé intended to guide people seeking to oppose communism. Indeed, in the introduction to the book, Selznick suggests that '[b]ecause of its stress on action rather than on ideological analysis, this volume may be used as an advanced-training manual for anti-communist forces.'[60] But it would pay those forces to be sophisticated, lest they misunderstand two central and interrelated features of what they read—its qualified political significance, and its scientific novelty.

Politically, it is important not to miss or misapprehend a point Selznick makes several times: even a successful organizational strategy is only a piece in the complex of assault and defence that compete within any society which contains (and seeks to contain) wielders of organizational weapons. Thus Selznick emphasizes:

> the *subordinate* role of organizational activity in the struggle against totalitarianism. . . . To speak of organizational strategy and tactics is to define a special sphere of interest and action. It must not be forgotten that this sphere is limited, providing special increments of power to political elites whose fundamental sources of weakness and strength must be looked for elsewhere. . . .

We must conclude, therefore, that in the long view political combat plays only a tactical role. Great social issues, such as those which divide communism and democracy, are not decided by political combat, perhaps not even by military clashes. They are decided by the relative ability of the contending systems to win and to maintain enduring loyalties. Consequently, no amount of power and cunning in the realm of political combat, can avail in the absence of measures which rise to the height of the times.[61]

Scientifically, and in explanation of this focus on a self-confessedly subsidiary—if crucial—matter, it is necessary to grasp the precise concern of Selznick's analysis, and its novelty. For this is the work of a theorist of, and self-consciously a study of, *organization*, who argues for the importance of this particular domain but does not consider it all important. In particular, the book is concerned not so much with how communists solve, or attempt to solve, the many political problems that face them. Rather it is concerned with an at once fundamental but second-order issue: how they create and sustain an *organization capable* of dealing with such problems.

Selznick's late colleague, Sheldon Messinger, made the point perceptively and

---

[59] For the enduring significance of those few Trotskyist years, see Selznick, *The Moral Commonwealth*, University of California Press, Berkeley, 1992, ix-xi, and Krygier, *Philip Selznick: Ideals in the World*, chapters 1 and 2.

[60] *The Organizational Weapon*, 16.

[61] *Ibid.*, 332-33. See also the Preface to the second edition, at v: '[T]he organizational strategies explored here, important as they are and have been, are not presented as the ultimate arbiters of victory or defeat in the struggle between totalitarian communism and the free world.'

well.[62] He distinguished between two levels of problem-solving engagement that a communist party must engage in. At the first level, such a party works in a context where its goals of achieving 'total power' are held illegitimate, as are the means they use to reach that goal. That being the case, they are presented with a 'level one problem' . . : what are the requirements of an organizational means which will be able to overcome such contextual blocks?' The novelty of Selznick's approach is that it concentrates on a deeper level of issues, what Messinger calls 'level two problems', that is *'what must we do to construct and maintain an organizational means which will fill the requirements at level one.'* Or as Messinger puts it in other terms:

> Michels revealed to us that administrators in carrying out day-to-day pursuits came to be guided by considerations specific to the means of action. He phrased this negatively . . . by telling us that ultimate goals tended to be lost sight of in the bureaucratic life. Selznick might be said to have drawn a profound lesson from this, namely, that one set of problems seldom enough considered is what one must do, from day-to-day, in order to have in hand a means appropriate to goal-achievement. Since TVA administrators were not especially cognizant of this problem, their means of action became ill-suited to pursuit of ultimate goals posited at the outset of their activities. The bolsheviks, on the other hand, *are* cognizant of this problem: thus it is possible for Selznick to view the construction of their means as illuminating 'those aspects of organization most important in the power process.'
>
> More important . . . is the implication of this point of view for research. It constitutes a directive . . . to make the leap from consideration of what one must do to achieve a given goal, to what one must do to construct and preserve means of action appropriate to a given goal.

This is an important corrective to many more common ways of studying power. And Selznick, who always sought the general message of particular truths, was not limited in his attention to communist parties. As in all his particular studies, larger theoretical stakes were in play. Another way to put the point, that could not have occurred to Selznick or to Messinger when they wrote, has been suggested by Jonathan Simon in his foreword to the Quid Pro Books reissue of Selznick's first book, *TVA and the Grass Roots*. Selznick shares with Michel Foucault a general orientation to the study of power that emphasizes 'the importance of methods, instruments, and techniques, asserting against the grain of most history, that purposes, goals, and objectives are almost always determined by the successes and failures of uncelebrated technologies of power.'[63] Simon quotes from a passage from *TVA* that, as he says, 'seems to anticipate Foucault's today better-known studies of power' and that reveals the motivation of his next work as well. In some ways the point is more strikingly apt for this book than for its predecessor, and I will quote from it at some length:

---

[62] In an unpublished paper, first written in 1954 or 1955, then rediscovered by its author and reproduced in 1962 (on file with Martin Krygier).

[63] *TVA and the Grass Roots*, Quid Pro Books, New Orleans, 2011, Foreword, iv.

If the problem of means is vital, it is also the most readily forgotten . . . the results which most readily capture the imagination are external, colourful, concrete. They are the stated goals of action. . . .

But methods are more elusive. They have a corollary and incidental status. A viable enterprise is sustained in the public eye by its goals, not its methods. Means are variable and expedient. Their history is forgotten or excused. Here again the concrete and colourful win easiest attention. Where incorrect methods leave a visible residue—a rubbled city or wasted countryside,—then methods may gain notice. But those means which have long-run implications for cultural values, such as democracy, are readily and extensively ignored.[64]

Selznick, we have seen, thought such ignorance unwise.

IV

All Selznick's work, I have argued elsewhere,[65] operates on several levels at once. Whatever he investigates, however particular and concrete, is subject to what he once identified as his 'generalizing impulse'. Though most of his books were directly, both ostensibly and really, concerned with a specific institution or class of institutions, other things were always going on as well. This lends a characteristic depth, richness, and complexity to his individual works, as it does to the *oeuvre* as a whole. There is always more than one might expect to find inside any one of them: more themes, more arguments, more applications, more connections with other works.

This is no less true of *The Organizational Weapon* than of other, better known, works. At its most concrete, and as we have seen, this work provides insights into pervasive features of communist organizational strategy and tactics. Even if that were only of historical concern today, it would be of enduring interest given the significance of communism in the past century.

However, communists are not the only people with an interest in converting adherents into 'deployable agents.' Modern terrorist organizations, radically different in their goals, have a similar organizational need and ambition. After all, it takes a lot, one would imagine, to become a member of a hunted, outlawed terrorist organization, let alone a suicide bomber. Students of other organizations that seek to convert adherents into 'deployable agents' might well find suggestive contemporary parallels, for '[n]o group has a monopoly on the use of organizational weapons'.[66] Wherever people seek to develop 'deployable agents' in hostile circumstances, they will require comparable organizational strategies and competences; '[s]uch a view is characteristic of groups which seek to catapult themselves out of obscurity into history when, as it seems to them, all the forces of society

---

[64]   *TVA and the Grass Roots*, 7.

[65]   *Philip Selznick: Ideals in the World*, esp. 276-77.

[66]   *The Organizational Weapon*, 4.

are arrayed in opposition.'[67] Marxist-Leninists made an art form of this, but it can be emulated, put to other uses, and re-created, doubtless in differing forms and in service to different gods. Thus it should not be surprising that one of the most penetrating analysts of global jihad, David Kilcullen, former Australian army officer and senior counter-insurgency advisor to the United States State Department and military, acknowledges *The Organizational Weapon* as a seminal influence.[68]

This is not to say, nor did Selznick say, either that there is nothing new under the sun or that communists were terrorists. As for terror, Communists had a purely tactical attitude to it, repudiating 'anarchic terrorism'[69] and evaluating other forms by their consequences. They were not drawn to it for its own sake, nor on the other hand did they have any principled objections to it, where it might serve the cause. More generally, no doubt different organizational weapons are differently constituted, and the differences may be systematic. That would be a topic worth exploring. This is a good place to start.

Moreover, apart from movements interested in taking over institutions of liberal-democratic institutions, there are questions about the character and vulnerabilities of these target institutions themselves, which can be considered in their own right. What makes an institutional target 'hard', what 'soft'? Here Selznick offers suggestions at the same time tied to their place and time of origin, and yet enduringly fertile. Thus, in the penultimate chapter of the book,[70] Selznick ventures some 'frankly preliminary' hypotheses as to sources of social vulnerability to political manipulation and penetration. He emphasizes that these sources are not only available for exploitation by communists, but by any outside political forces, whether of left or right. For they amount to weakened capacities of self-defence, whatever the source of attack. The key issue is 'the capacity of institutions to meet, within their own terms, the requirements of self-maintenance. Self-maintenance, of course, refers to the preservation of central values and purposes as well as to the bare continuity of organizational existence.'[71] That, in turn, depends upon the ability of culture-bearing elites to defend the character of their institutions, and that is eroded by the pressures of 'mass society', a concept that he took from discussions current before and after the Second World War, and a phenomenon he took to be increasingly, though variably, significant in the circumstances of modernity.

According to Selznick, 'mass' is itself a qualitative phenomenon. A mass society is not merely or even necessarily a large one. Rather, a society becomes a 'mass' to the extent that formerly potent sources of social cohesion, patterned differentiation, and cultural transmission have atrophied, been diluted and/or thinned, and replaced by agglomerations in which cultural attachments are weakened, social

---

[67] *Ibid.*, 113.

[68] See his *The Accidental Guerilla,* Oxford University Press, Oxford, 2009; George Packer, 'Knowing the Enemy: Can Social Scientists Redefine the "War on Terror"?', *The New Yorker*, December 18, 2006.

[69] *The Organizational Weapon*, 237.

[70] A large part of which also appeared in 'Institutional Vulnerability in Mass Society' (July 1951), 56 *American Journal of Sociology*, 320-31.

[71] *The Organizational Weapon*, 276.

differentiations have melted, culture-bearing elites have lost authority, social participation is highly fragmented. In such circumstances, novel challenges to the distinctive identities of institutions arise, for:

> The strength of cultural values depends on the ability of key agencies to transmit them without serious attenuation and distortion. But this in turn requires that these institutions be secure, that the elites which man them be able to maintain their distinctive identities. This becomes increasingly diffi-cult as powerful solvents—science, technology, industrialization, urbaniza-tion—warp the self-confidence of the culture-bearers and, at the same time, expose them to the pressures of an emergent mass.[72]

The key to institutional self-maintenance is leadership which sustains the institution's character; in a sense leadership which understands what communists understand:

> Vulnerability can be controlled only by the affirmation in practice of the moral ideals which define the character of an organization. This affirmation requires, above all, the shaping of individuals so that they become compe-tent to apprehend those threats, from within and without, which endanger the institution's self-image. It is the failure to do this that leaves the door open to *effective* penetration. . . . Unions, universities, and other agencies which embody values have most to fear when they become bound to the mo-ment, to the technical job at hand, to limited views of their social function. They are then softened for ideological and organizational manipulation: they will become unable to distinguish between those who defend treasured aspirations and those who corrupt them.[73]

Unfortunately, Selznick fails to explain why no successful Bolshevik revolu-tion ever occurred in modern massified societies, while all of them did in societies far less developed. Barrington Moore made the point well in an early review:

> [S]o far as Communism is concerned, it is quite clear that this doctrine fo-cuses attention on the wrong end of the horse. Communism has not gained a strong foothold in those advanced industrial countries where the processes alleged by Selznick to exist have supposedly been going on for the longest time. Instead, the Communist variety of totalitarianism has flourished best in peasant societies that for one reason or another were having difficulty in making the transition to an industrial order.[74]

This is not a refutation of Selznick's analysis of vulnerabilities of mass soci-eties, but it points to a significant gap in an attempt to explain the successes of

---

[72] *Ibid.,* 280-81.

[73] *Ibid.,* 313-14.

[74] Barrington Moore, 'Review,' in (1952), 46 *American Political Science Review,* 875.

communism in the twentieth century. In his preface to the 1960 reissue of *The Organizational Weapon*, Selznick implicitly takes the point, first by stressing that his 'frankly speculative' effort' was focused on 'institutions of the modern industrialized nations of the free world' (which doesn't fully explain the reference—in the book, though not in the 'mass society' chapter—to the Kuomintang Revolutionary Committee or the several references to the Philippines), that 'other conditions may also weaken institutions . . . [t]he processes of mass society are not the only ones at work in the world' and that the theory might be detached from its specific social sources in industrialized societies: 'The atomization of society, including the breakdown of "intermediate groups," may be brought about in a number of ways, including the sudden tearing of a traditional social fabric under conditions of rapid industrial, political, and cultural modernization.'[75] That may be so, but coming after the event it seems somewhat *ad hoc*, and the work of showing the relevance of an analysis that began elsewhere still has to be done. In the meantime, what we have is a penetrating analysis of a worldwide phenomenon from a particular and perhaps unrepresentative vantage point and moment—the United States in the early 1950s.

But we should recall that in his 1960 preface, Selznick observes that 'the vulnerability considered here is not uniquely a vulnerability to communism. The McCarthy episode in American life during the early 1950s reflected the same exposure of institutions to political assault. The diagnosis has to do with a lowering of resistance in specific ways. The attack may come from a number of different quarters.'[76] A few years later, some of his erstwhile friends, who were appalled by the student movement of the 1960s, which Selznick initially and for some time supported, reminded him of his earlier analysis, when he and they took different sides on the Berkeley Free Speech Movement of 1965.[77]

Wherever one came out on that debate, more recent observation of universities might suggest that attacks on weak defenders need not even be political or self-consciously subversive to be effective. They may not even be attacks. Members of modern cultural institutions, among them universities, who have lost confidence in ways of talking other than those generated by their new and pervasive neoliberal managers might come to find the deepest traditions of their institutions surprisingly vulnerable to erosion and corruption, not by determined subversives, but by outsiders who wish to do nothing but help. With no ill will from anyone, they may find their institutions' core values overridden by demands for justification and conformity that come from elsewhere, promote different and often incompatible incentives, reward different types of work (and workers), and come to colonise their institutions to such an extent that it becomes hard to recall, let alone voice and defend, what might once have been meant by a 'community of scholars,' or an 'academic vocation.'

---

[75] *The Organizational Weapon*, xviii.

[76] *Ibid.*, xvii.

[77] See the exchanges between Nathan Glazer and Selznick in *Commentary*, 1965, reprinted in Seymour Martin Lipset and Sheldon S. Wolin, eds., *The Berkeley Student Revolt: Facts and Interpretations*, Doubleday-Anchor, New York, 1965, 285-315.

In such circumstances, not universal but not unknown, cultural elites might come to find themselves at the same time dismayed and disarmed, less by the strength of forces arrayed against them, than by their uncertain and insecure grasp on what they and the institutions to which they belong, are for.[78] They could reflect on Selznick's observation, some sixty years ago, that in mass societies:

> Elites find it difficult to sustain their own standards and hence ultimately their special identity and function. This is most clearly evident in the institutions of higher learning: mass society threatens to transform them into institutions of specialized training. As higher education falls a prey to the mass, research as well as teaching is affected. . . . The result will be a decline in the university's ability to affect deeply the life of the student and, concomitantly, an increase in the vulnerability of both faculty and student to the stereotyped blandishments of the marketplace.[79]

As the philosopher Raimond Gaita has observed, '[i]mpressive technicality, a kind of high-flying thoughtlessness, can shine in such conditions,'[80] but a distinctive intellectual vocation is harder to sustain. Some might be led to recall Selznick's observation, clearly drawn from the reflections in this book, that a 'university led by administrators without a clear sense of values to be achieved may fail dismally while steadily growing larger and more secure.'[81]

This leads to a larger theme in Selznick's work, that of the key place of *institutionalization* in the life of organizations. Selznick's next book, *Leadership in Administration* was in part an ambitious attempt to distil and to generalize the findings of his first two works, *TVA and the Grass Roots* and *The Organizational Weapon*. In the process it became one of the foundation works in the early 'institutional' theory of organizations.

According to Selznick, a key process in organizations, and a key skill of a leader, is institutionalization, which Selznick defined as '[i]n what is perhaps its most significant meaning . . . to *infuse with value* beyond the technical requirements of the task at hand.'[82] In one sense, *TVA* could be understood as an attempt to understand a failure of organizational leaders to understand what such infusion involved, whereas *The Organizational Weapon* was, from this particular point of view, a study of institutional success.

Leadership in Administration seeks to generalize the 'leap' that Messinger identifies him to have taken in *The Organizational Weapon*, 'from consideration of what one must do to achieve a given goal, to what one must do to construct and preserve means of action appropriate to a given goal.' Institutionalization is a key to negotiating the space between.

---

[78]   See, for example, Simon Head, 'The Grim Threat to British Universities,' *New York Review of Books*, January 13, 2011; Stefan Collini, *What Are Universities For?*, Penguin, Harmondsworth, 2012.

[79]   *The Organizational Weapon*, 279-80.

[80]   At http://meanjin.com.au/articles/post/to-civilise-the-city.

[81]   *Leadership in Administration*, 7.

[82]   *Ibid.*, 17.

Processes of institutionalization—growth of group loyalties, commitments, particular attachments and idioms—are likely to happen over time and a leader must understand and work with them; ignored they will bite back, but a lot of organization theory had little to say about them. And apart from organic processes, Selznick identified institutionalization as a *project*, which was the special province of *leaders* as distinct from managers. Leaders need to be able to make *critical* decisions that have deeper, more pervasive consequences for the nature of the institution, than are involved in routine management. They need to be able to embody purpose in the life of the institution. This involves understanding the values and character of the organizations they lead and drawing support from them, or alternatively imbuing the organizations with values the leader considers appropriate (which means not merely valuable in principle or in general, but apt for *this* institution, with its particular history, character, values, competences, and specific commitments), and endeavouring to change them in some or other ways. These are complex and difficult tasks, but achievable by good leaders, as the Bolsheviks, certain churches, armies, and business organizations, showed. In this respect, *TVA* could be viewed as a study of well-intentioned failure while communist organizational strategy appeared to Selznick at the time to be ill-intentioned success.

Leadership in Administration draws from these and other exemplary organizational histories to analyze some of the ingredients of failure and success in institutional leadership, more generally conceived. Like all Selznick's work, it is also a book that operates at many levels, from concrete advice to leaders of business organizations (where it achieved great success) to reflections on the elements of statesmanship required of people exercising leadership properly understood, wherever they are to be found.

Though it builds on both earlier works, *Leadership in Administration* generalizes one respect in which *The Organizational Weapon* differs from *TVA*. If *TVA* exposed sources of failure to institutionalize values, *The Organizational Weapon* dealt with sources of a particular kind of institutional achievement. *Leadership in Administration* moves further, to explore the sources of such achievement more generally. But if the ambition was broader, and the sensibility was beginning to change in a more self-consciously constructive direction, the theoretical project was continuous. It drew upon and extended a distinctive understanding of the social character of organizations and institutions, and it did so with a view to exploring how values and ideals might be prone, on the one hand, to subversion and, on the other, to be realized.

At the time of writing *The Organizational Weapon*, Selznick did not inject his *own* theorization of what was valuable in the world. Rather, his question was: if you wish to achieve something you think valuable, what do you need to take into account and to do? In particular, how should you fashion the *means* you will need to achieve your ends? This was his stance too in *Leadership in Administration*. However, at least from the time he came to be interested in law in the mid-1950s, and then for the rest of his life, he was intent to explore the conditions of what was truly valuable in the world, not merely what someone valued. This led him deep into an 'ecumenical', '*humanist*' understanding of social science, according to which the fundamental questions have to do with what values and ideals are at stake in social arrangements, and the answers need to be sought wherever they might be found, whether in the investigations of 'value free' social scientists, the reflections of moral and political philosophers, the findings of historians, and reflections of humanists of other stripes as well. His later writings took up large questions concerning society, politics, institutions, law, and morals. They were pursued within general sociology, the sociology of organizations and institutions, management theory, political science, industrial sociology, the sociology and philosophy of law, political theory and social philosophy grounded in 'humanist science.'[83] They took him far from both the subject of *The Organizational Weapon* and the tone in which it was written. However, the continuities are deep. These were continuities both of focus and also of sensibility.

Selznick begins his last major, and magisterial, work *The Moral Commonwealth*, with reflections on his earliest intellectual preoccupations. These are worth quoting at some length, since—though Selznick's thoughts and political and moral beliefs developed hugely in the forty years between *The Organizational Weapon* and *The Moral Commonwealth*—the passages below give a context and a theme that connects the earlier book to all his works, at the same time as they convey the sensibility and central concerns of a distinguished mind, at work over a very long stretch of time and a spacious and varied terrain:

> In my late teens and early twenties I went through an intense, fruitful, and in some ways extraordinary experience. . . . I belonged for a time (1937-1940) to a Trotskyist youth organization. In those days the Trotskyists stood for militant anti-Stalinism as well as for revolutionary socialism. Beleaguered and despised in many quarters, the movement was nevertheless attractive to left-leaning intellectuals who were repelled by the tyranny and terror of the Soviet Union, the subservience and mendacity of American communists, and what they thought of as confusion and impotence among socialists and liberals. . . .
>
> At that time I was also an eager student of sociology and philosophy. The two parts of my life did not fit very well. . . . I could not be a Marxist and also respond as warmly as I did, during those same years, to the scientific humanism of Morris R. Cohen and, a bit later, to the pragmatism of John Dewey. . . . Together with some others, I soon left the organization. We were convinced that Stalinism was no aberration. Rather, the Leninist doctrine so faithfully preserved by Trotsky, and still adhered to by those who had recently rejected his leadership, was fully responsible for the dreadful outcome of the first Russian Revolution. . . .
>
> When I rejected Marxism/Leninism, and a few years later socialism as well, I did not suppose I was abandoning the faith that reason, love, and justice can be vital and transforming ingredients of human society. . . .
>
> I recite this brief memoir because my youthful encounter with revolu-

---

[83] And thus the title of his last book, written in increasingly difficult circumstances and published just two years before his death, *A Humanist Science: Values and Ideals in Social Inquiry*, Stanford University Press, Stanford, Calif., 2008.

tionary socialism established a theme that influenced my work over many years. I have in mind the fate of ideals in the course of social practice. Most of my specialized writings in the sociology of organizations and sociology of law have been preoccupied with the conditions and processes that frustrate ideals or, instead, give them life and hope.[84]

The last of these paragraphs is as deft a summary of a life of work on many subjects in many domains as one is likely to find. It can stand on its own. However, it gains resonance from the paragraphs that precede it. These evoke both the sources of his varied interests and the centrality through all of them, of his concern with 'the conditions and processes that frustrate ideals or, instead, give them life and hope.'

I have claimed elsewhere that there is a distinctive and attractive sensibility that connects Selznick's varied works, one that I think of as his Hobbesian idealism. That is not meant to be oxymoron or paradox, but simply to characterize his self-conscious determination not to succumb to either element of the coupling. Thus:

> Selznick recognized evil and the importance of resisting it. However, he refused to let that realism douse idealism: A forced choice between the two, he insisted, was commonly a false choice. It was possible—it was right—both to acknowledge that things could be worse while at the same time seeking to make them better. Security against the first was crucial; aspirations for the latter equally so.
>
> These are simple points to state but harder to appreciate and internalize, to *live*. They pull in different directions and typically appeal to people of different temperament. Selznick came to live them. He was that rare but distinguished type: a Hobbesian idealist, temperamentally and intellectually alert both to threat and to promise.[85]

Both these elements are already evident in *The Organizational Weapon*. They lie behind it and inform it. They help make of that work at once far more than an ephemeral political intervention and at the same time more engaged and engaging than is common in academic work. This is one more reason among several to commend this work, as indeed I commend all Selznick's works, to a new generation of readers.

MARTIN KRYGIER
Gordon Samuels Professor of Law and Social Theory, Law School,
University of New South Wales, and
Adjunct Professor, Regulatory Institutions Network,
Australian National University

Sydney, Australia
August, 2014

---

[84] *The Moral Commonwealth*, University of California Press, Berkeley, 1992, ix-x.

[85] *Philip Selznick: Ideals in the World*, 10-11.

Preface • 1960

Among the practical aims, and theoretical puzzles, of modern social science is the assessment of human institutions. Whether we speak of a trade union, a political party, a school, a business, a government agency, or any other complex enterprise, we wish to know what goals or objectives can be attributed to it, what capabilities it has, what strategies it lives by, and what its probable line of evolution may be. Assessments of this kind are necessary for the proper diagnosis of an organization's own troubles and for an understanding of how the organization relates to other institutions and to the community. This sort of understanding is especially relevant when groups are in conflict and we need to assess the possibilities of eventual accommodation or the likelihood of irreconcilable struggle.

The Organizational Weapon (reprinted now without alteration) was written with an eye to developing a theory of institutional assessment; and, at the same time, as offering a special key to the understanding of communism. These aims should be kept in mind by the reader, for they necessarily introduce a selective emphasis. The study is not a full account of communism in the modern world, nor does it attempt to explain everything about communism. Furthermore, the organizational strategies explored here, important as they are and have been, are not presented as the ultimate arbiters of victory or defeat in the struggle between totalitarian communism and the free world. My aim was to search out certain central features of the communist type of political party and to trace its characteristic role in the political arena. I hoped in this way to help sharpen our political intelligence, especially as applied to areas of the world where organizational stratagems could still have a great effect in transforming an ideologically isolated group into a powerful political instrument. Ideological isolation has been a perennial challenge to the communist strategists and tacticians. Organizational strategy is a way of overcoming that isolation, combining ideological deception with a special expertise and discipline. Obviously, however, communist ideological isolation has not been equally great everywhere or at all times. Therefore, the analysis presented in this book does not apply with equal cogency to every phase of communist history. It "fits" most adequately, the more remote and unappealing communist doctrine is within the population set up as a target. On the other hand, despite differences in degree, ideological isolation has plagued communism almost everywhere for long periods, and it loomed very large in the thinking of those who formulated the movement's organizational principles. For this reason, I believe the "model" developed in this book provides a fair interpretation of the communist "vanguard" or "combat" party, wherever it is found.

The comments that I can offer here will deal with two aspects of the study that have raised problems for some readers. First, there is the "logic" of institutional analysis, especially of the attempt to state the essential and distinctive features of a social institution. Second, I should like to discuss very briefly, the relation between communism and "mass society," a connection dealt with from a special point of view in Chapter 7.

Analyzing Social Systems

In contemporary sociology the word "institution" is used in two related senses. It may refer to an *organized group* having certain special attributes; or it may refer to an established *practice*, such as marriage or the secret ballot. In either case, the idea of institution suggests that the group or the practice has a special identity, which may mean that it has a peculiar capacity to do a certain kind of job, that it embodies a special set of values, or simply that it has had a significantly unique history. This discussion, of course, is mainly concerned with institutions as organized groups.

Among the problems that arise when we attempt to identify and diagnose institutionalized groups, three are of special interest here: (1) the justification for attributing to the group a special nature or identity; (2) the empirical testing of the theoretical model constructed; and (3) the risk that such treatments are "ahistorical" and radically defective on that account.

As a way of considering these issues, especially (1) and (2), I should like to develop the idea that the analysis of institutions calls for a logic of "interpretation," and that in this respect something can be learned from other interpretive fields of inquiry, especially psychoanalysis. We may speak of interpretive, or dynamic, or analytical sociology in much the same way as, in referring to psychoanalysis, we speak of analytical or dynamic psychology. I am thinking of all who work with the main tools developed by Freud, not just of orthodox Freudians. Indeed, the more recent emphasis on "ego psychology" is especially pertinent.

Although much has been said about the relation of psychoanalysis to sociology, and some important interdisciplinary work has been done, little attention has been devoted to the logical or procedural convergence of the two fields. The psychological interpretation of social events is not at issue here. The suggestion is, rather, that the logic or mode of analysis associated with dynamic psychology may be similar in essential ways to the analytical logic of sociology, at least when coherent, adaptive social organisms are being studied.

The characteristic quest of the interpretive analyst is not for a mere description or history. Nor is he interested in how selected variables are related to each other. The protocol of a free-association interview, or a life history, is scrutinized for "revealing" symptoms. What is revealed? The relation between id impulses, ego structure, and social pressure will form, it is presumed, a constellation inferable from the individual's overt behavior, including his verbal responses. The patient is studied for signs which reveal an underlying (latent) pattern. To expose this pattern, by way of the analysis of symptoms, is the goal of interpretation.

No given event is inherently a symptom. Thus Fenichel notes: "A patient used to dream exclusively about food, and the analysis apparently made no progress. It turned out that he actually did not have enough to eat. After he succeeded in getting a job, the 'oral' dreams disappeared and the analysis went on normally."[1] A dream about food, a slip of the tongue, or any other event which is potentially symptomatic, must be examined for its relation to other events, also symptomatic, before its evidential status can be assessed. This is not different logically from the role of a bellyache in routine medical diagnosis. A symptom is always part of a syndrome. It is the presence of the syndrome which permits inferences regarding the latent structure.

Similarly, interpretation in sociology scrutinizes a mass of data to find indicators of an underlying pattern. There is nothing interpretive about a public opinion poll until an inference is made about a latent structure. Even this is a low-order interpretation if it does nothing more than assess the validity of attributing a specific attitude to a population, say hostility or indifference toward a particular government program. We move toward fuller interpretation as we look for evidences of a constellation of attitudes, or at least of a single orientation so powerful that it shapes many aspects of behavior. Studies of apathy or impotence, or of the "mind" of military or political elites are interpretive in this sense. The essence of the interpretive process is the drawing of conclusions, from the study of observable "indicators," that some underling pattern or configuration exists. The sentiments, self-images, and dispositions of a population are, of course, not the only kinds of latent patterns that may be identified.

Psychoanalysis is often referred to as "depth" psychology. The analyst "probes." These metaphors lend emphasis to the search for hidden motives and commitments which shape overt behavior in unrecognized ways. Whether in the analysis of a personality or a social system, interpretive probing seeks to identify the latent motive or intent, the stake or interest, the implicit image of the self or of the other.

As interpretation develops in sophistication, it attempts to reveal self-activating, empirically closed systems which have, as is sometimes said, "laws of their own." It is this focus on self-activating systems which provides the "dynamic" element and name associated with psychoanalysis. Ego systems are constituted of empirically integrated strivings, conflicts, and defensive patterns. The "system" is not simply a set of logically related propositions, nor is it a set of arbitrarily isolated variables whose interrelations are studied. A particular ego system is an *organic* system, found in nature as such, analogous to a "solar system," "capitalist system," "circulatory system," or any other empirically isolable structure which, though never completely independent, is sufficiently autonomous to maintain its integrity as a system against at least some of the forces that would break it down. Characteristically, changes from within occur, serving a defensive function, and these defensive changes may result in pathological states.

Like other natural systems, ego systems are found inescapably bound to and conditioned by a larger empirical matrix. In inquiry, therefore, these systems must be treated as models, conceptually isolated, so that the specific potentialities of the system for influencing behavior may be explored. What the analyst does is something like this: He is faced with a specific problem, to make sense of a given pattern of behavior. He has available to him, as a sort of armory of analysis, a large

---

[1] Otto Fenichel, *The Psychoanalytic Theory of Neurosis* (New York: Norton, 1945), p. 24.

number of statements about personality, only some of which may be relevant to the case at hand. From among all these statements, he chooses a special set of connected ideas which seem to state the "essential features" of a latent psychic structure which, if it exists, will account for the patient's behavior.

In effect, drawing upon existing general knowledge, the analyst constructs a model of the psychic structure he is studying. Sometimes a standardized model is directly available to him, because certain recurrent syndromes and their under-lying psychic structures have been identified and are part of funded knowledge. He may have to develop a new one. In either case, he knows that the totality of concrete behavior is not explained by this model; neither does he justify it only because abstractions in general are justified. Rather, he hopes that he has hit upon the *proper* assessment of his patient's unconscious needs, ego strength, and other manifestations of a psychic state. He will then be able to explain and predict, not everything, but certain events, such as a flight from responsibility, which are relevant to the system he is studying. He knows, moreover, that the model will tell him only certain general potentialities, and that specific events will always depend upon many other factors.

Sociological interpretation treats social systems in much the same way. If we wish to study Athenian democracy, or the Roman imperial system, or the bol-shevik type of party, or any other institutional structure, we must treat it as an autonomous system, defined by inner potentialities and weaknesses, even though we know that this autonomy is limited and in fact the behavior we observe is a resultant of many interacting forces. The nature of Athenian democracy is not re-vealed to us by a complete description; we look for certain defining characteristics, such as, perhaps, dependence on slavery, and we try to draw out the implications of these special characteristics or commitments. In doing so, we set up a simplified model of the institutional system, and test it by seeing whether certain important events, otherwise inexplicable, are illuminated or predicted by it.

In studying personality, the analyst focuses attention upon inner forces tending to break down the system, especially upon conflicting needs and desires. Hence "conflict" is a very common word in the vocabulary of psychoanalysis. More generally, the study of inherent tensions is a crucial phase of interpretive analysis because this procedure helps to identify the system at hand. Systems may be lo-cated empirically by specifying their special, characteristic inner conflicts.

There is an important difference between disturbances created in a system by environing forces and those inherent tensions which arise from the system itself. Ego systems, like other natural systems, are "irritable" and respond to external stimuli in more or less predictable ways, e.g., in mustering defense mechanisms. But the tensions I am thinking of here are essentially *internal*, for example those created by the conflict between libidinal drives and dependency needs. Similarly, any organization may face a harsh environment, leading to inner stress and adap-tive change of both the organization and its environment. But these difficulties are externally derived. Inherent tensions are rather such as are generated by the very act of delegation, which creates new centers of interest and power, yet is an indis-pensable phase of organizational experience. Thus stress must be placed on the qualifier "inherent." The analyst is not necessarily interested in any disturbance, but primarily in those derived from the nature of the system itself.

Freudian analysis probes to discover the forces which *constrain and summon* behavior in determinate directions. The analyst is interested in what the individual *has* to do as a result of commitments from which he cannot readily escape. Commitments may change, but this involves a reconstruction of the system. Of the complaining wife, the therapist may ask: does she really want to leave her husband? Or is she in fact so committed to him that she must accept him and work out a solution on the basis of that acceptance? These questions have to do with the identification of a system of interpersonal relations. That identification proceeds through the discovery of latent commitments.

Social systems also are identified by latent commitments. An organization leader may ask, "What business are we really in?" In doing so he is trying to specify the social system of which he is a part by uncovering those involvements which in fact determine the purpose of the enterprise, a purpose not necessarily the same as what is formally acknowledged. Similarly, we identify the feudal system or the capitalist system or a bureaucratic system by discovering the set of commitments which uniquely characterizes each. If a man is a feudal lord, or a capitalist entrepreneur, or a bureaucrat, we infer from our model of the system which shapes him what he *must* do precisely because of his involvement in that system.

These remarks are meant to suggest, in lieu of a more extended analysis, a mode of interpretation applicable to both social systems and personalities. Stated elliptically, the basic idea is that sociological interpretation should be viewed as the search for "models" of "latent structures." This was the approach used in *The Organizational Weapon*.

What was presented for analysis in that study was the manifest behavior of certain groups called in common sense "communist parties." Much was known about membership in such organizations, about their leadership, and about the way they behaved vis-à-vis other groups in a large variety of settings. Many sophisticated observers understood that, in some sense, these political "parties" were decisively different from other agencies of political action. But the basis of this judgment had not been systematically explored. Therefore the rational ground for concluding, for example, that united action by liberals and communists was extremely dangerous for the former, had not been satisfactorily established. It was my belief that an adequate assessment of this institution demanded that special attention be given to the distinctive organizational characteristics of the communists, including their organizational strategies and tactics.

The basic intellectual task was to formulate a complex hypothesis stating the essential features of a going concern, a system, such that the most important distinctive attributes of communist political action would be accounted for. These attributes included the remarkable persistence of the communist core membership despite great fluctuations and turnover, and the persistence of strategies and tactics of power aggrandizement despite significant shifts in political "line." The search was clearly for a "latent structure," an emergent pattern of adherence and control, of self-perpetuating, interlocking commitments. The name "combat party" was devised to designate this system of interdependent behaviors, relationships, and beliefs.

The elements of this latent structure are developed in Chapter 1 and summarized on pp. 72-73. They consist essentially of distinctive modes of group membership and distinctive modes of social control. A system is created capable of making very large demands upon totally involved members. It is a system marked by a *distinctive competence to turn members of a voluntary association into disciplined and deployable political agents*. This competence, of course, does not extend uniformly to all members and under all conditions. But it does explain the creation and maintenance of the communist core, which is all that is really needed.

The hypothesis is elaborated by specifying a number of ways in which such a system is built and maintained. This elaboration is in turn a partial confirmation of the hypothesis, for we do not find the techniques that sustain such a system, playing so central a role in the life of the group, in the absence of the system itself. A similar logic applies in personality analysis. A particular assessment or diagnosis will be both elaborated and supported as the analyst discovers in the patient certain characteristic responses and mechanisms. Of course, there is the additional requirement that these discoveries be of central rather than marginal importance in the psychic economy of the individual. The same requirement applies to the study of social systems.

In addition to specifying the combat party's "distinctive competence," the system is identified in other ways. One of these brings to bear the idea of "inherent tension" discussed above. Thus the point is made (pp. 64, 73) that the combat party must continuously guard against certain characteristic dangers: excessive isolation on the one hand and liquidation on the other. To build and sustain the system requires a heavy emphasis on the withdrawal of members from society and upon ultimate doctrinal purity; at the same time the members must be deployed in the political arena. The first carries the risk that the party will be transformed into an isolated sect, the second that members will place the interests of target groups, such as trade unions, above those of the party itself. The working out of this inner conflict not only summarizes a considerable portion of communist history but also helps us to identify what the necessities of the system are, what has to be done in order to maintain its peculiar integrity. It also indicates that the system is not necessarily eternal, that there are points of special stress which, under appropriate circumstances, might lead to its transformation. On the other hand, one of the lessons of this analysis is that such a transformation cannot be expected so long as the special techniques that maintain the system remain in force. The period of Earl Browder's leadership of the American communists gave many outward signs of liquidation, but most of the fundamental mechanisms by which the communist core is recruited and maintained, including especially the unremitting effort to control and manipulate trade unions and peripheral organizations, continued in effect. The latent structure of communist politics is not completely revealed until the system is seen in action. The nature of the system unfolds as we identify its characteristic strategies, its special ways of perceiving the world and of relating to it. Four chapters are devoted to this phase of the study. They describe the specialized strategies developed to overcome the organizational isolation of the combat party (the strategies of "access" and "legitimation"), to bring the greatest benefit from whatever organizational conquests are made (the strategy of "mobilization"), and to forestall those who compete for the same target groups (the strategy of "neutralization"). In the course of this analysis we see that the combat party is also an "organizational weapon," an inherently subversive instrument unrestrained by the constitutional order of any arena within which it functions.

The capabilities of the combat party make subversion congenial to it. This, of course, is reinforced by the special political aims of communism. But the political and the organizational dimensions reinforce each other. We cannot truly determine the aims of an institution without knowing what it is as a social system—how it is held together, what resources it can muster and what it can do with them, and what its posture is in relation to other groups. The interdependence of strategy and distinctive competence is especially important; hence the study of institutional capabilities is a vital phase of institutional assessment. Only in this way can we distinguish effectively between merely verbal aims, or such as may be derived solely from doctrine, and aims that truly guide behavior because they are embodied in and supported by the social structure of the group.

In a work of this kind, the major concern is to identify the system, to state what the "nature of the beast" is. The task is to construct a conceptual model of a functioning institutional system. But this is also an exercise in typology. We view the structure we are studying as an instance of a class of objects whose general features are to be explored. The class may have only one member, but it is the kind of thing we are dealing with that interests us. We ask: what kind of a social system is the communist party? We answer by developing a model of the "combat party," including its strategies.

The testing of such a model presents some knotty problems. Since it is admittedly abstract and selective, it is not always easy to state the conditions under which it might be considered false. I think there are two ways of handling this problem, reflecting two different issues.

The first issue is whether the model fits in a particular case. For this purpose the model does specify certain crucial defining characteristics. These can be used to test its applicability. Thus the combat party is identified by (1) its capacity, relative to other political groups, to deploy members as controlled agents within target groups; (2) its use of techniques of indoctrination and mobilization that withdraw the member from other group loyalties; (3) its adoption of subversion, not only of government but of particular target institutions, as an acceptable mode of social action; (4) its use of characteristic strategies for the penetration and manipulation of institutional targets; (5) its tactical subordination of propagandistic aims to organizational needs (see pp. 137 ff.).

Taken together, as a syndrome, these elements permit an assessment of a particular organization to see whether it essentially conforms to the model. If it does, we may predict with some confidence that it will respond in determinate and characteristic ways when opportunities arise. For example, we expect this type of party to subvert a coalition government and to do so in predictable ways (see pp. 260 ff.); we expect it to eschew mass action under some conditions (see pp. 253

ff.) and to encourage it under others. Thus the model can be tested by determining how well it fits *the relevant features* of a particular organization.

The second issue is whether the model states an acceptable general theory regarding the nature of the communist type of party. Such a theory, of course, can only be offered as a "best fit," subject to deviations that can be accounted for by special circumstances. This is normal scientific procedure. We always need some theory of what the system is like in a "pure state," even if the theory is inadequate. To be sure, we expect that in due course a substitute or supplementary theory, able to account systematically for persistent deviations, will ultimately be formulated. But the mere fact that empirical deviations occur is no basis for rejecting a model that already accounts for a great deal of what needs to be explained. Certainly it is no ground for denying the quest for a general theory entirely.

Another problem that arises when a study places central emphasis on identifying the system is the appearance it may give of slighting historical change. Obviously, the very idea of a system, as used here, suggests that certain social configurations are viable and that they do persist through time. A corollary is that not all change is significant; many changes leave the system essentially as it was. Nevertheless, there is an important sense in which the analysis of social systems does deal with significant change.

At a number of points in this book, changes in communist strategy are explicitly discussed. Thus the evolution of communist "united front" policy is dealt with in some detail, pp. 126-144. Three stages of development are identified, culminating in a final, mature stage, in which unity with other groups is characteristically a cover for organizational maneuver. Similarly, a line of development is traced with regard to the communist technique of insurrection. "Bolshevism since Lenin has diminished its emphasis on stimulating mass energy and has increased its reliance on the party and its agencies" (p. 254). Bolshevism is seen as gradually detaching itself from any particular mass base, and from dependence on mass action. This is viewed, not as an adventitious historical trend but as a natural accompaniment of the system's growth to full maturity.

Clearly the study of social systems must take account of the fact that these entities do not emerge full-blown, ready to operate at peak strength. As organic unities they may exhibit stages of growth and decline. In other words, the significant history is *evolutionary*, identifying processes of fulfillment and decay, the unfolding of inner potentiality and the movement toward a stable configuration. Evolutionary trends are not always there to be found, but where they are found they provide the materials for a peculiarly relevant historical analysis. In the case of bolshevism, there is much evidence of a basic line of development, manifested in many different ways, from an early, inherently unstable Leninist phase to a more mature and stable Stalinist phase. These were stages in the development of a single system. Its potentialities took some years to unfold but its foundations were truly laid during the earlier period.

"Mass Society"

Chapter 7, "Vulnerability of Institutional Targets," was presented as a "frankly speculative" effort to specify some of the conditions under which institutions may be vulnerable to communist penetration and manipulation. The concern here was plainly with the sources of weakness in "our institutions," that is, the institutions of the modern industrialized nations of the free world. The basic thesis is that modern "mass" society runs the risk of exposing its institutions to subversive attack insofar as elites become insecure, mass behavior influences politics and culture, and values become attenuated.

Two cautions were explicitly introduced at several points. First the aim of the analysis was to identify some inherent tendencies of modern society (see pp. 279, 291). In other words, "mass society" is an analytical category, a way of summarizing a set of forces and relationships which will produce, in the absence of counteracting forces, some special weaknesses and evolutionary trends. Societies may display these characteristics in different degrees, but insofar as the model applies, it will help identify forces that are determining the viability of political and cultural institutions.[2]

Second, the vulnerability considered here is not uniquely a vulnerability to communism. (See p. 297.) The McCarthy episode in American life during the early 1950's reflected the same exposure of institutions to political assault. The diagnosis has to do with a lowering of resistance in specific ways. The attack may come from a number of different quarters.

Of course, other conditions may also weaken institutions, e.g., the dislocations of wars and economic crises. The processes of mass society are not the only ones at work in the world. And in the less industrialized areas, where communism has scored its greatest successes, we obviously cannot speak of mass society in the same sense. Nevertheless, the theory can have relevance even in those areas, if we introduce two simple modifications. We must reformulate the theory so that, instead of defining a type of society, it states relations between kinds of things, e.g. between the emergence of "masses" and institutional debilitation. We must also detach the theory from any *specific* set of conditions under which these relationships obtain. When this is done, we may discover a broader range of conditions producing essentially the same phenomena. The atomization of society, including the breakdown of "intermediate groups," may be brought about in a number of ways, including the sudden tearing of a traditional social fabric under conditions of rapid industrial, political, and cultural modernization.

No scientific theory can properly purport to predict the outcome of a theoretically identified process in the absence of known initial conditions. Under differing initial conditions, there will be expected variations in outcome. The ideal is to be able to state, given certain initial conditions, what will result after the known processes have had their effect. This in turn assumes that disturbing or counteracting forces have been controlled or accounted for; and it assumes that the theory is sufficiently well developed to be able to specify a *particular* outcome rather that a

---

[2]   See William Kornhauser, *The Politics of Mass Society* (Glencoe, Ill.: The Free Press, 1959), p. 228.

range of possible outcomes. It is obvious that this degree of rigor is not available to us so far as the theory of mass society, or of mass-elite relations, is concerned.

Nevertheless, the theory as it is being developed today can help us to order and explain a great deal about modern politics and culture. It is also germane to a theory of institutional assessment, in that it specifies a broad context within which institutional leadership is weakened and new forms of participation emerge.

P. S.

Berkeley, California
1960

Acknowledgments

This study owes much to the sustained collaboration of Joseph M. Goldsen, Paul Kecskemeti, and Hans Speier. They reviewed the entire manuscript in its various stages and wrote critiques on which I have relied heavily in preparing a final draft. Special thanks are also due to Harry S. Hall, who helped in many ways.

For expert assistance on trade-union and related matters, I wish to thank Daniel Bell of *Fortune*; Kermit Eby of the University of Chicago; William Gausman of Labor Press Association; Paul Jacobs of the Oil Workers International Union; and Murray Kempton of the New York *Post*.

Philip Selznick

Santa Monica, California
June, 1951

THE
ORGANIZATIONAL
WEAPON

INTRODUCTION

{page 1 in original}

This study has two objectives: (1) to analyze the use of organizations and organizational practices as weapons in the struggle for power and (2) to deepen our understanding of bolshevik strategy and tactics.

These aims sustain each other. Leninism, with its strong emphasis on the power of disciplined minorities, affords a most useful case history for the study of organizational weapons. At the same time, it is important to learn about organizational manipulation if we are fully to comprehend the bolshevik experience.

Using the special role of organization as a key, we may expect to learn something about the *inner dynamics* of bolshevism—that pattern of motivation and action which impels it onward to ever-renewed power struggles. Organizational analysis will illuminate the nature of bolshevism's central vehicle: the combat party. It will help us to understand the underlying organizational strategies that persist through many changes in the communist propaganda line. We shall be able to identify some of those special characteristics of bolshevism which, in many key areas, have given it strength beyond its capacity to win public support.

Throughout this study we shall be concerned with certain special aspects of *political combat*. Great social changes, however, can never be understood as the products of organizational or ideological maneuver. The day-to-day struggle must be viewed against the background of those less obvious shifts in the pattern of human life that create the historical alternatives confronting every age. A full appraisal of communism's impact on our own time, with conclusions for action on many fronts, would necessarily deal with that broad background. That task has not been undertaken here. It should therefore be remembered that this study is selective, dealing with only limited aspects of a far broader subject. {2}

What Is An Organizational Weapon?

It is a primary function of the constitutional order—whether of a particular organization or of the political community itself—to make power *responsible* by limiting the uses to which it may be put and specifying how it may be won. These limitations are designed to ensure that political contests do not undermine the central values of the community and the integrity of its institutions. The struggle for power is subversive when methods are used that do not heed these rules.

We shall speak of organizations and organizational practices as weapons when they are used by a power-seeking elite[1] *in a manner unrestrained by the consti-*

---

[1] Throughout this study, the term "elite" is used in its objective political and sociological meaning to denote those who, in any given social context, are the more influential, the more self-conscious, and the more manipulative elements. The term may be used to designate

1

tutional order of the arena within which the contest takes place. In this usage, "weapon" is not meant to denote *any* political tool, but one torn from its normal context and unacceptable to the community as a legitimate mode of action. Thus the partisan practices used in an election campaign—insofar as they adhere to the written and unwritten rules of the contest—are not weapons in this sense. On the other hand, when members who join an organization in apparent good faith are in fact the agents of an outside elite, then routine affiliation becomes "infiltration.

Organizational weapons exploit a source of power that is latent in every group enterprise. This is the capacity of almost any routine activity to be manipulated for personal or political advantage. For example:

1. A group of friends within an organization may become a power clique if the by-products of their association (the exchange of information, mutual support, etc.) are exploited systematically. The informal group may become a weapon in a hidden struggle for power, especially if there is some basis for cohesion beyond personal {3} ties and if the interests of the organization as a whole are subordinated to those of the clique.

2. In choosing among alternative courses of action, an official often has opportunity to influence the distribution of power, both inside and outside the organization. He may then modify his technical decisions so as to choose a policy that will aid his friends and hurt his enemies. From the standpoint of the power struggle, the official position then functions as an organizational weapon.

3. Proposals for administrative reorganization are often aimed at disturbing the existing power structure of an organization. An administrative unit seeking to extend its area of influence may screen its true activities behind proposals for more efficient internal organization or for closer cooperation with outside groups. Among experienced officials it is generally understood, although not always acknowledged, that such proposals will be closely inspected for their potential impact on the informal power structure inside the organization.

4. Most political parties, organized to function only in the electoral arena, mobilize their adherents only partially. Such groups are usually content to win a general loyalty, and to "get out the vote." This is consistent with their limited constitutional role. But if a fuller mobilization is attempted, integrating the members so effectively that they become available for continuous deployment in many arenas, a reservoir of energy will be developed that can be used outside the normal framework of political controversy. A source of power is tapped which may be used in conspiratorial ways to gain influence for an elite that cannot compete effectively at the polls.

5. Organizations established for limited purposes (trade-unions, civic groups, etc.) develop strength that may be diverted to other, more far-reaching aims. If irresponsible power-seekers gain control, this incidental utility may be exploited without regard to the limitations set by the initial character of the group. Every organization is in some respects useful to such elites, if only because funds, internal education, and jobs may be manipulated to serve a partisan interest. {4}

The exploitation of organizational potentialities in these ways entails secrecy

---

whole groups, and elite members may or may not be official leaders. The latter, if they are in fact covertly manipulated, may in the given situation be nonelite.

and subversion. Authority is used for unapproved ends, notably irresponsible power; and illegitimate channels for the attainment of influence are created. If, therefore, in the hiring of personnel, an official builds a personal machine, he will usually conceal this deviation from straightforward personnel administration. At the same time, he will be undermining the formal aims and constitutional order of his organization.

A constitution, it should be recalled, is not necessarily formalized. It includes all the traditional rules and expectations that define and control legitimate controversy. Moreover, in imposing its limitations on the struggle for power, the community continually extends the constitutional sphere to include new areas within which power is generated and won. The control of corporations, trade-unions, and pressure groups is a process of this sort, whereby society moves clumsily to an extension of responsible power beyond the narrowly political realm. By the same token, it is in those areas of power not yet fully recognized, or not readily controlled, that a struggle may take place divorced from ends and methods approved by the community.

The Relevance of Leninism

No group has a monopoly on the use of organizational weapons. But a functioning constitutional system minimizes the use of such devices by confining power-seekers to certain accepted arenas and methods. These restraints are not necessarily rigid or permanent, for constitutions continually accommodate themselves to new modes of action required by social change. In their turn, political parties, unions, pressure groups, and other agencies adapt themselves to the conditions set by the constitutional order; in doing so, they become ill-fitted for subversion. Upon this mutual adaptation of the recognized system of order and the instruments of action rests the continued stability of the political community.

A new social force, whose role in the community is unclear, may {5} sometimes appear to be subversive. The rise of trade-unionism, for example, was accompanied by fear that the new organizations would challenge the prevailing system of industrial and political governance. In time it became clear that the labor movement was not a basic threat to the constitutional order, even within industry, and that certainly room could be made for it within the going political system. *Its participation could be regularized because its aims were limited.* These limited aims are reflected in self-imposed restraints on the extension and use of trade-union power.

Communist subversion is of another order. The difference lies in the central aim of Leninism: the concentration of total social power in the hands of a ruling group. This is not the only goal of bolshevism, but this search for unlimited power decisively shapes the behavior of the communist parties. Whether or not we say that bolsheviks seek power for its own sake, or in order to further some more ultimate aims, makes little difference. For these distant goals do not restrain the power-seeking activities of the movement. Moreover, since the goal of total power necessarily entails the overthrow of a constitutional system granting only limited and temporary power to an elected government, there can be no question of absorbing communism into the established framework.

Nor is it to be expected that communism will adapt itself to the constitutional order. To be sure, other movements, as they have gained influence and a stake in the status quo, have altered their aims. But the problem is not one of goals alone, but of methods that have placed their stamp upon the character of this movement and are sustained in action wherever bolshevism exists. These methods are inherently subversive because they represent an unrelenting search for power in areas and by devices which know no constitutional restraint. The continued use of these methods holds communism to the revolutionary line.

The nature of bolshevism cannot be understood unless we grasp the fact that Leninist political doctrine rests upon a broad interpretation of the nature of power. In particular, bolshevik theory and {6} practice recognize that power is *social*, generated in the course of all types of action (not simply the narrowly "political") and latent in all institutions. This insight stems in part from basic Marxist theory and in part from the over-all aim of bolshevism—a total transformation of society that will invest every institution with political meaning.

Leninism views politics as omnipresent. As a consequence, bolshevik strategy has identified vast new areas of political potential in what are usually thought to be nonpolitical special-purpose social institutions and mass organizations. This theory of power has increased the sensitivity of bolshevik strategy to unconventional methods of gaining influence. Exploitation of these devices has helped to keep the communist movement from adapting itself to constitutional methods; in this way, it has rejected the path of accommodation taken, for example, by most sections of the international socialist movement.

The bolshevik pursuit of power is subversive (1) because it is not limited to the areas where constitutional, responsible power is won, but is carried on everywhere in the social structure, wherever an increment of power can be squeezed from control of an institution or a portion of it; and (2) because communism knows no stopping place in its search for power short of concentrating total control in its own hands. This unceasing and unbounded struggle, associated with the politicalization of every facet of society, is a basic characteristic of totalitarian politics. Many of communism's specific techniques are found elsewhere as well, but total subversion summons *all* the devices normally hidden in the interstices of a political order, emerging temporarily and episodically in times of constitutional weakness or crisis.

It is convenient for a subversive group to seek sources of power that may be won without bidding for direct popular support. Consequently it is better to work where small disciplined minorities can have their greatest impact. These are areas neglected by the major political forces, where the marginal strength of a minority can be {7} most effective. Recognizing the importance of such areas of operation. Leninism stresses the need to build organizations designed to compete effectively in nonelectoral arenas.

The sensitivity of communism to the social aspects of political power is reflected in its use of organizational weapons. Close attention is given to such problems as the social base upon which an organization rests, the social composition of its membership or personnel, the legitimacy[2] of its participation in political life, and the function of ideology in building morale. Thus not only are unconventional sources of power recognized and exploited, but specific organizations can be strengthened by taking account of sociological variables. Alertness to these variables is closely related to the stress on Marxist-Leninist political theory.

The analysis of Leninism is useful in identifying some of the action aspects of psychological warfare. For bolshevism has not been content to propagandize for its program; it has sought to control directly the *arena* of conflict. This has required the creation of unconventional tools of intervention (the combat party and peripheral organizations), the direct weakening of propaganda targets (through penetration of vulnerable institutions), and the development of an organizational strategy to maximize accessibility and neutralize opposition. It therefore becomes clear that the action aspects of psychological warfare are not restricted to "propaganda of the deed," important as that is, but include efforts to control the conditions under which agitation and propaganda are carried on.

Marxist doctrine stresses the division of society into segments having latent interests. According to this view, men are moved by social needs and pressures toward unity or into conflict. This theory pays little attention to mass psychology, to irrational forces, or to the techniques by which responses to emotional stimuli are evoked. Instead it emphasizes the vulnerability of broad segments of society to manipulation by elite groups that propose answers to day-to-day {8} problems. It becomes especially useful, therefore, to devise ways of attaining and coordinating positions of leadership among these "masses"—a type of action that can set the stage for a propaganda offensive.

Ideology and Organization

"The proletariat has no other weapon in the fight for power except organization . . . the proletariat can become and inevitably will become a dominant force only because its intellectual unity created by the principles of Marxism is fortified by the material unity of organization which welds millions of toilers into an army of the working class." This stress on organization is the kernel of Lenin's entire viewpoint; it is an emphasis that provides a thread of consistency through the variations in communist political warfare.

For Lenin, organization was an indispensable adjunct to ideology. He did not believe that he could win power by propaganda alone. Rather, he urged the need to forge a group which, beginning with an ideological commitment, would use whatever means were available to influence decision in society. For him, the task was not so much to spread the "truth" as to raise to power a select group of communicants. Given such a perspective, the role of ideology in bolshevism, while significant, differs markedly from its role in a simple propaganda organization. Many costly errors in appraising communist activities have been made because

---

[2] "Legitimacy" is used here to mean acceptability to the community, so that within popular sentiment the right to participation is granted. Similarly, legitimate monarchs are those whose authority is accepted by the community. No favorable or unfavorable evaluation by the author is entailed.

too little attention was paid to the hidden organizational meaning of seemingly straight-forward propaganda activities.

The most general of such implications is the subordination of propaganda to the needs of organizational strategy. If the struggle for access or legitimacy demands concealment of aims, then the communists will not hesitate to hide them. This becomes evident as attacks are launched within the movement itself against those who insist on open communist propaganda, especially against those who resist organizational maneuvers that seem to compromise the explicitly communist character of the movement in the interests of {9} tactical expediency. In his pamphlet on *"Left" Communism,* used as a training document in all countries and throughout all changes in propaganda line, Lenin made this point with uninhibited clarity: "We must be able to withstand all this, to agree to any sacrifice, and even—if need be—to resort to all sorts of stratagems, artifices, illegal methods, to evasions and subterfuges, only so as to get into the trade-unions, to remain in them, and to carry on communist work within them at all costs." Written in 1920, this was directed to communists in France, England, and Germany, not to the victims of tsarist repression.

Thus Lenin did not consistently adhere to the statement in the Communist Manifesto: "The Communists disdain to conceal their views and aims." He did not ignore the injunction altogether, however, for he accepted the necessity of plain statement to the vanguard itself. He distinguished between the role of doctrine when the weapon is to be *forged* and when it is to be *used:* "As long as the question was (and insofar as it still is) one of winning over the vanguard of the proletariat to Communism, so long, and to that extent, propaganda took first place; even propaganda circles, with all the imperfections of the circles, are useful under these conditions and produce fruitful results. But when it is a question of the practical action of the masses, of the disposition, if one may so express it, of vast armies, of the alignment of *all* the class forces of the given society *for the final and decisive battle,* then propaganda habits alone, the mere repetition of the truths of 'pure' Communism, are of no avail." An explicitly communist doctrine is important for orienting the vanguard to its proper task, but in attempting to mobilize the masses, the vanguard must be prepared to adjust its use of symbols to the needs of the struggle. The vanguard is *persuaded,* is won over to communism as a doctrine, but the masses are *maneuvered* into a position of struggle against the economic and political order.

This is consistent with the Leninist distinction between propaganda and agitation. "Propaganda," roughly equivalent to "indoctrination," is used to mean the dissemination of many fundamental {10} ideas to small groups. "Agitation" is the dissemination of a few ideas, or only one idea, to many people. In practice, this distinction means that only the vanguard is exposed to a full statement of communist aims and methods, whereas the mass is mobilized by anti-capitalist slogans and appeals for "peace," "bread," "land," and "unity."

Even this view of agitation is given an action content by Lenin's statement that "agitation among the workers consists in the active participation of the Social

Democrats[3] in the spontaneous struggles of the working class, in all the clashes of the workers with the capitalists." Agitation therefore includes not only techniques of communication, but disciplined penetration by indoctrinated cadres. This conception underlines the continuity of propaganda, organization, and agitation.

As a further aspect of the subordination of propaganda to organizational strategy, it should be recognized that some propaganda activities are related primarily to the facilitating of power-oriented organizational work rather than to the spreading of general gospel. The communists are interested in suppressing active anticommunist elements (as by defamation) and may at times support any formula (such as "national unity") which will enable them to function freely within the centers of power in the community.

Although ideology, to be translated into power, requires organization, effective organization also requires ideology. Much propaganda activity apparently directed outward is in fact designed to bolster the group's own ranks and supporters. Such propaganda plays an indispensable role in strengthening cohesion and discipline. In building an activist social movement, it is important to give the membership a sense of unique mission so that attitudes of dedication may be reinforced; this may be accomplished by special propaganda emphases. Similarly, the stress on action aids group solidarity by {11} maintaining a continuously alert membership. Personal commitment to the group is reinforced in the course of mutual support in action and as lives are organized around the group as a focal point. This internal relevance of propaganda and action is by no means unique to the communist movement, for in any political campaign many public meetings are held largely for the purpose of strengthening the morale of supporters. However, as in the case of other aspects of organization, the communists have made especially effective and self-conscious use of this principle.

The bolshevik emphasis on the power of the *vanguard* and on the consistent application of approved ideas operates to make political education paramount—another aspect of the importance of ideology for organization. A stress on political education follows from the assumption that the masses will move spontaneously but that the *direction* in which they move will depend on the leadership. This elite orientation makes the training of leadership a decisive element in communist organization.[4]

Finally, a stress on organized action is symbolically useful to a movement based on a negative ideology. Although socialism (identified with the USSR) functions as an integrating symbol for the communists, the ideological tenets effective for discipline and dynamic action are those which focus attention upon a threatening enemy: the bourgeoisie, the fascists, the Trotskyists, the Titoists, and the imperialists. This is a major difference between the socialist and communist

---

[3] *Read:* communists. Lenin's party was built within the Russian socialist movement; hence he referred to his own followers as Social Democrats until 1919 when the name "Communist Party" was adopted. Thereafter, "social democrat" became an epithet in the bolshevik lexicon. In this study, "communism" and "bolshevism" are not capitalized, except where a specific national party is designated, but reference is to the movement founded by Lenin.

[4] See pp. 36-42, where the role of "theory" in the organization of the combat party is discussed.

movements and helps to account for the relative weakness of the former.

The resources of hatred stimulated by this negative ideology—*against* dynamic evil forces rather than *for* an optimistic vision of the future—must be combined with positive elements, such as loyalty. These elements are supplied by an intensive emphasis upon the machinery of struggle itself—its historic leadership, its traditions, is strategy, its instruments. In this way, the organizational weapon {12} provides ample opportunity, not only for aggression, but for intensive self-sacrifice.

The Interpretive Model

No attempt is made here to present "the full story" of communism. With the perspective outlined above, our approach is necessarily selective. We are interested in constructing a model[5] that will effectively expose a *central* pattern of motivation and action, applicable in its basic features to the bolshevik movement in all countries and throughout its history. We have therefore emphasized what the record shows to be *general*, recognizing that there can be and are deviations in detail from one country or period to another, but that there *is* a persistent underlying pattern.

The task of interpretation is to identify significant patterns of motivation, interest, and need around which characteristic types of action are organized. Whether interpretation is focused on a single personality or on a political elite, the problem is one of isolating a set of interdependent variables forming a unique "system." When we have identified the system, we can tell something about the way behavior is summoned and constrained. This helps us to make predictions concerning certain likely responses. We say that the individual is "compelled" by the need to solve his inner problems to choose in characteristic ways among limited alternatives. We learn that leaders are "forced" to act in certain ways because of their commitment to specific conditions of institutional survival. The relevant system is identified by detecting repetitive symptoms. The task is always to choose that central pattern which will tell us most about the behavior we would like to predict or control.

A rigorous methodology of interpretation awaits the development {13} of new techniques of analysis; in the meantime, we must do the best we can with the available intellectual tools. In this study, an effort is made to identify the "nature" of bolshevism, as reflected in organizational practices, by defining a central institutional objective (the deployment of members as disciplined agents) and relating this objective to certain inferred needs (as for the party to engage in continuous political combat). In this process of interpretive model-building, a social system is defined, including its unique tensions (e.g., that the party is subject to the dual danger of assimilation to existing institutions and isolation from the sources of

---

[5] From among all the statements that can be made about organization, we choose a special set of connected ideas which seems to state the essential features of the phenomenon we are studying. Any such model, hence the "essential features" expressed in it, is constructed for the purpose of the inquiry at hand and is not meant to be an exhaustive description.

power), Once the model is built, it can be used to explain such apparently unrelated matters as the evolution of united-front policy.

A word may be said here concerning the observational standpoint assumed by this inquiry. Although historical materials were studied, the aim was not to write a history of bolshevism, but to explore the organizational aspects of its *operational code*. For this purpose, the main problem has been not so much to discover what the communists have in fact done, but what they would like to do and upon what principles they operate. These questions are, of course, related: an analysis of intent and strategy must be based on fact. But it is sufficient for our purpose to know, for example, that dual-power tactics are used to gain power in coup d'état, even if this has occurred only once.[6] Since tactical maneuvers are conditioned by opportunity, they may be part of the operational code even though the chance to use them arises only infrequently.

At the same time, in setting forth the general nature of bolshevism as it appears throughout the world, we have found a large body of evidence which supports the thesis that a central pattern of strategy and intent exists. Reports of communist party organization and action in Russia, the United States, France, Germany, China, the Philippines, {14} and Great Britain have been used to delineate the "model" analyzed in Chapter I, "The Combat Party." Although variations exist, the evidence fully justifies the interpretation presented there. Being abstract, it is necessarily a neater and simpler picture than would be found in any actual organization. The model necessarily speaks in terms of the code, as in the creation of a conspiratorial atmosphere or in the exploitation of the morale potentialities of Marxist doctrine; in fact, of course, no leadership ever completely fulfills its mission. The large membership turnover, splits, and other difficulties testify to the incomplete achievement. But if we wish to understand why they are able to achieve what they do, then it is to the model we must turn.

This study is based on an intensive review of the theory and practice of bolshevism.[7] The materials included: (1) the historical record, as that is available in published accounts[8] of the activities of the movement since its origin half a century ago; and (2) the voluminous self-analyses which have been produced by various members of the bolshevik elite.

It is recognized that most of the materials on bolshevism come from intensely partisan sources. Some may feel that such evidence should be disqualified. But this would be a hasty abdication of the responsibility to assess the data at hand. Materials used must be understood in their proper contexts and independent

---

[6] In the analysis of behavioral codes (as elsewhere in science), single instances are often crucial. Thus, in identifying the relation between the Communist Party and the Progressive Party in the United States, at the latter's 1948 convention, the single instance of changing the party program to conform to the official communist line on Tito is clearly crucial. Such instances become decisive because they crystallize a broader context of indirect evidence. A similar logic applies when we appraise an individual's character.

[7] Chapter VII, "Vulnerability of Institutional Targets," is a somewhat speculative effort in a field where only very poor and fragmentary data exist. Its purpose is to provide a context for the study as a whole and guides for further inquiry.

[8] Certain documentary materials were made available by various United States government agencies.

evaluations must be made, but to rule out such data would be to abandon all significant inquiry into social institutions and personalities.

From the bolshevik side, we have used extensively the self-analyses of the movement itself. A powerful social movement cannot hide its true face. It must train its members, evaluate its experiences, develop and communicate strategy and tactics. These tasks expose the true self-image, the operational goals, the basic commitments of the organization. In using bolshevik materials, *we have chosen, primarily, {15} those addressed to the initiates of the movement.* Here, in varying degrees, considerable frank discussion is available. The nature of bolshevism is thus spread upon a public record for all to read. One does not have to be an undercover agent to understand its basic features. But the communists can rely on the failure of all but a handful of outsiders to study the works of Lenin, Stalin, and their associates.

A similar approach would be necessary in studying any other social institution. In the case of a government agency or business organization, for example, the social scientist is especially interested in internal memoranda and working papers. These inevitably contain much of the self-analysis necessary for making important decisions. This is supplemented, of course, by observation of actual practice, but we do not throw out such precious data because the source is "colored" or "partisan." Indeed, we are somewhat better off in studying bolshevism because much of this internally oriented material is published, and because of the extraordinary self-consciousness of the movement.

As to anticommunist sources, we must necessarily make use of the testimony of participants, men who have found out the true nature of bolshevism during a sojourn in the party and have later chosen to reveal what they have learned. Similarly, much can be learned from those who have been in the thick of conflict against the communists. Such testimony must be evaluated for its internal consistency and its relation to other evidence. We neither accept it uncritically nor reject it out of hand. In many cases there is actually no contradiction between the testimony of such participants and the party's own affirmations. As in the case of many controversies over "the facts" concerning conditions in the Soviet Union, it is the *evaluation* of a practice which is in dispute rather than its existence.

We have also made use of the records compiled by official committees of inquiry, such as the Un-American Activities Committee of the United States House of Representatives. These investigations have often been conducted in a spirit rather far removed from scientific {16} objectivity. But this does not justify that indiscriminate repudiation which would enjoin independent research against use of the great body of documents and testimony gathered by these agencies.

A cognate matter is reliance, by the analyst, on "old" materials —books and pamphlets written as far back as fifty years ago. These include particularly the writings of Lenin, especially such tracts as *What Is To Be Done?*, *State and Revolution*, and *Left-Wing Communism*. These and similar works are bolshevik classics. They are such not in the sense that they are buried in libraries or read only for their historical interest. On the contrary, they have been reprinted in millions of copies and are used as *training documents* in all countries and throughout all changes in propaganda line. It is the *present* role of these documents which is significant. The works of Lenin and Stalin are not remote philosophical essays: they have almost solely a strategic and tactical content. The indoctrination of the movement along lines set forth in these basic works provides that sure source of continuity which is hailed as the "bolshevik unity of the party."

Because of its stress on action rather than on ideological analysis, this volume may be used as an advanced-training manual for anticommunist forces. The emphasis throughout is on making explicit the strategic and tactical doctrine as it is found in the literature of bolshevism and as it is reflected in bolshevik practice. This explicitness is often but little removed from the overt statements of the participants themselves, as many quotations in the text will show. But this reconstruction necessarily probes more deeply, revealing patterns of motivation and action of which many participants would not be fully conscious.

CHAPTER 1
THE COMBAT PARTY

{17}
"Our Party," the bolshevik leaders tell their ranks, "is not like other parties." By this they mean not only that it has special goals, or a unique place in history, but that it is organized in a different way, makes special demands upon its members, and has a vastly greater latent strength than the political party of western parliamentarism. There are many elements which contribute to this fundamental difference, but perhaps the most important is this: Bolshevism calls for the *continuous* conquest of power through full use of the potentialities of organization. These conquests are not restricted to the normal political arena and do not use conventional political tools. "Seizure of power" is a heady phrase connoting great events; yet a coup may occur in a trade-union or youth group as well as in a state. When these limited conquests are repeated and coordinated, when they are invested with great importance as preparing a "final battle," then the organization which makes them takes on a special character.

This continuous and ubiquitous search for power is directed toward readily defined and available targets. Because such targets exist, the seizure of power *somewhere* is always on the agenda, and realistic opportunities for the exercise of authority are offered even when state power is out of sight. This type of intervention renders inapplicable the normal criteria by which political power is appraised, such as size of vote; more important, it is associated with the use of covert power-oriented organizational practices.

An organization designed as a weapon is a specialized tool. Power as a goal requires technical skills, practices, and organizational forms. Therefore, an analysis of the bolshevik type of party, a designed weapon, should help to illuminate those aspects of organization most important in the power process. {18}

The Nature of Cadres

"Cadre" is a key word in communist parlance. It has a meaning consistent with but not limited to military usage. The "cadre" at an army training post is the permanent staff of leaders who train recruits and around whom new units may be built. More broadly, the term may refer to a corps of professional soldiers preserved in peacetime as a basis for the wartime army. Thus the Prussian military leadership after the victory of Napoleon and the German military leadership after World War I relied on the potentialities of a small army cadre which could later be easily expanded. It is in this sense that the communist membership functions as the cadre of a wider mass movement. Each member has special training and ideally should be able to lead nonparty groups as they may from time to time become accessible. The movement is expected to change in response to events, but, again ideally, the cadre represents a permanent core prepared to take advantage of opportunities as they may arise or be created. In sum, the cadre party is a highly manipulable skeleton organization of trained agents; it is sustained by political combat and is linked to the mass movement as its members become leaders of wider groups in the community.

Communist cadres, however, are more than just technically trained members of an elite group, and they may be less than hired personnel devoting their working days to an organization. Communist cadres are dedicated men. The idea of the "professional revolutionary" is not to be taken literally. It does not necessarily refer to full-time functionaries. The key element is personal commitment to the point where serious risks are accepted. This personal commitment has consequences for the individual's contribution of work and sacrifice. Indeed, a devoted participant may give most of his time to the party even when he has a full-time job.

The element of dedication is important for other reasons as well. Thus although military cadres *may* be simply hired personnel with special training and functions, an ideological component may also be present: for instance, when an officer is referred to as a {19} "West Point man" or as a "regular army man." This suggests a set of attitudes expressing institutional identification, but it also connotes systematic indoctrination leading to increased reliability in the execution of command. In general, wherever there is a job to be done which requires special loyalty or zeal, the potentialities of emotional commitment will be exploited. To undertake such an exploitation is to create cadres. The combination of specialized training, permanent status, and personal dedication is, of course, optimum, but the latter is most essential in the cadre.

The formation of cadres is a basic task of communist organization. The expenditure of years of effort on the gathering and development of the basic cadres is not begrudged, for they constitute the precious and indispensable vanguard of the revolution. The communists have never been dismayed by small numbers if these constituted an elite group which could be depended on to take advantage of any opportunity to participate in power. This requires, however, that the face of the party be turned outward, toward the arenas where power is won and lost. For bolshevik cadres cannot be created simply through indoctrination; they are trained and tested in the struggle for power. A leadership party must have something to lead, or some group for whose control a struggle can be carried on. This is one of the functions of continuous political combat in the communist movement, wherein targets (e.g., trade-unions) are always available and an opposition must always be destroyed. Hence communist infiltration tactics are valuable not only for the strategic objectives they win, but also for building the party. Work in other organizations multiplies many times the opportunity of the party member to exercise leadership in some context. Such work, moreover, deepens his commitment, tests his reliability, and trains him in the techniques of political combat.

The qualities required of communist cadres have been spelled out by Dimitrov as follows:

1. Absolute devotion to the cause of the working class, loyalty to the Party, tested in the face of the enemy—in battle, in prison, in court; {20}
2. Closest possible contact with the masses;
3. Ability independently to find one's bearings and not to be afraid of assuming responsibility and making decisions;
4. Discipline and Bolshevik hardening in the struggle against the class enemy as well as in irreconcilable opposition to all deviations from the Bolshevik line.[1]

Losovsky also emphasizes that "cadres refers not only to the narrow circle of leading workers but to all the activists from the shops to the leading organs."[2] This is one reason why even the smallest communist party will try to find some way of participating in a mass movement even if there is no real chance of influencing events. For the besetting danger to a cadre party is isolation, which removes those opportunities for continued elite action essential to the maintenance of effective discipline.

The formation of cadres fulfills a primary condition for transforming a voluntary association into a manipulable instrument. When members become cadres, they are no longer simple adherents; they become *deployable personnel*. Indeed, the issue of the nature of party membership created the crisis in Russian Marxism out of which bolshevism developed. Lenin insisted that a party member must be one who works actively in the party and accepts its discipline, not simply someone who agrees with its program. But although this controversy helped to sharpen the line which Lenin wished to draw between the revolutionary and reformist wings of Marxism, the difference over the formal conditions of membership does not of itself define the distinction between simple adherents and dedicated activists. The formal conditions of participation—acceptance of discipline, attendance at meetings—might easily be fulfilled without that dedication and full involvement which is the mark of the bolshevik. The process of changing an adherent into such a participant involves the formation of cadres, and this requires much attention to ideological indoctrination and practical training. {21}

A Manipulable Party Organization

The bolshevik type of party is an effective organizational weapon because it has solved many of the problems associated with transforming a voluntary association into a managerial structure. This is the key to whatever mystery there may be about the organizational power of communism, Put most simply, the process referred to is one which changes *members* into *agents*, transforms those who merely give consent into those (at an extreme, soldiers) who do work as well as conform. "The thing we need," said Lenin, "is a militant organization of agents."[3]

---

[1] Georgi Dimitrov, *The United Front*, International Publishers, New York, 1938, pp. 116*ff*.

[2] A. Losovsky, *Der Streik aft Schlarht*, Fünf Vorträge gehalten an der Internationalen Lenin-Schule zu Moskau, Januar–März, 1930, Sefer, Berlin [n.d.].

[3] V. I. Lenin, "What Is To Be Done?" (1902), *Collected Works*, Vol. 4, Bk. II, International Publishers, New York, 1929, p. 246. Note also the dictum of Michels: "The modern party is a fighting organization in the political sense of the term, and must as such conform to the

This structural transformation marks the great difference between the bolshevik party and other voluntary associations; and it is to effect this transformation that many of the special characteristics of bolshevik organization have been developed.

The forging of the bolshevik weapon on the basis of this organizational principle has been partly conscious, as reflected in Lenin's conception of the nature of the party; but there had to be more than conscious will to sustain so great an emphasis on discipline and on professionalism. The nature of the organization had to be consistent with its day-to-day functions. Such functions, to be effective in determining the structure of the movement, could not be merely propaganda or even ultimate revolution. The need was for continuing action to mobilize and train the party ranks. *The systematic exploitation of opportunities for power conquest in all social institutions was the answer to this need.* If this continuing struggle for power is kept in mind, it becomes easier to understand how Lenin's theory could be put into practice.

Lenin wanted an organization that could be mobilized for effective action and relied on to see the revolution through to the end. The {22} *Party Organizer* has summarized his organizational principles as follows:

1. The doctrine that the Communist Party is the vanguard of the working class.
2. The doctrine of the formation of the principle cadres of the Party, so-called professional revolutionaries.
3. Activity of all the members of the Party, their direct participation in the work of the organization.
4. The basis of the Party organization, its fortresses, are the factory nuclei.
5. The Communist Party, through Communist fractions in non-Party workers' and peasants' organizations, must link up closely with the masses of workers and peasants and take an active part in all their struggles against their exploiters and lead the struggles through the Communist nuclei and Communist fractions.
6. Democratic centralism in the Party and in the Communist International.
7. Iron discipline for the proletarian Party.[4]

Taken together, these principles defined a new type of voluntary association, one that could be built only over a long period and with great effort. Its function was to mobilize the resources of its members and to weld them into a reliable and manipulable instrument of struggle. This is one function of military organization. But where armies have legal authority to change recruits into soldiers, Lenin's task was to attain a similar objective at a time when he could not use the coercive powers of the state. He himself did not blink at the military analogy:

> Let us take a modern army, here is a good example of organization. This
> organization is good simply because it is flexible, because it knows how to

---

laws of tactics. Now the first article of these laws is facility of mobilization." Robert Michels, *Political Parties* [first published in 1915], The Free Press, Glencoe, Illinois, 1949, p. 41.

[4] *Party Organizer*, January, 1934.

impart a single will to millions of people. Today, these millions sit in their various homes at the different ends of the country. Tomorrow a mobilization order is issued and they gather at appointed places. Today, they lie in trenches sometimes for months at a stretch. Tomorrow, in a prearranged order, they march forward to storm the enemy. Today, they perform miracles in evading bullets and shrapnel. Tomorrow, they perform miracles in open battles. Today, their advance posts lay mines {23} under the ground; tomorrow, they cover dozens of miles in accordance with instructions from flyers in the air. That is what you call organization, *when in the name of one object, inspired by a single will, millions of people change the form of their intercourse and their action, the place and methods of their activity, their weapons and arms, in accordance with the changing circumstances and demands of the struggle.*[5]

The emphasis on manipulability is clear. Whereas the army creates a manipulable instrument for military purposes, Lenin wanted one that could be turned to account in political combat.

The *general* problem Lenin tried to solve was that of using the members of a voluntary association as managerial resources.[6] Normally, such members are involved only partially and give little beyond their consent to the activities of whatever officialdom the organization may be able to afford. On the other hand, the "members" of an administrative staff are subject to discipline and must work. If the work-discipline potential of the rank and file can be fully exploited, then the effectiveness of the organization is greatly enhanced. In military organization there is maximal use of personnel; they may be asked to do more work than ordinary hired employees, subordination to discipline is more complete, and manipulability is very high. But this represents only a full development of tendencies latent in all organization for action.

There is danger, while seeking an understanding of bolshevism, in {24} overstressing the military analogy. This may lead to an undue emphasis on the fact that both the bolshevik political army and conventional military organizations are interested in violence. But Lenin's stress on military organization had little to do with violence. Rather, he saw certain more general features: mobilization for

---

[5]   Quoted in F. Brown, "Lenin's Conception of the Party," *The Communist*, January, 1934. For a discussion of the military aspects of communist organization and practice, see William R. Kintner, *The Front Is Everywhere: Militant Communism in Action,* University of Oklahoma Press, Norman, Oklahoma, 1950.

[6]   "The whole art of conspiratorial organization consists in making use of *everything and everybody* and finding work for everybody, at the same time retaining the *leadership* of the whole movement, not by force, but by virtue of authority, energy, greater experience, greater versatility and greater talent. . . . The Committee should try to achieve the greatest possible division of labor, remembering that the various kinds of revolutionary work demand various capacities and that a person who is absolutely useless as an organizer may be invaluable as an agitator, or that a person who does not possess the endurance demanded by conspiratorial work may be an excellent propagandist and so on. . . ." V. I. Lenin, "A Letter to a Comrade on Our Problems of Organization" (1902), *Lenin on Organization,* Lenin Library, Daily Worker Publishing Co., Chicago, 1926, pp. 124-125.

action; discipline; and manipulability. His attention was drawn to these character-istics because he recognized their value for political combat as well as for technical military effectiveness. He also saw their special relevance for the task of creating an organizational weapon by transforming the partial consent of the membership into total conformance. To some extent, this would have to be recognized by any leadership attempting to exploit the members of a voluntary association as admin-istrative resources.

However, the communist elite has had special problems not necessarily faced by other leaders attempting to mobilize a voluntary association for action. These special problems increase the convergence between communist and military organization. In the first place, military recruiting tends to be nonselective, and much effort must be expended on re-educating the ranks. Although communist recruiting is far more selective than military recruiting, it faces a similar problem *because it wins members on ideological grounds and yet wishes to use them for the technical (though nonmilitary) work of power aggrandizement.* Hence the need for special indoctrination is pressing. This special problem is always present to some extent in voluntary associations, since the psychological factors that moti-vate joining may not sustain continued participation. But usually the split between the basis of recruitment and the work to be done is not so sharp as to require the reorientation demanded by military life and bolshevik activity.

Further, readiness for violence requires a single-mindedness on the part of the soldier difficult to achieve in normal human situations. This emphasizes the need to control the total individual. Similarly, the pressure of many diverse loyal-ties upon an individual makes it difficult for him to function consistently as an instrument of the {25} continuous conquest of power. Indeed, it may be more dif-ficult to induce such single-mindedness in the power context than in the military one, since the latter is reinforced by direct threats to the individual in combat. In both situations, there is need to exercise maximum control over the individual to minimize the deviations induced by his multiple interests and obligations.

Therefore in considering the nature of communism's basic organizational weapon—the combat party—two forces must be kept in mind: (1) the consequences for organizational structure of any effort to exploit the work-discipline potential of a voluntary association; and (2) the special consequences of any effort to commit the total life of the member to a power-oriented group.

Total Control of the Individual

An army demands that at its convenience a soldier's entire life be subordi-nated to military aims. This is accomplished by the exercise of special legal powers plus physical isolation. A bolshevik party does not have these powers but must accomplish the same objective. Normally, a hired employee is involved in his job only partially, with limited psychological commitment, for prescribed periods and in a set place. His job is usually isolated from other aspects of living. But political cadres should be emotionally dedicated, physically mobile, and prepared to sacrifice time, career, and life itself. Such a pursuit seriously affects family life, education, recreation, and other sectors of experience which are usually relatively independent. Therefore, so long as the party permits the individual freedom to order the "nonpolitical" sectors of his life, there is loss of manipulability. This is the import of Lenin's injunction: "What we need is a military organization."[7]

Total control in voluntary associations may be achieved by *insulation* and *absorption*. These are reciprocal, since insulation frees the individual for fuller absorption and the process of absorption aids {26} insulation. The means of achieving insulation are partly ideological. Thus one aspect of indoctrination in the communist movement is the creation of a separate moral and intellectual world for the party member. The emphasis on theory extends to all realms of thought, not simply political strategy and tactics. This is one of the significant organizational functions of Marxist philosophy, sociology, and economics and helps to explain the heavy emphasis upon this type of doctrine. In a bolshevik organization, all leaders should be willing and ready to discuss problems of philosophy so as to give prestige to levels of thought which in most action groups would be relegated to the limbo of "long-haired impracticality." A party official writes:

> The first and most basic task of the Party in developing the struggle on the ideological front is for the political leadership of the Party to take the guidance and development of this struggle in hand. . . . Our leading committees and individual leaders of the Party must set an example not only by attention to and direction of this work, but also by their personal participation in the ideological struggle. We must make Marxist ideology at home in our organization . . . by creating the proper atmosphere for its study and for the grounding of our cadres in Marxist theory. We must ourselves take the leadership in the fight against narrow practicalism, against any manifestation of contempt for theory.[8]

The consequence of "waging a struggle" in political economy, philosophy, history, etc., is to provide the member with a sense of identification extending far beyond the conventional political arena. Such an emphasis on the existence of two hostile worlds, one the Marxist, the other bourgeois, has the great advantage of identifying political opponents (including organs of the state) with a whole system of purported evil.

Other devices for insulation are less purely ideological. The emphasis on illegal work creates a conspiratorial atmosphere; this has the dual consequence of disintegrating normal moral principles, thereby reducing inhibitions that might hamper manipulability, and of increasing the dangers (real or imagined) of leaving the organization. {27} Again, the prohibition of personal contact with enemies of the party—expressly included in the constitution—is a measure enforcing insulation from personal friends and relatives who might have a corrupting influence.

Absorption may be accomplished by organizational measures. The most obvious is the sheer volume of activity. Meetings, demonstrations, literature distribu-

---

[7]   As quoted by Boris Souvarine, *Stalin: A Critical Survey of Bolshevism,* Alliance Press. New York, 1939, p. 41.

[8]   Max Weiss, "The Struggle on the Ideological Front," *Political Affairs,* Vol. 25, September, 1946, p. 9.

tion, and recruiting may easily consume all the member's available time, leaving little chance for thought beyond the moment (hence minimizing opportunities for disaffection), defining a way of life that will be relinquished only with difficulty, and creating an immediate social context of party affairs commanding the individual's entire span of attention. At the same time, this high pitch of involvement gives the member a sense of meaningful activity: he is made to feel that he is "achieving" something, rather than passively waiting for the millennium.

Less obvious is the way a cadre party relates its members to a firmly integrated but at the same time highly filiated organization. The member is not simply an adherent within an amorphous group, as in the case of most voluntary associations, but is absorbed into a network of subordinate organizations and offshoot bodies which are able to bind him effectively into the party structure. Unit organizations are often very small, not merely because of conspiratorial advantages gained when a party member knows only a few of his comrades, but perhaps more especially because such extreme subdivision makes possible full use of the energies of the membership.[9] In addition, any given member may be required to function in several party groups. i.e., in neighborhood, shop, or professional units, in fractions, in compulsory classes, and in a large number of committees and subcommittees of all sorts. Absorption into such a network in effect multiplies the memberships of the individual. He is not simply a cardholder related in a formal but very partial way to some central {28} office, or at most to a central office plus a branch; rather, membership in a communist party carries with it affiliation to subgroups that give a political meaning to, and derive a political worth from, all facets of social life.

Of course, all organizations attempt, to some extent, to involve members in work through committees, etc., but in the bolshevik party we find a systematic exploitation of this multiple affiliation. Each subgroup makes its own demands upon the member, evokes its own identification, and has independent opportunity for supervising thought and action. Absorption through multiple affiliation is a potent method of increasing the subordination of the individual to the party and its leadership.

These techniques of absorption and insulation help to ensure submission to iron discipline and thus to transform simple adherents into "soldiers of the revolution." This change takes place *after* the new member has joined the party. If the "bolshevik man" is contemplated with wonder, it is this transformation that deserves special attention, perhaps more than why individuals join the party.

It is apparent that there are other ways (as in religious orders) of assuming control over an individual's whole life. What distinguishes these is their consistency with *mobilization for action*. The paramilitary character of the cadre party is a product of training and control that prepares the individual for conquests in which he may participate directly. The bolshevik effort to identify and fill all areas of political vacuum is intrinsic to its paramilitary character. Ideally, every party

---

[9] Note also in this connection: "An organizational structure based on groups of three lends itself to the selection and training of new leaders, if only because it multiplies posts of responsibility. . . . The essential things are to distribute and graduate the various tasks in such fashion as to utilize and develop all available capacities. . . ." A. Rossi, *A Communist Party in Action*, Yale University Press, New Haven, 1949, p. 195.

member is deployed along some front, engaged in some power struggle. It is in this sense that we may speak of communist parties as combat organizations.

As a result of this pattern of total involvement, the "bolshevik man" becomes a member of a nuclear "bolshevik society." This exists within a larger, hostile, bourgeois society but successfully replaces it as a matrix of social action. Membership in the cadre party does not mean the performance of a political role, in the sense usually understood, but the determination and shaping of the individual's entire life, including his political activities. {29} This total commitment is emphasized by the denial of the right of voluntary withdrawal. As in a wartime army, the leadership reserves the right to decide who may quit the service. To leave the party is not simply to dissociate oneself from a program, but is regarded as desertion in battle. This calls for a maximum penalty which, in a party not in power, is expulsion, ostracism, economic boycott, defamation and, occasionally, assassination.

Managerial Leadership

Bolshevik organization is characterized by the intimate union of political and administrative goals and methods. The context is always political, the aims of the organization are political, and the fundamental commitment of the ranks to the party and its leadership is political. Yet a full understanding of bolshevism requires that we recognize the continuous pressure to emphasize the administrative side at the expense of the political. The reason for this is simple: it stems from the need to transform members into agents and to exploit as fully as possible the potentialities of the membership for work, for the execution of predetermined tasks. We use the term "managerial" to refer to these politico-administrative patterns.

Leadership in a normal voluntary association must continuously win the consent of the membership to ensure its tenure in power. In this sense, the role of the trade-union leader is a political one when, as in the conduct of collective-bargaining negotiations, he must take account of the possible defection of his rank and file. In the interests of effectiveness, however, an organization meant to function as a manipulable instrument must avoid imposing such limitations on the decisionmaking of the leadership. In the bolshevik party this freedom is guaranteed by the strong emphasis on discipline. But it is important to understand that the member can accept this discipline because it is consistent with the day-to-day functioning of the organization. The continuous exploitation of opportunities for action provides a routine justification for submission to command. This {30} mitigates (without eliminating) the need to introduce special emotional patterns of self-abnegation.

Since the communist party member is by definition one who must carry out certain tasks, this poses the problem of supervision. It becomes the duty of the party leadership to establish an administrative apparatus to see that the work gets done and that executive control over the membership is maintained. This system of accountability is established through a hierarchy of committees. "Every elected Party committee must report regularly on its activity to its Party organization. It must give an account of its work. The lower party committees and all Party members of the given Party organization have the duty of carrying out the decisions of the higher Party committees and of the Communist International. In other words, decisions of the C.I. and of the higher Party committees are binding upon the lower bodies."[10] The formal structure of committees—unit, section, district, national—is actually misleading, since in effect the committee hierarchy is transformed into a hierarchy of responsible *individuals*. Each such committee has a center or "buro" and this, in turn, has an organizer or secretary. The latter bears the burden of administrative accountability, and so the necessary clarity of the chain of command is maintained.

This emphasis on accountability and on forceful leadership in mobilizing the members for party work explains the often-noted power of the secretariats in communist parties and party-controlled organizations. An unusual emphasis on exploiting the potentialities of the membership for work, combined with a prizing of practical activity as an important means of indoctrination, naturally concentrates special responsibilities and powers in the hands of administrative officers. In effect, the emphasis on membership work reverses the line of responsibility typical of conventional voluntary associations, wherein the leadership must prove its accomplishments to the {31} members. On the contrary, in the bolshevik movement the members elect taskmasters whose function it is to wring the greatest possible activity from the very persons who elected them.

The election of the committee hierarchy might seem, however, to introduce a strong democratic element into the organization. This would be so if the elections were meaningful, i.e., if there were contending leaders bidding for the support of the party electorate. Such contention would maintain the party as a political arena and undermine administrative effectiveness. But elections in the communist parties do not involve the normal processes of faction and debate: A fundamental Leninist principle states that "no movement can be durable without a stable organization of leaders to maintain continuity."[11] Challenges to the leadership as a whole are not tolerated in a communist party. However, this does not mean that changes do not occur. But the replacement procedure should fill the need for effective mobilization and minimize internal controversy. To accomplish this, the leadership itself is made responsible for introducing changes in its own ranks. Elections become administrative devices, not only because the leading committee itself recommends a slate of candidates to a convention, but because this slate is based on a *technical* evaluation of the relative merits of individuals. "In the place of the formal routine election of functionaries we have had up to now, we must establish the system of political examination and review of their activities as the basis for the election of functionaries."[12] Under such conditions elections become equivalent to promotions rather than political contests. The name for this administrative way of selecting new leaders is "co-option." To be sure, co-option

---

[10] J. Peters, *The Communist Party — A Manual on Organization,* Workers Library Publishers, July, 1935. Reprinted in *Hearings,* Appendix, Pt. I, U.S. House Special Committee on Un-American Activities, 76th Cong., 1st sess., Washington, 1940, p. 697.

[11] V. I. Lenin, "What Is To Be Done?" (1902), *Collected Works,* Vol. 4, Bk. II (1929), p. 198.

[12] C. Smith, "The Problem of Cadres in the Party," *The Communist,* February, 1932. See also Rossi, *loc. cit.:* "The Party is an army in which promotions are made on the basis of performance."

has a political meaning, since it is often a device for perpetuating the power of an elite by absorbing new elements into it, thereby legitimizing its authority and disarming potential enemies. But in the communist party, the administrative dimension—wherein advances {32} in the hierarchy take on the character of selection and promotion in bureaucratic structures—is of special significance. For this is a phase of the general effort to transform a voluntary association into an effective instrument for the execution of tasks set by the leadership.

When the communists speak of a "cadre policy," they mean what is normally known as "personnel policy," more consistent with the nature of an army than with a voluntary association. A communist cadre policy calls for: (1) systematic analysis of personnel resources in the membership; (2) proper classification and assignment of all members to party tasks; (3) continuous upgrading of rank and file elements who show leadership ability; (4) hierarchic control, including indoctrination, detailed direction of day-to-day tasks, and reprimand; (5) safeguarding of cadres by withdrawing them from danger situations when necessary, providing replacements, and maintaining secrecy of operations.[13]

The implementation of such a policy requires measures hardly customary in voluntary associations. Thus the party's leading committees issue directives to subordinate committees and secretariats. These directives are not the general "appeals to the membership" for action, common in groups that are organized but are in effect unmobilized; these are, on the contrary, specific orders and detailed critical analyses of methods of work. Party experiences in the unions and elsewhere are subjected to exhaustive analyses so that the "lessons" may be recorded for training purposes. And attention is focused on the key questions of action: what to do now and what to do next.

In keeping with the managerial character of the organization, great emphasis is placed maintaining the stability of authority. Official policy is therefore presented as unified, public utterances of members are controlled, and efforts to change policy, except through approved internal channels, are prohibited. This is normal in administrative structures and in armies, but not in conventional voluntary associations. Here too, moreover, the bolsheviks exaggerate normal managerial imperatives. The bolshevik is taught to see all {33} aspects of experience through political eyes. This sustains the authority of the leadership, much as ecclesiastical authority may be upheld by asserting the relevance of religious judgment to all human experience. In addition, this doctrinal foundation (again as in a church) places the stability of authority on an impersonal basis, so that the office is haloed and not the person. Individual leaders may then be scrapped without excessive cost to the authority structure of the organization.

Finally, the priority of managerial imperatives is evident in the bolshevik attitude toward criticism or opposition. In the mature bolshevism of Stalin, some degree of criticism is permissible within a communist party, but on two conditions: (1) the criticism must be self-criticism, of the party in general, and not so formulated as to constitute an attack on the central leadership; (2) the criticism may not be organized—no factions and no opposition press.

---

[13] Dimitrov, *loc. cit.*

"Bolshevik self-criticism" plays a large role in the communist movement, and especially in the Soviet Union. The Soviet press is replete with references to self-criticism and from time to time encourages attacks on various classes of officials. The idea of such criticism is raised to a basic organizational principle, and ability to engage in it is a much-glorified trait of the "bolshevik man." It takes the place, in bolshevik organizations, of "discussion" in nonbolshevik organizations and lends itself to exploitation in fighting deviationists. The latter point is especially important. For example, in the fight against Tito, a Cominform communiqué of June 28, 1948, stated:

> The information bureau considers that the criticism made by the Central Committee of the Communist Party of the Soviet Union (B) and central committees of other Communist parties of the mistakes of the Central Committee of the Communist Party of Yugoslavia, and who in this way rendered fraternal assistance to the Yugoslav Communist Party, provides the Communist Party of Yugoslavia with all the conditions necessary to speedily correct the mistakes committed.
>
> However, instead of honestly accepting this criticism and taking {34} the Bolshevik path of correcting these mistakes, the leaders of the Communist Party of Yugoslavia, suffering from boundless ambition, arrogance and conceit, met this criticism with belligerence and hostility. They took the anti-party path of indiscriminately denying all their mistakes, violated the doctrine of Marxism-Leninism regarding the attitude of a political party to its mistakes and thus aggravated their entire party mistakes.[14]

The proper response is capitulation and self-accusation. Of course, an attack upon Stalin's stewardship would not be treated as proper self-criticism.

A crucial resolution on factions, adopted by the CPSU at its Tenth Congress (1921), stated:

> It is necessary that every Party organization pay strict attention to the undoubtedly necessary criticism of the failings of the Party, to the analysis of the general policy of the Party, the summarizing of its practical experience, the control of the execution of decisions of the Party and the rectification of any errors, etc., being conducted not by discussions in groups organizing themselves on some "platform," etc., but by discussions among the entire membership of the Party.[15]

The carrying on of discussions "among the entire membership" without factional meetings, platforms, or states of candidates in effect eliminates the possibility of developing new centers of power within the ranks and thus guarantees the

---

[14] *The Soviet-Yugoslav Dispute*, Royal Institute of International Affairs, London, 1948, p. 65.

[15] "Resolution of the Tenth Congress of the Russian Communist Party on Party Unity," (1921) *Lenin on Organization*, pp. 217-218. The editors of this volume state that the resolution was "drafted by Bukharin in close collaboration with Comrade Lenin."

continued dominance of the existing leadership. It is significant that despite the continued possibility of discussion without factions, the abolition of factions at the Tenth Party Congress is a landmark in the development of Soviet totalitarianism. Whether or not Lenin meant this policy to be temporary, his successors accepted it as basic party doctrine:

> Achievement and maintenance of the dictatorship of the proletariat are impossible without a party strong in its cohesion and iron discipline. But iron discipline in the Party is impossible without {35} unity of will and without absolute and complete unity of action on the part of all members of the Party. This does not mean of course that there will never be any conflict of opinion within the Party. On the contrary, iron discipline does not preclude but presupposes criticism and conflicts of opinion within the Party. Least of all does it mean that this discipline must be "blind" discipline. On the contrary iron discipline does not preclude but presupposes conscious and voluntary submission, for only conscious discipline can be truly iron discipline. But after a discussion has been closed, after criticism has run its course and a decision has been made, unity of will and unity of action become indispensable conditions without which Party unity and iron discipline in the Party are inconceivable.[16]

But Stalin here obscures the issue, which is not whether discussions are held but whether independent centers of power are permitted. On this point he is very clear:

> It follows that the existence of factions is incompatible with Party unity and with its iron discipline. It need hardly be emphasized that the existence of factions leads to the creation of a number of centres, and the existence of a number of centres connotes the absence of a common centre in the Party, a breach in the unity of will, the weakening and disintegration of discipline, the weakening and disintegration of the dictatorship. It is true that the parties of the Second International, which are fighting against the dictatorship of the proletariat and have no desire to lead the proletarians to power, can permit themselves the luxury of such liberalism as freedom for factions, for they have no need of iron discipline. But the parties of the Communist International, which organize their activities on the basis of the proletariat, cannot afford to be "liberal" or to permit the formation of factions. The Party is synonymous with unity of will, which leaves no room for any factionalism or division of Party control.[17]

This is taken to justify a monopoly of power, not only for the Russian government in its sphere, but for the leadership of all communist parties. The elimination of opportunities for organized opposition is entirely consistent with the process of

---

[16] J. Stalin, *Foundations of Leninism,* International Publishers, New York, 1932, pp. 116-117.

[17] *Ibid.,* pp. 117-118.

turning a voluntary {36} association into a managerially controlled organization of disciplined agents. Only "constructive" criticism is permissible in managerial contexts. When a free association allows administrative criteria to shape its character in a decisive way, it loses its freedom.

The Role of "Theory"

Education and training play a vital role in the transformation of simple adherents into reliable and deployable agents. These functions are, of course, not unique to bolshevism, for they must play some part in all organizations characterized by extensive delegation of functions. The more esoteric the activities of the organization, the less it can rely on the general education provided by the community, the greater the need for internal "orientation." Bolshevism's radical split from the community, and the need to ensure an extraordinary degree of reliability, greatly increase its dependence on an official doctrine. Such a doctrine normally aids communication and morale, functions effectively performed by Marxist ideology in the communist movement.

The role of "theory" is heavily stressed by communist leaders. Indeed, a favorite method of "self-criticism" is to bewail the failure to apply Marxist-Leninist principles to party organization and action. A recent internal document of the Communist Party in the Philippines emphasized this source of weakness:

> It was only under the Japanese regime that our Party undertook a serious study of Marxist-Leninist theory. It was only then that the whole Party was involved in a serious study of what is our strategy and tactics.
> . . . Before the war, mention has been made by our leading cadres of what is strategy and tactics, but as to its real content there has been no clear understanding. A great number of our party members thought that strategy and tactics was a maneuver, a trick by which we can push our plans through. . . . We committed serious mistakes of right opportunism and left sectarianism. . . . Lack {37} of theory has been primarily responsible for our past opportunist mistakes.[18]

Here there is the assumption that a doctrine exists which, if only it were understood, would provide a key to correct policy. The labels "right opportunism" and "left sectarianism" bolster the omnicompetence of theory, for they leave no room for simple error. Every deviation has a political meaning and is understandable within the terms of Marxism-Leninism. This competence extends not only to questions of general political policy, but to organizational practices as well:

> In practice, as a result of this lack of theory we were not in a position to visualize and actually grasp some intricacies of organizational work. We have not masterfully welded theory and practice. For example: for about a period of three months, the Party did not know how to channelize Party lead-

---

[18] "Report on the Political Situation," report of the General Secretary of the Partido Kommunista sa Filipinas, undated but probably written in late 1946 or early 1947.

ership within the CLO [Congress of Labor Organizations], how the Political Bureau and the Marcom [Manila-Rizal Committee] should work within the CLO, who should directly hold the leadership. It was only through trial and error method that we finally formulated the correct system of channelizing Party leadership in the CLO. Another example: there was a certain period in 1945 when the different P Coms [Provincial Political Committees] did not exactly know, were not so sure of themselves about how to channelize Party leadership in the PKM [National Peasants Union], DA [Democratic Alliance], Youth and Women's League. Another example: because of the low political level of the rank and file Party members they have failed to perform their role as leaders within the local branches of the PKM and the Democratic Alliance. In many instances, Party nuclei were lagging behind the local mass organizations; instead of performing the role of leaders they were being led.

Poor theoretical leadership means also poor organizational leadership.[19]

The report of the General Secretary then proceeds to castigate the leading committee of the party for theoretical weakness. And further:

{38} The weakest link in the Political Bureau is the Education Department. What has the Education Department done within a period of more than a year? It has translated the Foundations of Leninism [by Stalin] and had it printed; it put out two issues of the Ang Kommunista and took charge of two National Training Schools. This is all that the Education Department has done. It was not able to put out documents, save the Ang Kommunista, It has not assumed active leadership of the work of the Education Departments of the P Coms. It has not put out a single propaganda material. It was decided that the Education Department should put out a regular theoretical organ of the Party, but the ED did not execute this decision.[20]

In keeping with this emphasis, the Secretary's summary of the party's organizational tasks gives high priority to education:

1. Consolidate our leading organs: systematic work, prompt fulfillment of decisions, raising of political level of members of the Political Bureau . . . by organized study and self-study.
2. Improve the theoretical level of our Party membership: (a) acquire mastery of strategy and tactics; (b) possess complete knowledge of what we are going to establish within the present bourgeois stage of our revolution: (c) improve our inner Party educational system by putting out more documents to be studied by the whole membership; (d) regularly put out a mimeographed theoretical organ of the Party; (e) serious at-

---

[19] *Ibid.*

[20] *Ibid.*

tention should be paid to translation of Marxist-Leninist classics into Tagalog.[21]

These emphases and proposals in the small Filipino party echo those which have long characterized the parties of the west. The report incidentally offers evidence both of the universality of communist organizational methods and of their recent application.

It is clear that the communists do have a body of principles useful to them in the struggle for power. However, it is not clear that these principles are relevant beyond organizational structure (the creation of the vanguard party and its agencies) and organizational strategy and tactics (methods which maximize the utility of the movement's organizational weapons). It is no longer possible to predict whether communists will support a "bourgeois" candidate — {39} *e.g.*, Osmena in the Philippines, Roosevelt in the United States—on the basis of any principles reflecting class-struggle doctrine. Mature communism is associated with rampant opportunism. This has two sources: the use of propaganda to conceal conspiratorial struggles for power, especially organizational work; and the shifting needs of Soviet foreign policy. Indeed, it may be said that Stalinism has developed most fully the Leninist modification of Marxism, namely, the subordination of all doctrinal precepts to the needs of the struggle for power. Wherever, as in the Philippines case cited above, the relevance of doctrine as a guide to action seems most cogent, the application is to organizational problems. How shall we get into the trade-unions? How control them? How increase the leadership capacity of our members? How avoid isolation? The Marxist theory of the stare, as the "executive committee of the ruling class," might once have determined policy on political candidates; it does not do so now. The doctrine of class struggle might once have effectively shaped communist trade-union policy, but it is not now a reliable indicator. However, Leninist doctrine regarding *organizational* practices continues to guide behavior.

Communist "theory" cannot be understood solely as a guide to action. It is partly that but doubtless of equal significance is the managerial function Marxist-Leninist doctrine fulfills. Communists, says Dimitrov, are people of action. And "it is precisely this *practical* task that obliges Communist cadres to equip themselves *with revolutionary theory.* For, as Stalin, that greatest master of revolutionary action, has taught us, theory gives those engaged in practical work the power of orientation, clarity of vision, assurance in work, belief in the triumph of our cause."[22] The utility of doctrine as a morale builder is here made explicit.

The Marxist portion of Marxism-Leninism plays the decisive role in fulfilling this morale function. It provides categories of thought—the class struggle, theory of the state and of economic crisis, the nature of historical development—which can be manipulated to bolster Leninist aims. Party purges may be more easily accepted if {40} their justification rests on the idea that the class struggle is reflected within the party. Ruthless suppression of anarchist and socialist opposition is defended on the theory that these groups "objectively" serve the class enemy. The

---

[21] *Ibid.*

[22] Dimitrov, *op. cit.*, p. 124.

very category of "objective" or historic function gains credence if the members can be immersed in an Hegelian doctrine such as Marxism. This ideology also aids effective communication. It offers a common language and approach for formulating specific directives.

Perhaps the most important contribution of Marxism to communist morale is the doctrine of the inevitability of socialism. A belief in ultimate triumph, or at least in the consistency of action with the basic forces of history (a secularized form of "God's will") seems to be a necessary condition for high morale in apocalyptic movements.

Recognition of the significance of Marxist doctrine in the bolshevik movement should not, however, lead to the unwarranted assumption that communists are excessively deviant in their everyday language. These basic doctrinal tenets may be (and have been in the past) associated with the use of easily identifiable modes of expression—strong hostility to all "bosses," liberal use of such a term as "bourgeois" as an epithet—but need not be. Indeed, the communists have decreased their vulnerability by increasing their ability to reserve the use of Marxist clichés to inner circles. When a cadre group is heavily indoctrinated in a special way, as in the case of the Nazi attitude toward Jews, it is vulnerable because members are easily spotted, and their freedom of tactical maneuver is restrained. Marxist doctrine, the defense of the USSR, and principles of organizational strategy do not necessarily have such consequences for day-to-day attitudes. This bears on the difference between modern communist cadres and those of an earlier day who more consistently reflected the common image of the "red" fanatic.

Although not altogether separable from Marxism, it may be said, nevertheless, that it is Leninism that offers the doctrinal guide to action which the communist leaders value. An understanding of {41} this special role of Leninism will help avoid confusion regarding the meaning of reaffirmations of allegiance to Marx, Engels, Lenin, and Stalin. If their ideas contained only broad philosophical, sociological, and economic principles, or even if the allegiance were directed solely to Marx and Engels, it would be difficult to draw any conclusions regarding communism as such. Many noncommunist groups identify themselves with Marxism.

What is significant, however, is the *coupling* of the names Marx-Engels-Lenin-Stalin whenever the doctrinal allegiances of communists are identified. The other Marxist groupings do not accept this constellation of heroes. Marxist socialists (some socialists are not Marxist at all) are divided from communists in rejecting the Leninist road to power. It is Lenin, not Marx, who is communism's special hero, for it was Lenin's form of organization, with its implications for strategy, that gave birth to communism as a distinct trend within Marxism. When a group arises out of a vision of the "true road" to salvation, allegiance to *method* becomes psychologically more important than acceptance of the presumptive goal, because it is assumed that no one can really accept the goal who does not accept the method. This is not essentially different in religious controversy. Although both Lutherans and Roman Catholics profess to be Christians, different views concerning the way to salvation are crucial. Catholics do not accept Luther as a defining hero any more than socialists accept Lenin.

In Trotskyism, the roster of heroes is Marx-Engels-Lenin-Trotsky. Bolshevik organizational form and strategy is explicitly accepted, but certain Stalinist developments of Leninism are rejected. Neither Trotskyism nor Stalinism would abandon Lenin in the process of self-identification. Neither is content to identify itself as simply "Marxist." Leninism has specific relevance to the struggle for power. Allegiance to Leninism can have no meaning save acceptance of his basic ideas about methods of political combat. Hence it is misleading to suggest that the most important part of the doctrine of Marx-Engels-Lenin-Stalin is economic or sociological. *Leninism is above {42} all a political doctrine, and more specifically, an organizational one.* It is a detailed design of weapons and strategy for continuous conquest of power. Leninism is not subject to the diverse "interpretations" characteristic of a broad social theory such as Marxism. No group accepts Lenin as mentor which is not prepared to use his basic methods.

It is therefore of the greatest importance, in analyzing the communist movement, to recognize the significance of continued use of Lenin's political pamphlets as training materials. Such works as *"Left" Communism* and *What Is To Be Done?* are standard texts to be read and learned by communist recruits. The main content of these works has to do with specific methods of organization and detailed injunctions as to strategy. Nor is the fact that they were written in 1920 and 1902, respectively, of any significance; the current use made of them as training documents shows their relevance to the movement.[23]

Party Allegiance

Like all organizations, but more urgently than most, bolshevism needs to develop a sense of allegiance, not simply to a set of ideas, but to specific institutions. The two major institutions around which the movement is organized are the party and the Soviet Union. Loyalty to abstract ideals such as "socialism" or even "revolution" is always somewhat tenuous, since the individual's commitment is not sufficiently concrete to be readily and clearly defined. In its search for reliable adherents, an elite attempts to focus loyalty on dramatic symbols, traditions, heroes, and established forms of work, rather than solely on doctrinal tenets. At an extreme, permitting virtually {43} unrestrained manipulability, personal fealty is won by a single—often charismatic—leader.

These institutions also help to form a channel through which action can be directed; they provide focal points of attack and defense. Neither abstract moral ideals nor antagonisms rooted in frustration, both sources of adherence to communism, are themselves able to offer motivational sustenance beyond weakly joined or temporary action. Institutional patriotism therefore helps to increase the power potential of the organization; at the same time it is a value for the followers

---

[23] The basic principles of Leninism are reaffirmed, with copious quotations from Lenin's early works and examples from the history of bolshevism in the *Short History of the Communist Party of the Soviet Union (Bolsheviks)*, published in 1939 (International Publishers, New York) and distributed in millions of copies and in twenty-four languages throughout the world. This text was first announced as prepared by a "Commission of the Central Committee of the CPSU," but more recently authorship has been attributed to Stalin himself.

themselves in that it adds concrete meaning to the original ideological grounds for participation.

The creation, protection, and aggrandizement of the party as the indispensable tool of revolutionary struggle is a primary theme of Leninist doctrine:

> The Party is the political leader of the working class. I have spoken above of the difficulties encountered in the struggle of the working class, of the complicated nature of this struggle, of strategy and tactics, of reserves and manoeuvering operations, of attack and defense. These conditions are no less complicated, if not more so, than war operations. Who can understand these complicated conditions, who can give correct guidance to the vast masses of the proletariat? Every army at war must have an experienced staff, if it is to avoid certain defeat. All the more reason, therefore, why the proletariat must have such a general staff if it is to prevent itself from being routed by its accursed enemies. But where is this general staff? Only the revolutionary party of the proletariat can serve as this general staff. A working class without a revolutionary party is like an army without a general staff. The Party is the military staff of the proletariat.[24]

And Trotsky:

> To overthrow the old power is one thing; to take the power in one's own hands is another. The bourgeoisie may win the power in a revolution not because it is revolutionary, but because it is bourgeois. It has in its possession property, education, the press, a network of strategic positions, a hierarchy of institutions. Quite otherwise with proletariat. Deprived in the nature of things of all social advantages, an insurrectionary proletariat can count only on its numbers, its solidarity, its cadres, its official staff.[25]

These are almost random quotations from a long record of bolshevik emphasis on the historic importance of the party. A *mystique du parti*[26] is created:

> The Party is above everything else! To guard the Bolshevik unity of the Party as the apple of one's eye is the first and highest law of Bolshevism![27]
>
> For the proletarian revolutionist the party is the concentrated expression of his life purpose, and he is bound to it for life and death. He preaches and practices party patriotism, because he knows that his socialist ideal cannot be realized without the party. In his eyes the crime of crimes is disloyalty or irresponsibility toward the party.[28]

---

[24] Stalin, *op. cit.*, pp. 106-107.

[25] L. Trotsky, *History of the Russian Revolution*, Vol. 3, Simon and Schuster, Inc., 1932, p. 168*f*.

[26] See Rossi, *op. cit.*, Chap. 25.

[27] Dimitrov, *op. cit.*, p. 138.

[28] J. P. Cannon, *The Struggle for a Proletarian Party*, Pioneer Publications, Inc., New York, 1943, p. 35.

The emphasis on loyalty to the party as an institution is so great, indeed, that it has apparently played a large role in motivating "confessions" at such events as the treason trials in Moscow during the nineteen-thirties.[29]

With this ideological basis for party allegiance, loyalty to the party quickly becomes loyalty to the party *organization*. A halo is raised over party leaders, party organs, party decision. Thus the Canadian Royal Commission found:

> A further objective, pursued through the study-group, is gradually to inculcate in the secret membership of the Communist Party a habit of complete obedience to the dictates of senior members and officials of the Party Hierarchy. This is apparently accomplished through a constant emphasis, in the indoctrination courses, on the importance of organization *as such*, and by the gradual creation, in the mind of the new adherent or sympathizer, of an {45} over-riding moral sense of "loyalty to the Party." This "loyalty to the Party" in due course takes the place in the member's mind of the earlier loyalty to certain principles professed by the Party propaganda.[30]

Extreme forms of party patriotism serve to transform the nature of political affiliation, as reflected in charges of "treason" and "betrayal" against those who simply withdraw. This is consistent with the paramilitary character of the organization and is reinforced by the intensive use of symbols—Trotsky, Lovestone, Browder, Tito—which emphasize the heinous quality of defection. Party patriotism, like other extreme forms of flag-waving, is closely associated with hatred toward presumptive enemies within and without the community.[31]

An important qualification is in order here, however. Although the cadre party effectively generates organizational loyalty and pride, it strenuously rejects "organizational fetishism." This means that loyalty is fixed upon a continuing

---

[29] See Arthur Koestler, *Darkness at Noon* (The Macmillan Company, New York, 1946), a novel which probes the motivation of those who "confessed" at these trials. A forthcoming RAND study by Nathan Leites and Elsa Bernaut will provide a systematic treatment of this subject.

[30] Report of the Royal Commission to Investigate the Facts . . . Surrounding the Communication, by Persons in Positions of Trust of Secret . . . Information to . . . a Foreign Power, Ottawa, 1946, pp. 74-75, hereinafter cited as Report of the Royal Commission.

[31] The widely distributed and studied *Short History of the Communist Party of the Soviet Union (Bolsheviks)* is replete with such "lessons." Of the six chief lessons cited in the conclusion, the third "teaches us that unless the petty-bourgeois parties which are active within the ranks of the working class and which push the backward sections of the working class into the arms of the bourgeoisie, thus splitting the unity of the working class, are smashed, the victory of the proletarian revolution is impossible." And the fourth promises that "unless the Party of the working class wages an uncompromising struggle against the opportunists within its own ranks, unless it smashes the capitulators in its own midst, it cannot preserve discipline and unity within its ranks, it cannot perform its role of organizer and leader of the proletarian revolution, nor its role as the builder of the new, Socialist society." The struggle against all types of deviation is given great emphasis. It is well to recall that this book, for which the greatest promotion campaign in the history of communist education was conducted, presents a basically orthodox Leninist position, and was issued during the period of "popular front" and democratic phraseology preceding the Stalin-Hitler pact.

group, leadership, and tradition independently of the name or external form which may from time to time be assumed. Such flexibility is essential in the use of organizational weapons, since that demands a high degree of opportunism. The essentials of the weapon to be manipulated must be understood {46} so that it may be stripped to those essentials when attacks from the outside or opportunities for covert organizational maneuver occur.

This qualification, however, refers only to *overt* aspects of organization. Despite radical external changes—even to the extent of formal liquidation by merger with some larger political group—the cadre group will maintain its existence, retaining the main elements of Leninist organization. The party simply assumes the form of a "progressive group" within the larger organization, with its own national committee, educational apparatus, literature, and devices of penetration and control. This entails great flexibility, but the emphasis on maintaining lines of communication intact keeps the party together. A classic example in the history of bolshevism is the entry of the Trotskyists into the socialist parties of France, United States, and elsewhere. This maneuver entailed no break in the continuity of the party; it quickly found new forms of self-expression. Control of a Socialist Party newspaper in California soon served as a substitute for the administratively indispensable party press.[32]

The official communist movement, since it began with a sizable force, has perhaps never engaged in such a drastic tactic, although various "unity" parties under communist control have been formed and have required similar adaptations. However, the example of the Trotskyists is important because theirs is the same type of party and it is by no means excluded that, in some new period of Browderism, The Communist Party might simply "dissolve" itself and try to join, say, the Democratic Party. The history of the Trotskyist maneuver of the mid-thirties would then become very relevant. Training in the psychology of underground operation is thus effective preparation, not only for general illegality, but also for covert operations within target groups.

Loyalty to the USSR is developed along the same lines as loyalty to the party. "Defense of the Soviet Fatherland" is taken as the prime objective of all communists. The abstract ideal of socialism is associated with a country and a ruling group which may easily be defined as in continuous danger. The ideal itself is then thought to {47} be threatened, resulting in added and persistent stimulus to action. Leninism recognizes implicitly that proximate, operational goals are more important in the struggle for power than abstract, ultimate goals. An appraisal of the individual's relation to relevant power structures is crucial for the communists. They ask: How will what he does help or hinder the party as an organization? They are only secondarily interested in the question: What are his ultimate goals? Someone who competes with the party for its clientele, or who undermines loyalty to the party leadership or to the Soviet regime, is anathema regardless of any agreements on ultimate goals or even on rather specific political objectives. On the other hand, someone (e.g., Henry Wallace in 1948) who can serve the immediate opportunistic interests of the party and of Soviet policy, but who has

---

[32] For a frank description of this exploit, see J. P. Cannon, *History of American Trotskyism*, Pioneer Publications, Inc., New York, 1944.

many programmatic disagreements, will be very welcome. When power is central, ideological agreements that do not "pay off" in organizational strength must be deemed of little consequence. The mark of the muddlehead, in Leninist terms, is the barter of concrete advantages (with respect to actual or potential power) for verbal commitments.

Institutional loyalties are fostered as a way to give abstract ideals a content that can effectively summon psychological energies. The same function may be served by linking ideals to a continuous conquest of specific targets in the struggle for power. An important Leninist principle is reflected in the rule that organized education and self-study must be supplemented by participation in communist activities. The primary function of each type of education is to steel the loyalties of the party member, to immerse him in the movement, and hence create a life-commitment—in a word, to "bolshevize" him. "Bolshevization" involves more than ideological instruction, however effective and intensive that may be. It includes training in "the school of the class struggle." The indispensability of both types of education is explicitly understood:

> The new members, whom we want to involve actively in the work of the Party, do not enter our ranks with a full knowledge of the Party's program, theory, tactics, or methods of work. This {48} they will achieve, ultimately, in two ways: (1) Through active participation, under the guidance of the Party, in the activities and struggles of the masses. (The key to this is the Party club.) (2) Through systematic and organized education and self-study—guided not only by the club, but by the Section or County Party Committee—as well as through regular reading and study of the Party press and literature.[33]

It is in the "mass movement"—which means, less dramatically, in trade-unions, in youth, veterans, and parent-teachers organizations, in unemployed councils, in public forums—that the member learns "the line" in the process of fighting for its implementation under the guidance of more experienced comrades. He learns to identify the enemies of the party and those who may be used to serve its ends. He is exhilarated by identification with an elite group which seems to know what it is doing and where it is going. He learns how to *be* a communist. Moreover, party work in his place of employment offers the individual the opportunity to invest an often routine and emotionally unrewarding job with a moral significance. His job takes on a new meaning, that of the struggle for power, adding new and often welcome responsibilities and status. Thus the very activities which extend the influence of the party also strengthen the party organization by increasing the competence and the commitment of the rank and file. This dovetailing of functions is a key source of strength in the combat party.

---

[33]   J. Williamson, "Improve and Build Our Communist Press—The Next Step in Party Building," *Political Affairs*, Vol. 25, September, 1946, p. 9.

The Press as Collective Organizer

The communist press is more than a medium for the dissemination of party propaganda. An incidental potentiality for mobilizing the membership is explicitly recognized and exploited. The great emphasis on the importance of the party press—far in excess of that normal in political organizations—is due as much to the organizational {49} utility as to the propaganda potential of the material issued. Lenin stressed this point repeatedly:

> A paper is not merely a collective propagandist and collective agitator, it is also a collective organizer. . . . With the aid of, and around a paper, there will automatically develop an organization that will be concerned, not only with local activities, but also with regular, general work; it will teach its members carefully to watch political events, to estimate their importance and their influence on the various sections of the population, and to devise suitable methods to influence these events through the revolutionary party. The mere technical problem of procuring a regular supply of material for the newspaper and its regular distribution will make it necessary to create a network of agents of a united party, who will be in close contact with each other, will be acquainted with the general situations, will be accustomed to fulfill the detailed functions of the national (All-Russian) work, and who will test their strength in the organization of various kinds of revolutionary activities.[34]
>
> To train a network of agents for the rapid and correct distribution of literature, leaflets, proclamations, etc., is to perform the greater half of the work of preparation for an eventual demonstration, uprising. It is too late to start organizing literature distribution at a moment of interest, a strike, or ferment; it must be done gradually, distributions being made twice or even three times a month. . . . The distribution machine must in no case be allowed to remain idle. We must try to bring the machine to such a pitch of perfection that the whole working class population can be advised, and, so to speak, mobilized overnight.[35]

Here Lenin identifies two functions of the party press especially important in a movement using organizational weapons. First, the press can communicate tactics—what to do and how to behave in relation to specific targets and enemies. The communist press contains detailed (though often oblique) instruction for communists and sympathizers on day-to-day problems of the mass movement. Readers of the *Daily Worker* look for the general line of the party {50} but more especially for discussions of internal problems of unions and other organizations, including left-wing anticommunist groups. Such a function is not vital to a group interested only in general propaganda, but it is indispensable if members are thought of as

---

[34] V. I. Lenin, "Where To Begin" (1901), *Collected Works*, Vol. 4, Bk. 1 (1929), p. 114.

[35] V. I. Lenin, "A Letter to a Comrade on Our Problems of Organization" (1902), *Lenin on Organization*, pp. 57-58.

shock troops to be armed with knowledge that may spell the difference between defeat and victory in combat situations.

Secondly, for Lenin the newspaper is a collective organizer in the sense that it is a focal point around which action can be centered, e.g., by offering definite things to do and goals to accomplish. The very task of building a newsgathering and distribution system can help train, prepare, and unite the rank and file. Consider the following analysis of the *American Daily Worker* made by a committee of the Communist International:

> The paper must very soon take steps to create a strong network of worker-correspondents in the localities, in order to instruct and help them in writing their letters and to raise their political level; not only to print letters, but to point out the political importance and the lessons of any given fact. . . . The Daily Worker does not deal with questions of building the party. And yet these questions are of decisive importance for development of the CPUSA, its transformation into a mass party, its bolshevization. The paper must create a section of party life and party construction. . . . In this section, the paper must, in the first place explain the line of the party on the most important current questions and fight for this line; secondly, it must fight for a check-up on the execution of the party's decisions, of the tasks set by it, showing how the execution is going on, explaining the tasks of the party with concrete examples, and showing how to carry them out, and so on; thirdly, it must particularly give information on the tasks and methods of masswork of the Communists, particularly the trade unions; fourthly, it must popularize the experience of the organizational building of the party, the work of the cells, the fight against bureaucracy, for discipline, against membership fluctuation, recruiting work, work among new members, and so forth; fifthly, it must give information on questions of propagandist work, on the work of the school, on questions of agitation, on the work of factory papers. . . . The paper must have permanent connections with the active party members in the trade unions (in order to systematically popularize the tasks of the party in this work) — {51} explain to non-party workers the current tasks of trade union work, with workers' letters, at conferences with worker readers of the paper, etc., so that not the least detail of trade-union life, of the trade-union policy, and work of the party should remain unexplained to the non-party masses; and particularly questions of opposition work in AFL, work in independent unions, questions of trade union unity, attitude toward Musteites, etc.[36]

The use of "worker-correspondents" (in practice probably party members) and of the membership for distribution of the paper at union halls, demonstrations, etc., is an additional method of involving adherents in active work. This type of activity is especially useful for institutionally unattached elements who cannot be involved

---

[36] *Communist International*, October 15, 1933.

in an immediate power struggle.[37]

When party members are schooled in the use of the press as an organizational weapon, it becomes especially dangerous to permit dissident groups within the party to have publications of their own or even to have access to the party press:

> The party press is the decisive public agitational and propagandist expression of the Bolshevik organization. The policies of the press are formulated, on the basis of the fundamental resolutions of the congresses and conferences of the International, the conventions of the party, and decisions of the National Committee not in conflict with such resolutions. Control of the press is lodged directly in the hands of the National Committee by the convention of the party. The duty of the editors is loyally to interpret the decisions of the convention in the press.
>
> The opening of the party press to discussions of a point of view contrary to that of the official leadership of the party or of its programmatic convention decisions must be controlled by the National Committee which is obligated to regulate discussion of this character in such a way as to give decisive emphasis to the party line. It is the right and duty of the National Committee {52} to veto any demand for public discussion if it deems such discussion harmful to the best interests of the party.
>
> The petty-bourgeois opposition in our party demonstrates its hostility to Bolshevik organization by its demand that the minority be granted the right to transform the press into a discussion organ for diametrically opposite programs. By that method *it would take control of the press out of the hands of the National Committee* and subordinate it to any temporary, anarchist combination which can make itself heard at the moment.
>
> By the same token the demand of the petty-bourgeois opposition for an independent public organ, expounding a program in opposition to that of the majority of the party, represents a complete abandonment of democratic centralism and a capitulation to the Norman Thomas type of "all-inclusive" party which is inclusive of all tendencies except the Bolshevik. *The granting of this demand for a separate organ would destroy the centralist character of the party,* by creating dual central committees, dual editorial boards, dual treasuries, dual distribution agencies, divided loyalties and a complete breakdown of all discipline. Under such conditions the party would rapidly degenerate into a social democratic organization or disappear from the scene altogether.[38] [Emphasis supplied]

The above is particularly revealing as reflecting the *general* nature of bolshevism because it is written by one who accepts Leninism but who is not Stalinist. Even

---

[37] Emphasis on reporting news of special party interest has the incidental consequence of weighting content in favor of unions and other organizations in which communists are active, although the fact of communist participation may not be openly admitted. However, with some margin of error, knowledge of this organizational use of the press should make it possible to identify areas of communist concentration during a given period.

[38] J. P. Cannon, *The Struggle for a Proletarian Party*, pp. 243-244.

this relative freedom of Trotskyism—as reflected in the fact that factions are countenanced at all—is incompatible with a dual press. Bolshevism cannot endure any break in the unity of command, and so long as the press is viewed as a power vehicle (in the sense of creating power-oriented organization), a multiple party press expressing divergent views is intolerable. In addition to the general fear, on other grounds, of even esoterically divergent opinions, there is the special fear of administrative dualism—in distribution agencies, treasuries, and ultimately in decisionmaking. When this is understood, the consistency of centralized control over the press with paramilitary bolshevism becomes apparent. {53}

The Role of Conspiratorial Activity

Conspiratorial activity is intrinsic to communism, regardless of fluctuations in the respectability of its immediate program. Leninists accept the importance of carrying on illegal operations as a matter of course. Traditionally, this has been motivated by revolutionary aims and the expectation of repression. Thus two of the "Twenty-one Conditions of Admission to the Communist International" (1920) read as follows:

> 3. The class struggle in almost every country of Europe and America is entering the phase of civil war. Under such conditions the Communists can have no confidence in bourgeois laws. They should create everywhere a parallel illegal apparatus, which at the decisive moment would be of assistance to the party to do its duty toward the revolution. In every country where, in consequence of martial law or of other exceptional laws, the Communists are unable to carry on their work legally, a combination of legal and illegal work is absolutely necessary.
>
> 4. Persistent and systematic propaganda and agitation must be carried on in the army, where Communist groups should be formed in every military organization. Wherever owing to repressive legislation agitation becomes impossible, it is necessary to carry on such agitation illegally. But refusal to carry on or participate in such work should be considered equal to treason to the revolutionary cause, and incompatible with affiliation to the Third International.[39]

But illegality does not cease under less repressive conditions:

> A Communist representative [in a parliament], by decision of the Central Committee, is bound to combine legal work with illegal work. In countries where the Communist delegate enjoys a certain inviolability, this must be utilized by way of rendering assistance to the illegal organizations and for the propaganda of the party.[40]

---

[39] Reprinted in *Blueprint for World Conquest*, ed. by W. H. Chamberlin, Human Events, Washington, 1946, pp. 66-67.

[40] "The Communist Party and Parliamentarism," *ibid.*, p. 97.

Indeed, the traditional formula calls for illegal work wherever governments are "in the hands of the bourgeoisie or the counterrevolutionary {54} Social Democrats.[41] In other words, wherever the communists have not yet seized power, they are enjoined to combine conspiratorial activity with legal work.

It would be wrong, however, to assume that illegality is necessarily tied to *revolutionary* aims. Such aims, plus the conditions in pre-Soviet Russia and the repression (real and threatened) suffered elsewhere after the revolution, did indeed constitute the traditional and recognized rationale for illegal activity. But even the founders of bolshevism may not have realized the general applicability of the methods of work they devised.

Conspiratorial organization in bolshevism stems from the continuous and systematic search for "pieces of power," regardless of whether this search ultimately leads to the overthrow of a government. It serves these revolutionary aims, but is useful for more immediate goals as well.[42] Such a pattern of power-seeking leads to the use of conspiratorial methods in attempting to seize control of target groups and in utilizing them as casual organizational weapons. Since the use of such a group for power purposes involves potential, and often actual, subversion of the purpose for which the group is maintained and of the principles upon which it is organized. Such operations cannot well be carried on openly. {55}

To be sure, even apart from revolution and repression, conspiratorial activity can be partly explained by the bad repute of communists, leading them to hide their affiliations and views in order to qualify for leadership. But no group seeking naked power can long avoid reliance on conspiratorial methods. Racketeers and self-serving bureaucrats are inevitably driven toward illegality. This is emphasized in the case of the Leninists, because the power-seeking of one party faction is to be coordinated with that of others, multiplying the chances that the interests of the manipulated groups will suffer. This is to say nothing of the inherent illegality of so-called "opposition work"—outright subversion of organizations (e.g., socialists) competing for the same clientele.

On this theory, it should be anticipated that conspiratorial activity *increases* rather than decreases as (nonideological) communist influence is extended. The

---

[41] "The Role of the Party in the Revolution," *ibid.*, p. 83.

[42] This is consistent with the following analysis of the role of the Latin-American communist parties: "This unsuccessful *putsch* [of Prestes in 1935] has had great significance for the entire Communist movement in the Western hemisphere. It convinced the Comintern that the Communist parties of America could be used for better purposes than mere propaganda outlets. . . . Prestes formulated the transformation of the formerly insignificant Communist propaganda groups south of the Rio Grande into Russian pressure organizations with sharply defined objectives The Stalintern demands from its Latin-American adherents no revolution, but participation in power, be it ever so small. Its pressure groups are advised to utilize all means that will serve the purpose; to enter into any combination with political or military groups, be they democratic. fascist, or socialist. They are absolutely free to move as it seems best to them on one condition—a common minimum program of direct or indirect support of Russia's acts and activities in the Western hemisphere." Ypsilon, *Pattern for World Revolution,* Ziff-Davis Publishing Company, Chicago, 1917, p. 406f. Note also the events at Bogota in April, 19-18. The radical opportunism induced by support of Russian foreign policy is consistent with the central pattern of Bolshevik action: the use of organizational weapons in a continuous search for bits of power.

more the communists penetrate and control *non*communist groups, the more urgent is the need for conspiratorial work. If the mass organizations themselves are or become ideologically communist, the need for illegal work abates. In the United States, where the possibility of open communist control of mass groups is very limited, reliance on conspiratorial methods is correspondingly great. Although the communists were overtly more "red" in the nineteen-twenties than in the thirties, it is probable that the relative weight of illegal work was much greater in the later period than in the earlier. During the nineteen-twenties, the communists were largely isolated, using strongly leftist phraseology and talking openly about illegal activity. But, since the early peripheral organizations, and the "red" trade-unions, were largely composed of communists and very close sympathizers, the need for practical conspiratorial work was not urgent. Later, when new opportunities and methods permitted the party to break through this isolation, gaining access to noncommunist groups, the need for covert organizational practices was more pressing. Naturally enough, conspiratorial *phraseology* became a handicap when there was real work to be done. {56}

Organizational Character-Definition

The "character" of an organization may be regarded as a product of its ingrained methods of work, its natural allies, its stake in the course of events, the predispositions of its personnel, and the labels (deserved and undeserved) which have become attached to it. These characteristics reflect the organization's controlling roles and purposes; they generate those established patterns of expectation with which the organization is uniquely identified. Not every organization has a set character. Where goals are highly specialized and technical, where individuals and groups have only a narrow relation to the organization as a whole, few character-defining commitments may develop. But where some special mission, or a tong history, results in more than a purely formal administrative structure, there emerges a quality of uniqueness that suffuses the entire organization. When this occurs, two general consequences are discernible: on the one hand, the organization becomes well adapted to the fulfillment of its own purposes and, especially, to its own methods of operation; on the other hand, it becomes ill adapted to the fulfillment of other purposes, even those closely related to it. Hence, as in government, new agencies are built and old ones cast aside simply because of the fear that the "character" of the old organization would inhibit effective adaptation to a new program or new methods of work.

In the case of an organizational weapon, whose explorations in the search for power are always hazardous, the need for character-definition is especially urgent. For example, if the relation of members to the combat party is unclear—if the role of the member as agent is only poorly understood—then a trade-unionist may place his union's interests before that of the party. One of the many differences between the character of the socialist movement, at least in the United States, and that of the communist movement lies precisely here. A socialist member is not essentially an agent, though he may function partially as such. Indeed, it has been one of the ironic roles of the socialists to train many future trade-union leaders who later leave the party after attaining positions of prominence. The communists {57} are consequently highly conscious of the differences between themselves and the socialists on these character-defining issues. They are issues which identify the unique nature of the communist type of party as against other political organizations.

Nor are differences of this kind simply *resolved* into existence: a long process of indoctrination and action is required to inculcate methods of organization and work so deeply that they select and create congenial personality traits. One way of analyzing the character of the communist movement is to trace its own efforts to distinguish itself from the socialists. This would include not only Lenin's controversy with Martov, very early in the century,[43] concerning the nature of party membership, but also some less well-known matters, such as the following:

> Our present organizational structure, based primarily on arbitrary territorial divisions, is a heritage from the Socialist party. The Socialist party was and still is first and foremost an election apparatus. Consequently, it was based simply on the territorial divisions most convenient for the bourgeoisie in their organization of election campaigns. In short, the territorial basis and the decentralized, the federalist character of the Socialist party cannot be separated from its all-important tasks of participating in the parliamentary campaigns and striving to reform the capitalist order.
>
> Our Party is suffering too much from this heritage. The time is at hand to cast overboard whatever structural forms we have inherited from the Socialist party. The time is at hand to remove completely the vestiges of social-democratic organization noticeable in our Party. The time is at hand to eradicate these serious {58} obstacles to developing our Party into a genuine Bolshevik organization.[44]

A combat party, which seeks a larger arena than the purely electoral, must reorganize, must escape from earlier commitments into new ones better adapted to a more general struggle for power. But this requires the "eradication" of a "heritage," a basic shift in the nature of the party structure.

Or changes in the role of leadership may, when combined with related transformations, help to crystallize a definite social character:

---

[43] In 1901, Lenin sharpened his conception of Bolshevik organization by insisting, against Julius Martov, upon a party of professional revolutionaries. Martov "wanted a broad party, not a party of professional revolutionists alone, but one open to all workers and intellectuals who believed in its program and were willing to work under its direction." B. Wolfe, *Three Who Made a Revolution,* Dial Press, Inc., New York, p. 241. Lenin's insistence on a definition of the member as one who recognizes the Party's program and supports it by material means and by personal participation in one of the party organizations," as elaborated, meant that he wanted a party of men who put themselves at the disposal of the leadership, accepting full discipline and responsibility. The looser formulation, characteristically social-democratic, which was supported by Martov, would have permitted the party member to have a more ambiguous, less total, relation to the party organization.

[44] J. Lovestone, Introduction to "The Party Organization" [c. 1925]. Reprinted in *Hearings,* Appendix, Pt. 1, p. 296.

The pre-war Social Democracy was a sprawling, slow-moving reformist organization which proceeded on the theory that it had unlimited time to advance to socialism at a snail's pace in a completely normal evolutionary process, uninterrupted by wars and revolutions, The leadership in the main corresponded to the character of the party. Lawyers, doctors, teachers, preachers, writers, professors—people of this kind who lived their real lives in another world and gave an evening, or at most two evenings, a week of their time to the socialist movement for the good of their souls—they were the outstanding leaders of the pre-war Socialist Party.

They decided things. They laid down the law. They were the speakers on ceremonial occasions; they posed for their photographs and gave interviews to the newspapers. Between them and the proletarian Jimmy Higginses in the ranks there was an enormous gulf. As for the party functionaries, the people who devoted all their time to the daily work and routine of the party, they were simply regarded as flunkeys to be loaded with the disagreeable tasks, poorly paid and blamed if anything went wrong. A prejudice was cultivated against the professional party workers. The real honors and decisive influence went to the leaders who had professional occupations outside the party and who, for the most part, lived typical petty-bourgeois lives which were far removed from the lives of the workers they were presumably "leading."

When we organized the Communist Party in this country in 1919, under the inspiration of the Russian revolution, we put a stop to all this nonsense. We had the opinion that leadership of the revolutionary movement was a serious matter, a profession {59} in itself, and the highest and most honorable of all professions. We deemed it unworthy of the dignity of a revolutionary leader to waste his time on some piddling occupation in the bourgeois world and wrong for the party to permit it. We decreed that no one could be a member of the Central Committee of the party unless he was a full time professional party worker, or willing to become such at the call of the party. I think we had the right idea in 1919. . . .[45]

The reorientation described here is not simply one of technical organization, but of restructuring the *attitudes and actions* of the membership. The habits of political activity on an electoral basis are not easily altered when established in the course of years of effort; so too with the attempt to increase the stature of the full-time worker and to alter the relation of the ideological leader to the party. These attitudes toward organization generate commitments which contribute to the character of the organization as a whole.

The ideology of a group is, of course, also important in shaping its character, particularly if the doctrine affects strongly the individual's participation. The doctrinal commitments of the Democratic, Republican, and similar parties are only weakly consequential in this way and therefore are inadequate to give these groups distinctive characters; moreover, little effort is made in these parties to create a "new man." through indoctrination. But in the communist movement the

---

[45]   J. P. Cannon, *The Struggle for a Proletarian Party*, pp. 23-24.

character-defining role of ideology is of great significance. This is reflected in the "great teacher" as defining hero—Marx, Engels, Lenin, Stalin—as well as in special methods of work.

Moreover, Marxist doctrine in its tenets on morality helps to create and to attract the kind of personality congenial to bolshevism. Marxism holds that all moral concepts are necessary reflections of the prevailing socioeconomic order. Hence there is no universal morality and, indeed, it is futile to consider moral questions on their merits. What one has to do is (1) to "unmask" the morality of a bad (nonsocialist) social system as a moral "fable," and (2) to change the system by revolutionary action. Such views bolster the amoralism of participants who are trained to view all human situations {60} in terms of power relations, who are withdrawn from normal loyalties and ambitions, and who make the party and its struggles the receptacle of meaningfulness. "Our morality," wrote Lenin, "is deduced from the class struggle. . . . Communist morality consists entirely of compact united discipline and conscious mass struggle against exploiters. We do not believe in eternal morality, and we expose all the fables about morality.[46]

Another aspect of organizational character-definition is control over the social composition of the membership. It is generally true that where the class, family, sectional, or ethnic origins of personnel are uncontrolled, unanticipated consequence for decisionmaking may ensue. Organizations which are self-conscious about their characters—an officers' corps, an elite school, etc.—normally attempt to control composition by selection with respect to origin. The communists are likewise concerned about composition but are not prepared to be completely selective. As a consequence, their problem becomes one of devising special measures for the reorientation of personnel whose origins may raise doubts as to reliability and utility. Such doubts arise in the relation of the party to members recruited from among doctors, writers, teachers, and other professionals. The party meets this organizational problem in three ways:

1. *Selective Recruiting.* "Only those [professionals can become members] who show by practical work that they definitely understand the party line, are prepared to put it into effect, and especially display a thorough readiness to accept Party discipline. . . . There must be selective recruitment far more than in the case of miners. longshoremen, railroad workers, etc."[47] The intellectual joins out of conviction rather than out of "class interest." But convictions may change and are potentially divisive; hence the party is wary of those who join on intellectual grounds.

2. *Intensive Education.* Once accepted into the party, a compulsory schedule of indoctrination through discussion groups, party {61} schools, and literature oriented to intellectuals is instituted. It is here that the nuances of Marxist doctrine—such as the theory of "historic function" which may justify any excess in the here and now—come into play as effective contributors to reliability.

3. *Mass Work.* The professional is asked to participate in the organization of

---

[46] V. I. Lenin, "The Tasks of the Youth Leagues" (October 2, 1920), *Selected Works,* Vol. 9, International Publishers, 1937, pp. 475, 478.

[47] W. Z. Foster, "The Communist Party and the Professionals," *The Communist,* September, 1938.

the rank and file of his own calling; to accept assignments which will link him to the mass movement—e.g., a communist intellectual may be assigned to a maritime trade-union fraction[48] to act as secretary, educational director, etc.; and to defend publicly the party and Marxist viewpoint whenever opportunity arises. All of these functions serve to guarantee his involvement in and commitment to the basic power-seeking functions of the party.

The most dramatic effort to define the character of the communist movement was probably the promulgation of the famous "Twenty-one Conditions for Admission to the Communist International" in 1920. A whole series of political and *organizational* commitments was exacted. It is instructive to review the list:

1. General propaganda and agitation should have a "really Communist character." All publications should be subject to the control of the presidium of the party, whether legal or illegal. "It should in no way be permitted that the publishers abuse their autonomy and carry on a policy not fully corresponding to the policy of the party."

2. "Every organization desiring to join the CI shall be bound systematically and regularly to remove from all the responsible posts in the labor movement (party organization, editorship, labor unions, parliamentary factions, cooperatives, municipalities, etc.) all reformists and followers of the centre, and to have them replaced by Communists, even at the cost of replacing at the beginning 'experienced' opportunists by rank-and-file workers."

3. The affiliating parties must have "no confidence in bourgeois laws" and must combine legal and illegal work.

4. Willingness to conduct illegal work in the army is an indispensable condition for affiliation. {62}

5. Rural districts should not be slighted in communist work or relinquished to "untrustworthy half reformists."

6. [A political condition: against "social pacificism."]

7. Complete rupture with "centrists" (mostly socialists) must be recognized as necessary and all parties "must advocate this rupture amongst the widest circles of the party membership, without which condition a consistent Communist policy is impossible."

8. [A political condition: on the colonial question.]

9. Systematic work must be carried on in labor unions, cooperatives, and other "organizations of the working masses." The communist nuclei organized for this purpose should be completely subordinated to the party.

10. Affiliates must carry on a struggle against "the Amsterdam 'International' of the yellow labor unions."

11. All parliamentary fractions must be subordinated to the Central Committee of the party, "not only verbally but in reality," and the party must demand that each communist representative in parliament "subject his entire activity to the interests of real revolutionary propaganda and agitation."

12. "Democratic centralization"[49] must be the rule in all parties.

---

[48] See footnote 54, p. 67, for discussion of the difference between "fraction" and "faction."

[49] More often: "democratic centralism." This refers to the pattern of a hierarchy of party organizations and committees, each of which is elected by the next lower body, but once

13. "The Communist parties of those countries where the Communist activity is legal should clean out their members from time to time, as well as those of the party organization."

14. [A political condition: defense of the USSR, to be implemented by inducing workers to sabotage transport of equipment used against the USSR and by propaganda among troops.]

15. All ex-socialist parties must draw up a new program to be approved by the International.

16. Rulings of the International and its executive are binding for all parties.

17. Affiliates should change their names, so that "every rank-and-file {63} worker should be able clearly to distinguish between the Communist parties and the old official 'Social-Democratic' or 'Socialist' parties, which have betrayed the cause of the working class."

18. The leading organs of the parties must publish the important documents of the International.

19. Parties wishing to affiliate must convene an Extraordinary Congress within four months after the Second Congress of the Communist International.

20. Parties wishing to join the Communist International, but which have not demonstrated a radical change in tactics, should, prior to joining, "take care that not less than two-thirds of their committee members and of all their central institutions should be composed of comrades, who have made an open and definite declaration prior to the convening of the Second Congress, as to their desire that the party should affiliate to the Third International."

21. "Those members of the party who reject in principle the conditions and the theses of the Third International are liable to be excluded from the party."

It is characteristic of the commitments enjoined here that they are more than merely verbal. They required implementation through a reorientation of structure, doctrine, and symbols which took years to complete. Especially noteworthy is the effort to sever sharply the new communist groups from their socialist antecedents. The need to do this reflects one of the key imperatives to self-conscious character-definition in the communist movement. Unless its special character is clearly defined—not in words only, but in a set of behavioral commitments—there is the danger of backsliding into socialist methods of work. This danger exists not so much because of received habits and ideas as because of the inherent tendency of a working-class party to be caught up by and dissolved into the labor movement. It was precisely this danger which Lenin noted and fought, and which in the early days played an important role in identifying the nature of bolshevism. The danger is mortal, for it threatens to destroy the capacity of the party to function as an organizational weapon. Furthermore, {64} confusion of the socialist and communist movements results in a softening of the demand for exclusive leadership and permits the socialists the right of access to the working class; but this is precisely what cannot be permitted without restraining the continuous struggle for power.

---

elected the higher bodies exercise executive control over the lower ones. Typically, it is the latter aspect which is stressed, elections becoming ratifications of choices made by the permanent leadership.

This sensitivity to character-definition is related to a theory of inherent dangers, of potential sources of corruption which must be guarded against continuously. Typically, bolshevism catalogues these threats in a systematic way: "All Communist parties achieve their unity, ideological clarity, and strength only in constant struggle against opportunism—Right opportunism and Leftist sectarianism—in their own midst."[50] When the ideological trappings are stripped away, these classic "deviations" come to this: "Right opportunism" refers to any policy which tends to liquidate the party as an organizationally distinct vanguard group. Under this heading would be classified efforts to subordinate political leadership to trade-union leadership or to weaken the organs of party control in the labor movement. "Leftist sectarianism" refers to policies which tend to isolate the party from the mass movement, as in insistence on openly communist trade-unions.

These labels are not always used consistently and accurately. Often, they serve merely as convenient pejoratives to stigmatize a dissident element or to justify a purge. Nevertheless, these trends are inherent in an activist ideological movement such as the communist and much effort is expended in an attempt so to commit the party as to avoid both liquidation and isolation. The willingness of the membership to participate in power struggles; organization of the party along lines which emphasize work in industry; absolute subordination of the press and of the leaders of mass organizations to the center; inculcation of an amoralism which loosens normal inhibitions against treachery and deceit; doctrinal emphasis on the indispensability of the vanguard; special education and involvement for {65} potentially unreliable elements—all of these and similar practices create predispositions helping to keep the party in line against corruptionist tendencies which would decrease its utility as an organizational weapon.

To set the character of the organization in this way may seem to be inconsistent with the central rote of manipulability in the designed organizational weapon. Clearly, the more firmly established the character of an organization becomes, the less readily can it be adapted to purposes not in accord with its own nature. In this sense manipulability is limited. But it will be noted that the kinds of commitment which have been established are those which increase the capacity of the leadership to mobilize and "hurl" the organization against strategic targets in the struggle for power. It is in this sense that organizational weapons, not unlike military units, are manipulable.

One of the advantages of a firmly established organizational character is the possibility of increasing decentralization without sacrificing unity of policy or stability of command. There is a normal tendency in organizations to permit a loosening of formal central controls after the character of the organization has been established. In the cadre party, with its heavy emphasis on indoctrination and institutional character-formation, this means that party members may be relied on to carry our party policy even under conditions which do not permit direct control over the member by regular party organs. This lends support to the interpretation that the dissolution of the Communist International in 1943 was not a mere sham but was a recognition of the possibilities of decentralization of

---

[50]   A. Bittelman, "The Twenty-seventh Party Anniversary," *Political Affairs*, Vol. 25, October, 1946, p. 10.

tactical decision to the constituent parties.[51] This is not to deny that it was basically deceptive in the attempt to convey the impression that an internationally directed communist movement no longer existed, or that the timing of the dissolution was a matter of psychological warfare. {66}

Organs of Infiltration

Nuclei of communists in target institutions have always been the primary components of the communist organizational weapon. Among the "theses" of the second Congress of the Communist International (1920) we find:

> The fundamental principle of all organization work of the Communist Party and individual Communists must be the creation of Communist nuclei everywhere where they find proletarians and semi-proletarians—although even in small numbers. In every Soviet of Workers' Deputies, in every trade and industrial union, cooperative association, factory, tenants' union, in every government institution everywhere, even though there may be *only three people* sympathizing with Communism, a Communist nucleus must be immediately organized. *It is only the power of organization* of the Communists that enables the advance guard of the working class to be the leader of the whole class. Communist nuclei working in organizations adhering to no political party must be subject to the party organization in general, whether the party itself is working legally or illegally at the given moment. Communist nuclei of all kinds must be subordinated one to another in a strictly hierarchical order and system. [Emphasis supplied]

Nor is this an outmoded emphasis. It has never been repudiated as basic principle, and as late as 1938 the *Party Organizer* published an article which identified the shop units as the basic organization of the party.[52]

At first glance, the utility of insisting on organized nuclei even of very small groups of co-thinkers may seem doubtful. The problem, however, is always one of *relative* weight. A few individuals—when they are virtually the only ones acting in concert for power goals—may be very effective. Whereas others will use many varying criteria in arriving at decisions, these will use but one: power aggrandizement. In a university faculty, for example, a few men in strategic places can be very influential. But they will not be effective, no matter how close their ideological agreement, unless they are organized. They must consistently exploit opportunities for {67} concerted action—as in recommendation of personnel, promotions, departmental prerogatives, or defamation of an enemy—and, above all, they must not permit other considerations (e.g., technical academic criteria) to qualify their dedication to power-seeking. This transformation of mere general agreement into effective action requires meeting, planning, and discipline.

---

[51] In addition, it is likely that there was a desire to be rid of the Comintern *headquarters,* which occupied an anomalous position in the Moscow hierarchy and had already experienced some blows.

[52] F. Brown, "Essential Problems of Organization," *Party Organizer*, May, 1938.

According to Lenin, "every nucleus and every Party workers' committee must be a base supporting the agitational, propaganda and organizing work among the masses, i.e., they must go wherever the masses are going and at every step endeavor to direct their consciousness towards Socialism, they must associate every private question with the tasks of the proletariat, they must use every attempt at organization to further the cause of class consolidation, and by their energy and moral influence (and not, of course, by their titles and ranks) gain the lead in every legal proletarian organization. . . . Under all conditions and circumstances, and in every possible situation, they will carry on a *Party* policy, they will influence their environment in the spirit of the Party and will not allow their environment to engulf them."[53]

Carrying out a "party policy" requires the maintenance of lines of authority and communication, which is to say, organization.

Coordination of party activity "in the field" has received considerable attention. Thus in 1932 the Presidium of the Executive Committee of the Communist International defined the role of factory nuclei in relation to party fractions in the trade-unions.[54] Since any {68} given factory might include members of several different unions, a coordinating center would be needed. This function, it was pointed out, should be performed by the factory nucleus, which must guide all the trade-union work in the factory. The factory fraction groups of the various trade-unions were to work under the direct leadership of the factory nucleus. The chain of command would therefore run from the local party committee to the nucleus, with the trade-union fraction restrained from giving direct orders to the factory fraction. Presumably this would mean that the fraction would communicate its directives through the party committee, which could then make modifications in the light of the total trade-union situation at the area level. This is an example of the classic need for area-functional coordination in administration. In theory, the directive of the Comintern[55] would seem to be based on the view that power in a given factory rather than in a union per se should be the central objective.

Although analyses of this kind reflect a high order of administrative self-consciousness, it is not known to what extent this sort of coordination has been effec-

---

[53] V. I. Lenin, "On the Road" (1909), *Lenin on Organization*, p. 202.

[54] The terms "fraction" and "faction" are not always used consistently in bolshevik parlance. However, the dominant usage conforms to the following restatement. A communist "fraction" is an association of all party members belonging to a nonparty organization in a given shop, city, or country. Thus the communist fraction in the United Automobile Workers coordinates all activities of communists within that union on a local and national scale. More generally, a fraction is a working group of those agents of an outside elite who are concentrated in a given organization. A fraction is not necessarily the same as a "faction," however. A faction is a group united on a common platform with respect to a given organization, often openly contending for power within that organization. The communist fraction will usually combine with other elements to form a "unity" or "progressive" group within a union or other association. Conceivably, the fraction could divide its forces among several factions, or it could itself function as a faction. Open inner-party factions are prohibited within communist parties, although covert ones do exist from time to time. The distinction between the fraction and the faction is one of agency rather than of legality.

[55] See *The Communist*, August, 1932.

tive in practice. It is known that difficulties have occurred which have necessitated changes in organizational form and practice. Thus words like "nucleus" and "cell" have been dropped, and "branch" substituted. This represents partly an effort to avoid prejudicial terminology, but it is also a reflection of the need to avoid organizational methods which would isolate the party from possible nonparty support in the factories and unions. It is probable that shop branches continue to exist and play an important role, but the importance of controlling unions (rather than factories) for the pressure-group goals of the modern communist party—as well as the prevalence of industrial unionism—indicates that the importance of the shop nucleus as a coordinating group has diminished.

It was announced in 1938 that "Party general fractions" in trade {69} unions and mass organizations had been or would be abolished except "where reactionary bureaucrats use their usurped power to prevent democratic participation of the workers in the affairs of the organization."[56] Since the communist use of the term "reactionary" is, to say the least, elastic, this hedge could be interpreted to mean that wherever the communists are under attack—whether by arbitrary means or not—the organization of party fractions would be justifiable. However, it was felt that "organized fraction work may build artificial barriers between Communists and non-Party workers [since the] holding of general fraction meetings to discuss problems coming before the union is bound to create the feeling among non-Party workers that we have no confidence in them, that we are trying mechanically to influence and control the policies of the organization."[57]

If anything was liquidated as a result of this directive, it was probably the fraction *meeting* rather than the fraction itself. There is no evidence that communists ceased functioning in the unions as agents of an outside group, that the party's power struggles were uncoordinated, or that the flow of information on trade-union affairs to national headquarters was stopped. The shift was simply from methods which could not be easily concealed to more conspiratorial ones. Evidence developed during hearings conducted by the CIO in 1950 makes it clear that secret communist steering committees functioned in unions dominated by the party during the late nineteen-forties.[58] Given the discipline of the party and the ability to communicate directives through other channels, general meetings of the entire fraction in a union are not essential.[59] Hudson's use of {70} the term "party *general* fractions," noted above, is significant in this connection.

---

[56] R. Hudson, "Work among the Masses: A Discussion on Fractions," *Party Organizer*, May, 1938.

[57] *Ibid.*

[58] See "Report of the Committee to Investigate Charges against the International Union of Mine, Mill, and Smelter Workers" and "Report of the Executive Board Committee Appointed by President Murray To Investigate Charges against the International Longshoremen's and Warehousemen's Union," Congress of Industrial Organizations, Washington, D.C., 1950, mimeo.

[59] Hudson also pointed out that "if we are to lead, not through organized fraction work, but through greater Communist understanding, responsibility and work, then there will have to be greater emphasis upon individual responsibility, ability, and knowledge." This would mean, he went on, more education, more critical review, more discipline, and greater em-

The restriction of fraction meetings is consistent with the rule that the more legal and acceptable communist activities become, the more dependent they are on conspiratorial methods. They must hide evidences of disciplined party control over mass organizations. In addition, it should be pointed out that communist organizational forms and methods, though they reflect a consistent operational code, can be very flexible. This is especially true of the period since the adoption of tactics promulgated at the Seventh Congress of the Communist International in 1935.[60]

The Espionage Potential

An incidental utility of the paramilitary combat party is the conditioning of its personnel for espionage, both to support the party's political functions and as a direct aid to the USSR. This does not mean that communist parties are espionage agencies, but it does mean that they are *linked* to such agencies; that they serve as effective and secure *sources* for the recruitment of spies; and that they provide the motivation necessary for the participation of otherwise respectable and idealistic individuals in an international underworld of espionage and violence.

The basic facts about the relation between the party and the Russian espionage network were uncovered by the Canadian Royal Commission in 1946:

> It became manifest at an early stage of this Inquiry, and has been overwhelmingly established by the evidence throughout, that the Communist movement was the principal base within which the espionage network was recruited; and that it not only supplied personnel with adequately "developed" motivation, but provided {71} the organizational framework wherein recruiting could be and was carried out safely and efficiently. . . . In every instance but one, Zabotin's Canadian espionage agents were shown to be members of or sympathizers with the Communist Party. . . . The evidence shows that the espionage recruiting agents made use in their work of reports, including psychological reports, on Canadian Communists which had been prepared as part of the routine of the secret "cell" organization of that Party.[61]

The security of espionage recruiting is greatly enhanced when individuals, being approached and refusing, will not denounce the solicitor. This is precisely the kind of security offered by a communist party and its close periphery:

> By concentrating their requests to assist in espionage within the membership of secret sections of the Communist Party, the leaders were apparently able to feel quite confident—and apparently with reason based upon

---

phasis on the work of the shop, industrial, and branch units. Thus other, less formal, means of communication were to be emphasized with the "liquidation" of the fractions.

[60] See the discussion of unity tactics, pp. 126-163; see also the comments on flexibility in techniques of penetration and control, p. 199n.

[61] Report of the Royal Commission, p. 44f.

an experience in Canada over a period of at least eleven years—that even if the adherent or member should refuse to engage in activities so clearly illegal and which constitute so dear a betrayal of his or her own country—such adherent or member would in any case not consider denouncing the espionage recruiting agent to the Canadian public or to the Canadian authorities.[62]

The impact of communist indoctrination is to create a basic cleavage between the adherent and the institutions of "capitalist" society. This has the useful consequence of dissolving sentiments of loyalty and removing inhibitions inappropriate to a paramilitary context. Working for government and even private employers is viewed as an opportunity for helping the party. This does not mean that party members automatically enter the Russian secret services, but it does mean that they have gone through an initial course of training which will make them available for further participation. Given the necessary safeguards, espionage agents drawn from this milieu are more reliable than those recruited on a purely monetary basis, for their {72} loyalty is not for sale; they are committed to the party and to the "worker's fatherland."

Although only specially chosen members of the party and its periphery will be recruited for systematic espionage work (and these will drop their open association with the movement), it is to be expected that incidental espionage activity may be carried on by a large number of party members. This applies not so much to industrial or scientific espionage, although the latter is not excluded, as to the transmission of information of political interest to the party hierarchy. Given the nature of the party and its adherents, it is to be expected that individual party members who come across confidential information which would be of obvious interest to the party will pass it along, ultimately to be received by the official network. No distinction would be made between information of interest, say, to the communist leadership of a trade-union (as picked up by a corporation employee) and strategic intelligence of interest to the USSR. Consequently the uncovering of amateurish efforts to procure and transmit information is not necessarily inconsistent with the general nature of communist espionage.

Summary: The Operational Code

The preceding analysis simply details the basic code of the Bolsheviks as it bears on their conception of the combat party. This code, as distinct from party ideology or doctrine, may be summarized as follows:

1. The objective of bolshevik party organization is the creation of a highly manipulable skeleton organization of trained participants. This organization is sustained by continuous political combat and is linked to the mass movement as its members become leaders of wider groups in the community.

---

[62] *Ibid.*, p. 77. We are here discussing the espionage potential of the *party*. It is not to be inferred from this that communist espionage solicitation occurs exclusively within the party. Moreover, there is some evidence that many recruits are not so openly approached as to be given information which can be exposed prior to commitment.

2. Adherents, giving only partial consent, are to be transformed into agents from whom total conformance can be demanded.

3. The party, through activity and indoctrination, absorbs and {73} insulates the member, severing his ties to the outside world and maximizing his commitment to the movement.

4. To avoid the divisive and action-frustrating nature of democratic participation, bolshevism requires that political contention within the party be minimized. Power centers which challenge the official leadership are prohibited.

5. The keynotes of party organization are *mobilization* and *manipulation*. Everything must be subordinated to maximizing these values, for they define the combat character of the party.

6. The full potentialities of Marxist ideology for morale-building are to be exploited, but "dialectical" adaptations of doctrine to the requirements of the tactical situation are desirable. At the same time, Leninist organizational and strategic principles are to be maintained.

7. The party is to be safeguarded against the twin inherent dangers of liquidation and isolation. Consequently there is constant emphasis on maintaining the integrity of the party organization and its access to the sources of power in society.

8. The party organization can be maintained only by a continuous struggle for power in every conceivable arena.

9. The party engages in conspiratorial activity regardless of fluctuations in the respectability of its immediate program and irrespective of the degree of political freedom in the arena. This is required by the aim of subordinating target groups to the party organization.

10. Public (legal) activity is always to be combined with conspiratorial (illegal) work, the latter supporting and advancing the former. The struggle for legal standing, the right to have an open communist organization, is therefore an essential part of communist activity.

CHAPTER 2
THE VANGUARD AND THE MASS

{74}

The construction of a bolshevik party consolidates the communist elite, readies it for action. This vanguard, however, can fulfill its function, and indeed sustain itself, only as it finds a way to the sources of power. In meeting this need, the communist movement has before it an image of a *manipulable mass*—a great potential source of energy which can be mastered by those who have the knowledge and the will to do so. The problem is then one of strategy and tactics: how to make best use of the combat party, and especially how to manipulate groups and institutions that lie outside the constitutionally controlled arenas of the struggle for power. These techniques are not randomly selected. They depend on the nature of the tools to be used as well as on the goal of total power.

Strategic Principles and Organizational Weapons

Strategically valuable positions may be afforded by nature or history, as when a mountainous terrain offers defensive advantages, or when a fund of traditional loyalty is available in case of need, or when conjuncture of economic interest creates allies. However, similar advantages may also be gained when tactics are organized according to a *strategic principle* so that many diverse actions are given a unified focus and objective: annihilate the enemy; confuse him; exhaust him. These principles provide guiding concepts for exploiting tactical opportunities. They are dynamic and action-oriented, focused upon a changing situation rather than upon such specific objectives as the attainment of atomic weapons or control over a key geographic area. In a sense, the application of strategic principles is a substitute for the possession of natural strategic advantages.

{75} In addition, and of special importance here, strategic principles may be *tool-oriented*. Tools and techniques have strategic import when they directly affect the outcome of a general struggle. So with strategic bombing; so too we speak of a "strategy of terror" when this means that some action is of itself competent to create an overall advantage for the power-seeker. We speak of terrorist tactics when these are merely adjuncts of a general line of action to which they add an incidental effectiveness.

When techniques are used strategically, an effort is made to exploit their full potentialities. Thus terror as a strategy may be implemented by the tactical use of assassination and defamation. The strategic problem is not how best to execute terrorist activities under various circumstances (tactics) but rather what changes in the environment (e.g., elite morale) will be most favorable to, or place limitations upon, the use of terror. The strategic use of naval, air, psychological, or organizational weapons attempts to maximize their utility as direct sources of power. This is not a matter of manipulating planes or propaganda for greatest effectiveness in a specific situation; it is a matter of increasing or conserving the *general* utility of the weapon. Strategic principles focus attention upon the nature of the weapon in question, exploring its limits and potentialities, and upon the environmental conditions which affect the fulfillment of these potentialities.

The principles applicable to strictly organizational strategy may be best approached if we first consider the *political* strategy of bolshevism. Stalin has presented this in his own way:

> Strategy is the determination of the direction of the main blow of the proletariat at a given stage of the revolution; the elaboration of a corresponding plan of disposition of the revolutionary forces (the main and secondary reserves); the struggle to carry out this plan during the whole period of the given stage of the revolution.
>
> Our revolution had already passed through two stages and, after the October Revolution, entered upon a third stage. Our strategy was changed accordingly.
>
> *First stage, 1903, to February, 1917.*
>
> Aim: to overthrow tsarism and completely liquidate the survivals of medievalism. {76}
>
> The main force of the revolution: the proletariat.
>
> Immediate reserve: the peasantry.
>
> Direction of the main blow: the isolation of the liberal-monarchist bourgeoisie which was striving to win over the peasantry and liquidate the revolution by compromising with tsarism.
>
> Plan for the disposition of forces: alliance of the working class with the peasantry. . . .
>
> *Secondary stage, February, 1917, to October, 1917.*
>
> Aim: to overthrow imperialism in Russia and to withdraw from the imperialist war.
>
> The main force of the revolution: the proletariat.
>
> Immediate reserve: the poorest section of the peasantry.
>
> Probable reserve: the proletariat of neighboring countries.
>
> Favorable circumstances: the protracted war and the crisis of imperialism.
>
> Direction of the main blow: isolation of the petty bourgeois democrats (Mensheviks and Socialists-Revolutionists) who were striving to win over the toiling peasantry and put an end to the revolution by *compromising* with imperialism.
>
> Plan for the disposition of forces: alliance of the proletariat with the poorest section of the peasantry. . . .
>
> *Third stage, after the October Revolution.*
>
> Aim: consolidation of the dictatorship of the proletariat in one country, using it as a fulcrum for the overthrow of imperialism in all countries. The revolution goes beyond the confines of one country and the period of world

revolution commences.

The main force of the revolution: the dictatorship of the proletariat in one country and the revolutionary movement of the proletariat in all countries.

Main reserves: the semi-proletarian and small peasant masses in the advanced countries and the liberation movement in the colonies and dependent countries.

Direction of the main blow: the isolation of the petty-bourgeois democrats and the isolation of the parties of the Second International which constitute the main support of the policy of *compromise* with imperialism.

Plan for the disposition of forces: alliance of the proletarian revolution with the liberation movement of the colonies and the dependent countries.

Strategy deals with the main forces of the revolution and their reserves. It changes with the transition of the revolution from one {77} stage to another, but remains essentially unchanged throughout the entire duration of a given stage.[1]

Stalin's analysis might be reformulated in part somewhat as follows:

1. The bolsheviks constitute a revolutionary leadership group which seeks to concentrate a monopoly of social power in its hands. This elite is ideologically prepared to link itself to whatever social forces are set in motion against existing authority. The content of bolshevik agitation varies with the nature of these forces.

2. In Russia and in other parts of the world, the industrial workers in a primary way, and the peasantry secondarily, represent vast potential social power; these groups are indispensable and precious levers which can catapult a revolutionary elite into power. It will be noted that concentration upon these social forces is constant through all of the "stages" identified by Stalin.

3. The main enemy, the target, of this strategy is not the class of power-holders (feudalists, monarchists, capitalists, etc.), but rather that group which competes for the control of the proletariat and the peasantry. In each of Stalin's stages "the main blow" is directed against liberals, democrats, and socialists. This, too, is a constant factor in Leninist strategy.

The *organizational* strategy of bolshevism is, of course, shaped by these political aims. But it has a logic of its own. Its goal is to maximize the capacity of organizational weapons to increase the power of the controlling elite. In other words, in the special nature of these tools we see needs that must be fulfilled before their power potential can be realized. The identification of these needs yields organizationally relevant strategic principles.

The first and most important of the strategic needs of organizational weapons is *access*. Isolation must be avoided and techniques devised that will aid penetration of target groups and institutions. The tactical creation and manipulation of peripheral organizations {78} is one important way of fulfilling these aims; it occurs not only in communist tactics, but in the more innocent attempts of other elites to extend their influence.

But this strategy of access is especially important to a group that searches for

---

[1] J. Stalin, *Foundations of Leninism,* International Publishers, New York, 1932, p. 87f.

power everywhere in society. Finding it difficult to justify intervention, it must resort to covert and devious methods of entry. The development of a deceptive cover for organizational penetration is discussed in Chapter III, "The Strategy of Access," in connection with communist "unity" tactics.

Around this central need for access there are other closely related needs. As defined in the introduction (p. 2), organizations function as weapons "when a power-seeking elite uses them to maximize its own influence in a manner unrestrained by the constitutional order of the arena within which the struggle for power takes place." We may expect, therefore, that there can be no question of ordered competition with organizational rivals, especially those appealing for support to the same social groups. Such rivals must be eliminated, by whatever means are available and expedient, if the character and utility of the organization as a weapon is to be maintained and fully exploited.

Since such competitors threaten a leadership at its most sensitive point, the social base upon which it rests, they are, quite objectively, the main enemy—but only if the effective goal is a monopoly of power, or, what is much the same thing, if the elite is convinced that it alone has the historic right to fulfill a given program. In the bolshevik movement, this *strategy of neutralization* has played a large role in the relation of the communists to socialists and other left-wing oppositional groups. If the importance of this strategy is understood, then the bitterness generated among elements which are apparently kindred ideologically, but which compete for the same social base, can be properly appraised.

Another consistent strategic pattern has to do with the relation between the organizational weapon and public opinion. The problem here is not that of direct popular support; it is rather to find some {79} means of winning acceptance of the organization as a legitimate instrument of action. Many groups, of course, have little popular support; but their right to function is not challenged. For communism, however, the *strategy of legitimacy* is of peculiar importance because it faces precisely such a challenge.

An important variable in the organizational process is participation. The relation of the individual to an organization may vary widely in meaning for him and consequently in potential power for the leadership. In pursuing the *strategy of mobilization* a controlling group attempts to transform the nature of participation so that partial adherence may become total involvement. The objective is to mobilize fully the energies of the members, through various techniques of indoctrination and participation, so that their full, rather than partial, availability for action is won. In this pattern, the range and intensity of action undertaken by the membership is increased at the same time as critical attitudes toward the leadership are lowered. As a result, the controlling elite consolidates its position internally and wrings from the organization its maximum potential for influence on the community.

These principles—access, neutralization, legitimacy, mobilization—identify strategic objectives to be gained by appropriate tactical measures. The systematic exploitation of such devices marks the difference between casual bureaucratic maneuver and the struggle for power in society.

The Image of the Mass

There are two major sources of confusion about the nature of bolshevism. The one, usually associated with political innocence, is to identify the communist party with the working class, or to see the interests of the two as convergent, and to assume that communists are simply "good trade-unionists," "consistent idealists," and the like. The other, less naïve, is to emphasize the Blanquist and paramilitary aspects of communism, to see it as an elite corps which utilizes conspiracy and violence for sabotage and for coup d'état. It is true that {80} the communists are an elite corps and that they are interested in conspiratorial subversion and insurrection; but in fulfilling these interests they attempt to retain an intimate relation to "the masses." In Leninism, the twin emphasis on elite formation and on mass involvement is fundamental:

> The Party must first of all constitute the *vanguard* of the working class. . . . But in order that it may really be the vanguard, the Party must be armed with a revolutionary theory. . . . The Party cannot be a real Party if it limits itself to registering what the masses of the working class think or experience, if it drags along at the tail of the spontaneous movement, if it does not know how to overcome the inertia and the political indifference of the spontaneous movement; or if it cannot rise above the ephemeral interests of the proletariat, if it cannot raise the masses to the level of the class interests of the proletariat.[2]

The party instructs the masses as to their true interests. "The Party must take its stand at the head of the working class, it must see ahead of the working class and lead the proletariat and not trail behind it."[3] That is what it means to be a vanguard.

Nevertheless:

> The Party cannot be merely a *vanguard. It* must at the same time be the vanguard of the class, be part of that class, intimately bound to it with every fibre of its being. The distinction between the vanguard and the main body of the working class, between Party members and non-Party members, will continue as long as classes exist, as long as the proletariat will continue replenishing its ranks with newcomers from other classes, as long as the working class as a whole is deprived of the opportunity of raising itself to the level of the vanguard. But the Party would cease to be a party if this distinction were widened into a rupture; if it were to isolate itself and break away from the non-Party masses. The Party cannot lead the class if it is not connected with the non-Party masses, if there is no close union between the Party and the non-Party masses, if these masses do not accept its leader-

---

[2] *Ibid.*, p. 105*f.*

[3] *Ibid.*

ship, if the Party does not enjoy moral and political authority among the masses.[4]

{81} There is a continual and admitted tension between the bolshevik elite and the contaminable mass it seeks to lead, but the tension would not exist were not both inescapably bound together in a grand strategic design.

If large population groups are to be used as social levers," where is the arm to move the fever? How should this arm grasp the lever? How may its hold be maintained? The special problem of leadership posed to Leninism is that of joining a revolutionary elite to the social force which it hopes will carry it to power. This relationship must (1) hold the leadership group together and (2) bind it firmly to the mass.

Here the utility of organization becomes apparent. On the one hand, the creation of the combat party welds the elite into a fighting weapon. Thus is created the arm to move the social lever. It is this party—an organized elite, or, as Stalin says, an organized detachment—that must find an intimate relation to the mass if its leadership potentialities are to be fulfilled. At the same time, apart from the use of broadside propaganda, the party cannot be related to an *amorphous* mass. Its articulation must be to something definite so that clear lines of access and command may be established. Hence the party must seek a path to, or create if they do not exist, specialized groups which are part of the mass and may form a leading segment of it. The need for organization does not stop with the building and use of the combat party; there must also be devices that provide the party with links to a social base.

The bolshevik concept of "masses" is tough-minded and flexible; it is always relative to the power position and tactical or strategic aims of the revolutionary leaders. It should be clearly understood that in technical communist usage the term "masses" is not simply a romanticized symbol—although it is partly that—but is a way of identifying the manipulable environment of the power-seeking elite. Power is the universal keynote and touchstone.

The Leninist rule is: go to the masses, for they are the font of power. This is very different from the "go to the people" slogan of {82} religious and political groups whose sense of mission is primarily educational. In such cases, the people are valued for themselves, as individuals who must be transformed in order to be saved. But when power is the decisive aim, then education will be valued only in so far as it contributes to that end. If the mass can be utilized for power purposes without a spiritual lesson, then that will be foregone. Moreover, as soon as the justification for action is removed from immediate values, and is relegated to some transcendental realm, the door is opened to coldly manipulative use of the targets of missionary enterprise. In the bolshevik movement both of these qualities converge. Power is the decisive rationale of "going to the people," and justifications are left to History. The leadership is thus freed for a purely technical approach to mass manipulation.

In the bolshevik image, the mass is not homogeneous. Some sections are more valuable than others as targets. This value in part depends on the incidence

---

[4] *Ibid.*

of social unrest. It also varies with the potential capacity of groups to influence decisionmaking in society and government. Thus steel workers, concentrated at centers of industrial power, have a greater political worth than drug store clerks. Since such utilities vary, a rational approach to the struggle for power entails a breakdown of the "mass" into elements according to strategic position. Therefore, although certain basic targets are given by the nature of industrial society, the role of population groups as masses is conditioned by their availability for bolshevik exploitation and control.

The most important condition of readiness for bolshevik exploitation is that the masses be separated from their nonbolshevik leaders. The latter, "who are very frequently hopelessly infected with petty bourgeois and imperialist prejudices . . . must be mercilessly denounced and driven out of the labor movement."[5] The mass, however, is to be approached "with patience and caution, and with {83} an understanding of the peculiarities, and the special psychology of each stratum."[6] This recognition of strata within the mass distinguishes the basic bolshevik conception from the notion that the mass is an amorphous and undifferentiated lump of humanity.

The essential characteristic of the mass in bolshevik terms is its manipulability. Unless a group is susceptible to manipulation, at least after some preparation, it does not qualify for the distinction of being part of the masses. It follows that it is not number which defines a mass, although the larger a group the more likely it is to be susceptible to manipulation. A very small group, say of workers or students, would be a "mass" group *if* it were subject to control for power purposes. Class position is a more useful criterion because it is more closely related to manipulability than is mere number. Groups identified by their common interests (labor, farmers, unemployed, etc.) are unifiable on nonideological grounds. Such unification always creates potentiality for covert manipulation. The nonideological aspect is important because attention is then centered on bread-and-butter issues, with little sensitivity to the political consequences of apparently neutral commitments.

Within ideological groupings, however, potential manipulability depends on toleration of communist participation. Once this is denied, not bureaucratically, but by the self-conscious choice of the membership, the group is no longer part of the mass, but becomes an "empty shell" or "petty-bourgeois." In ideological groups, a situation analogous to bread-and-butter trade-unionism may develop if interest is formally restricted to local issues, consumer welfare, or to administrative efficiency in government. These too are associated with limited sensitivity to the broader issues in the interests of which narrower decisions may be covertly controlled.

If *manipulability for purposes not recognized by the group* is essential to the bolshevik image of the mass, then it will be apparent that the communist movement itself is composed of layers of adherents who, relative to a controlling group, function as masses. First there is the hard core of self-conscious agents within the

---

[5] Theses of the Second Congress of the Communist International (1920). Reprinted *in Blueprint for World Conquest,* ed. by W. H. Chamberlin, Human Events, Washington, 1946, p. 51.

[6] *Ibid.*

party who {84} are fully aware of the central role of power in bolshevism. Their commitment is so deep that it need not be shored up by hatreds, by symbols, or by other forms of mass persuasion. These are the steeled cadres upon whom the continuity and the basic power of the party rest. They constitute the fundamental support of the decisionmaking group because they identify with the power aims of the movement and are ready to defend twists in the party line before the general membership. This group may constitute no more than one-tenth of a large party such as the French Communist Party; among American party members the proportion is probably higher.

Around this group, and manipulated by it, is a large number of ideologically committed communists who must be continually convinced that there is a relation between the ultimate professed aims of the party and its current political action. It is to this stratum that emotional appeals to communist traditions may be made; it is this group which had to be held in line at the time of the Stalin-Hitler pact. These elements are masses relative to the self-conscious elite; their loyalty must be maintained by indoctrination, demagogy, and other forms of persuasion. Nevertheless, these are staunch communists who for most purposes can be counted as cadres. They need, as it were, to be fed with arguments, but in respect to wider groups they themselves are leaders.

Beyond this group, but still within the party, there are elements of varying political reliability who for the time being accept communist discipline. For this stratum, which may be very large in a period of rising communist power, belonging to the party is not the momentous experience that it is for those who are more deeply committed. For this group, mass-persuasion techniques are especially important. Meetings must be large and well run, so that morale will not deteriorate. They may be expected to derive satisfactions from mass gatherings and demonstrations of all sorts, while the elite elements either stay away or attend only because they have a special job to do or are subleaders who must appear for the benefit of unit discipline. An elite communist is not concerned about such frills. He {85} will attend a meeting in a bare hall in an atmosphere of despair, and he will conceive it to be his job to bolster the morale of the five or ten "mass" party members and supporters who have come. The mass member is dependent, the elite member is responsible.

Despite the mass character of much party membership, even the party masses are elite with respect to peripheral and target elements on the outside. Any party member must be responsible in relation to a sympathizer; he must play upon his prejudices and clamp down on any deviations. In some cases, the party member must be ready to use all-out deception, as in approaching Catholic workers. Here the fundamental antagonism of communism to religion will be set aside, or even denied, so that the Catholics can be proselytized "on the basis of urging them to carry into practice their own Catholic ideals and aspirations."[7] Or institutional loyalties will be utilized for immediate purposes, as in exploiting the warning of a Cardinal against red-baiting. Indeed, it is the process of manipulating mass elements which is probably the most important educational technique in the communist movement, for it sharply reinforces the loyalty and the power sensitivity

---

[7] "Some Experiences on Work among Catholics," *Party Organizer*, May, 1938.

of the rank and file. A "mass" party member, when supported and directed by an organization, can be a useful soldier on the line in the unions and other target groups. The mere fact that he has an outside commitment—to the party—will force him to function in elite terms and to participate in the manipulation of workers so that a party-approved shop steward will be elected, and in the manipulation of union meetings so that the party slate will win. This will provide him with a strikingly sharper insight into events than that possessed by his fellow workers and hence will bolster his sense of special mission.

Lenin once suggested that "the meaning of the term 'masses' changes in accordance with the changes in the character of the struggle."[8] At that time he was arguing for the importance of winning a majority of workers and peasants as a condition for seizing and maintaining power:

> {86} At the beginning of the war several thousand real revolutionary workers were sufficient to be called masses. . . . When the revolution has been sufficiently prepared, the term "masses" acquires a different meaning. Then, several thousand workers can no longer be called masses. . . . The term masses then means the majority; not merely the majority of the workers, but the majority of all the exploited.

The mass is always the *relevant* mass, depending on the power goals of the party. In the distinction made by Lenin, the problem is one of identifying targets in a period of simple intervention, when the movement is being built, as against one in which the possibility of victory is posed. There is no question of democracy here, but of victory. "But in order to achieve victory you must have the sympathy of the masses. An absolute majority is not always essential, but in order to achieve victory, in order to retain power. . . ." The criterion of relevance is power. At one stage it may be necessary to orient to the "radicalized workers," especially those who follow a social-democratic leadership; the "socialist masses" will then be the relevant target, although this may represent a very small and selected group in the population. At another stage, the masses may indeed represent the bulk of the population.

Exploitation and control involve each other. The overwhelming importance of leadership to the Leninists is implicit in their conception of the masses as inherently subject to control by *some* elite. It is, in this view, the inevitable role of the mass to be exploited for power purposes. The only question is: who will do the exploiting? Hence it becomes just as important to know what groups can function as elites as to know the special characteristics of strata in the mass. Moreover, if the mass is to be *used* rather than simply proselytized, it is necessary to create organs of control and to guarantee the unchallenged ascendance of the party. The necessity for this ascendancy is formulated in a doctrine of the chosen vanguard, whose basic assumption is that bolshevism represents the historic interests of the working class. But it is not enough to have symbolic leadership. The working class must not only give assent, but must do work for the revolution: it must

---

[8] V. I. Lenin, "In Support of the Tactics of the CI" (July 21, 1920), *Selected Works,* Vol. 10, International Publishers, New York, 1958, pp. 286-287.

submit itself to the organizational leadership of {87} the communist party. The party manages the revolution and hence must be the controlling force among the institutions of popular expression:

> The Party is the organized detachment of the working class. But the Party is not the only organization of the working class. The proletariat has in addition a great number of other organizations which are indispensable in its struggle against the capitalist system—trade unions, cooperative, factory and shop organizations, parliamentary fractions, non-party women's associations, the press, cultural and educational organizations, youth leagues, military revolutionary organizations (in times of direct revolutionary action), soviets of deputies, which is the state form of organization (where the proletariat is in power), etc. Most of these organizations are non-party and only a certain part of them adheres directly to the Party and thus may be regarded an offshoot of it. . . . But how can unity of leadership become a reality in the face of such a multiplicity of organizations? . . . the activities of these organizations ought to be directed into a single channel, as they serve *one* class, the proletariat. The question then arises: who is to determine the line, the general direction along which the work of these organizations is to be conducted? Where is that central organization with the necessary experience to work out such a general line and also able, because of its authority, to prevail upon all these organizations to carry out this line, so as to preclude the possibility of working at cross purposes?
> This organization is the Party of the proletariat.[9]

Just as within the party the ranks must be effectively subordinated to a managerial party leadership, so must the mass organizations be coordinated and directed by the party as a whole. The party, writes Stalin, is, by reason of its experience and authority, the only organization capable of centralising the leadership of the struggle of the proletariat and in this way transforms each and every non-party organization of the working class into a serviceable functioning body, a transmission belt linking it with the class." The key phrase here is "serviceable functioning body," for we thus see explicitly identified the utilitarian role of such groups for bolshevik power objectives. Other Marxists might see these organizations as "objectively" {88} and "ultimately" leading to desired social change without, however, requiring control by a political elite. But for bolshevism, although historical forces must be understood and their potentialities used, they cannot be relied on of themselves to fulfill communist aims. The party must intervene to serve as indispensable arbiter and guide. This is true even in relation to the most "advanced" forms of mass Organization:

> The origin of the Soviets as an historically basic form of the dictatorship of the proletariat, in no way lessens the guiding role of the Communist Party in the proletarian revolution. The assertions made by the "left" Communists of Germany . . . that the party must always adapt itself to the idea of Soviets

---

[9] Stalin, *op. cit.,* p. 112*f.*

and assume a proletarian character, is nothing but a hazy expression of the opinion that the Communist Party should dissolve itself into the Soviets, that the Soviets can replace the Communist Party. This idea is essentially mistaken and reactionary.

There was a period in the history of the Russian Revolution when the Soviets were acting in opposition to the party, and supported the policy of the agents of the bourgeoisie. The same has happened in Germany, and may take place in other countries.

In order that the Soviets may perform their historic mission, a strong Communist Party is necessary which should not merely adapt itself to the Soviets, but on the contrary should take care that the Soviets do not adapt themselves to the bourgeoisie, and to the white guard Social Democracy; that with the aid of the Communist factions in the Soviets the latter be brought under the banner of the Communist Party.[10]

Thousands of words have been written by Bolshevik leaders to hammer home the thesis that the masses are sources of power for the party *if* manipulative control is established. Least of all are the thoughts of the workers to be taken as guideposts for the party. "Thus, for instance, it is clear that notwithstanding the disposition or prejudices of certain parts of the working masses during the imperialist war, the workers' parties ought to have counteracted these prejudices, defending the historical interests of the proletariat, which {89} demanded of the proletarian parties a declaration of war against war."[11] It is the party, not the workers, which is the arbiter of these historical interests. The workers are continuously susceptible to "reactionary prejudices," to being misled, deceived, betrayed, corrupted. The party is the great stabilizer which holds the class to the course fixed by history. It is the cleanser and the purifier, the teacher, the judge, and, at the inevitable hour, the jailer.

This is not to say that the bolsheviks do not cater to the mass, nor even that its authority is not from time to time invoked. As noted above, the masses are approached with "patience and caution." This is in part related to the task of exploiting resentment in the mass. Care must be taken that the summons to disaffection from the existing order is accompanied by reassurances that present values will not be lost. Hence patience means that certain ultimate goals must be held in abeyance until the time is ripe, and caution means that statements which would make a potential sympathizer fearful of the implications of the intended change must be avoided.

Further, the *movements* of the mass are watched with care—e.g., as to whether there will be a significant trend toward the American Federation of Labor, or whether veterans will join the older veterans' organizations or the new ones—as a basis for the rational deployment of communist forces. But this is simply to specify the conditions of action. When the authority of the workers is invoked, it is usually in order to chastise dissident elements or to justify some policy when there is

---

[10] "The Role of the Party in the Proletarian Revolution," Theses of the Second Congress of the Communist International (1920). Reprinted in Chamberlin, *op. cit.*, p. 79*f*.

[11] *Ibid.*

evidence that worker elements within the party support it. This is to make use of the moral prestige of the working class within the communist movement when it is convenient to do so. But expediency, not democracy, is the rule.

In harnessing the forces created within the working class, the party faces a problem similar to that of mobilizing its own ranks. But while the same type of political-managerial relation is involved, the process is initially reversed. Within the party, as we have seen, political hegemony, on the basis of voluntary adherence to a program or ideology, must be linked to managerial control so that members {90} may become "soldiers." In dealing with the mass, however, the process begins with managerial leadership (of unions, cooperatives. etc.) and results in the transformation of such leadership into political hegemony. In both cases the process is voluntary:

> [The guiding role of the Party] does not mean, of course, that non-party organizations like trade unions, cooperatives, etc., must be formally subordinated to Party leadership. It means simply that the members of the Party who belong to these organizations and doubtless exercise influence in them, should do all they can to persuade these non-party organizations to draw nearer to the Party of the proletariat in their work and voluntarily accept its political guidance.
>
> That is why Lenin says that "the Party is the *highest* form of class association of proletarians" whose political leadership ought to extend to every other form of organization of the proletariat.
>
> That is why the opportunist theory of the "independence" of the non-party organizations (which theory is the progenitor of *independent* parliamentarians and publicists who are *isolated* from the Party, and of *narrow-minded* trade unionists and officials of cooperatives whose *psychology* has become warped into that of petty-shopkeepers) is wholly incompatible with the theory and practice of Leninism.[12]

But this voluntary acceptance means little when the political hegemony of the party is won by conspiratorial means. The party does not confuse itself with the masses. They belong in nonparty organizations that are formally independent. But if the party is to be a general staff guiding and deploying these forces, it must exercise control. This aim is fulfilled, not by forming openly communist mass organizations, but by covertly manipulating groups composed primarily of non-communists.

This system of subordinating mass organizations to the bolshevik vanguard is also useful *after* the seizure of power. Unions, cooperatives, youth leagues, etc., are all expected to participate in building the communist-managed society:

> In the process of fulfilling these tasks of the proletarian dictatorship, a radical change takes place in the tasks and functions {91} of the mass organizations, particularly of the labor organizations. Under capitalism, the mass labor organizations, in which the broad masses of the proletariat

---

[12] Stalin, *op. cit.,* p. 113*f.*

were originally organized and trained, i.e., the trade (industrial) unions, serve as the principal weapons in struggle against trustified capital and its State. Under the proletarian dictatorship, they become transformed into the principal levers of the State; they become transformed into a school of Communism, by means of which vast masses of the proletariat are drawn into the work of Socialist management of production; they are transformed into organizations directly connected with all parts of the State apparatus, influencing all branches of its work, safeguarding the permanent and day to day interests of the working class and fighting against bureaucracy in the departments of State.[13]

The classic example of this process is the fate of the Soviet trade-unions, which have become part of the state administration, shorn of independent power. Thus the inner dynamic of bolshevism disposed of the issue which divided Lenin and Trotsky in 1920. Lenin had championed the independence of the unions against Trotsky's theory that unions could not defend the workers against "their own" state. But though Lenin won the majority, it was Trotsky's theory which prevailed under Stalin. Nor is this a purely Russian problem. The experience of trade-unions under communist governments established after World War II has been similar. The communists are not insensitive to the inherent potential of unions to function against any state if permitted the freedom to do so. The trade-unions and other mass organizations are useful, even indispensable, to communist aims, but the vanguard must gather all the reins into its own hands.

Vanguardism in Semicolonial Areas

Because the Leninists have, in their own way, continued to use the Marxist doctrine of evolutionary "stages" of development, and to identify themselves most clearly with the transition to the proletarian {92} dictatorship, it is sometimes believed that the communists will forego the seizure of a monopoly of power in economically less advanced areas of the earth. In fact, however, "ripeness" has to do only with the strength of the movement. If the party is able to take power, it will do so. This is sometimes concealed behind phraseology which, were it not for the nature of the communist concept of organization and leadership, might indeed imply that power would be shared. But the necessity for the ascendance of the bolshevik vanguard in colonial and semicolonial areas has been settled communist policy for many years. Thus, in 1920, one of the "theses" of the Second Congress of the Comintern read as follows:

> The revolution in the colonies is not going to be a Communist revolution in its first stages. But if from the outset the leadership is in the hands of a Communist vanguard, the revolutionary masses will not be led astray, but may go ahead through the successive periods of development of revolutionary experience. Indeed it would be extremely erroneous in many of

---

[13] "Program of the Communist International" (1928). Reprinted in Chamberlin, *op. cit.,* p. 203.

the Oriental countries, to try to solve the agrarian problem, according to pure Communist principles. In its first stages, the revolution in the colonies must be carried on with a program which will include many petty bourgeois reform clauses, such as division of land, etc. But from this it does not follow at all that the leadership of the revolution will have to be surrendered to the bourgeois democrats. On the contrary, the proletarian parties must carry on vigorous and systematic propaganda of the Soviet idea and organize the peasants' and workers' Soviets as soon as possible. These Soviets will work in cooperation with the Soviet republics in the advanced capitalist countries for the ultimate overthrow of the capitalist order throughout the world.

Many adaptations of program may be required, and such adaptations are always permissible; the one indispensable requirement is that communists not surrender the stuff of power to some other group simply because the "proletarian" stage of the revolution has not been reached. Nor was this policy abandoned, as one might conclude from Trotsky's critique of Stalin from the perspective of "permanent revolution." A new and more flexible terminology was designed for the same basic strategy. On March 7, 1948, a New China News {93} Agency release of the Chinese Communist North Shensi broadcast stated:

> The Declaration of the Chinese Democratic League on 5 January 1948 and the Declaration and Action Program of the Kuomintang Revolutionary Committee on New Year's Day show the broadness of the United Front of the national democratic movement. . . . Without the broadest united front, comprising the overwhelming majority of the entire national population, the victory of the "Chinese New Democratic Revolution" is impossible; but this is not all—this United Front must also be under the firm leadership of the Chinese Communist Party. Without the firm leadership of the Chinese Communist Party, no revolutionary United Front can be victorious.

The meaning of this "firm leadership" became clear after the victory of the Chinese communists. Thereafter, a new designation, "the dictatorship of the people's democracy" was used to describe a system based on the union of the workers and peasants and led by the working class (through the Communist Party). This dictatorship must function in accordance with the international revolutionary forces. This is our formula, our main experience, our main program.[14]

The Leninists do not propose to wait for some historic hour of the working class, standing to one side or helping along the bourgeois revolution. History cannot be entrusted to other hands. With respect to the semicolonial areas, the communists do indeed have maximum and minimum programs, but the essential point is that *both* are to be instituted under communist domination.

Similarly, in the Philippines, failure to distinguish between program and power may lead to confusion regarding the "motives" of the Filipino Communists. But when the communists speak of a "bourgeois stage" of the revolution, they

---

[14] Mao Tse Tung, "The Dictatorship of the People's Democracy," *Pravda*, July 6, 1914. Reprinted in *Soviet Press Translations,* September 1, 1949, p. 460.

do not mean to suggest that they have removed the conquest of power from the agenda until that stage has been completed. If it is understood that the "motives" of the PKP [Partido Kommunista Pilipinas] and other such parties {94} are only incidentally programmatic and are basically those of the search for a monopoly of power, then it will be seen that there is no inconsistency, no retreat, no abandonment of goals. It is simply that in semicolonial areas the road to power is through an emphasis on agrarian reform and anti-imperialism. The Secretary General of the Filipino party is not unfamiliar with the flexible vanguard theory:

> The Communist Party of the Philippines as the vanguard of proletariat *must set itself at the head* of the Philippine national emancipation movement. It must be the most energetic and consistent fighter for the establishment of a democratic republic *of a new type* at the present stage. . . . The carrying out of the bourgeois democratic revolution—establishment of a democratic republic—is the task to be accomplished during the whole stage and this will not change until the task has been accomplished. But conditions within the whole stage may change and have changed and because of this our programs do change corresponding to the changes that have taken place and will take place.[15] [Emphasis supplied]

Since a "bourgeois republic" existed in the Philippines at the time this was written (1946 or 1947), the call for a change in the character of the state (rather than simply a new administration) and the qualification of the phrase "democratic republic" by "of a new type" indicates that the proposals are for something rather more drastic than appears at first sight. In fact, political dictatorship by the communist vanguard is envisioned; this dictatorship will have "bourgeois" components only in the sense that the program to be executed will retain certain sectors of private enterprise. But, in both the Chinese and the Filipino programs, this private sector is to be restricted to a minor role, while the major industries, the banks, and the means of transportation would be taken over by the government. Strict definitions of what is "socialist" in orthodox Marxist terms are used as a basis for propagandistic efforts to obscure the actual goals of the movement.

Even with respect to programmatic goals, apart from the conquest {95} of power, the PKP has explicitly called for the following as part of what it terms the bourgeois democratic revolution: "(1) Large haciendas and public lands will be broken and divided among the peasants who work the land; (2) All enterprises in the nature of monopolies, banking, public utilities (railways, electric power, shipping, transportation) will be owned and operated by the state."[16] The nationalization of key industries is not only a traditional socialist goal, but even more important, it is the indispensable basis for the maintenance of unchallenged predominance by a governing elite. The communists have no intention of sharing significant power even in the "bourgeois" stage of a revolution.

---

[15] "Report on the Political Situation," report of the General Secretary of the Partido Kommunista sa Pilipinas, undated but probably written in late 1946 or early 1947.

[16] *Ibid.*

The meaning of bolshevik vanguardism is found in its implementation. Leadership is, for the communists, never simply ideological or symbolic; it is always concrete and total. To have leadership is to have a command function, and this means the establishment of organs of control, from censorship to concentration camps. This follows not from any obvious evil-mindedness, but from simple assumptions as to the nature of governance. These assumptions apply within the party and in all institutions over which the communists are able to exercise control. They include (1) the Bonapartist assumption that the delegation of authority by the ranks to a leadership places the latter in unlimited control during its period of office; (2) the belief that the regime established is identical with the state or organization and that consequently attacks upon the regime are equivalent to treason against the state or the group; (3) the belief that truth is partisan and that the masses must be protected from exposure to ideas which might poison their minds; (4) the acceptance of purges of all institutions as a normal and acceptable tool of governance; and (5) the assumption that the masses must be subject to thorough control through a unified political apparatus.

These principles have been applied with consistency wherever the bolshevik vanguard leadership has assumed power, even to the extent of introducing "democratic centralism" into nonparty organizations. In other words, wherever the "firm leadership" of the {96} bolsheviks is to be established, this leadership is exercised in such a spirit and with such tools as to guarantee the gathering of a monopoly of power into communist hands.

It is important to be clear regarding these effective goals of communism in order to avoid confusion as to the use to which its organizational techniques and strategy are put. There is no relaxation in the search for power, nor could there be, for the entire basis of the movement, the system of action which keeps it going, is the continuous search for power.

The Strategy of Mobilization

For the bolsheviks, the masses represent a vast reservoir of potential energy which can and must be summoned to fulfill the strategic and tactical plans of the vanguard. The revolutionary heroics which dramatize this summons may seem to limit it to "great events"; but the effort to involve mass elements in communist enterprises extends all the way from insurrection to the organization of a political club or a guerrilla unit. This would be sociologically trivial were it merely a matter of increasing the *numbers* of those involved; in fact, however, it refers to a process which effectively transforms the nature of group relations.

Most voluntary associations (including the democratic state) are skeletal in the sense that they are manned by a small core of individuals—the administration, the local subleaders, a few faithful meeting-goers—around whom there fluctuates a loosely bound mass of dues-payers. This type of membership has, on the whole, only a very limited relation to the organization; its agreement with it may be of the vaguest sort; it may give little or no time to the organization nor be guided by its pronouncements save, as in unions and professional groups, on very narrow issues; in short, the power implications of membership are minimal.

Such a situation is both a challenge and an opportunity for the {97} commu-nists.[17] It is, for them, intolerable that an organization or leading group should pay so little attention to the political potentialities of changing the nature of mass participation. At the same time, their own sensitivity to such potentialities and their special competence in this field are a source of tactical advantage in the struggle for power.

Mobilization as Subversion

The communists have learned, through their experience with the combat party, that organizational power can be increased by maximizing the involvement of the membership. In a communist organization, the party ranks are a source of influence for the leadership to a far greater degree than is common in voluntary associations. Hence one aim of the communists is to create and shape target or-ganizations in the image of the party in the sense of maximizing involvement and discipline. Then, if control can be established, the power exercised will be that much greater. Thus communists will not ordinarily be content with the kind of weak membership participation which exists in many unions; they will attempt to mobilize the membership so that the union leadership can be an effective political leadership as well. This emphasis on mobilization is what often gives a pseudo-democratic cast to communist-controlled activities, including guerrilla organizations, since a high pitch of mass participation is generated. In fact, this mobilization is always effectively controlled, so that decisionmaking powers are in no way abandoned by the communist leaders.

Superficially, this would seem to be inconsistent with the dictum, many times repeated, that "the Bolsheviks never substituted methods {98} of leading the Party for methods of leading the masses."[18] This distinction, however, is usually offered as a warning against sectarianism which, overestimating the revolutionary devel-opment of the masses, seeks to "leap over the difficult stages and the complicated tasks of the movement." But the transformation of skeletal organization into mass organization discussed here does not necessarily imply that communist symbols will be used or that adaptation to the political level of the mass will not be made. On the contrary, the practice is useful precisely because it creates opportunities for communist control through organizational devices which permit wide varia-tion in propaganda content.

So confident are the communists of their competence to control the process of changing skeletal organizations into mass organizations that they are able to use it as a strategic orientation in the attack upon target groups. This was set forth explicitly and boldly by a communist leader, William Z. Foster, during the period

---

[17] As it is, of course, for other groups. The bolsheviks have no monopoly of techniques of mobilization; but it may be said that here, as in the case of other practices analyzed in this study, the pattern of action is especially characteristic of communism—in the sense that it "comes naturally." The party is readied, both by its internal organization and its doctrine, for exploitation of these techniques.

[18] Georgi Dimitrov, *The United Front,* International Publishers, New York, 1938, p. 113.

of the "democratic front" in the United States, marked by an orientation to the Democratic Party in some areas, notably California.

Foster called for changing the "two old parties out of which the democratic front is largely being born" into a "new type of political mass organization."[19] In the case of the Democrats, strengthening the "democratic front" forces must include measures which will unloose the "firm grip and sabotage of such elements as the conservative AFL officials, the Southern Bourbons, the Tammany reactionaries, the Hague clique and many similar groups."

Characteristically, the communists were directed to rely on new organizational practices to solve the problems of "apathy, demagogy and sabotage":

1. *Political Education.* Foster called for a great intensification of political discussion reaching down to the lowest levels of the party. "Every ward, club, or branch should be made a center of continuous mass education, carried on with all the modern techniques of intense {99} agitation and propaganda." This means an emphasis on frequent and colorful meetings, widespread distribution of literature, discussion groups, party schools—in short much the same type of apparatus, though with a different content, as is used within the communist party itself. As a result, the nature of membership undergoes a change: the party as an institution comes to have a greater meaning in the life of the individual; he is more fully shaped by it and is more readily mobilized to support its aims and activities. Such a transformation offers an opportunity to the communists because the initiative becomes theirs and they are prepared to seize control of the machinery through which the new educational work is carried on.

2. *Patronage.* This is by no means to be abolished, but its mechanism is to be changed. "The democratic front should take firm responsibility and not leave appointments to the personal control of political overlords." A secret communist caucus would take control of the party committees and would eliminate the power of the old machine politicians. The party structure, manipulated by the communist caucus, would replace prominent individuals as the focus of attention and loyalty. Patronage would then be truly party patronage, rather than patronage by individuals, and those who controlled the local party apparatus would be able to reap the benefits. Further, party patronage would then become "principled," i.e., it would be based on political reliability rather than on immediate expediency. In addition to the normal practical value of dispensing jobs, this type of patronage control contributes to the general politicalization of the organization.

3. *Political "Fixing."* The ordinary forms of political graft—obviously corrupt practices such as taking bribes, or improperly influencing officials—may well be eliminated, resulting in a general aura of efficiency and honesty. But the important process of "doing favors" for the voters which is so useful to a political machine is by no means to be abandoned. According to Foster: "The new type of political mass organization will succeed, not by disregarding the pleas of the masses for effective service, but by being even more responsible {100} to them than the old party machines have been. Every ward club, as well as higher party unit, will have to be literally a grievance committee of the people." Such grievance committees

---

[19] W. Z. Foster, "New Methods of Political Mass Organization," *The Communist,* February, 1939.

are methods of *public* witness; they function best when supported by demonstrations, picket lines, and similar techniques. Thus the (target) party is to become a mass pressure group. By substituting these methods for the "dry" ones—such as a simple call by a local machine politician at a city hall—the masses are taught "to rely upon themselves." In practice this form of self-reliance simply means that a new type of machine, using techniques of mass manipulation, is swung into action. Since such techniques are congenial to communism, the use of them is promoted.[20]

4. *Social Activities.* Far from spurning the traditional social activities of political clubs as frivolous or unimportant, Foster's program would have the communists and their allies in the Democratic Party engage in a "bigger and better" program of recreational activity. "Every ward club should not only be a vital social center itself, but should also see to it that all the playgrounds, sports activities, etc., in its community are raised to the highest level of development." In communist terms, this means turning every community gathering-place into a center of party activity and influence. The organization of boys' clubs and other groups by machine politicians is far from unknown, but their loyalty is usually focused upon some individual. A well-developed "red" neighborhood would be united on the basis of certain common political symbols. For example, the word "fascism" would summon resources of hatred in the playground, at a union meeting, or among gossips at a local store. {101}

5. *Finances.* An organized system of dues-paying, not excluding the collection of a per capita tax, would be substituted for reliance on relatively few contributions from officeholders and wealthy individuals. This would sharpen the individual's awareness of his membership in the party and would spur him to greater involvement.

6. *Relation to Other Mass Organizations.* This "new type" of party should find ways of establishing intimate connections with other mass organizations, such as unions, cooperatives, parent-teacher associations, tenant groups, professional associations, community clubs, and the like. This may take the form of "people's legislative conferences" which "are in no sense rivals of or substitutes for the mass party, but are powerful supporters of it by grouping about it the organized armies of toilers." This technique not only makes possible the concentration of pressure-group resources for support of some immediate objective, but also would provide the (Democratic) party members with a sense of relatedness to a broad and widely supported movement. This might be largely artificial, of course, because of the

---

[20] The official communist movement—as distinguished from certain splinter groups—does not consider itself committed beyond recall to the use of any given method of action. Like other weapons, the transformation of skeletal organizations into mass organizations is a practice available for use; but this does not mean that it will always be used. In general, mass involvement seems to be preferred because it is associated with methods of control with which the party can deal; and, in general, dependence on some single leader—rather than on an organizational apparatus—will be avoided. But if gains can be made through special individuals—the case of Vito Marcantonio may be in point—these will not be foregone simply because they may entail unbolshevik methods. Indeed, no tactic is unbolshevik so long as it offers an increment of power. But some are more characteristic of bolshevism than others.

manipulation of multiple memberships and interlocking directorates by communist fractions.

The objective of these procedures is explicit: "the political organizations of the democratic front must take on a really mass character instead of their present skeleton forms." Here "mass" is not used vaguely or symbolically, but is given a definite technical meaning. It refers to participants who have, through the use of designed organizational forms and practices, been made *mobilizable*. For the communists, there is no significant line to be drawn between appealing to the masses and taking them in tow. To place a group under the banner of "communism" is primarily an exercise in social control.

Mass Organization in Strike Tactics

The use of techniques which transform organizationally skeletal operations into mass operations is well exemplified in communist strike tactics. The communists have always paid close attention to {102} the problem of strike organization, for it is an especially pertinent challenge and opportunity. Here the necessity to combine strong leadership with wide influence is most sharply posed; here too is the chance to make a sudden leap over the barriers which isolate the party from the masses. Nor are the bolsheviks insensitive to the opportunity for "war games"—to prepare for insurrection and to test the mettle of party cadres and organization.

Perhaps the most explicit statement of communist strike strategy and tactics is contained in the lectures given by Losovsky, formerly head of the Red International of Trade Unions, at the Lenin School in Moscow.[21] Here Clausewitz is explicitly cited as an authority, and an attempt is made to adapt his teachings to the economic struggle.[22] A difference exists, however: the general rules, although accepted, are supplemented by methods especially useful in this type of conflict, namely, politicalization and mass involvement.

Communism stresses the primacy of political action over economic action. The strike, just as the military organization, must have its political commissars, although in this case the office is not formalized. Here too politicalization has two elements. On the one hand, decision making must be controlled by political criteria.[23] At the same time, the consciousness of the strikers themselves must be raised to political levels. The strike should be a school of struggle in which all the general problems are posed, so that even a defeat may be a victory if the workers have become more deeply committed to their communist leadership and have been taught to respond to the right political symbols.

---

[21] A. Losovsky, *Der Streik als Schlacht,* Füns Vorträge gehalten an der Internationalen Lenin-Schule zu Moskau, Januar-Mätz, 1930, Sefer, Berlin [n.d].

[22] But see Stalin's letter on Clausewitz (1946), *Military Affairs,* Vol. 13, No. 2, Summer, 1949.

[23] "In our movement we never played with the absurd idea that only those directly connected with a union are capable of giving assistance. Modern strikes need political direction more than anything else." J. P. Cannon, *History of American Trotskyism,* Pioneer Publications, Inc., New York, 1944, p. 148.

Apart from the need for general politicalization, Losovsky offered the following rules of strike strategy: {103}

1. Offense is the best defense. The strike leadership must at all times be prepared to seize the initiative.

2. Bold use of the "proletarian hinterland." In order to strengthen and broaden the strike forces, the entire network of party-influenced mass organizations, as well as others which can be induced to lend support, should be mobilized for the purpose of favorably influencing public opinion, securing funds, mass picketing, and other duties as required.

3. Heightening of the activity and initiative of the masses. The strikers should be kept busy—demonstrations, mass meetings, and picketing are valuable aids to morale, especially in maintaining the commitment of the strikers to the struggle.

4. Establishment of uninterrupted lines of communication between all parts of the army of strikers and their general staff. According to Losovsky, this is even more important in a strike than in war because of the voluntary character of the former. This is consistent with the view set forth above that in the effort to establish managerial controls over voluntary groups, a special emphasis on effective communication is necessary.

5. Opposing forces must be broken up. This involves special concentration upon the use of political weapons against citizen armies (National Guard) which may be mobilized against the strikers.

6. The battle must be carried on with all means. The rule is: "All means are good which lead to victory over the bourgeoisie except those which result in the disintegration of your own army."

It is plain that these principles are related to a basic communist sensitivity to the importance of mass involvement, so that operations traditionally carried on by skeletal organizations can be transformed into a broad movement capable of stirring deep social forces. The ultimate utility and meaning of the mass strike was set forth by Lenin:

> Prior to January 22 (January 9, old style), 1905, the revolutionary party of Russia consisted of a small handful of people, and the reformists of those days . . . derisively called us a "sect." . . . Within a few months, however, the picture completely changed. The hundreds of revolutionary Social-Democrats "suddenly" grew {104} into thousands; the thousands became leaders of between two and three million proletarians. . . . The principal means by which this transformation was brought about was the *mass strike*. The peculiar feature of the Russian revolution is that in its social content it was a *bourgeois-democratic* revolution, but in its methods of struggle it was a *proletarian* revolution. It was a bourgeois-democratic revolution since the aim toward which is strove directly and which it could reach directly with the aid of its own forces was a democratic republic, an eight-hour day and the confiscation of the immense estates of nobility. . . . At the same time the Russian revolution [of 1905] was also a proletarian revolution, not only in the sense that the proletariat was the leading force, the vanguard of the movement, but also in the sense that the specifically proletarian means of

struggle—namely the strike—was the principal instrument employed for rousing the masses and the most characteristic phenomenon in the wave-like rise of decisive events.[24]

To be able to use the strike as a means of catapulting a small party into the decisive arena of history is the dream of every bolshevik group, however small it may be. It is the belief in the possibility of such transformations referred to by Lenin which helps to maintain the high seriousness and continued operation of apparently futile "splinter" groups.

It would be a serious error, however, to assume that it is only the revolutionary perspective which sustains an emphasis on mass involvement in strike strategy. As in the case of other aspects of bolshevism, the immediate goals of the movement may be served by techniques very similar to those which, in a favorable historical situation, may be turned to revolutionary ends. What began as a technique fundamentally related to insurrection, has turned out to be very useful for more limited goals. Thus, if we follow communist strike strategy in the United States, we can see that the use of Losovsky's rules of class struggle can be related to tactical effectiveness rather than to revolutionary aims. This does not mean that the revolutionary aims are abandoned, only that the technique {105} of struggle—and more specifically, the process of mass involvement—is useful for objectives short of insurrection.

The note of mass involvement runs through all of Foster's "propositions" on organizing methods in the steel industry.[25] The relevant directives are summarized or quoted below, following the document's major headings, which in themselves are illuminating.

1. *General.* "A central aim must always be to draw the largest possible masses into participation in all the vital activities of the union; membership recruitment, formulation of demands, union elections, strike votes, strike organization, etc."

2. *Organizational Forms and Functions.* Paid organizers should be supplemented by a corps of volunteer organizers, the former acting as captains of crews of volunteer organizers. Supporting committees should be established by central and allied unions, as well as among community groups where sympathizers for the strike can be found.

3. *Mass Agitation.* "The main objectives of the educational work should be to liquidate the fear and pessimistic moods among the workers; to convince them of the necessity for trade-unionism to win their demands, and the possibility for success in the present campaign; to rouse the enthusiasm, confidence, and fighting spirit of the workers; to win public sentiment behind the campaign." This must be implemented by proper slogans and intensive use of all available avenues of publicity, as well as by mass meetings and demonstrations. The importance of the latter is justified as follows:

---

[24] V. I. Lenin, "Lecture on the 1905 Revolution" (January 22, 1917), *Collected Works,* Vol. 19, International Publishers, New York, 1942, p. 389*f.*

[25] W. Z. Foster, "Outline of Organizing Methods in the Steel Campaign" (1936). Reprinted in *Hearings,* U.S. House Special Committee on Un-American Activities, 75th Cong., 3d sess., Vol. 1, Washington, 1938, p. 227*ff.*

The actual gathering together of workers in mass meetings and demonstrations is fundamental to the carrying on of a successful organization campaign. It gives the workers confidence bred of their own numbers, and it enables the organizers to reach them personally with their educational appeal and organization methods. But such meetings, to achieve their best success, must be of the broadest mass character. This means that they have to be thoroughly prepared, and all the batteries of publicity, organizers, etc., should be coordinated and devoted to their organization. {106} The entire agitation among the workers should aim directly at holding such mass meetings. One good mass meeting is better than two dozen bad ones.[26]

We must infer that by "mass character" Foster means not simply large attendance, but a meeting which creates the conditions for crowd behavior: symbolic unity, high emotional pitch, circular response, manipulability.

It should also be noted that in the above quotation Foster identifies two distinct functions of personal gatherings of the workers. They heighten morale and "they enable the organizers to reach [the workers] personally," i.e., they make the target population more accessible to the propaganda and control devices of the elite. These two functions, morale and managerial accessibility, are characteristic of efforts to absorb mass elements into a system of action so that they can function as more effective tools. This mass absorption is often confused with democracy, but in fact, and not only among communists, there is no question of permitting decision-making power to escape from the hands of the controlling elite.

4. *Company Unions.* Groups organized under hostile auspices are not written off if they can be won to a new leadership. Unions organized by employers, largely to avoid the entry of an outside power into the factory, are normally highly vulnerable to reorientation because, among other reasons, the employers who stimulate this mass organization are not competent to control it. *The peculiar* {107} *competence of the communists is not that they set masses into motion—this may be the unintended consequence of decisions by many different elements—but that they are able to take advantage of this stirring to channelize it in desired directions and to institute controls over it.* This general approach doubtless influenced

---

[26] Or, similarly, on picketing: "But the most important of all forms of mass strike activities is mass picketing. Good picketing is a decisive factor in every big strike—that is why employers are so rabidly opposed to it. Picketing is usually grossly neglected in the ordinary A.F. of L. strike, only a few workers carrying it on, and then merely in a desultory fashion. The consequence is a great loss in the holding power of the strike. The best way to conduct picketing is on a mass basis. Not only should all the strikers be mobilized for picketing, but their women and children as well. In addition, prominent liberals and others should be brought into the strike areas from the outside to march in the picket lines. Where one or more industries are striking, joint picketing should be organized. The unemployed can play a most important part in picketing and the members of non-striking unions should also be systematically drawn into the work. Women's and children's picket lines should be organized on special occasions. This system of mass picketing raises enormously the political level, enthusiasm, and resistance power of the strikers." W. Z. Foster, *Daily Worker,* January 10, 1937. Reprinted in *Hearings,* U.S. House Special Committee on un-American Activities, 75th Cong., 3d sess., Vol. 1, Washington, 1938, p. 246.

Foster's ability to design rules for turning company unions into a strong force for organizing the steel industry:

> All activities within the company unions should be undertaken with flexible tactics in the sense of utilizing the company unions as an auxiliary force to the building of the trade-union, with the aim of eventually incorporating the company union membership into the Amalgamated Association.
>
> The general policy in the company union should be directed toward bringing the masses into conflict with the bosses, to awaken the workers' fighting spirit, to demonstrate to even the most backward workers the insufficiency of company unionism. . . . This should be the policy rather than making important settlements through the company union with the bosses and thus create illusions that the company unions are effective and that the trade union is not necessary.

Even given control over the company union, the latter should identify itself with the trade-union demands, and any important concessions should be won directly by the trade-union in order to avoid strengthening company-union illusions. In other words, though the current leadership of the company union may be acceptable, the institution should be weakened. However,

> Minor shop demands should be freely submitted by the company unions, efforts being made at the same time to develop the local company-union forces into shop grievance committees of a semi-trade-union character. . . .

Here, as so often in bolshevik strategy, the emphasis is on changing the nature, in structure and function, of the organization being manipulated. Again,

> Efforts should be constantly made to have the company unions in practice break with their narrow constitutions by holding mass local and district conferences, by issuing independent papers and bulletins, by meeting off company property, etc.

{108} This is very similar to the approach to student organizations, which are encouraged to become independent of the campus administration, to take on wider functions, and to become associated with outside organizations, not always of a purely student character. Throughout, the objective in such target groups is not merely to seize control, but to transform them—primarily in a "mass" direction, i.e., one which permits maximum mobilizability. In completing his directives with regard to the company unions, Foster warns:

> In working out the company-union policy the great danger to avoid is that of the organizing forces of the trade-union losing the initiative and hence the leadership of the masses of the company unions. The main source of this danger would be: first, failure of the union to come forward militantly with the advocacy of its demands and active organization work; and second,

to take a standoff attitude toward the company unions and fail to give them the necessary leadership.

It would, in this view, be criminal for communists to overlook the energy resource represented by the company unions. For these are not merely diffuse worker groups; they are organizations, and as such provide definite targets in the struggle for access to and control over the men in the plant. Moreover, to fail to give them the necessary leadership would run the risk that they would be left to some other power group, always an important consideration in bolshevik strategy.

5. *Special Organization Work.* Here Foster turns to Losovsky's principle of mobilizing the "proletarian hinterland." The task is one of gaining support from elements within the community which command the loyalty of the workers. Thus Foster emphasizes the importance of using the resources of religious organizations. The communists never confuse their own attitudes toward religion with those of the masses. Nor does the status of the church as an "historic" antagonist interfere with the use of it in concrete circumstances, as an auxiliary in the power struggle. Indeed, the general Leninist image of the world as purely a field of power potential releases any inhibitions which might otherwise exist regarding the manipulation of "nonpolitical" institutions.

{109} In addition, fraternal organizations should be mobilized; the solidarity of the unemployed workers with the organizing campaign should be guaranteed, not merely by broadside propaganda, but by specific organizational methods, such as the employment of representatives of unemployed organizations as hired organizers in the steel campaign, and the recruitment of volunteers from the rank-and-file unemployed.

Readers experienced in the labor movement will note correctly that Foster's organizing methods are not uniquely communist and, in fact, are used by noncommunist unions. We need not be embarrassed to find that certain portions of the bolshevik operational code, and in particular this emphasis on mass involvement, are found elsewhere in behavior. This is a familiar problem in the analysis of individual and group character. The integrated commitments which we refer to as character are reflected in predispositions to act in "characteristic" ways. There are always some who behave in similar ways (without sharing the total constellation), but who are not especially predisposed to do so. Thus when noncommunist labor leaders use techniques of mobilization, their actions reflect efforts to solve immediate problems rather than a consistent pattern associated with a basic way of dealing with the world. Similarly, the fact that withdrawal responses are found in ordinary behavior does not lessen the significance of identifying the predisposition to withdrawal as part of a syndrome of psychic disorder. Because for them it does reflect a strategic perspective, we may say that the communists are peculiarly sensitive to the utility of mass involvement, use it in many different contexts, and are probably especially competent in exploiting its potentialities.

This principle of mobilization—in the profound sense of institutional transformation, wherein segmental operations are given a mass character—is not explicit in bolshevik "theory." It is, however, easily inferred from even a casual survey of bolshevism in practice. The great emphasis in communist training on the study of actual combat situations reflects the existence of strategic principles and tactical applications which have been only inadequately verbalized. {110}

The "Free" Mass Base

Sensitive to the power implications of mobilization, the communists seek opportunities to win control over a mass base created by some other leadership. Consider the following statement by Foster:

> The Roosevelt administration has been unique in following a policy of stimulating the growth of mass organizations. [Labor, farmers (cooperatives, referenda, committees), youth, women, negroes, national groups, health, peace, the South.] The Roosevelt administration, while definitely favoring such mass movements, cannot be expected to (nor would it be desirable that it should) carry through directly the job of organizing them. That is the task of the masses themselves.[27] [Brackets in original]

In effect, the Roosevelt administration—perhaps without any self-conscious policy of doing so—was building a mass base by helping to create organized groups through which its adherents might be mobilized. This was perhaps most explicit in the case of labor. Here we see the communist leadership ready to seize upon any degree of innocence which would make possible the capture of this base.

The communists welcomed the creation of instrumentalities through which the people could be approached and manipulated; it was hoped and anticipated, largely correctly, that the New Deal would take its own democratic slogans seriously and thus fail to institute effective controls over the groups thrown up by its new programs. Even more, Foster denies to the Roosevelt administration the function of organizing these groups; it would be well for it to restrict itself to giving official approbation and creating friendly government agencies, whereas the actual task of putting organizers in the field should be left to those forces which deserve to be put in direct charge. The "task of the masses themselves" is, in proper translation, that of groups accessible to communist control.

The organization of the masses, even under alien auspices, is always a good thing so long as the issue of control is left in doubt. Normally, there is no advantage to the communists when conscript {111} armies are created, or when other totalitarian groups mobilize mass support, for in these cases a system of rigid control is instituted. It may then become necessary to undermine rather than to use these organizations. But when the process of mass involvement takes place in a loose and uncontrolled fashion, it affords an opportunity for bolshevik action. This is not necessarily a matter of formal democracy; it may simply reflect laxness on the part of the mobilizing elite. The only relevant criterion is the availability of the organization for communist infiltration and manipulation.

It follows that it would be a mistake to expect the bolsheviks to use criteria of political acceptability in appraising the potential value of a mass organization for

---

[27] W. Z. Foster, "New Methods of Political Mass Organization," *The Communist,* February, 1939.

their purposes. On the contrary, such criteria are explicitly rejected:

> The Communists have no fear of the largest workers organizations which belong to no party, even when they are of a decidedly reactionary nature (yellow unions, Christian associations, etc.). The Communist Party carries on its work inside such organizations and untiringly instructs the workers. . . .[28]

The concept of what it means to "instruct the workers" has varied considerably since Lenin died, and other advantages of organizational control have become more important. But the basic directive remains: communists are not to be dissuaded from doing their work within mass organizations simply because of a "reactionary" leadership or program. Better a difficult target than none at all, and it is the organized mass which makes a target. Hence it is wisdom to support the creation of mass organizations so long as the possibility of communist access remains. In wartime, the communists might look with favor on the creation of the kind of a mass base for the war effort represented by civil defense organizations reaching into every locality, since infiltration of these might pay rich dividends. This tactic may be anticipated regardless of the communist attitude toward the war. {112} These remarks on the "free" mass base may be summarized as follows:

1. Bolshevism is highly sensitive to the power implications of mass involvement, even when this takes place under the aegis of some other leadership group.

2. A noncommunist leadership may create a mass base over which, however, it does not establish effective organizational controls. When this occurs, the communists may attempt to intervene to harvest the fruits of the mobilization.

3. When mobilization is effectively controlled, the communist objective is to isolate or undermine the newly created mass organization.

4. The potential value of a mass organization to the bolsheviks is largely independent of the ideological program to which the members of the organization subscribe.

5. Finally, as a major presupposition to all of the above, bolshevik strategy recognizes that it is the *organized* mass which constitutes a target.

---

[28] Theses of the Second Congress of the Communist International (1920). Reprinted in Chamberlin, *op. cit.,* p. 79.

CHAPTER 3
THE STRATEGY OF ACCESS

{113}

Communism is pre-eminently a movement based on will. Force is the final arbiter, vigorous intervention is the keynote, and victory goes to those who have the courage and the discipline to see things through to the end. Such a view is characteristic of groups which seek to catapult themselves out of obscurity into history when, as it seems to them, all the forces of society are arrayed in opposition. A movement dedicated to moral principles and to a program may be unconcerned about just who gets the chance to put them into practice; but things are very different when it is assumed that the ascendance of a specific leadership is indispensable to the fulfillment of a prophetic vision. This again sheds light on the difference between socialism and communism. In general, the socialists are willing to rely on the independent development of forces which they help to set in motion. They may speak of the utility of a "socialist leaven" in the trade-unions without implying that rigid controls should be instituted or even that leadership must be assumed. They tend to welcome the spread of socialist ideas among other groups without insisting on organizational ties. This emphasis on program rather than on power led the Russian socialists in 1917 to accept the coming of a capitalist era in which they would function as a minority opposition. This is not to deny that socialists have sacrificed program for office or, in general, have functioned as quite ordinary politicians. But even the acceptance of office under capitalism has been a reflection of the belief that the final achievement of socialism might well be left to other hands under more auspicious circumstances.

The bolsheviks have a quite different view. For them, a small group of obscure men becomes hallowed when it accepts the Leninist program. To be a Bolshevik is not simply to say that communism will win, but that we will seize the power, *our* nerve will not fail, {114} to *us* will come the victory. Such a view does not permit reliance on the long run, on the dissemination of ideas, or on the building of forces which will of themselves lead to the desired goal. On the contrary, nothing can be relied on save will. To be sure, the workers are counted as a "force" and the peasantry as "reserves," but these are of no account save as the revolutionary leadership devises effective means of mobilizing and wielding them. Lenin wanted power for himself and his party, and this perspective could not brook reliance on the gradual development of historical forces. It is impossible to be content with gains for an idea when what is really important is power for the party. Nor can the development of this power wait upon the occurrence of propitious events. "We must find a way to the masses" is at once a wail and a battle cry—one which reflects the determination of the movement to plunge itself into the struggle for power, almost, as it were, in the teeth of history.

Without recognizing the importance of will in bolshevism it is difficult to understand the ceaseless effort of the movement to create opportunities for the wielding of power, for access to its sources, for full exploitation of that which is available.[1] This is not merely a matter of alertness, of seizing advantages as they arise, or even of fomenting discontent or otherwise creating conditions under which communist ideology would be more easily disseminated. Rather, the Leninists reach out to restructure their environment by creating new centers of power which may serve to increase the utility of the combat party. The party does not merely link itself to the masses, but in a significant sense "creates" them. *It does so by establishing organs of access and control which transform a diffuse population into a mobilizable source of power.*

Peripheral Organizations

Peripheral organizations play an important role in the strategy of access. They may be thought of as auxiliary weapons used by the {115} combat party (1) to create a useful, i.e., manipulable, mass out of a diffuse target population; and (2) to penetrate and control further targets, more remote from direct access by the party. Bearing in mind the central importance of access as a strategic aim, it is instructive to review the development of communist tactics in the creation and manipulation of these peripheral organizations.

The simplest form of peripheral organization is that which mobilizes party sympathizers. This form belongs to an older period in the communist movement, before the tactical utility of such organizations was fully understood. Its function was to direct the efforts and maintain the loyalties of persons who could not be persuaded to enter the party or who were insufficiently reliable to be acceptable to it. Such persons, if effective lines of communication were established, could be useful in supporting communist fractions in trade-unions, in providing numbers for demonstrations and mass meetings, and, in general, in offering an immediate and receptive audience for communist agitational and propaganda efforts. They might also be a source of funds for party causes and for the party itself, a purpose for which feelings of guilt on the part of nonparty communists for not taking the final step might be exploited effectively. These early "mass organizations"—John Reed Clubs, Anti-Imperialist League, Trade Union Educational League, International Labor Defense, Friends of the Soviet Union—were not covertly communist, although some of them later attempted to become so. There was no question of deception, but only of providing vehicles through which elements which were *ideologically* on the periphery of the party could be made useful. Later it was realized that ideological adherence was not a necessary condition for political exploitation.

One of these "mass revolutionary organizations" which has attempted to become more useful as a weapon is the International Workers Order. This is a mutual-benefit society having insurance, social, and educational functions, the membership being largely composed of so-called "national" sections, i.e., sections

---

[1]   The importance of will is further reflected in the bolshevik emphasis on militant activism under a dedicated leadership as the only basis of true legitimacy. See below, pp. 245*n*, 273, and 270.

drawn from immigrant groups in the United States. It originated in 1930 {116} when left-wing elements split off from the Jewish socialist fraternal order, the Workmen's Circle. Later, Croatian, Serbian, Italian, and other national sections were established. For a time, this simply reflected the existence of a large immigrant population having radical sectors which could be brought within the communist movement. The IWO for a long time made little effort to hide its special identity. Prominent members of the communist party were among its leaders, the party press treated it in a brotherly way, it supported communist candidates in elections, served as a communist recruiting agency, helped raise funds, and, in general, gave material and moral support to the activities of the party.

It soon became apparent, however, that the accidental "nationality" (many were United States citizens) of the IWO members could have its own role to play in communist politics. The organization could be used as a specialized weapon to attain specific objectives, rather than remain simply a sort of political halfway house. This utility of the IWO is based on the fact that immigrant groups in the United States take a special interest in their homelands and may often exert pressure upon the United States government to attain desired policies. Since communist interests are world-wide, and the influence of the immigrant groups is considerable, a definite target for the IWO was offered:

> Among immigrants from Europe, the CPUSA and its sympathizers form a distinct political *bloc* within each national or ethnic group, agitating on behalf of Soviet interests as they relate to this group. . . . As a rule, the bloc is represented by a foreign language newspaper closely following the party line as laid down by the Daily Worker. At present, there are just short of 30 foreign-language Communist-line newspapers, with a total *circulation* of over 400,000. Further activities among East-European and Italian immigrants follow the established pattern of social gatherings and political activities focused around mutual benefit insurance societies. The IWO, with a membership of nearly 136,000 scattered amongst these ethnic and cultural groups, represents the Communist faction in each of them.[2]

{117} Presumably, the IWO can carry relatively more weight in its special area than the communist movement can carry in the country as a whole because of its ethnic appeal and the fact that it operates where there are relatively few organized centers of power. Since the target ethnic community is broadly cultural rather than specifically political, possibilities for covert manipulation for political ends are readily available.

This manipulation is abetted by the characteristic use of organizational measures. For example, certain IWO sections have penetrated noncommunist groups within their ethnic communities (e.g., the Croatian Fraternal Union), acting within these groups as a power bloc to further communist aims. It is not only the party, but the peripheral group as well which builds new mass organizations and penetrates suitable targets. Further, the communist groups, in this

---

[2] Barrington Moore, Jr., "The Communist Party of the USA: Analysis of a Social Movement," *American Political Science Review,* February, 1945, p. 38.

case the various sections of the IWO, function as a network, centrally directed, which permits mutual reinforcement and concerted effort against a broad target such as the Slavic population. When critical issues arise, as in the case of the Tito-Mikhailovitch controversy, this apparatus can be set in motion with telling effect.

This tactical reorientation, in which a simple device for the control of an ideological periphery became a weapon of offense against target groups, was revealed very clearly in 1944. At that time, organizational changes were introduced in an attempt to transform the ethnic sections which composed the order into "mass membership societies." This was to be accomplished by so changing the names of the sections of the Order and of the Order itself as to make it more acceptable—and hence afford it greater access—to the ethnic communities. For example, the large Jewish Section had attempted to gain admittance into the councils of the Jewish community. It had even muted its traditional antagonism to Zionism in the name of "unity." Yet when the Section attempted to participate in the American Jewish Conference in 1943, it was refused admission on the ground that it was part of a multinational order and not a distinctively Jewish organization. It was to overcome such barriers that {118} the reorganization was instituted. Originally, the executive board voted to drop the word "International" from the name of the Order, but in the face of membership resistance to a change in the familiar name, the board retreated on this point. However, the several sections were to be renamed so that, for example, the Jewish-American Section became known as the Jewish People's Fraternal Order, while other sections identified themselves with national heroes. It was hoped that the transformation of the IWO sections into "autonomous societies" would help to remove obstacles to the participation of the IWO in the ethnic communities while altering nothing essential in the existing relationships. In addition to changing the names of the sections, the rules of admission were liberalized, making insurance optional and thus stressing the social and political meaning of membership.

Thus the earlier emphasis, in which the political meaning of the immigrant sympathizers, as ethnic groups, was considered minimal and of declining importance, underwent a radical change. (Assimilation had been expected ultimately to eliminate this fringe around the party.) It may be that this reorientation in part reflected an increased ethnic self-consciousness, especially among groups whose homelands have undergone major political and social changes in recent years. At least of equal importance, however, is the full recognition by the communists of the special role which such national groups can play in their own right, rather than as merely general-purpose adjuncts of the party organization.

Just as the party associated itself openly with such groups as the IWO, there has never been any secret about the general tactic of building organizational links to target populations. Stalin speaks (see above, p. 87) of transforming "each and every non-party organization of the working class into a serviceable functioning body, a transmission belt linking it with the class." And even more explicitly, another party leader has written:

> [In order to transform ourselves from a propaganda into a mass party]
> we must break definitely with the conception that Communist work con-

sists solely in direct efforts to build the Communist Party and in recruiting new members. *We must learn to set {119} up and work through a whole series of mass organizations and in this way also develop our Party work.* Our chief error is our failure to understand the role of and to systematically utilize mass organizations (T.U.U.L[3] Unemployed Councils, I.L.D.[4], W.I.R.[5], L.S.N.R.[6], etc.) *as transmission belts* to the broad masses of non-Party workers. The Communist Party is necessarily composed of the most conscious and self-sacrificing elements among the workers. These mass organizations, on the contrary, with a correct political line, can be made to reach many thousands of workers not yet prepared for Party membership. Through these organizations, led by well-functioning fractions, the Party must necessarily find its best training and recruiting ground. They are the medium through which the Party, on the one hand, guides and directs the workers in their struggles and, on the other hand, keeps itself informed on the mood of the masses, the correctness of the Party slogans, etc.[7]

As the use of these organizations was developed, the party became increasingly aware of the great value of secret control by a party fraction, especially for tactical flexibility. So long as this leadership was maintained, it was possible to extend the influence of the party in many directions and, especially, into areas where the ideology of communism was completely unacceptable. Since the face of the party had to be hidden, this might seem to be self-defeating. In fact, however, there was much to be gained from the creation and manipulation of ideologically noncommunist groups:

1. The manipulation of groups which did not subscribe to communist ideology became increasingly useful as the communist parties oriented more and more to the defense of Soviet foreign policy. As the emphasis on propagandizing for communism as such declined, and the specific task of promoting immediate objectives useful to Moscow rose in importance, the so-called "minimum program" of {120} the communists assumed a new character. It was no longer simply a programmatic adaptation consistent with the revolutionary goals of the party but limited by the need to avoid isolation. The problem was no longer to build up the self-consciousness of the workers, to have the masses "learn for themselves through struggle," or to build up general disaffection from the capitalist order. These traditional Marxist goals were subordinated to the attempt to function as a pressure group implementing the current policies of the Soviet Union. The defense of the "workers' fatherland" had, of course, been a cardinal principle of communism since the revolution, but now it became the primary effective goal. It followed that the communists were now free to approach more diverse sectors in society, to

[3] Trade Union Unity League.

[4] International Labor Defense.

[5] Workers International.

[6] League of Struggle for Negro Rights.

[7] C. A. Hathaway, "On the Use of 'Transmission Belts' in our Struggle for the Masses," *The Communist, May,* 1931. Reprinted in *Hearings,* Appendix, Pt. I, House Special Committee on Un-American Activities, 76th Cong., 1st sess., Washington, 1940, p. 484.

make any compromise with avowed principle if this had some immediate utility in mobilizing public opinion for some goal of interest to the Soviet Union. Therefore any group was useful, however remote its potentialities for revolution, if it could be made to contribute to these immediate ends.

A word of caution is in order here, however. Although it is true that the communist parties have become, increasingly, simple agents of the Soviet Union, it does not follow that all Leninist strategy and tactics have been abandoned. The strategy of pursuing presumptive class goals has become, indeed, considerably attenuated. Thus the idea of independent working-class action in politics—so that class lines will not be blurred—has long been set aside. None of the many political (programmatic) consequences of a class view of the world—from "revolutionary defeatism" in war to opposition to the speed-up in industry—is any longer a reliable basis for predicting communist policy. However, it is necessary to distinguish between (1) policies reflecting revolutionary socialism, and (2) strategic and tactical goals determined by what has to be done to maximize the utility of the basic weapon of bolshevism, the combat party. The nature of the tools available, and of the arena, makes for a basic continuity of bolshevik practice. Despite many changes in propaganda line, the bolsheviks have not abandoned their fundamental reliance on the combat party, and this has a dynamic of its own {121} which pushes on to the continuous conquest of power for its own sake. Moreover, this activity is useful for more than one goal; it can be at least temporarily freed from revolutionary socialist aims and directed to pressure-group action in the interests of the Soviet Union. Older Marxist-Leninist policy would have dictated a rejection of support for the "bourgeois politician" Henry Wallace, but the abandonment of that doctrine by no means implies that the techniques of winning and maintaining power for the party have been rejected. On the contrary, it is precisely because the use of organizational weapons has been perfected that the party can permit itself increased opportunism without fear that the basic loyalties of the movement will be endangered. Moreover, regardless of their relation to revolution, control of the trade-unions is still a significant source of power. The change to a pressure-group party in no way requires an abandonment of orientation to the unions. It must also be remembered that the nature of the combat party, and the use of such tinderbox devices as political strikes, always leaves open the possibility of return to the program of revolution whenever that is expedient. Stalin has made use of the naked power potentialities of the communist parties, but this has not changed their essential nature or their tested techniques. It has only freed them from the necessity of weighing the means they use according to traditional class-struggle criteria.

2. Peripheral organizations are useful in mobilizing many persons indifferent to or even opposed to communist ideology for the defense of the public existence of the party. The rallying cry is "civil liberty."

This is the role of numerous "defense committees" which spring up whenever a leading communist faces some form of attack in the courts. Apart from immediate gains which may be won by such activity, its most important function is the establishment of the legitimacy of the party by associating it with a traditional democratic principle.[8] It is not so much that the persons influenced come to {122} agree with the party's program, or even to accept it as a champion of civil rights; these things occur, of course, but the basic gain is the creation of a climate of opinion which accepts the communists as normal contenders for power within the democratic process. In the course of such operations, the party must take care to hide its real antagonism to civil rights. It does not favor freedom for its enemies, or ultimately even for those who presently consider themselves its friends. Conspiracy is inherent in bolshevism, for the moment it attempts to mobilize support on a noncommunist basis—and this is fundamental to its political strategy—it must train its agents in deception.

3. The widespread use of peripheral groups is in part motivated by incidental organizational utilities. For example, much of the activity of such groups consists of fund raising, and it has been held to be "the considered opinion of all responsible investigators that not more than 50 percent, and frequently much less, of all funds raised by these front groups ever goes to the cause for which the group publicly is working. In some cases funds raised for a so-called worthy cause are diverted to the Communist Party by direct theft and dishonest bookkeeping transactions. In other cases money is diverted by payment of large sums to communist agents, lawyers, publicists and workers within the particular group, who turn over substantial amounts of their wages and fees to the party.[9] On the whole, however, it seems doubtful that the raising of funds for the party is very significant in explaining the proliferation of these organizations, although it may be so in special cases, as in the large-scale collections during the Spanish Civil War and the use of these groups for access to wealthy individuals in Hollywood and elsewhere. Probably of much greater importance is the considerable opportunity created for channeling energies mobilized by the party. Professionals and other middle-class communists are given a chance to participate in revolutionary [*read:* conspiratorial] work"; many cadres are made available for part-time or even full-time party work {123} while filling posts created by such organizations; a focus for individual recruiting is offered. In addition, some groups may be useful as covers for espionage recruiting.

Once a network of peripheral groups has been established, new ones can be created with ease, since an initial core of supporters can be readily mobilized. This has a purely commercial aspect. If, for example, a book club were organized by the communists, it would be able to secure an initial membership by using the already established network of peripheral organizations. The club would then become a *going* concern with only a minimal outlay for promotion.

Out of these activities is created a disciplined nonparty organizational network which, in combination with party-controlled unions and other functional groups, can be mobilized for concerted attack on a specific objective. These orga-

---

[8]   Of course, the party itself rejects the traditional democratic principle of legitimacy esoterically. The esoteric legitimacy which the party professes is based on an activist interpretation of democracy which, pushed to its conclusion, is subversive of constitutional parliamentary democracy. See Chap. 5.

[9]   Fourth *Report* of the Senate Fact-Finding Committee on Un-American Activities, California Legislature, Sacramento, 1948, p. 34.

nizations become chessmen in the hands of the party tacticians; they are created, transformed, and dissolved in accordance with the current party strategy. Thus, in 1947, the National Negro Congress was merged with the Civil Rights Congress. The latter undertook the function of acting as a cover for what was in effect the liquidation of the Negro group. This liquidation, in turn, may have been a prelude to penetration of established Negro defense organizations, such as the National Association for the Advancement of Colored People. This is manipulation in accordance with an organizational strategy and is less well known than the birth and demise of peripheral groups—e.g., American Peace Mobilization—for more obvious political reasons.[10]

Of course, the availability of peripheral organizations for tactical maneuver presupposes unquestioned dominance by the party. This is usually guaranteed at the outset, by the way in which the group is organized. The process may be set forth as follows:[11]

1. A group of reliable nonparty friends of the communist party—or secret party members—acts as an initiating nucleus in issuing a {124} call for the establishment of the organization. This committee draws up a provisional program which has the approval of the party.

2. On the basis of this provisional program, a larger group, but still not the public at large, is canvassed in a search for a list of sponsors who can invest the new organization and its program with the requisite legitimacy.

3. A provisional secretary is appointed, usually a party member, whose access to the files and personnel of the organization may be exploited for party purposes. In some cases, the secretary is given unusual powers in conducting the affairs of the organization.

4. An effort is made to have some prominent public figure assume the presidency; if such a person is likely to balk at communist control, it is desirable that he be one who is occupied with other affairs and hence unable to follow the activities of the organization too closely. In any case, such a person can easily be surrounded with a dependable executive board so that in case of conflict he would have no recourse but to resign.

5. The provisional program and provisional secretary assume the status of accomplished facts and are usually confirmed when the organization meets. In effect, these matters are never opened for serious discussion.

It should be noted, however, that save for the element of conspiracy, and the special role of the secretary, the establishment of *initial* control (its maintenance is another matter) according to the pattern just described is hardly unique to communism. Associations organized on the basis of ideological aims rather than functional interests normally follow a similar pattern. A small nucleus usually initiates the organization, and this group is permitted to lay down its fundamental character. Those who join subsequently, even as members of a leading committee, are expected to operate within the established terms of reference or to withdraw.

---

[10] See below, pp. 151-153 and 163-166, for other examples of the tactical manipulation of groups according to an organizational strategy.

[11] See the testimony of Benjamin Gitlow, *Hearings*, U.S. House Special Committee on Un-American Activities, 76th Cong., 1st sess., Vol. 7, Washington, 1940, p. 4717.

Such a pattern cannot be so easily followed, however, when the organization reflects more than ideological interest, as in the case of trade-unions.

The early peripheral organizations created by the communists {125} were known, quite openly, as "innocents' clubs." This contemptuous label reflects a general communist attitude toward those who are unwittingly manipulated for power purposes. The "innocence" of these groups, moreover, did not consist in ignorance of communist auspices; the John Reed Clubs and similar groups were very radical affairs, with no lack of open espousal of communist ideology, association with communist leaders, and denunciation of social democracy. Rather, their innocence consisted in a failure to recognize that they had no independent existence, that they were completely subordinated to the organizational interests of the communist party, that they were not established simply to promote literature, workers' relief, or any other such objective for its own sake. The members of these groups were often interested in the Revolution, but they did not always understand that the party gave its own content to this romantic dream—a hardheaded, single-minded emphasis on increasing its own power as an organization. This involved tactics which were not necessarily consistent with the idealism of many adherents. In this context, a man loses his innocence not when he adopts the communist label, but when he accepts the subordination of all principle to the naked pursuit of power.

These peripheral organizations were always formally independent, though "under the leadership" of the communists, but informal identification with the party was general. Consequently, the potentialities of these organizations as power weapons were severely limited. As this became apparent, the party moved to give them an appearance of greater independence without, however, relaxing its covert control. This not only improved the utility of groups created by the party, but permitted an orientation toward actually independent elements which could serve as targets. Perspectives regarding the use of peripheral organizations were thus broadened so that (1) certain types of organizations not created by the communists, or at least not by them alone, might be captured and brought within the party periphery; and (2) the peripheral organizations created or captured could be used to win over rank-and-file elements of {126} competing organizations, to win positions of influence for party members, to gain entry into ideologically noncommunist circles, to exert pressure upon government, and, in genera], to serve as weapons directed against definite targets. We have seen, in the case of the International Workers Order, the attempt to transform a peripheral organization of the early type into such a weapon. It is necessary now to consider organizational weapons of a more complex type, whose utility is in part based on the involvement of actually independent forces, rather than simply sympathizers or even noncommunists as individuals.

The United Front

One of the most common, and most deceptive, of the communist slogans is "unity." It is a word which is associated with their tactics all the way from a trade-union local with its "unity caucus" to a coalition government. It is an emphasis which is based, in large part, on the potentialities of organizational manipulation. So long as one side is in a position to establish organizational control, and makes *that* its target, it enters with what is often an overwhelming tactical advantage. This advantage underlies the communist eagerness to enter unity ventures of all kinds, in the confidence that they can gain something and lose nothing, whereas other organizations may be unwittingly staking their lives on the outcome of the maneuver.

Before considering these organizational implications, it is necessary to review the meaning of the communist "united front" policy. This has been at once one of the most important and the most ambiguous of communist political formulae, and any attempt to arrive at a consistent and meaningful interpretation is necessarily hazardous. But if attention is focused on power objectives, and especially on organizational ones, rather than on verbalized programs, the pattern is not too difficult to discern.

The problem of blocs and alliances has, of course, always been present for bolshevism, as for all political movements. Most of Lenin's career was spent in at least formal collaboration with leaders {127} of opposing tendencies; a great deal of his writing is devoted to the drawing of lines between his group and others. Yet the very fact that there was this great emphasis on sharp differentiation presupposed an underlying unity, a "natural" tendency for banners to be confused. Consequently, for bolshevism, the problem of cooperation with other groups was complicated beyond the normal exigencies of politics. It had its special source in the peculiar origin of bolshevism as an offspring of the general socialist movement. The latter split into what ultimately became two radically different branches, the one clinging to democracy, the other embracing totalitarianism. However, while the depth of the cleavage was apparent very early, the contending leaders had always to face the insistence of rank-and-file adherents that internal squabbling be eliminated and a common front against the main enemy established. This is a normal response, for the ranks are always interested in the fulfillment of a program and are ready to work with anyone who professes to share it. The attention of leaders, on the other hand, is focused on the choice of means and on the consequences of action for the wellbeing of the organization as such, to say nothing of the security of their own authority.

This problem was especially acute for bolshevism because Lenin was committed to the organizational and political independence of his forces and to a struggle against liberals, democrats, and evolutionary socialists. He was therefore faced with the need to escape a continuing dilemma: an insistence on independence would alienate rank-and-file support, and the maintenance of unity would be incompatible with his revolutionary objectives. It followed that the relations between world communism, newly founded as an independent force in 1919, and the reformist movements would require the most serious strategic and tactical attention.

Lenin's general attitude toward cooperation with others who agreed with him on specific issues was hardly that of the loyal collaborator, nor could it be, given the depth of his indignation against those whom he considered betrayers of the

Marxist mission. Thus {128} Wolfe reports[12] that as early as 1899 Lenin criticized the socialist Axelrod for his attitude toward the democratic opponents of tsarism: "In my opinion, *utilize* is a much more accurate and appropriate word than *support and alliance*." As Wolfe points out, "this attitude toward 'allies'—the determination to 'utilize' them rather than to give them mutual support and genuine alliance—remained a characteristic Leninist view for the rest of his life. And today, as in the past, it is a distinguishing feature of every united front or alliance entered into by any of the communist parties." This judgment must extend to communist policy in international relations as well as in domestic policy. Alliances must be justified on the basis of expediency, with no nonsense about lasting cooperation for common ends among forces inherently contradictory.

It is not suggested, of course, that all nonbolsheviks enter alliances with clean hands and with no attempt to "utilize" their collaborators. On the contrary, political and administrative cooperation is always shot through with power considerations. But—and this is characteristic of bolshevism as a whole—an explicit recognition of underlying power motivations becomes transformed into an exclusive emphasis on them, so that what is normally only an aspect of cooperation emerges, for bolshevism, as its total meaning.

As a general and explicitly formulated policy, the idea of a "united front" seems to have been put forth only after World War I, when the organization of the Communist International posed the problem of relations to other groups, and especially to the socialists, on a world scale. By 1921, it was apparent that the world revolution was to be postponed, and that the communists had succeeded only in isolating themselves from the trade-union and socialist workers. The united front became a device for establishing contact with the masses—in the first instance the "socialist masses"—without compromising the organizational independence of the communist parties. The strategic problem was ideological and organizational access, but the tactics varied according to historical opportunity, as well as in {129} response to the shifting anxieties and factional interests of the communist leaders.

In the history of the Comintern, three main phases of united-front activity may be identified, each involving a different ideological and organizational content:

1. *The Leninist Phase: The United Front Links Class Aims and Party, Power.* During the period of the first four congresses of the International,[13] official formulations followed a relatively straightforward, though hardly simple, approach. Basically, this was a policy which stated that the communist parties had an obligation to join with other working-class parties and organizations to promote united action on specific issues. In this phase, party strategy was to be based, in part, on the "objective interests" of the proletariat; although these interests are ultimately served by the victory of the party, there are nevertheless immediate gains which are important to the class and which should be furthered by cooperative action.

The first general statement of the nature of the united front to be adopted by the Comintern was probably that written by Trotsky in March, 1922.[14] The

---

[12] Bertram D. Wolfe, *Three Who Made a Revolution,* Dial Press, Inc., New York, 1948, p. 122.

[13] Seven congresses were held: 1919, 1920, 1921, 1922, 1924, 1928, 1935.

[14] "The Tactics of the United Front." Reprinted in *Fourth International,* March, 1941.

Communist Party, it was held, must fight to win a majority of the working class. This presupposes organizational independence, but such independence is only the beginning and not the end of communist wisdom:

> Any members of the Communist Party who bemoan the split with the centrists in the name of "unity of forces" or "unity of front," thereby demonstrate that they do not understand the A.B.C. of Communism, and that they themselves happen to be in the Communist Party only by accident.
>
> But it is quite self-evident that the class life of the proletariat is not suspended during this preparatory period during the revolution. Clashes with industrialists, with the bourgeoisie, with the state power, on the initiative of one side or the other, run their due course.
>
> In these clashes, insofar as they involve the living interests of {130} the entire working class, or *its* majority, or this or that section, the working masses feel the need of unity in action—of unity in resisting the onslaught of capitalism or unity in taking the offensive against the latter. Any party which mechanically opposes itself to this need of the working class for unity in action will unfailingly be condemned in the minds of workers.[15]

In other words, a sharp distinction must be drawn between (1) unity which compromises the ability of the combat party to assert its independent strength and (2) the day-to-day need to work together with other forces, even if they are politically unclean, when there is some goal at stake in which sections of the working class have a conscious interest.

The united front is (in this view) not a decisive practical question when the communists are numerically insignificant, and of course it does not arise when the party is the only leading organization based on the workers. But when the party forces are large but not decisive, the question of the united front is sharply posed.

> If the party embraces a third or one-half of the proletarian vanguard, then the remaining half or two-thirds are organized by the centrists. It is absolutely self-evident, however, that even those workers who still support the reformists and centrists are vitally concerned in maintaining the highest material standards of living and the greatest possible freedom for struggle. We must consequently so devise our tactic as to prevent the Communist Party, which will on the morrow embrace all the three-thirds of the working class, from turning into—and all the more so, from actually being—an organizational obstacle in the way of the present struggle of the proletariat.[16]

But there is no question of simply working for immediate class aims. This task is not only necessary for itself, but more important plays a strategic role in the struggle for a monopoly of power:

---

[15] *Ibid.*

[16] *Ibid.*

Still more, the party must assume the initiative in securing unity in this current struggle. Only in this way will the party draw closer to those two-thirds which do not as yet follow its leadership, which do not as yet trust it because they do not understand {131} it. Only in this way can the party win them over.

If the Communist Party did not seek for organizational avenues to the end that at every given moment joint, coordinated actions between the Communists and the non-Communists (including the Social-Democratic) working masses were made possible, it would have thereby laid bare its own incapacity to win over—on the basis of mass actions—the majority of the working class. It would degenerate into a society for Communist propaganda but never develop into a party for the conquest of power.

It is not enough to have a sword, one must give it an edge; it is not enough to have an edge, one must know how to use it.

After separating the Communists from reformists it is not enough to fuse the Communists together by means of organizational discipline; it is necessary that this organization should learn how to guide all the collective activities of the proletariat in all spheres of its living struggle.

This is the second letter of the ABC of Communism.[17]

It is clear that there already existed a "left-wing" tendency which called into question this version of the united front, especially the idea of united action "from above," i.e., with the social-democratic leaders. For Trotsky goes on to raise the question:

Does the united front extend only to the working masses or does it also include the opportunist leaders?

The very posing of this question is the product of misunderstanding.

If we could simply unite the working masses around our own banner or around our practical current slogans, and skip over reformist organizations, whether party or trade union, that would of course, be the best thing in the world. But then the very question of the united front would not exist in its present form.[18]

It should not be supposed, however, that there was anything conciliatory about this "rightist" position. The problem is not one of friendly relations, but of revolutionary tactics, of "dragging the reformists from their havens and placing them alongside ourselves before the eyes of the struggling masses." At the same time, the {132} masses "will draw from our conduct the following conclusion: that despite the split we are doing everything in our power to facilitate for the masses unity in action." And further:

It is possible to see in the policy a rapprochement with the reformists only from the standpoint of a journalist who thinks that he removes himself

---

[17] *Ibid.*

[18] *Ibid.*

from reformism by ritualistically criticising it without ever leaving his editorial office and who is fearful of clashing with the reformists before the eyes of the working masses and giving the latter an opportunity to appraise the Communist and the reformist on the equal plane of the mass struggle. In this seeming revolutionary fear of "rapprochement" there lurks in essence a political passivity which seeks to perpetuate an order of things wherein the Communists and reformists each have their own rigidly demarcated spheres of influence, their own audiences at meetings, their own press, and all this together creates an illusion of serious political struggle.

We broke with the reformists and the centrists in order to obtain complete freedom in criticising perfidy, betrayal, indecision and the half-way spirit in the labor movement. For this reason any sort of organizational agreement which restricts our freedom of criticism and agitation is absolutely inacceptable to us. We participate in a united front but do not for a single moment become dissolved in it. We function in the united front as an independent detachment. It is precisely in the course of struggle that broad masses must learn from experience that we fight better than the others, that we see more clearly than the others, that we are more audacious and resolute. In this way, we shall bring closer the hour of the united revolutionary front under the undisputed Communist leadership.[19]

Whatever the changes in content, unity for communists has always been a matter of tactics. But as the movement evolved, these tactics were more and more closely adapted to the organizational struggle, less and less related to "working class" aims. The early Leninists were totalitarian in seeking a monopoly of power, but they operated within a context of purported class aims which, while sometimes imaginary, had at least a restraining function. Their Stalinist heirs, however, took the road of emancipating the movement from its {133} class commitments so that it could become more readily usable for defending the Soviet power. This change coincided with a shift of attention from an impending revolution in the west, especially in Germany, to the consolidation of the Russian dictatorship. The united-front tactic then became subordinate to the needs of a *state* and had to be detached from its original relation to a presumptive set of proletarian *class* aims.

The "sincere" phase of the united-front policy—involving a stratagem but a minimum of deception—was inherently unstable. Given the nature of bolshevism and its propaganda, this policy was psychologically and organizationally very difficult to maintain. It must be remembered that this idea of a united front was being put forward very shortly after the communists in most countries had split from the socialist parties amid great factional strife. In their daily propaganda, the communists were committed to a ceaseless war against the socialists, whom they considered the mainstays of capitalism. As bolsheviks, they were schooled to place the power needs of the party above all else. With such a background, the chances of loyal and sustained cooperation at any level were very slight. Only recently created, the communist parties had to re-emphasize most vigorously their break from the social-democratic tradition. Moreover, the drive to continuous organizational

---

[19] *Ibid.*

aggrandizement would make a mockery of any united-front agreement, for the communists could hardly avoid seizing the opportunity to vie for leadership over the cooperating groups. In the course of this struggle, the joint goal might well be subordinated to the immediate interests of the party, and especially to the aim of destroying the hegemony of the social-democratic leaders. Only the greatest restraint, based on an ideological clarity and unity of purpose which did not exist at the time, could have held the communist parties to the difficult tactic first envisioned.

Thus it may be suggested that even the early, apparently straightforward, rendering of the united front was not platonic, and, if applied in practice, might well have yielded results not very different {134} from the later Stalinist versions. For the inner dynamic of bolshevism is its continuous struggle for power; and this would not permit participation in a united-front action without a struggle for control, without an ideological and organizational offensive against the leaders of the other participating groups. The problem is not one of "incorrect" Stalinist tactics, but of the nature of bolshevism itself.

2. *The Consolidation of Stalinism: The United Front as Propagandistic Cover for Ultra-Left Isolation.* In a context of general confusion, aggravated by the struggle for leadership during Lenin's illness and after his death, marked shifts occurred in policy regarding the united front and related matters. Though not without ambiguity, the united front "from above" was emphasized at the Fourth Congress in 1922, following the main lines of the tactic as just outlined. This "rightist" policy was soon set aside, however, for by 1924, at the Fifth Congress, a new turn to the left was instituted, the earlier policy being "explained away" as tactical deception.[20] Although followed by episodic and opportunistic maneuvers which sometimes reflected a more moderate attitude toward labor and socialist leaders, the basic line of united front "from below" was established and later reaffirmed at the Sixth Congress in 1928. This ultra-left period continued until the major turn to the right in 1934-1935.

The leftist phase of united-front policy did not envision any effective coalition with democratic or socialist forces. The latter were presented as "social fascists," against whom all means, including violence, were in order. Indeed, during this period, the struggle against the German Social Democracy included tactical cooperation with the fascists against the "social fascists." This occurred not only in the German Parliament in the early thirties, but also in certain strikes, such as the Berlin transportation strike in 1932. The communists had two strategic goals: (1) to neutralize the socialist leadership; {135} and (2) to gain access to the rank and file. As always, the Bolsheviks could not simply write off these organizations as enemies; they had to devise special means of dealing with them which would permit a struggle for control over the mass of adherents. In this period, the tactics chosen were fundamentally propagandistic. The leaders would be isolated by "exposing" them before the workers, and the ranks would be won by appealing for unity in the struggle against capitalism. This dual objective was sufficiently explicit:

---

[20] See Nathan Leites, "The Third International on Its Changes in Policy," in H. D. Lasswell (ed.), *The Language of Politics,* George W. Stewart, Publisher, Inc., New York, 1949.

The executive committee emphasizes that the application of the united front tactics is the duty of every Communist Party, that this tactic constitutes a powerful means of exposing the opportunism of the reformist leaders and of *dissociating the toiling masses from the leaders,* and also of *uniting* the proletarian masses *under the banner of the Comintern.*[21]

Hence "unity" meant persuading the workers to leave their present leaders and join the communists. Of course this was not an easy position to maintain, as Karl Radek (who seems to have opposed the ultra-left policy) pointed out at the Fifth Congress:

How are the Social Democrats to be unmasked? We know that the Social Democrats can and will fight. But we propose to them that they should fight with us in order that we may unmask them. Treint (the French delegate) knew perfectly well that the Social Democrats would never join us in form-ing a bloc, and we were able to permit ourselves the luxury of offering them this union. They have refused it; therefore, they now stand unmasked. But we rather spoil the effect of this unmasking when we announce beforehand: "Our object is not a common struggle, what we are out for is to unmask you."[22]

These caustic comments scored the public way in which the communists stated their aims, a frankness which inevitably decreased the effectiveness of the tactic. Discussions at the Fifth Congress were especially explicit, for there it was neces-sary to leave no doubt among {136} the participants as to the real meaning of the united front. In discussing a cognate matter, the slogan of a "workers' govern-ment," with its implication that several parties would be represented, Zinoviev said:

For pedagogical reasons we did not say to the social democratic worker: We are against a coalition with other "workers' parties," because their lead-ers are counter-revolutionary. We rather told him: We are ready to enter a coalition, if your social democratic leaders accept these elementary condi-tions (which, as is well known, are not acceptable to these gentlemen).[23]

This is the well-worn device of loudly calling for unity on the basis of obvi-ously impossible conditions. It is hoped in this way to place the onus of division upon the opponent, without risking acceptance. As a result, the question of unity is shifted away from those limited objectives on which there is agreement, and becomes purely a propaganda weapon.

---

[21] Komor, *Ten Years of the Comintern,* quoted in August Tyler, *The United Front,* Rand School Press, New York, 1933.

[22] Fifth Congress of the Communist International. *Abridged Report* of meetings held at Moscow, June 17 to July 8, 1924, published for the Communist International by the Com-munist Party of Great Britain, p. 54.

[23] Quoted in Leites, *op. cit.*

In an effort to avoid the tactical weakness resulting from open identification of unity with simply joining the communists, the united front "from above" was permitted *if* it was combined with the kind of propaganda which would separate the masses from their existing leaders, Thus, Zinoviev said:

> United front from the bottom—nearly always; united front from the top—fairly frequently and with all the necessary guarantees as to the tactics of mobilization that would facilitate the revolutionizing of the masses; united front from the top alone—never.[24]

Since "revolutionizing the masses" requires the unmasking of their misleaders, this simply means that after reaching an agreement with socialist leaders, the communists would immediately set to work to agitate against them, and this would soon become their main activity, in order that the opportunity for access to the social-democratic workers be not wasted. This was of course another impossible condition, which could only be fulfilled episodically and briefly, on the basis of deception. The problem was to establish the appearance of {137} unity, even to the point of arranging formal agreements, but always as "a method of agitation and mobilization of the masses, and not a method of political coalition with the Social Democrats."[25] The basic point is that the communists wished to exploit the sentiment for unity among the masses while avoiding any implementation of it which would blunt their attack upon the labor-socialist leadership.

We shall see that after 1935, coalitions made with socialists were quickly subverted, but this was done by organizational means and not by agitation for communism. The ultra-left period was characterized by aggressive presentation of communist symbols; the later period avoided these symbols (when working in mass organizations) but depended on the power of communist organization to undermine the socialist leadership.

The united front from below could only result in organizational isolation. In a sense, it was a great failure, for it only succeeded in isolating the communists ideologically as well; it was based on a woefully incorrect appraisal of the historical situation and of the public mind. This is so even if we take into account the Soviet appraisal of the world situation, which minimized the importance of fascism and saw the greatest threat to the USSR in the western powers. For the "failure" was not simply that fascism was inadequately fought, but that the ultra-left policy divorced the communists from the masses. At the same time, however, this long period of isolation served to consolidate the power of the Russian party over the International, to test and train the party cadres, and to intensify reliance on conspiratorial methods. Out of this period of ultra-left phrases, revolutionary adventures, splits, purges, and intensive indoctrination there emerged the steeled movement we know today. This is not to say that the communist leaders designed it so. But the modern communist movement is a product of its history: it owes elements of strength, as well as of weakness, to the apparently irrational period of "social fascism" and "united front from below."

---

[24] Quoted in Tyler, *op. cit.*

[25] *Ibid.*

3. The Maturity of 'Multinational Bolshevism: Reinstatement of Unity in Action as a Cover for Organizational Maneuver. It was {138} stated above that the original concept of the united front was inherently unstable. On the one hand, it was overly optimistic about the ability of bolsheviks to accept joint action with the socialists, given the context of antagonism and the need to consolidate the split on a world scale. As we have suggested, it was the function of the ultra-left period to wipe out all vestiges of social-democratic tradition and thus to guarantee the fundamental difference between communism and socialism. In Russia, this problem did not arise in a significant way because the bolshevik bid for control of the masses was compressed into a very short period, and ended with a successful coup d'état, following which the socialists were simply removed from the political arena. Bolshevism in Russia established its totalitarian character while it was in power. In other countries, however, the transformation of the totalitarian potential, implicit in Leninist doctrine, into a living reality had to take place while the new communist parties were competing in open political contest. These parties had to turn inward, and to take extreme ideological positions in order to define their character so as to be impermeable to corruption from without.

In addition, the original doctrine was unstable because it assumed that communists could enter cooperative ventures without subverting them. But in fact the whole impact of Leninist doctrine was such as to emphasize the seizing of all available opportunities for organizational aggrandizement. Hence, when the communists were ready to leave their character-forming isolation, it was inevitable that all unity activities should degenerate into mere shields behind which the pursuit of bits of power would be carried on. This would probably have been the case even if the specifically Stalinist transformation of the International had not taken place, although of course the latter decisively reinforced the inherent tendency.

After Hitler seized power in Germany, the Comintern executed a turn to the right. Evidences of the shift appeared in 1934 and full validation took place at the Seventh Congress the following year. Great emphasis was placed on the united front, and a new era of {139} communist tactics was begun. The united front became a method of action, no longer merely an agitational slogan. Organizational isolation was definitively—and permanently—rejected. *It is important to be clear regarding the meaning of this change, for during the period which followed the Seventh Congress, practices were instituted which persisted through all subsequent changes in propaganda line.*

In presenting the new policy, Dimitrov[26] did not content himself with calling for joint action of the labor-socialist organizations on specific issues. To be sure, the simple united front, long rejected, now became important. "We must not confine ourselves to bare appeals to struggle for the proletarian dictatorship, but must also find and advance those slogans and forms of struggle which arise out of the vital needs of the masses, and are commensurate with their fighting capacity *at the given stage of development.*"[Emphasis supplied] Communists were now to strive for agreements with the social democrats and the trade-unions; even more,

---

[26]   Georgi Dimitrov, "Speech at Seventh World Congress of the Communist International" (August 2, 1935). Reprinted in *The United Front*, International Publishers, New York, 1938. The following series of quotations is from this document.

they were to create *new* organizations, "non-partisan class bodies" to reach the unorganized workers. Communist unions were to be a thing of the past.

But the acceptance of the simple united front as legitimate was only the beginning. It now became permissible to leap over the class lines to establish the "anti-fascist people's front," so that coalitions might be established even with organizations having outright "bourgeois" leadership. There was to be an end all along the line to what frequently occurs in our practical work—the ignoring of or contemptuous attitude towards the various organizations and parties of the peasants, artisans, and urban petty-bourgeois masses. This new line was to be implemented by the creation of new organizations which would not necessarily be limited to the working class. Speaking of America, Dimitrov said:

> Under these circumstances [of incipient fascism], can the American proletariat content itself with the organization of only its class conscious vanguard, which is prepared to follow the revolutionary path? No.

{140} That had been the policy of the earlier period, when the united front was a mere slogan. But now:

> It is perfectly obvious that the interests of the American proletariat demand that all its forces dissociate themselves from the capitalist parties without delay. It must at the proper time find ways and suitable forms of preventing fascism from winning over the broad discontented masses of the toilers. And here it must be said that under American conditions the creation of a mass party of the toilers, a *"Workers' and Farmers' Party,"* might serve as such a suitable form. *Such a party would be a specific form of the mass people's front in America* that should be set up in opposition to the parties of the trusts and the banks, and likewise to growing fascism. Such a party, of course, will be *neither* Socialist *nor* Communist. But it *must* be an antifascist party, and must *not* be an anti-Communist party.

The "toilers" were now to include, moreover, the members of the "liberal professions, the small business men, the artisans."

The keynote was simple: an end to isolation, ideologically and practically. The old appeals for unity did not work, for they were belied in action. The communists had been for unity on the basis of their own program. But all that was to be changed:

> Yet we must base our tactics, not on the behavior of individual leaders of the Amsterdam unions, no matter what difficulties their behavior may cause the class struggle, but primarily on the question of wh*ere the masses are to be found.* And here we must openly declare that work in the trade unions is the sorest spot in the work of all Communist Parties. We must bring about a real change for the better in trade union work and make the question of trade union unity the central issue.

The communists must no longer stand outside the mass labor movement in revolutionary dual unions—a general but not uniform practice during the ultra-left period—but return to the basic Leninist formula: go where the masses are.

The earlier period was one of steeling the revolutionary cadres, and this required a struggle against "right opportunism" which might infect the communist parties with reformist and legalist illusions. But, complains Dimitrov, the struggle against sectarianism was {141} largely neglected, This was now the major problem; after strengthening bolshevik unity and fighting capacity, it was necessary to abandon positions which hindered the access of the party to the sources of power. Dimitrov's attack on sectarianism is instructive:

> Is it not a fact, comrades, that there are still not a few such doctrinaire elements left in our ranks who at all times and places sense nothing but danger in the policy of the united front? For such comrades the whole united front is one unrelieved peril. But this sectarian "stickling for principles" is nothing but political helplessness in face of the difficulties of directly leading the struggle of the masses.

Characteristically, Dimitrov repudiates the past policy of the entire International in the guise of attacking certain individuals. The day for worrying about the communist integrity of the parties is past; the basic weapon has been forged; the time for wielding it effectively has arrived. Insistence on correct ideological formulae is to give way to more flexible slogans, and organizational practices are to be adapted to the conditions of the arena:

> Sectarianism finds expression *particularly* in overestimating the revolutionization of the masses, in overestimating the speed at which they are abandoning the positions of reformism, in attempts to leap over difficult stages and over complicated tasks of the movement. Methods of leading the masses have in practice been frequently replaced by the methods of leading a narrow party group. The power of traditional contacts between the masses and their organizations and their leaders has been underestimated, and when the masses did not break off these contacts immediately, the attitude taken towards them was just as harsh as that adopted towards their reactionary leaders. Tactics and slogans have tended to become stereotyped for all countries, and the special features of the specific conditions in each individual country have been left out of account. The necessity of stubborn struggles in the very midst of the masses themselves to win their confidence has tended to be ignored, the struggle for the partial demands of the workers and work in the reformist trade unions and fascist mass organizations have been neglected. The policy of the united front has frequently been replaced by bare appeals and abstract propaganda.

All of this has kept the party in isolation and has made it overly dependent {142} on revolutionary slogans. It has also given a one-sided development to bolshevik training, which has emphasized ideological loyalty but has "hindered the correct selection of people, the training and developing of *cadres connected with the masses, enjoying the confidence* of the masses, cadres whose *revolutionary mettle* has been *tried* and *tested* in class battles, cadres that are capable of combining the practical *experience of mass work* with the *staunchness of principle of a Bolshevik.*"

In sum, the communists had to find a road out of their isolation; and the name of this road was unity.

For the spokesman of the International at the Seventh Congress, and for the leading communists who attended, there was no question of altering basic perspectives. In attacking sectarianism, Dimitrov was scoring a method of action, not a set of alien goals. To be sure, the Congress laid down a new tactical orientation to fulfill the strategic goal of access; but the entire discussion presumed the continuity of basic communist aims and characteristic methods. Lest there be any mistake, Dimitrov warned:

> While fighting most resolutely to overcome and exterminate the last remnants of self-satisfied sectarianism, we must increase to a maximum our vigilance in regard to the struggle against *Right opportunism* and against every one of its concrete manifestations, bearing in mind that the danger of Right opportunism will increase in proportion as the wide united front develops more and more. Already there are tendencies to reduce the role of the Communist Party in the ranks of the united front and to effect a reconciliation with Social-Democratic ideology. Nor must the fact be lost sight of that the tactics of the united front are a method of convincing the Social-Democratic workers by object lesson of the correctness of the Communist policy and the incorrectness of the reformist policy, and *that they are not a reconciliation with Social-Democratic ideology and practice.* A successful struggle for the establishment of the united front imperatively demands constant struggle in our ranks against tendencies to *depreciate the role of the Party,* against legalist illusions, against reliance on *spontaneity and automatism,* both in liquidating fascism and in conducting the united front against the *slightest vacillation at the moment of determined action.*

{143} The party was not to abandon its program or to develop "legalist illusions." In other words, revolution when expedient, as opposed to revolutionary phraseology, was still in order, and conspiratorial methods were not renounced. Moreover, the united front, far from replacing the party, offered a grand opportunity for leadership:

> The more the united front of the working class extends, the more will new, complex problems rise before us and the more will it be necessary for us to work on the political and organizational consolidation of our Parties. The united front of the proletariat brings to the fore an army of workers which will be able to carry out its mission if this army is headed by a leading force which will point out its aims and paths. This leading force can *only be a strong proletarian, revolutionary party.*

The party cannot take advantage of the new opportunities created if it allows itself to be weakened; hence the need for "political and organizational consolidation" as united-front activities proceed.

Dimitrov's address was directed to his own comrades; since it was to be used as a source of authority for the communist leaders throughout the world, it had to be reasonably explicit. Doubtless, if its full contents had been generally understood, the great psychological coup which followed the Congress would have been thwarted, or at least made more difficult. For the communists, the new policy offered freedom to practice deception on an unprecedented scale. This was true both on the ideological and the organizational front. Perhaps the most striking aspect of the former was a new emphasis which marked the beginning of multinational bolshevism. In discussing the "ideological struggle against fascism" Dimitrov said:

> We Communists are the *irreconcilable opponents, on principle,* of bourgeois nationalism of every variety. But we are *not supporters of national nihilism,* and should never act as *such.* The task of educating the workers and all toilers in the spirit of proletarian internationalism is one of the fundamental tasks of every Communist Party. But whoever thinks that this permits him, or even compels him, to sneer at all the national sentiments of the broad toiling masses is far from genuine Bolshevism, and has understood nothing of the teaching of Lenin and Stalin on the national question. . . . We must at the same time prove by the very {144} struggle of the working class and the actions of the Communist Parties that the proletariat in rising against every manner of bondage and national oppression is the *only* true fighter for national freedom and the independence of the people.

Out of this directive grew Earl Browder's "Communism Is Twentieth-Century Americanism" and similar slogans throughout the world.

On the organizational front the new turn permitted a wide range of targets, a multiplicity of new devices and maneuvers, unrestricted by the need continuously to repeat revolutionary phraseology. It opened up a whole new arena for political intervention from which the communists have not retreated despite subsequent major shifts in the party line. During the "left" period of the Stalin-Hitler pact, and that following the expulsion of Browder, this version of the united-front tactic was not abandoned. Indeed, the first major success of the American party in building a noncommunist national political party—the Progressives in 1948—occurred during the latter period. Similarly, the coalitions established as forerunners of the "dictatorship of the people's democracy" in the postwar period carried forward the basic tactic first clearly delineated at the Seventh Congress. These experiences have shown that communism supports other parties in the same way, as Lenin once said, "as the rope supports a hanged man." Dimitrov's speech, and the resolutions of the Congress, reflected a permanent effort to break through longstanding isolation by the free use of deceptive symbols and organizational techniques.

The "Front" in Unity Tactics

With this background in mind, we may now proceed to consider the role of communist peripheral organizations as they reflect the ubiquitous striving for unity. The older peripheral groups were simply a means of establishing organizational control over individuals who were close to the party ideologically. But now they were conceived of as weapons which would permit the party to gain {145} organizational access to and control over broader sectors of the population having no ideological commitment to communism or even to Marxism.

The use of the term "front" to characterize communist peripheral groups, and the relation of the latter to united-front tactics, may be the source of some terminological confusion. The word "front" in the phrase "united front" refers, characteristically, to the military context, in the sense of an alignment against an enemy formation. It is in this sense that the word is used by the communists themselves. On the other hand, the phrase "front organization" is not a communist one, and is derived from the architectural idea of a facade. The peripheral organization is a "front" to the extent that it functions as a cover behind which the political activities of the party are carried on.

Although deception is by definition involved in the use of "front" organizations, it was not always a dominant aspect of united-front tactics. Just as in the case of the early peripheral organizations, the communists did not hide their participation in united-front actions. On the contrary, it was deemed essential that the party openly present its banner and its leaders, for the early history of communism, after the founding of the International, was one of *direct* appeals to rally the masses behind its banner. In 1935, however, this orientation underwent a basic change. It was a change which is generally regarded as a shift in political line, i.e., the relaxation of aggression against western democracy. In fact, however, the shift represented something additional and even more fundamental: the historic culmination of the logic of Leninism, wherein deception became recognized as communism's most useful and characteristic tool. Bolshevism was now to wrap itself in any ideological banner, or to infest as a parasite any expedient host, which would yield increments of power to the party, even though this power could not be exercised in its own name. Thus after the Seventh Congress the united front became essentially deceptive; the party retreated from open participation, relying more and more on the covert maneuverability of its {146} cadres and on the use of peripheral organizations as shields for this secret penetration and control. Hence the old "open" peripheral organizations, when used to implement the new unity tactics, inevitably became "fronts."

This pattern is well exemplified in the case of the American League against War and Fascism, whose history reflected the major shift following the Seventh Congress.[27] The League was originally formed in 1933 as a peripheral organization with open communist participation. There was no secret about its auspices,

---

[27] The basic data on this and other organizations of that period were gathered by the Dies Committee and reported in *Hearings*, U.S. House Special Committee on Un-American Activities, 75th Cong., 3d sess., Vol. 1, Washington, 1938. On the use of these data, see above, pp. 15-16.

though as usual formal independence of the party was maintained. Earl Browder was made a vice-president, and many well-known communists appeared on the executive board. Although even then conceived of as a united-front organization, the communists were in fact the only political party affiliated with the League. This was consistent with the general tactic of the so-called "third period"[28] in which the party would "unite" with its own periphery to form a propagandistic "united front."

At the Seventh Congress, however, stress was placed on the importance of using the widespread antiwar sentiment, which had nothing to do with communism, as a base from which new increments of covert communist power could be gained. In emphasizing the need for antiwar propaganda, the organizational aspect was not neglected:

> We must penetrate among the pacifist masses and carry out the work of enlightenment among them, using forms of organization and action which are adapted to the level of consciousness of these masses and which give them the possibility of taking the first step in the effective struggle against war and capitalism. We must take two things into account. The *first* is that the organization of the pacifist masses cannot and must not be a Communist organization, {147} the second is that in working in this organization Communists must never give up explaining with the greatest possible patience and insistence their own point of view on all the problems of the struggle against war.[29]

The organizers of the League responded to the directive of the Seventh Congress by retiring the Communist Party from open participation. By 1937, a proposal was adopted to prohibit any political party from having delegates at the League's convention. There was no objection from the communists, the only political group which had been affiliated, and Browder said that for their part they were "perfectly satisfied to have our representation through those who are elected as representatives of non-party organizations through their own recognized work in those organizations . . . . I myself am not only a fraternal delegate from the Communist Party but also am an official delegate from the International Workers Order, a fraternal organization of 135,000 people, and in that capacity I want to take my part in this Congress and the work of the league hereafter." Thus the party would be content to exercise control through the manipulation of representation from the many organizations affiliated with the League. Of course, this had been the source of control even earlier, for the party had no official authority over the League. But now the party was to hide its face, though of course not sacrifice control. At the same time, the name of the League was changed to American League for Peace and Democracy. This change of name in part reflected new political slogans—from

---

[28] This phrase is commonly used to designate the period of ultra-left isolation described above. In that scheme, the preceding periods were those of War Communism, immediately following the bolshevik revolution in Russia, and the period of the New Economic Policy, involving a shift to the "right" in 1921.

[29] Dimitrov, *op. cit.*

isolationism to collective security—but it also made possible a fresh start for the organization as a true "front," i.e., one in which the role of the communist party was discernible only to the careful observer. The party did not have to cover its tracks completely, because the "innocent" affiliates, both organizations and individuals, were not accustomed to close inspection of the programs or personnel of those who proposed these broad cooperative ventures.

Earl Browder called the League the party's "most successful application of the united front." In fact, of course, it had nothing to do {148} with the classic position of uniting organized segments of the working class against capitalism, but rather it functioned as a great pressure group which gave the party access to the American middle class. Eugene Lyons sums up the work of the League in this way:

> In eight years of existence under changing names this League probably reached more Americans with its propaganda than any other foreign agency in the whole history of our country. By a generous definition of the "democracy" it ostensibly defended, the organization worked busily with all other communist stooge groups. This process of mutual help expanded the clamor and impressiveness of the incredible revolution immensely—a sort of multiple-mirror trick. The League published a monthly magazine, distributed millions of pieces of literature, staged scores of parades and mass meetings, lobbied for legislation, sent its speakers into hundreds of clubs and churches, promoted plays and motion pictures in line with its policies, and developed hundreds of contact points in our Federal and local government.[30]

Through the use of the League and similar groups, the communist party turned its attention to that portion of the population which was most susceptible to ideological appeals. To be sure, they could not be approached with undiluted communist propaganda, but the party learned how to exploit symbols such as peace, democracy, and unity. Beginning with limited ideological acceptance, covert organizational controls could be established.

In general, the American communists have been most successful in their propaganda efforts among middle-class elements, rather than among workers. Power among the workers has been established not through ideological operations, but by penetrating the unions. It should be noted, however, that in each case a *limited* interest is used as a basis for action to create an arena within which power may be sought. The middle class has few and weak organized centers through which access can be gained; hence it is necessary to create such centers. At the same time, the common nonideological interests of the middle class are weak, and psychological vulnerability is high so that it pays to create organizations which exploit the symbols of {149} liberalism. Among the workers, psychological vulnerability is *low* and common interests are strong so that functional organizations (existing or created) are the best means of access. Whether functional or ideological, it is the "nonpolitical" character of these groups which makes them ready targets.

---

[30] Eugene Lyons, *The Red Decade,* Bobbs-Merrill Company, Indianapolis, 1941, p. 199.

In the case of the American League for Peace and Democracy a peripheral organization was created, with the participation of many noncommunists but without the involvement of independent political forces. Throughout the history of the League the participating individuals and groups could easily be subordinated to the communist machine. This lack of another power center was in part due to the fact that the League in its original form was a product of the ultra-left period, and was later simply transformed into a broader organization by involving only mass elements rather than other leadership groups.

For organizations created after the Seventh Congress, the pattern could be somewhat different. This pattern is also somewhat more instructive because the full potentialities of unity tactics, and especially the impact of organizational weapons, are displayed in the attack upon other power centers rather than in the simple involvement of masses. The new policy now permitted the communists to engage in actual organizational relations with the socialists and other self-conscious political elements. Hence the mass organizations to be brought into the communist periphery could *begin* with a united-front agreement among competing elites. This would have many advantages, including a firmer initial respectability, access to potential cadre recruits, and an opportunity to undermine the power of the competing leaders.

This process is well exemplified in the communist attempt to gain control over the youth and the unemployed. These sectors of the population, like the middle class in general, are highly vulnerable to propaganda and do not have stable functional organizations. Neither the youth nor the unemployed can establish a strong, nonpolitical bread-and-butter leadership. Yet in times of economic stress, {150} a basis for temporary union may be available; as a result a dynamic situation emerges in the absence of stable leadership—an optimum environment for communist political activity.

In 1935, a merger took place between the Student League for Industrial Democracy and the National Student League to form the American Student Union. The SLID was part of the socialist movement, the NSL was communist. Thus the ASU was formed on the basis of an agreement reached by two sets of leaders, the socialists indeed having the larger organization. However, very shortly following the merger, the communists made a determined effort to oust the socialists from the leadership. They did this not by agitating against the socialists from the standpoint of communist ideology, but by capturing segments of the organization through the disciplined use of rationally deployed cadres. As contrasted to the ultra-left period described above, the communists now avoided ideological isolation by adapting themselves to symbols acceptable to the student membership. (In the same way, communists in the unions learned to talk as "good trade-unionists," abandoning the revolutionary phraseology which had been used during the stage of ultra-left isolation.)

The highly disciplined communist organization was a far more effective weapon than the loose socialist party. The young socialists themselves were infiltrated by the communists, and some of their leaders were won over. In addition, the Young Communist League organized a power caucus in the ASU which was able to seize control over most of the chapters and, ultimately, the national office.

Indeed, at the time of the merger itself the posts most useful for carrying on an organizational struggle were gained by the communists, whereas the socialists were given the more prestigeful but less powerful positions. As a result, by means of an initial tactic of actual unity with the socialists, the communists were able to gain control of a large organization and bring it within its manipulable periphery. The ASU which resulted from the merger became recognized as the major student organization and was able to attract large {151} numbers of nonpolitical elements on the basis of its wide publicity and prestige. When the socialists left, they found that they had been skillfully used to lay the foundations for a communist peripheral organization.

In the broader youth field, a very similar tactic had been used in the communist capture of the American Youth Congress. The first congress was held in 1934, when the communist line was already changing and the socialists were heavily infiltrated. At that time, the socialists combined with the communists to take the Congress away from its original founders. The communists won key positions and, with control of the American Student Union, were soon able to turn the American Youth Congress into a peripheral group under their complete domination.

A similar development took place among organizations of the unemployed. Before the turn to the right of 1934-1935, the communists had organized a National Unemployed Council under the direct leadership of well-known party members, although it was formally independent of the party. Socialists and liberals had organized a much more successful unemployed movement, known as the Workers Alliance. In 1934, the communists convinced the socialists of their sincere interest in unity, and a merger ensued. In a very short time, the communists emerged in undisputed control of the Alliance, with the socialists ousted from the leadership. As in the case of the American Student Union, the socialists soon left the organization altogether, since the task of regaining the leadership was too great. Another parallel with the student case is that the major socialist leader among the unemployed was induced to join the communist forces.

Earlier we described the use of the International Workers Order as a weapon of offense against target groups. The Workers Alliance, after it came under communist domination, performed a similar function. An example is available from the struggle for control of the Minnesota Farmer-Labor Association. In 1934, the communists were attaching Farmer-Labor Governor Floyd Olson as "one of the most {152} dangerous enemies of the working class . . . the executive head of capitalism's state machinery in Minnesota."[31] By 1936, however, a new policy called for support of the Minnesota Farmer-Labor movement, the communists joining the organization to "build it and make it a more effective instrument of the working people." After the election of Elmer Benson as governor in 1936, the communists claimed that they had "contributed by their political clarity, by their discipline and energy, a great measure of the success of the Farmer-Labor victory."[32]

---

[31] Quoted from a communist paper, published in Minneapolis, in testimony before the Dies Committee. See *Hearings*, U.S. House Special Committee on Un-American Activities, 75th Cong., 3d sess., Vol. 2 (1930), p. 1360.

[32] *Ibid.*, p. 1361.

To implement this unity, the local branches of the Workers Alliance were effectively deployed. As described in testimony before the Dies Committee,

> The Workers' Alliance has many locals, and the Communists used the Workers' Alliance as an instrument by which they could obtain control of the Farmer-Labor Association. This was carried out by having each local affiliate with the Farmer-Labor Association, and send delegates to the executive committee. In Hennepin County this worked so well that the Workers' Alliance, with a membership of less than 12,000, had more delegates than the Farmer-Labor clubs to the central committee.[33]

The success of this tactic was made possible by the loose structure of the target organization, characteristic of many similar groups:

> The Farmer-Labor Association county central committee is composed of delegates from Farmer-Labor ward clubs, A.F. of L. local unions. Communist "fronts" such as the Workers Alliance, International Workmen's Order, International Labor Defense, American League for Peace and Democracy, and a score of other language groups and fraternal lodges. The Communist, being of the "professional joiner" type, usually succeeds in having himself elected as a delegate if not from one from another of the various organizations to which he belongs. In this way the Communists {153} have been successful in capturing control of the county central committee of the Farmer-Labor Association.[34]

This case illustrates the pattern in which a target, won as a result of merger tactics, itself becomes a weapon for further penetration of a more important target.

The import of these events is plain. The new turn heralded by the Seventh Congress did actually result in united action with competing groups; but these were simply tactical efforts to create new centers of influence over which exclusive leadership could ultimately be established—not by propaganda, but by organizational maneuver. It is significant that the new policy tended to blur the distinction between the united front and "organic unity." The latter phrase refers to mergers of two or more organizations into one, whereas the united front in its original sense contemplated only temporary blocs between independent organizations for the achievement of specific objectives. But the early concept of the united front did not reckon with the utility of mass nonparty organizations. These now permitted a united front *and* organic unity. Thus in the formation of the American Student Union and the Workers Alliance the decisive agreement was reached between the socialists and the communists, both retaining their independent political organizations. But this agreement permitted a merger of the respective mass organizations. As a result unity was not restricted to temporary political accommodation, but involved organizational interaction. The latter being permitted, the communists were offered what amounted to a decisive tactical advantage. If the Student

---

[33] *Ibid.*, p. 1374.

[34] *Ibid.*, p. 1387f.

League for Industrial Democracy, or the premerger Workers Alliance, had simply agreed to work together on specific issues with the National Student League and the Unemployed Councils, respectively, this advantage might have been denied the communists. However, as noted above, this simple form of the united front is exceedingly difficult to maintain. If there is enough common ground for unity in action, it is often difficult for the rank and file to understand why there should not be organic unity, so that the real alternatives are either to build up {154} strong antagonism, precluding any kind of cooperation, or to capitulate to the appeals for merger. Moreover, unless strict measures are taken, the communists will infiltrate the organization with which they are negotiating and create an internal pressure group clamoring for unity with the communist-dominated organization. During the early nineteen-thirties, the socialists were ideologically unprepared to take the necessary steps to preserve their integrity as a political movement.

A major example of the unity-based peripheral organization appeared after World War H in the form of a World Federation of Trade Unions. It is desirable to examine this case in somewhat greater detail in order that the utility of such organizations as weapons may be clearly discerned. Superficially, the WFTU might seem to be a functional organization, such as an ordinary trade-union, and therefore more properly discussed in that connection. But in fact we are considering not the constituent trade-union centers, but the confederation itself. The latter was established primarily for ideological reasons and only incidentally to perform trade-union functions. It was created in order to add a new international dimension to the world communist movement; and it will be sustained only as long as it serves that purpose.

The WFTU was formally established in Paris in October, 1945. The new labor body replaced the old Red International of Trade Unions (Profintern) on the left and the International Federation of Trade Unions on the right. The former was a product of the period of communist isolation and had represented no major trade-union center save the government-controlled Russian federation. The IFTU was generally, but not uniformly, socialist in orientation and had included the legitimate labor movements of most western nations. Hence the WFTU reflected the new power of world communism, in the emergence of Russia as a great power, in the establishment of communist dominance in eastern Europe, and in the capture of the great trade-union federations of France and Italy. At its foundation, the WFTU claimed the affiliation of 65 national labor centers in {155} 44 countries and 12 colonies. These, in turn, claimed a total of 66 million members. A novel feature, not unconnected with the heavily political orientation, was the admission of trade-union organizations from colonial and semicolonial areas. These represented nearly one-fourth of the national centers affiliated with the WFTU.

The formation of the World Federation came largely at the initiative of the Russians, who took advantage of the existence of a wartime Anglo-Soviet Trade Union Committee to push the proposal. The British were hesitant but finally agreed to the holding of a conference in London in February, 1945. Here the Russians mobilized support for the formation of a new world labor body. They were supported by the French and Latin-American unions, as well as by the American Congress of Industrial Organizations. It appears that the British agreed to enter,

despite serious misgivings, because of their desire to effect a general rapprochement with the Soviet government in the immediate postwar era. The CIO wished
to assume a role in the international arena which had long been denied it by the
opposition of the American Federation of Labor. Thus the new power of world
communism was reflected in its ability to extract a united-front agreement from
legitimate and normally right-wing trade-union centers. This was a considerable
advantage over the earlier capacity to win such agreements from infiltrated and
radicalized socialist groups, resulting in such mergers as the American Student
Union and the Workers Alliance. The consequences of the alliance were fundamentally the same, however, and were readily predictable by those familiar with
the earlier events. On the basis of a unity agreement, an organization was set up
which could be made to serve the interests of the Soviet Union.

The socialist capitulation to the united-front blandishments of the communists in the early nineteen-thirties was largely a reflection of political innocence,
though in part also a controlled maneuver effected through the deployment of
communists within the socialist organizations. The left-wing socialists naïvely
believed that they could engage in unity ventures without having them subverted
in the {156} interests of communist power. Similarly, some CIO leaders believed
that the WFTU would build "unity" among peoples and ultimately among governments, that it was a good thing to raise the political consciousness of workers, to
bring them together in order to eliminate suspicion born of ignorance. But these
"pure and simple" limited ideological objectives must gain some content in action,
and when those who control the instruments of decision are committed to specific
power objectives, the subversive potential is apparent.

The Russians held an undoubted majority in the WFTU. This power stemmed
from control over most of the important member federations—a control exercised
prior to and largely independently of the world federation. Thus the Soviet trade-
unions, the French Confederation of Labor, the Italian Confederation of Labor,
the Latin-American Confederation of Labor, the Polish, Czech, and Balkan unions,
the All-India Trade Union Congress, and a number of smaller centers were led by
the communists. However, in order to maintain the indispensable participation
of the British and of the CIO, the Russians did not exercise control by using this
mechanical majority. On the contrary, many concessions were made in order to
ensure Anglo-American participation, for this was essential, at least in the beginning and probably permanently, to give the new federation authoritative status
among the peoples of the world and in the councils of government. The problem
of the communists was not so much to make the WFTU their own—indeed it is a
defeat for them that it should now assume the role of a new and enlarged version
of the Profintern[35]—but to *use* it. For this purpose it had to remain useful, i.e., still
within the framework of an actual alliance with other forces.

Therefore, rather than bring to bear their direct political weight within the
organization, the communists relied on indirect means of making the WFTU an
effective organizational weapon. This is not to say that the techniques were subtle
or unrecognized, but that the problem of decision was never posed explicitly.

---

[35] In 1949, most of the free trade-unions of the western democracies withdrew from the
WFTU to form the International Confederation of Free Trade Unions.

Characteristically, {157} reliance was placed on organizational sources of power. First, control over the secretariat, located in Paris under the direction of Louis Saillant, was ensured. The latter was also secretary of the communist-led French Confederation of Labor and could be expected to so staff the secretariat and to so execute his office as to fulfill the tactical and strategic objectives of the communists. Thus entrenched they could rely on the exercise of administrative discretion so that, in the fulfillment of generally agreed-on objectives, the incidental political consequences would be controlled.

The most obvious utility of the WFTU for communist aims is as a propaganda vehicle. This role is especially important in the colonial and dependent areas of the world. Because of the vulnerability of the western world to charges of imperialist exploitation, the WFTU has paid special attention to these areas, as reflected in the representation given them in its organization and in the investigating commissions sent to politically unstable areas such as Indonesia and Iran. The WI·7U functioned as a means of access, permitting partisan propaganda to be disseminated under the auspices of a recognized and accepted agency of world labor. Important here is the opportunity available to exercise discretion in the choice of propaganda issues. The WFTU was quick to seize upon issues which would reflect discredit upon the western democracies, but it avoided any problems which might embarrass the Soviet Union. In order to expedite such purposes, it was not difficult to arrange for appeals from the national centers on political matters, e.g., the appeal of a communist trade-union conference in North China asking the WFTU to demand early withdrawal of American troops from China.

Not less important than the propaganda potential, although less readily apparent, is the utility of the WFTU in pursuing specifically organizational objectives having political import. This arises from the opportunity available to the WFTU leadership to intervene in local situations selectively, in ways that will strengthen the hand of the communists. Thus the WFTU group sent to Korea in March-April, 1947, {158} identified itself with the communist faction of the labor movement. The activities of this mission have been described as follows:

> The program of factory inspection tours and conferences with key government personnel and Korean labor leaders which had been arranged was ignored and the delegation promptly met with a small group of Leftists headed by a local Communist who announced himself as the delegation's "official" interpreter. During their stay in Seoul [in the American-occupied area] the delegation, accompanied by the Soviet Liaison Officer, visited Leftist leaders in their homes. After ignoring the request of the Public Relations Officer for a press conference, the delegation finally agreed to meet with representatives of the noncommunist labor federation. This meeting apparently impressed the CIO delegate (Townsend) who apologized for the actions of his fellow delegates. The Korean Federation of Trade Unions (Chun Pyung), which is under CP influence, appeared to be well informed regarding the WFTU and the delegation seemed to have been well briefed on the key figures and facts regarding the Federation. The delegation appeared more interested in establishing liaison with the leadership of the

Federation than in discovering for itself the actual labor conditions, and declined to confer with the local U. S. Department of Labor representatives on any matter.[36]

In this way, the WFTU lent the weight of its prestige to the communist faction. Although this would not be of great importance in the United States, it could be influential in countries having weak labor movements or where the ideology of working-class unity has taken firm root. The possibilities of direct pro-Soviet propaganda were not neglected:

> On return of the WFTU delegation to Seoul from Pyong-Yang in the So-viet Zone, Saillant stated in an interview that the workers of Northern Korea reported that they enjoyed "much greater freedom of organization" than the workers in Southern Korea. He also stated that the WFTU delegates were leaving Seoul "with the feeling of unwanted guests" while Northern Korea they were warmly received. He did not mention that the SCAP [General MacArthur's headquarters] representative who accompanied the {159} delegation and his interpreter were detained in their hotel rooms during their stay in Pyong-Yang.[37]

Similarly, in Iran, a WFTU delegation arrived under the leadership of a Lebanese communist who, in turn, looked to a Russian delegate, in close contact with the Soviet Ambassador, for direction. "The activities of members of the mission, with the exception [of the delegate from the British Trade Union Congress] were of such a character as to make it clear that they were endeavoring to strengthen those elements of the population of Iran which depend on Russia for support and to undermine the prestige of the Iranian government among the Iranian workers."[38]

The WFTU has done its part to lend support to the communist effort to gain control of the German trade-union movement. A commission which visited Germany in February, 1946, gave its stamp of approval to developments which were questionably democratic but were consistent with communist power aims:

> The Commission ignored evidence that while it was visiting Germany a series of rigged elections were being held in the Berlin and Soviet Zone FIDGB,[39] culminating in the Berlin convention of February 2-3 and the Soviet Zone convention of February 10-11. In these elections, the previous, Soviet-appointed officials, mainly communist, were given every advantage and no legal opposition to them could exist. Although the majority of FDGB members was anti-communist, the allegedly non-partisan electoral procedure did not permit them to know in most cases that they were voting for communists. Moreover, in certain places in the Soviet Zone where an

---

[36] From an unpublished report by an American official observer, June, 1947.

[37] *Ibid.*

[38] *Ibid.*

[39] Freier Deutscher Gewerkschafts Bund (Free German Trade Union League).

unusually large number of noncommunists was elected, the results were simply falsified. So patently undemocratic were these elections and so much resentment did they create that at the Soviet Zone convention, by order of the SMA,[40] a large number of Social Democratic and Christian Democratic "guest delegates" was seated and given the voting privilege in order to even up the political party balance. Nevertheless, the {160} communists retained a comfortable majority and re-elected themselves to the Directing Committee.[41]

It is especially important to note that the noncommunist members of the WFTU commission were involved in this endorsement, although in at least one case the delegate did not support communist aims and was probably aware of the true state of affairs. Since the communist elements had a firm policy, and also a majority, it would fall to the lot of the noncommunists to "raise difficulties." Hence silence is enjoined as the price of continued participation. The British, beginning with a wish to make a gesture of friendliness to the Soviet Union, were forced, through exigencies of organizational participation, to make concrete political concessions.

Another case of WFTU intervention in Germany occurred in connection with a meeting of its General Council, held at Prague, in June, 1947. The WFTU invited an interzonal conference of German trade-union leaders to send representatives to the General Council meeting. The Soviet delegation to the trade-union conference urged early affiliation with the WFTU. Since the communists were in favor of early national unification of German labor, such affiliation could serve as a step in that direction, for the WFTU was bound to help unite the unions in member countries. The delegates from the western zones were more doubtful about a commitment to the WFTU but presumably could hardly take vigorous exception to so generally popular a slogan as unity, especially when the labor movements of the western powers, aside from the American Federation of Labor, were members of the world federation. The principle of affiliation was accepted, and delegates were sent to the Prague meeting.

The result of even this tentative involvement was to create a sense of commitment to the WFTU among the trade-union leaders in the western zones. This tended to inhibit them from establishing contacts with other international groups. Such a commitment can arise because, once involved, the union leaders are subject to attack on the charge of "betraying unity." Although such a tactic may not be {161} ultimately decisive, it can effectively introduce confusion and weakness in the ranks of the opposition, making it difficult for them to take an independent line.

The ability to intervene selectively in a situation charged with conflict is a normal, if usually incidental, prerogative of broad administrative discretion. It is this utility which was exploited by the communists in using the WFTU as an agency for supporting communist-led factions in the labor movement. This occurred not only in Germany, but throughout the world, wherever opportunity for selective intervention was available. In considering this problem, it should be recalled that

---

[40] Soviet Military Administration.

[41] From an unpublished report by an American official observer, July, 1948.

the WFTU can always act in conjunction with local supporters, and need not come as an unwanted intruder. Thus, in the Greek situation—in which the WFTU was very active both propagandistically and organizationally—the ERGAS[42] could insist on the participation of the WFTU in all unity negotiations and could invoke its authority in support of the communist proposals. Even if the WFTU did nothing more than issue a statement from its Paris headquarters, it could still be a potent weapon to confuse and weaken the opposition, for the local communists would see to it that the statement was given its full measure of publicity. In other words, the power of the WFTU, as of all communist peripheral organizations, is considerably enhanced by its ability to rest upon the organizational machinery of the communist parties for vigorous grass-roots support.[43]

There are many additional functions which an organization such {162} as the WFTU can serve. Unity on one level can become a device of pressure for unity on other levels. Thus the participation of the British labor leaders in the WFTU probably increased their vulnerability to the demand by the British communists that they be permitted to enter the Labor Party. And ultimately, if it could be firmly established, the communists would not hesitate to use such a federation as a means of exercising centralized control over the world labor movement. In 1945, at the foundation of the WFTU, the Russians wanted to construct a centralized organization whose decisions would be binding on all member unions. They were restrained by the opposition of the British and Americans. What is important is not that any noncommunist unions would bind themselves by formal commitments to an international organization under communist domination, but that a national trade-union center under communist control could use the decisions of a WFTU to justify pro-Soviet action. The world labor federation would then become a means of transmitting the decisions of the communist leadership. Given communist domination in Europe, the WFTU would take its place among the instruments of mass control as a coordinating center through which Russian power could be exercised.

Indeed, the life history of peripheral organizations may be viewed in the following way: (1) as devices for mobilizing nonparty communists and sympathizers; (2) as instruments and products of unity tactics; and (3) as devices for establishing control over the mass once power is achieved. Just as the trade-unions begin as vehicles of mobilization for offense but end up (under communism) as organs of

---

[42] Democratic Union of Anti-Fascists, the communist labor organization.

[43] The utility of this communist backbone for "front" organizations was evident in the United States during the presidential campaign of 1948. In politics, the existence of a reliable core of experienced supporters is of fundamental importance, and this is what the communists were able to supply to the Progressive Party. Indeed, they functioned so well as to deceive many observers, and perhaps even themselves. Usually, this core of professional or semiprofessional supporters. although indispensable and costly, nevertheless reflects widespread support among the voters, who are not easily mobilizable for meetings or doorbell ringing. The communists, on the other hand, were able to supply the meeting-goers and doorbell ringers, and this gave the impression of wide support on the basis of normal political calculation. But in fact the situation was artificially contrived, and the communists represented hardly anyone but themselves plus the periphery which they had built up in the course of years of effort.

control, so too are peripheral organizations useful, in the period after power has been won, as means of establishing effective control over the citizenry at large. One observer in Germany, after noting the widespread development of organizational confederations of all sorts in the Soviet Zone, made the following comment:

> The significance of the "mass organizations" is apparent. Through them the SED can bring into action from four to five million individuals who are not members of the Socialist Unity Party. Taken together, the "mass organizations" form almost an alternative governmental structure, and in some cases may be {163} regarded as more effective than the governmental structure. . . . A citizen of the Soviet Zone may refuse cooperation with the SED on the grounds that he does not agree with the principles of that political party, but if he refuses cooperation with a body purporting to represent *all* organizations of the zone, or *all* workers, or *all* youth, or *all* women, he is in danger of being labeled an enemy of the people and subject to severe social and economic sanctions.[44]

In the totalitarian state, the individual must be subordinated not only to governmental power, but to organizations established to control all the facets of his life.

Other Tactics

The communist attitude toward peripheral organizations is entirely secular, bare of all sentimental attachments. Only the party—and not even the name or the external form of the party, but its aims, basic methods, and leadership—is the object of idealization. Other organizations may be freely created or dissolved, depending on the exigencies of the political struggle. This is in keeping with their status as tools, whereas the power of the party is an end in itself. A striking illustration of this attitude toward peripheral groups is found in a communist leader's matter-of-fact discussion of what should be done with the United Farmers League, after the line had changed and the tactic of building these "red" organizations was repudiated:

> There is no doubt that tendencies toward liquidation of the UFL reflect a desire to duplicate the changes made in our trade-union policy. This in some cases has been furthered by the correct directives given to our farm comrades to concentrate on the penetration of the mass farmers' organizations. [But] the main problem is to utilize the UFL as an instrument for the development of the united front with other farm organizations, locals, {164} county bodies, etc., which are ready to fight on the basis of a class struggle program.[45]

---

[44] W. F. Davison, "The Organization of Power in the Soviet Zone of Germany," unpublished MS, 1947.

[45] C. Hathaway, "Let Us Penetrate Deeper into the Rural Areas," *The Communist*, July, 1935.

Hathaway opposed the immediate liquidation of the League on the theory that the organization, even if it only existed on paper, could be useful for bargaining purposes. The "representatives" of the League could approach other groups with proposals for a merger in the hope of securing posts or other concessions which might not be forthcoming if they entered as individuals. Moreover, paper organizations are always useful for the purpose of increasing communist representation in "roof" organizations, i.e., broad confederations or congresses which hold infrequent conventions and elect directing or continuation committees.

The tactical advantage which the communists gain in the course of unity maneuvers is not based on episodic or "clever" manipulation. It derives from the fundamental increment of power offered by the combat party. The latter creates a corps of disciplined cadres dedicated to the ubiquitous pursuit of power. In this sense the basis of communist influence is real and not illusory. The ability to deploy forces in a controlled and systematic way makes possible minority control in large organizations, especially in an environment of general apathy and in the absence of competing power centers. Normally, civic or humanitarian gatherings lack any strong political machine. Leadership falls to almost anyone who is willing to accept responsibility. The group is usually split many ways, and the selection of leadership is very difficult in the absence of superficial unanimity. The communists enter such a situation—say a World Youth Congress—with a ready-made machine. The latter avoids the difficulty faced by what is usually its nearest analogue, the sectional group which may sometimes seek to dominate such gatherings. The communist machine can easily give the appearance of geographical representativeness, usually a maximum condition required of the new leadership.

Not only can the communists coordinate their forces once the {165} meeting is begun, but they can make ample prior preparations which will give them a tactical advantage. Most of the organizations invited to such gatherings will not send all the delegates to which they are entitled, because they do not anticipate a power struggle. They will send only token delegations, and these will often be composed of those within the organization who are most eager to go or who offer to finance themselves. In such circumstances, it is relatively easy for many of the token delegations to include those who will obey communist discipline at the meeting. On the other hand, if a communist-controlled organization is invited, it will send all the delegates to which it is entitled, and hence will in fact be disproportionately represented at the conference. In addition, paper organizations will be brought to life, whose "representatives" will often be seated without challenge as a matter of courtesy and recognition of interest.

In order to make full use of the potentialities of the combat party—to make every individual count—it may be useful to attempt to transform a confederation of organizations into an individual-membership group. According to a report issued by the Nationalist Government in China,[46] this tactic was followed in the Democratic League. The latter was organized in 1940 as the League of Chinese Democratic Political Groups, a loose confederation of political factions. A reorganization took place in 1944 which changed the conditions of membership and

---

[46] "Why the Government Bans the Democratic League," Government Information Office, Nanking, 1947.

tightened the organizational structure. These changes permitted the communists to join the League as individuals and made it easier to harass an opposition and to create conditions which would make continued participation by unwanted groups exceedingly difficult and ultimately intolerable. From a loose grouping which would tolerate many differences and permit varying tactical orientations, the League became more disciplined, permitting the expulsion of member groups which did not follow the line of the leadership. The change in the conditions of membership gave the communists full freedom to deploy their forces within {166} the organizations, and the tightened structure made it possible to eliminate other power centers and absorb the League into the communist periphery. As in the instances cited above, an *initial* united front with other power centers was the basis for the eventual creation of a peripheral organization.

Although the tactic of individual affiliation may often be useful, especially as a means of gaining access to an organization, it does not follow that the communists will always use it. This was an issue in the struggle for control of the New York American Labor Party in 1943-1944. The victorious group (composed of the communists plus Sidney Hillman's forces in the New York labor movement) had proposed a plan which was characterized in the following way by a right-wing leader:

> Mr. Hillman . . . has proposed a plan for the ALP which, if successful, would place the communists in effective control of the party. The Hillman plan ignores the New York election laws for the democratic composition of all political parties. It gives to a few trade union leaders control of the party and recognizes the right of communists to participate in the party councils. It would deny a voice in party affairs to those numerous middle-class liberals who have voted the party ticket and who have worked with devoted enthusiasm. . . . Criticism has led Mr. Hillman to agree to make a place in his scheme for non-union groups, but only as window-dressing. Final authority would still reside in the trade union superstructure. Our county and district organizations would be dummy organizations, shorn of the rights given to them by the New York election laws.[47]

In this situation, the problem was not one of access—already available—but of finding a means to establish tight control over the organization once power had been captured. The large number of communist-controlled unions in the New York area made possible reliance on control of the ALP by the union representatives. At the same time, the middle-class liberals who might ultimately be able to recapture control of the party would be effectively neutralized.

As a rule, control of peripheral organizations will be maintained {167} by granting large powers to a secretariat, dominated by the communists, which is able to give decisions political import. The work of such permanent officials is not restricted to neutral administrative affairs. This was the case, for example, in the World Federation of Democratic Youth, established at a World Youth Conference at London in 1945. The permanent officers who controlled the secretariat held

---

[47] George S. Counts, *New Leader*, February 5, 1944.

the real power in the organization. They settled questions of representation and procedure, made up the agenda, guided the discussion, possessed the knowledge upon which the infrequently meeting bodies of the WFDY would have to depend.[48] Moreover, the secretariat can busily turn out resolutions, sponsor delegations, and carry on factional activities against an existing or potential opposition. Its press can be used for partisan propaganda, and leading opponents can be forced out, either by arbitrary expulsion or by creating conditions which leave no alternative but resignation. It is interesting, in this connection, that in communist-controlled organizations the catalogue of crimes which merit expulsion includes any effort to organize an opposition to the existing leadership. The communists tend to carry over into their peripheral groups the opposition to internal factions which characterizes the party itself.

But it would be a mistake to conclude that Bolsheviks never deviate from the policy of seizing the organizational apparatus. This is uniformly the ultimate goal, but often any concession will be made, including temporary self-restraint in seizing key organizational posts, in order to gain access to the membership of a target group. Thus, in discussing the negotiations of the Trotskyists with A. J. Muste's American Workers Party, Cannon pointed out:

> We proposed that Muste should be National Secretary and that I should be editor of the paper. . . . We knew what it meant to them, with their overemphasis on purely organizational matters, to have the secretaryship because the secretary, theoretically at least, controls the party machine. We were more interested in the editorship {168} because that shapes directly the ideology of the movement. Similarly, with the posts of labor secretary and educational director. We proposed to take the latter and give them the former, or vice versa, as they saw fit.[49]

This flexibility was based on the assumption (1) that the bolshevik faction under Cannon would maintain itself intact after the merger had taken place, so that the power of the National Secretary would always be limited by the prior allegiance of the Trotskyists to their factional leaders; (2) that in preparation for a struggle for control of the organization, it might be more important to conduct the fight on the ideological front and hence it would be better to have the advantage of control of the paper and the educational machinery; (3) that the Musteites, wary of bolshevik organizational tactics, could be disarmed by granting them the coveted secretaryship, while preparing the way for eventually taking it away; (4) that the real point of the merger was to win new cadres—an ideological task—and not to wield the practically non-existent power of this splinter organization. For any of these reasons, communists can be expected to adopt a tactic of disinterestedness

---

[48] These powers are of course latent in the secretarial function as such and are often exercised in noncommunist contexts. But there is a great deal of difference *between* the potential power of a secretariat, or of power wielded occasionally, and the *systematic exploitation* of this incidental capacity of administrative personnel to influence substantive decisions.

[49] J. P. Cannon, *History of American Trotskyism,* Pioneer Publications, Inc., New York, 1944, p. 180.

with respect to organizational power when that seems expedient. In order to understand this, it is essential to recall that in making such a gesture they would not be abandoning the permanent source of their own power—their own disciplined membership—which could, at some later time, be utilized in a frontal struggle for power within the organization.

Other evidences of this flexibility in using peripheral organizations include, for example, the apparent paradox that the less obvious the communist relations with a group, the tighter their control may be. Consider the following report:

> In October 1945, at the 7th Congress of the KKE,[50] it was decided, apparently because EPON's[51] true character was becoming so publicly known as to reduce its value as a "front," that all ostensible ties between EPON and the KKE would be severed. Accordingly {169} the KKEN[52] was formally dissolved, and secret orders were given that all Communist Party members under 22 years of age were to relinquish party membership and to join the EPON. In this manner, while outward evidences of the integration of EPON with the KKE were artificially removed, by making EPON membership an acceptable substitute for party membership, the EPON became even more firmly a party instrument.[53]

In this transformation, the peripheral youth group became a substitute for the party youth organization even though formal ties with the party were severed.

In considering any particular peripheral group, it must be remembered that once control is established the organization is absorbed into a *network* of groups which follow the party line. With the party performing general-staff functions, it then becomes possible for members of the network to reinforce each other. For example, an important advantage of control over an office-workers' union is the opportunity to create reliable office staffs—whose first allegiance is to the party—in the peripheral organizations and controlled functional groups. Usually, the latter will sign a contract with the controlled office-workers' union and will use its placement service in the hiring of personnel. The union understands that it is its function to send only politically reliable persons to work for the peripheral Organization. The noncommunist members of the union are sent to politically unimportant jobs, and the communists can be readily concentrated where they will do the most good. The communist office staff will provide an additional arm of party control.[54]

Finally, the emphasis on access in this analysis should help to avoid the naive assumption that any organization which is defended or publicized by the communists is necessarily controlled by them. The communists are highly sensitive

---

[50] Communist Party of Greece.

[51] National Panhellenic Youth Front.

[52] Or KN, Communist Party Youth or Young Communists.

[53] From an unpublished report by an American official observer, May, 1917.

[54] See *Hearings,* U.S. House Special Committee on Un-American Activities, 75th Cong., 3d sess., Vol. 2, Washington, 1935, p. 1418. See below, p. 190, on the use of similar methods to support communist leadership in unions.

to the importance of an *arena,* and it is that which they may be defending and publicizing at any given time. The CIO has been important for the communists, not {170} because they control it, or ever did, but because it offered a field within which the struggle for power could be carried on. And the most bitterly attacked opponents of the communists are those who threaten to deny them access to a target group in which they are interested.

CHAPTER 4
PENETRATION OF
INSTITUTIONAL TARGETS

{171}

The peripheral organizations discussed above are, in general, devices for establishing access to and control over unorganized sectors of the population. In creating such weapons, the communists seek to generate a useful "mass" by transforming an unstructured segment—youth, unemployed, intelligentsia—into one which has an established leadership and effective channels of communication and mobilization. But the unstructured quality of these target sectors is not accidental; it is a product of the natural instability of the groups in question, of their tenuous relation to the anchoring points of the economy and the social structure. Hence there is always a forced and artificial aspect to these peripheral organizations. They have usually been created or sustained only to serve the aims of the communist movement; they have no firm basis apart from those aims. Ideological currents and direct political demands normally constitute the effective content of their programs, and these, in themselves unstable, reflect the temporary unity and weak commitment which binds the group together. It is not surprising, therefore, that the peripheral organizations, although they absorb considerable energy and have many advantages both in building the party and in propaganda work, are not the major source of communist power.

Communism in its political strategy seeks to base itself on forces set in motion by permanent and reliable tensions within modern industrial society. These forces, moreover, are those important to society because they can strike paralyzing blows at the economy. The communists seek to place the party's agents at the leadership of whatever social forces set masses in motion. This means an orientation first toward the labor movement, secondly toward the peasantry where oppressive semifeudal conditions remain, and, beyond these, toward any objective situation which generates resentment. Thus the basic communist perspective is not to create a mass movement, {172} but to link itself to one which history has already begotten, to establish leadership over it, and to ride to power upon its shoulders. Although the communists may help to build the labor movement where it is weak, in order to create a source of power, organized labor under capitalism is born and grows to maturity independently of communist activity. It achieves a recognized status in society, develops a stable leadership, and fulfills a needed function in economic life. We may speak of labor unions as "functional organizations" in the sense that they exist to fill some gap in the institutional structure, to serve a purpose which helps to maintain the society as a going system. Although often supported by ideologies, they are not the products of ideological commitment and do not depend for sustenance on their ability to service a political elite.

These functional organizations—business, government, labor, church, traditional political parties—are the established value-impregnated associations which fulfill enduring needs and which, taken together with the systems of belief and practice that sustain them, constitute the institutional structure of a society. Those portions of this structure which are vulnerable to communist attack become the institutional targets against which organizational weapons are directed. It is just because these institutions are important to society that the penetration and exploitation of them may yield significant increments of power. The communists understood very early the importance of labor for this purpose, but in recent years a more flexible and varied approach has been apparent. The new tactics have emphasized especially an offensive against the state itself, in which an older rejection of "bourgeois" government has been modified tactically to permit covert penetration of its agencies.

The term most frequently applied by the communists to what we have here called peripheral and functional organizations is "mass organization." In line with the preceding discussion of the communist attitude toward the mass, this general designation is acceptable. The key quality of the mass is its manipulability, and it is upon this that the communist interest in these organizations is focused. In both {173} types of organization, the foundation of manipulability is the same. The stated goals are proximate, emphasizing immediately urgent problems or limited by the need to fulfill specialized functions, whereas the ultimate commitments remain undetermined. This is obvious in the case of trade-unions and similar groups organized for collective bargaining or other limited objectives. But it is just as true in the case of ideological or humanitarian groups which meet to create sentiment for peace, tolerance, or civic virtue. In both cases participation is gained on the basis of limited agreement but the very existence of the organization creates the opportunity to use membership loyalty as a basis for further ventures beyond the originally stated aims, as well as the possibility of exploiting the incidental prerogatives of administrative discretion.

Ideological groupings whose agreement is based on unanalyzed abstractions—unity, peace, democracy—are vulnerable to manipulation because these notions must be given some definite content when positions are taken on specific matters, and it is usually the permanent officialdom that decides, when the membership lacks political acumen, just what content will be given to the glittering generalities that adorn convention resolutions. Similarly, the unavoidable political consequences of trade-union activity leave an area of significant decision to the discretion of the union leadership. And in general, the leadership of any organization is invested with the incidental responsibility of maintaining morale and of creating and preserving the organization's traditions. In carrying on these educational functions, a politically self-conscious leadership can provide its own emphases and thus lay the basis for more general commitments than those upon which the group was founded.

These considerations are not lost to the communists. Indeed, a very similar analysis was made by Foster, in 1939, in a series of articles devoted to instructing the membership on the potentialities of various types of mass organizations and the attitude which communists should take toward them. As usual, the problems were posed elliptically, avoiding direct statement, but the articles could {174} form the basis for more explicit discussion in face-to-face educational meetings. In one of these articles, Foster distinguished between the "primary" and "secondary" aspects of mass organizations in the following way:

> The primary purposes of mass organizations of workers, farmers and other toilers are the fundamental aims for which they are organized; their secondary aspects are the effects, intangible or concrete, produced within them by the impact of other movements and social forces.[1]

The secondary aspects are of special interest, for these define the area within which the communists can make their special contribution. Foster distinguishes further between the ideological and functional secondary aspects. The former include "capitalist illusions," religion, Americanism, racism, discrimination against women and youth; the latter include politics, social activities, fraternal insurance (when promoted incidental to primary purposes, as a stabilizing factor) social activities, and education. These secondary aspects may be found in all organizations in varying degrees, no matter what the primary purposes may be. They are, further, usually uncontrolled elements left to the discretion of the leadership, which may invest them with a special content if it is disposed to do so. The communists, being always so disposed, are directed to exploit fully the incidental advantage thus offered to those who assume leadership ostensibly to promote the primary aims of the organization. This leadership provides access to the members, whose attitudes on social and political matters may often be manipulated, and it offers the opportunity to make decisions that will gain for the party the maximum benefit from whatever incidental political impact the organization may have.

The utility of existing mass organizations for the communists may be summarized as follows:

1. They may command access to decisive sources of social power, as in the capacity of unions to halt production. {175} All have incidental or secondary aspects, such as internal education, which may be exploited for the benefit of the party.

2. They represent areas of untapped political potential, in which the relative weight of even small communist groups can be very great.

In the political community at large, there is ample contention for power, and the basic trends of opinion are reflected in the established political leadership. But inside a student body or a trade-union, or even in a church, the centers of power are few, and the chances are good for small cliques to exercise influence far beyond the weight of their numbers. Functional organizations are not normally considered arenas of political struggle, yet their political potential can be considerable; hence they represent areas of political vacuum which power-oriented minorities can readily exploit. In the United States, it is of first importance for the communists to have such an arena of action. Since they are largely excluded from direct appeals to the citizenry on the basis of the communist program, they

---

[1] W. Z. Foster, "Secondary Aspects of Mass Organization," *The Communist,* August, 1939.

can play but a small role in the general electoral arena. Therefore the possibility of gaining power within functional groups is especially important.

Labor Unions as Institutional Targets

Lenin had no illusions about any "natural" relation between trade-unionism and communism. Indeed, it was for him a fundamental tenet that workers will not of themselves arrive at revolutionary conclusions. The functional organizations of the workers, he saw, become an integral part of the existing order:

> Since the development of an independent ideology among the workers, as a result of their own struggle, is out of the question, there is thus possible either a bourgeois ideology or a Socialist ideology, and the question is: Which of the two shall it be? The blind unfolding of the labor movement can lead only to the permeation of that movement with a bourgeois ideology, because the unconscious growth of the labor movement takes the form of trade unionism, and trade unionism signifies the mental enslavement of the workers to the bourgeoisie. Therefore, our task as Social {176} Democrats is to oppose this blind process, to divert the labor movement from the unconscious tendency of trade unionism to march under the protective wing of the bourgeoisie, and to bring it under the influence of Social Democracy instead.[2]

The unions had to be *acted upon* if they were to serve the revolution; they were to be targets against which the combat party was to be directed. What Lenin identified was the revolutionary and power-creating *potential* of the unions, and this could be exploited only if the party retained its independent and disciplined existence. The source of this potentiality is readily discerned:

1. Although the unions are, in general, adaptable to the status quo, nevertheless they are from time to time set in motion against it. Strikes are threats to public order, and, in carrying out its function of maintaining order and the continuity of essential production, the state may be cast in the role of strikebreaker. The economic struggle, even for conservative unions, may then have explicit political implications, with significant consequences for the attitudes of the workers and the actions (however reluctant) of the leadership. Normally, acute social cleavages of this sort are only episodic, and basic loyalties, buttressed by practical compromises, ultimately prevail. But the communists see the revolutionary possibilities of mobilizing a great social force against the state if partial crises can be generalized and if their party can assume the leadership.

2. Even if the communists were not interested in revolution through mass upheaval at all—and latter-day bolshevism is not necessarily committed to that road to power—penetration of the unions would still be a vital source of power for

---

[2] Quoted in David Shub, *Lenin,* Doubleday & Company, Inc., New York, 1948, p. 54. This is the main theme of Lenin's famous "What Is To Be Done?" (1902). "Social Democrat" here refers to the Russian Social-Democratic Labor Party, from which the bolsheviks later split off, taking the road to totalitarianism.

the party. It would be a means of intervention into a significant political arena, especially when other forms of intervention are unavailable. This is the primary role of communist activity in the trade-unions in the United States. With its agents deployed as the leaders of (some) labor organizations, the party's headquarters in New York becomes more {177} than a center for a small ideological grouping. The trade-union committee of the central executive comes to function as a board of strategy. It can split the CIO, call a crippling strike in an essential industry, merge one union with another, break a strike in order to undermine a political opposition—and these decisions will be effectively communicated and promptly executed. No other political group in America has this kind of power. An organization of liberals such as the Americans for Democratic Action might have considerable ideological support from powerful elements in the unions, but if it set up a trade-union committee, this committee could only make studies and give advice. It would not have the power to issue directives to an ADA-minded union leadership (say, the United Automobile Workers) as to how union decisions should be made. There are other political influences in the labor movement, but only the bolshevik cadre party has the kind of linkage, based on the discipline of agents whose only commitment is to the party, which can give a central leadership the power of strategic and tactical command.[3]

In order fully to understand the nature of modern communism it is essential to bear in mind that the sources of, and techniques appropriate to, revolutionary action contribute to the power of the party regardless of whether or not it takes the revolutionary road. The penetration of institutions that have important social functions, the stimulation of mass action as a means of political intervention and of establishing the leadership of the party over the unemployed or the youth, and the mobilization of the party cadres for political combat these were, for Lenin, indispensable elements of proletarian revolution. But actually they may have a more limited function: simply that of placing unconventional but weighty sources of influence in the hands of a political elite. Within broad limits, this elite can {178} dispose of this power *as it sees fit*. Hence a bolshevik party, using Leninist tactics, may function merely as an effective pressure group, as an adjunct to power based on Soviet arms, and even, from time to time, as an overtly legitimate participant in a "bourgeois" government or parliament.

Lenin thought he was defining the conditions for revolution, as indeed he was, with his insistence on revolutionary policies such as defeatism in war and intransigent opposition to all "capitalist politicians"; but in fact the heart of his teachings was separable from these objectives. The fundamental nature of the bolshevik party and the strategies of access, mobilization, and neutralization were primarily means of creating power for the leaders. With the maturity of communism, these essential teachings were retained. Programmatic objectives could be sloughed off in the interests of a more flexible approach and complete subordination to the

---

[3]   In periods of strength, the socialists have derived power from their influence in the unions, but this has always been weak and incidental (1) because the socialists have had, primarily, an electoral orientation; and (2) especially because there has been no serious pressure to place the interests of the party above those of the union. In addition, "the tail has sometimes wagged the dog," the union leaders setting party policy.

interests of the Soviet Union. The latter might or might not at any given period require the seizure of power. At the same time, the traditional revolutionary objectives remain consistent with (although not indispensable to) modern bolshevism. They can be brought into focus whenever required. The point is that bolshevism in its maturity has achieved freedom from specific programmatic objectives, although some are, of course, congenial to it and will be utilized in the absence of conflicting opportunistic needs.

The import of recognizing the separability of bolshevism from revolutionary objectives is this: if it can be shown that at a given period the communists have apparently set aside their revolutionary goals, it does not follow that the nature of bolshevism as a social force has changed. Quite apart from the justifiable assumption that the ultimate goals have been only *temporarily* set aside, it must be understood that the communists will seek to establish their power monopolies wherever they can gain a foothold. The inner dynamic of bolshevism drives it on to build the cadre party; and this process is inseparable from a continuous struggle for power in the community. They may avoid a frontal attack upon the state, but they will not abandon pursuit of total power in more limited areas.

{179} In seeking to maximize its impact upon society, bolshevism concentrates effort in key industries. This has never been a secret:

> The Party should concentrate all its forces and energy to build Shop Units, first of all in the basic industries.
>
> Basic industries are those upon which the whole economic system depends. They include:
>
> 1. Those which produce material for production, like steel, mining, oil, chemicals.
>
> 2. Those which deliver material to the place of production or consumption, like railroad, trucking, marine, etc.
>
> 3. Those which produce power for running the wheels of industry, electric power plants, steam and hydroelectric plants, etc.
>
> It is also important to concentrate all our energy to build the Party in the auto, textile, and packing house industries because of their strategic importance in the economic system. Strong Party organizations (Shop Units) in these basic industries with a mass following could really influence and lead the millions of workers engaged in these as well as in all lesser industries in their daily struggles, and deliver decisive blows to capitalism.[4]

The main targets against which organizational effort is to be directed are identified by the political strategy of bolshevism, which links the party to the proletariat on the theory that the latter, having access to the instruments of production, can wield decisive social power. But the focus on power aims, rather than simply vague or propagandistic identification with "the workers," calls for sharper distinctions. Not all segments of the working class have equal potential for social power: the

---

[4] Peters, *The Communist Party—A Manual on Organization*, Workers Library Publishers, July, 1935. Reprinted in *Hearings*, Appendix, Pt. I, U.S. House Special Committee on Un-American Activities, 75th Cong., 1st sess., Washington, 1940, p. 707.

coal miner, the seaman, the steelworker, the teamster, the trainman and the like are more important to the revolution—or for the power of a pressure-group party—than are the textile workers or retail clerks.

As always, bolshevik sensitivity to the importance of key industries means more than generalized support of union organization in those areas, or verbal broadsides to the workers in them. The political principle, identifying the source of power, is implemented by diligent {180} organizational measures. Existing communist forces must be effectively exploited:

> The stronghold, the fortress of the revolutionary movement, is in the factory. But in order to build the revolutionary movement there, we must organize all Party members working in one factory into a Shop Unit. The main difference between the Communist Party and the Socialist Party form of organization is that the Socialist Party organizations (branches) are built on the basis of bourgeois election wards and districts while the Communist Party is built on the basis of the place of employment. Party members who work in the same shop cannot belong to different Street Units. If such forms of organization were permitted, Party members working in the same factory and not knowing each other, would carry on their Party work in an anarchistic way. Each one individually would try to give leadership to the other workers.
>
> The first step, therefore, in building the Unit in a factory *is to find who the Party members are.* This can be done by checking the membership registration or by getting information from the fraction of the union. If we find three or more members, a Shop Unit should be immediately organized.[5]

First, individual forces in the shop are consolidated; then, the local party organization is mobilized to support their work. Two or three unaffiliated individuals who would like to carry on political work in a shop can be very lonely indeed. Not so with the communists where a party organization exists. The handful of communists can receive advice, sometimes funds, and auxiliary political support, such as the distribution of party literature at the factory gates or defense in case of trouble. Thus the Peters manual points out:

> Besides these organizational measures, there are various other effective methods for organizing and strengthening the Shop Units. The best method is the *concentration* of our best forces around the factory. This concentration work consists of systematic mass agitation and propaganda among the workers in the selected factory through distribution of the Daily Worker, Party pamphlets, and other literature at the factory gates or at the workers' homes, combined with the holding of shop-gate meetings. This {181} mass agitation will help prepare the ground for the carrying on of successful work by our members inside the factory.[6]

---

[5] *Ibid.*, p. 707f.

[6] *Ibid.*, p. 708. But see above, p. 68, on the shift from an emphasis on factories to an emphasis on unions.

The same principle of concentration would lead to special effort to organize an International Workers Order branch in the target area, so that workers recruited into this peripheral group could be proselytized to join or work with the party in the shop. Although the communists have altered their propaganda methods, especially in more frequently hiding the face of the party, there is no reason to believe that principles such as this have been abandoned.

Another important tool for linking the local party organization to the shop unit is the following:

> A Shop Unit consisting of three members can be strengthened by adding one or two of the best, most developed, most reliable comrades from the Street or Town Unit. These comrades, as regular members of the Shop Unit, help in working out policies and making decisions for activity in the factory. They help the Shop Unit keep connection with the Section Committee, and help guide and participate in the mass work outside of the factory. It is absolutely essential that *outside* members (from the Street Units) be always in the *minority* in the Shop Unit.[7]

Thus is applied, in the most concrete way possible, the general Leninist dictum that although the workers are the source of power, it is the party which must provide leadership. There can be no question of reliance on the worker elements, even though they are members of the party, without day-to-day direction from those who know how to put political considerations first. This device of adding outside members to the shop unit is also a useful method of "bolshevising" middle-class elements by involving them in the labor movement.

An obvious step in the building of communist strength in the factory is to recruit among the workers themselves; but here too the rule is careful analysis and systematic concentration. The party has already had access to many workers in some way, and this resource should be fully exploited. "There are thousands of very close sympathizers, {182} readers of our press (Daily Worker or the language papers), members of the unions and various fraternal and cultural organizations, who are working in important factories. Conscientious effort will help us to recruit them into the Party and thus build the Shop Units."[8]

The communists, always military minded, are highly conscious of the need to *deploy their forces* in the most effective way possible. For example, the 1935 manual on organization we have been following states: "Since the most effective work of the Party is inside the factory, it is necessary to find ways and means whereby developed Party members can get a job in a given factory, and in this way to start building the Party there."[9] Communists should be assigned to train for and find jobs in target factories so as to be able to join the union and begin the fight for power. Deployment of this type is known as "colonization." The ability of the party to call on its members in this way is dramatic evidence of the authority

---

[7] *Ibid.*

[8] *Ibid.*

[9] *Ibid.*

it asserts, for colonization often demands a complete change of life perspective on the part of the individual, especially when students or white-collar workers are sent into industry.

On the whole, however, colonization is not and could not be a major means of building communist power in the factories. It can be used relatively extensively only when the party is very small, and desperate measures seem necessary for access to the labor movement. It can continue to be used only for highly important work, as in the penetration of key defense industries or scientific organizations. There is no evidence of any wholesale shifts of garment workers to the steel industry, or any similar activity, nor could there be, because colonization requires intensive retraining which is not feasible except on a small scale. Perhaps its most effective use on a relatively large scale would be in wartime, when large numbers of youth may enter war industries after short training periods. Personal incentives would then be coupled with party needs. Although in practical terms the power of the party to deploy its membership in such a manner is {183} limited, the existence of this latent authority is of great significance, because in some areas, notably espionage, there is no question of large-scale movements and the control of the party over the individual may be ample.

Although the main trade-union targets are in the basic industries, the utility of power in the labor movement is so general that the party is quite willing to undertake secondary concentrations in less vital areas of the economy. Vital or not, industries characterized by mass employment offer opportunities for building the party through the manipulation of the unions. As the Peters manual states: "While it is of the utmost importance to concentrate all energy of the Party to build and strengthen the Units in the basic industries, the other industries cannot be neglected. The Party systematically builds Units in light industries (clothing, shoe and leather, etc., in offices, stores, laundries, hotels and restaurants, etc.).[10]

The party could not well avoid work in the service and light-industry fields, since these are so important a source of mass employment in great urban centers such as New York. And it is precisely in these centers that the ideological influence of the party is greatest. Penetration of the unions in these areas is therefore not a means of achieving commanding positions in the economy but of serving more immediate political needs of the movement.

Control of urban light-industry unions makes possible (1) the mobilization of mass backing for current political aims, especially through support of peripheral organizations and publicity-oriented demonstrations, calling for a large turn-out in the streets or in great assembly halls; (2) the recruitment of party cadres, more readily than from other unions because of the general atmosphere of political self-consciousness and the easier acceptance of procommunist ideology; and (3) the building up of large union treasuries which may be partly diverted to party causes. It is precisely in the urban centers that these functions can be most effectively performed, so that there the unions are more political auxiliaries to the party than they are sources of economic power.

{184} Indeed, this light- versus heavy-industry problem highlights a dilemma faced by the communists in many parts of the world, and especially in the United

---

[10] *Ibid.*, p. 707.

States. The groups most readily susceptible to communist ideology are not in fact located in the basic industries.[11] The difficulty is resolved by using the light-industry unions as party-building resources; the party thus strengthened can then be used to assault those areas where ideological influence is small but where potential social power is great. These assaults are organizational and covert: they are, essentially, forays into a hinterland where power must be based on contrived and tenuous devices, drawing its main sustenance from localized but substantial centers of ideological strength. The party is strongest in the less decisive areas of the economy, and this emphasizes the need to rely on organizational measures to win strength in the key centers of industrial power.

Tactics in the Maritime Industry

A good illustration of communist technique in target unions is afforded by the maritime industry. Here the development of specialized techniques has been particularly important, and information is available as a basis for describing in some detail the practices that facilitate penetration and control.[12]

Seamen have always occupied a special and honored place in the communist movement. The revolt of German sailors at Kiel during World War I; revolutionary Kronstadt; support by foreign merchant seamen of the Soviet cause against the Allied Expeditionary Force: the general way of life which detaches the sailor from society and may easily pit him against the forces of law and order; the enormous power which small crews can wield in embargo operations; the opportunity for international communication—all of these elements give the seamen an aura of revolutionary power.

In 1943, at a meeting of the communist Waterfront Section in {185} New York, Earl Browder is reported to have said: "Seamen are the most basic section of the working class, the Communist Party cherishes and is proud of them. They are the truly international members of our Party and the vanguard of the vanguard. They are socialists at heart, internationalists by occupation, the backbone of international workers' solidarity and the leaders of the revolution throughout the world."[13] The sections of the working class gain status according to the capacity they have to provide the party with increments of power; and the more directly they can serve the interests of the party, the more praiseworthy is their role. This status is not without its privileges. Communist leaders in the maritime industry are granted special respect as well as more autonomy than are other industrial groups under party discipline. Doubtless this autonomy is also related to the peculiar international status of the maritime sections, some of whose key leaders in the United States have been trained in Moscow and have spent some time in the Soviet armed forces.

Party work in the maritime unions follows the classic Leninist formula of "combining legal and illegal work," with an open organization paralleled by an

[11] See above, pp. 148-149, and below, p. 196.

[12] The following is in part based on an unpublished report prepared in 1947 for a United States government agency.

[13] Quoted in the report cited in footnote 12, above.

underground one. The "legal" organization is made up of Waterfront Sections, bringing together a number of different branches that can be coordinated for penetration of a port area. A section may include the following branches: (1) seamen; (2) longshoremen; (3) teamsters; (4) maritime communications workers; (5) communist youth; (6) shipyard workers; and (7) women's auxiliary, composed of wives of seamen, female maritime workers, and office employees of the maritime unions. Thus the administrative groundwork is laid for mobilizing all the vital elements of the port, supplemented by auxiliaries such as the youth and women, for a communist-led labor offensive. Full-time, paid functionaries lead the Sections and the large branches. Many of these men are communists who have been exposed and who are no longer able to operate covertly in the unions.

This apparatus is sufficiently elaborate, but it is complicated further {186} by the existence of distinct chains of command. Formally, the Sections are responsible to the County, State, and National Committees of the party, but actually this channel relates only to routine party business, such as distribution of the *Daily Worker,* participation in all-party campaigns, and similar matters which do not call for directives on distinctively maritime matters. Apparently the actual direction of the Waterfront Sections by-passes the usual party hierarchy' to create a separate chain of command having major responsibility in the New York section organizer plus international agents working out of the national headquarters. Probably because of the mobile membership, the integration of the maritime industry, the specialized knowledge necessary, and secret functions such as international communication, the maritime organization has a special coherence within the party structure. There is doubtless some tendency for the geographic chain of command to break down generally, when a distinct occupational group has a nation-wide target, but the pressure toward coherence along occupational lines is probably greater in maritime than elsewhere.

The technique of colonization has been especially important in this industry, because of the importance of the target, the relative ease with which it is possible to become a seaman, and the many opportunities for carrying on party work which the irregular life (with its long full-time stretches "on the beach") affords. On colonization in maritime, Gitlow reports:

> The Party overcame the deficiency in seamen by sending large numbers of selected communist party members to sea. Most of them made just one trip in order to acquaint themselves with the seamen's lingo and to learn just enough about a ship and the sea to pass off as a bona fide sailor. These synthetic sailors, trained communists, who knew what the Party was after on the water front, became the backbone of the Party among the seamen and the drive to get them all organized into a powerful national seamen's union.[14]

This not only created the basis for strong communist fractions in the {187} unions, where they might otherwise not have existed at all, but permitted the party to

---

[14] Benjamin Gitlow, *The Whole of Their Lives,* Charles Scribner's Sons, New York, 1948, p. 281.

avoid reliance on "native" elements in the industry by sending in men who could be trusted fully to grasp and obediently to execute the policy of the party.

The problem of deployment is especially acute in maritime, because the floating "shop" is subject to continuous reorganization. Opportunities for establishing nuclei of communists among the crews are afforded by the constant shifting of personnel, and the neatly isolated and mobile targets call for special controls. The more the crews change the more necessary it is to maintain an adequate system of intelligence and to establish a party center to guide the activities of the communist seamen. Hence the latter ship out under orders of the waterfront organizer. Whereas seamen may normally use purely personal interests as a basis for deciding (where choice is available) upon destination and ship, the party moves in to introduce political-organizational criteria into the decisions of its members. In this way, the organizer can plan to have a nucleus of adequate size on each important target, and the composition of the nucleus itself can be controlled. Moreover, communist seamen are sometimes ordered to ship to definite destinations for the purpose of delivering party correspondence, the maritime members thus functioning for the party as a secure and inexpensive international messenger service. The seaman is enjoined to report to his local organizer before sailing as well as to the organizers at his ports of call. At conferences with the waterfront organizer, the political complexion of the crew and the tasks during the voyage will be discussed; this discussion is based on information gathered by the organizer from the reports of other party members.

Aboard ship the communist nucleus (usually three to six members) attempts to establish its leadership in the crew. Party members are instructed to take the initiative by calling a union meeting at the beginning of the voyage. The very fact of assuming the initiative helps to establish their role as union leaders aboard the ship, even though they might have no official standing in the union. Beginning {188} with simple nonpolitical objectives, such as the enrollment of all members of the crew in the union, the communists are to institute political action. As a basis for initiating political discussion, resolutions are to be introduced at the ship's union meetings. These may then be followed by the establishment of Political and Educational Committees whose leadership, usually falling to volunteers, can readily be assumed by the communists. Using these committees, the party members attempt to lead the crew from unionism to acceptance of the party's ideology.[15] In the course of this work, individuals who might be especially valuable for "development" can be identified and given special attention on the homeward journey. At the end of the voyage the communists may attempt to have the crew donate to the party any funds remaining in the ship's treasury. These activities on shipboard can also be supplemented by such tactics as having a party member volunteer to act

---

[15] One of the most serious errors made in analyzing communism is that of focusing attention on the formal program of the party, so that it is assumed to be a partial fulfillment of the party's propaganda goals to create sentiment for unionization or similar "immediate" objectives. In fact, however, the significant partial goals are of two kinds: the promotion of current propaganda objectives of interest to the Soviet Union (e.g., opposition to the Marshall Plan), and, equally important but less well understood, the inculcation of attitudes which neutralize the opposition to communism and create a favorable atmosphere for open communist activity.

as ship's librarian, a position which makes it possible not only to weed out books under the party's interdict,[16] but also to incorporate the party's own literature into the library.

When the voyage is completed, the communist seamen are expected to turn in a "ship's report" to the waterfront organizer. This provides information on personnel—new sympathizers as well as avowed anticommunists—and a review of political activities. General intelligence on the ship's officers, cargo, and working conditions is collected, all of which is useful for determining the relative utility of assigning men to the ship. During the war the organizers also {189} gathered data of military importance: troop movements, cargoes, convoys, and similar matters.

Not only do the communist seamen serve the international organization, but the latter is itself helpful in establishing the party in the industry. With communist organizations in most major ports, the party member need not share the feeling of being alone in a strange country. He has ready-made affiliations, friends, and an exciting job to do. American seamen are sometimes enrolled as honorary members of foreign branches, and these associations are useful as inducements in recruiting, the party card being recognized as a means of admission to a social circle when few, if any, alternatives exist. Common affiliation to the international party provides a basis for communication that readily overcomes language barriers. Thus, far from being a disintegrative force, the dispersion of communist seamen reinforces their allegiance to the movement.

During periods ashore at home, the activities of the communist seamen do not abate. Those not assigned to tasks in the union may be detailed to work in the longshore, teamster, or other branches of the Waterfront Section. Volunteer work at party offices, in peripheral groups, and in support of current party campaigns can also absorb available energies. Opportunities for training are also offered during these periods ashore. In New York, a party school supplies instructors for the Waterfront Section, and seamen are admitted to courses at such communist schools without charge. It is reported that some waterfront party members are enrolled in every session of the secret National Committee Training Courses.

The party's main target in the industry is, of course, the union. The struggle for control is unrelenting, and all of the party machinery is dedicated to that end. But even prior to control, especially when the existing leadership is nonpolitical, the communist fraction will attempt to exploit the untapped political potentialities of the union organization. This may begin with the creation of the position of educational director, later that of political director. The communists will seek to control these posts and thus have a means of {190} influencing the membership and of involving the union in political activity. Control of the speakers bureau, union library, and bookstore will be sought, and they are often available simply for the asking. Given communist control, these positions will all be pre-empted by party members, ensuring proper "education" of the ranks. This is another instance

---

[16] Again, superficially this might seem to refer to materials extolling capitalism or otherwise running counter to the formal program of the party; actually, however, the main targets are those which expose the party's conspiratorial tactics or which charge it with abandoning socialist ideals, as well, of course, as any books which attack the Soviet Union.

of the principle suggested above: the organs of mobilization become instruments of control.

As in the case of peripheral organizations, the effective coordination of communist forces is well exemplified in the use of office-workers' unions. The latter can, by selective placement, staff the maritime union's offices with party members. These form a spy network for the party which can be exceedingly useful during a struggle for control of the union, since confidential information is then available to the communist opposition. In other words, an approach to the union's own employees is a good auxiliary tactic supplementing the main effort to win the leadership through parliamentary channels.

Once in control the party can use the union machinery for building its own organization. Communist organizers can be placed on the union payroll, a type of patronage which is useful not only for maintaining control over the union, but to increase the number of full-time persons furthering the party's interests. Such positions as that of waterfront patrolman are especially useful for recruiting and fund raising, since the patrolman has special access to the crews and, speaking in the name of the union, may promote party causes. The communist leadership may also tap the union treasury by proposing (with decisions often involving minimal member participation) donations to communist peripheral organizations, or even to the *Daily Worker*. One device for milking the union treasury is based on the ability of the leadership to exercise discretion in administrative matters. For example, it is reported that the communists owned two printing corporations in New York, occupying the same premises and sharing equipment and personnel. One of these corporations printed party literature at little cost to the party, its {191} deficit being made up by the other corporation, which accepted printing contracts from communist-led unions and peripheral groups. Since the awarding of such contracts will be made by party members, prices paid may be only indifferently inspected, so that the union ultimately helps to pay for the cost of publishing open party materials. The establishment of interlocking directorates linking party and union leads naturally to devices not unusual in such combinations.

After his break with the communists, Joseph Curran revealed some of the tactics of the party during its leadership of the National Maritime Union. Thus, on the relation of the union leaders to the party, Curran states:

> Certain leading NMU officials in New York meet regularly with top Party leaders to discuss policy and program for our Union. The fact that these Party leaders are not members of our Union, and have no right to interfere in our affairs, is of small concern to the NMU officials who meet with them. The decisions of these secret meetings of the Party bosses are then relayed to other Communist Union officials, and to paid Party organizers, in every port, where Party meetings are then held to organize to enforce these decisions upon our Union, whether the rank and file agree with them or not.[17]

---

[17] Joseph Curran, *President's Report on the State of the Union,* Sixth National Convention of the National Maritime Union (CIO), September 22, 1947, p. 108.

In communicating these decisions, the party can use the union machinery not only in such minor matters as telephone service, but more significantly:

> In major matters, when the Party wants to get their outpost officials into New York, it is easy for them to call a special Council meeting for this purpose, or to call them in to headquarters to "discuss Union business," with the Union paying transportation and expenses. The proof of the system's operation is shown, for example, by the many instances when the same resolution, sometimes with the exact wording, has been submitted at membership meetings all held on the same day, in a dozen different ports, separated by thousands of miles. Another example is the fact that more than one Party member may be nominated for the same post in a Union election, but it will be noticed that all but one will {192} withdraw according to plan, and the final slate of Party candidates will be uniformly circulated throughout all ports.[18]

In addition, the national convention offers an opportunity for the accomplishment of party tasks. Many party members attend the union gathering as delegates, so that secret conferences of the communist fraction from the entire country can be held at union expense. These are important occasions, since they permit personal discussion of tactical problems and effective communication of the party's directives, as well as morale-building activity. The secret meeting has an air of special authority because it is attended by the prominent union executives who publicly deny affiliation with the party and by the international agents who guide the party's maritime activities.

In the National Maritime Union, as elsewhere, the communists wielded the full power of their disciplined membership to impose a minority will. The following report by Curran is typical of many others

> The record of membership meetings in New York shows that the Communists show up in force, including members working ashore whom they permit to retain their Union books. They come early and stay late. Their patrolmen are the ones to count the votes. Whenever one of their people is chairman, only Party members are recognized, although they constitute a small minority of the members present. Their booing squads harass all non-Communist speakers. The meetings are filibustered until it is necessary to recess or adjourn before vital work or resolutions are discussed and acted upon.[19]

These tactics of delay and harassment are often reported. Sometimes, they involve heated debates and even violence, with organized and systematic effort to deny the floor to the opposition. At other times, the tactics are those of what might be called "attrition through tedium," which is perhaps even more effective. These tactics are described by one union leader as follows:

---

[18] *Ibid.*

[19] *Ibid.*, p. 109.

By wearing them down I mean this: For instance, if an election whereby a change of officers may occur is held, and the Commies {193} were to be unseated, they would arrange for that evening a very lengthy agenda and at the tail end of the agenda they would have the election. The meeting may start at 6:30, and it may wind up at 12 or 1 o'clock in the morning, depending on how successful they were in wearing down the right-wingers, causing them to leave and go home. They are usually successful in doing that, because the average individual who is not union-conscious sufficiently, or is not diligent enough to want to overthrow these Commies—they want to, in a lackadaisical way, but they will not spend 5 hours or an evening to sweat it out to unseat them. Or, when the agenda is read, they will not challenge the agenda and have additions or corrections made on the agenda so that the all-important thing, the election, may come up first, and the lesser things come up secondary or last. They wear them down. They tire them out. . . . And they embarrass and scream down the opposition so that they lose heart and go home, and the different Commies at strategic places take a count and if they find out they are in the majority then they give the signal to the Chair to proceed with the agenda, and come to the final decision, the election. They spring the election, and the minority is the majority.[20]

Whether by disruption or attrition, the result is minority decision. Thus, Curran continues:

The following day they hold "continuation" meetings in the hall, during the morning or the afternoon, when the majority of the membership is working or not available. At these "continuation" meetings, the Communists, who always show up in force, jam through their disruptive policies and programs. These same methods are used in all other ports where the Communists have control. . . . The powers of special meetings, or "continuation" meetings, to decide policy, or commit our Union to any program, must be drastically curbed.[21]

The Leninist subordination of all practices to the extension and maintenance of the party's influence leaves no room for inhibitions induced by respect for democratic procedure. This does not reflect on the abstract idealism of the bolshevik cadres, for they can preserve {194} that by the simple expedient of arrogating to the party the right to decide upon the "historical interests" of the workers. This decision uniformly supports whatever means may be necessary for placing party members in positions of authority. Actually, of course, cynicism and corruption are a normal outcome when moral principles have no restraining consequences, and the actor is his own judge. For the Bolsheviks, democracy implies no restraints

---

[20] Testimony of Paul P. Milling, "Investigation of Communism in New York City Distributive Trades," *Hearings,* U.S. House Committee on Education and Labor, 80th Cong., 2d sess., Washington, 1948, p. 731*f.*

[21] Curran, *op. cit.,* p. 109.

and, indeed, reaches its fulfillment with the establishment of a monopoly of power by the party.[22]

A review of the rise and fall of party influence in the National Maritime Union offers some insight into the possibilities and limits of communist penetration and control. Early concentration in the maritime industry was effected through the Marine Workers Industrial Union, a product of the ultra-left "third period," which was able to play a significant role in the San Francisco dock strike of 1934. With the organization of the CIO, and the communist shift to participation in the accepted labor movement, the communists liquidated the Marine Workers Industrial Union and helped to set up in its place a National Maritime Union. The communists took control of the new organization from its inception, but their problem was complicated by the existence of an opposition known as the Mariners Club. Since the active defense of its regime required an appeal to the membership, the small communist fraction found it necessary to lean on the support of a noncommunist seaman, Joseph Curran, who was personally popular among the rank and file. Curran agreed to work with the communists, and became president of the union. Since he had no independent machine, he became completely dependent on the party. The party did not fear this arrangement, which was by no means unusual, because with a majority of the powerful National Council, and control of key posts such as {195} treasurer, it could make Curran its prisoner. If necessary, he could be presented with the alternative of capitulation or resignation."

The bloc between Curran and the party lasted until about 1944, when the first indications appeared of an impending split. At that time, Curran was virtually helpless, having little effective support against the communist fraction. Without relinquishing his post as president, however, he turned to the ranks to begin building an independent group, and began to establish personal contact with Philip Murray, president of the CIO. It is doubtful that he could have prevailed had it not been for events that were taking place within the party itself during that period. A combination of difficulties beset the party, beginning with a personal conflict within the New York Waterfront Section and continuing with a series of disaffections from the party that took place after the ousting of Earl Browder. It appears that a conflict between two leading communists in the Waterfront Section led finally to a major break in the communist ring around Curran when the union treasurer left the party. At the same time, or soon thereafter, other prominent communists in the union resigned, on political grounds. Their reasons for leaving the party were not uniform—some split off as Browderites, others with those who believed the party had not gone far enough to the left—but regardless of these differences they allied themselves with Curran in the struggle to oust the party from its leadership in the union. Following their victory in 1948, the *Daily Worker* (July 28, 3948) pointed out that "the main instruments for Curran's caucus were

---

[22] It is especially important to bear in mind that this concept of democracy is world-wide in the communist movement and is applied in specific institutions such as trade-unions. All the evidence indicates that the USSR, far from being a special case, is the prototype of communist domination wherever the communists can gain power, whether in a state as a whole or in a private association.

the renegades from communism. Of 32 top officers and port agents elected, 17 are former communists."[23]

The strength of the communists in the union lay entirely in their ability to so manipulate the fraction of about 500 members as to establish organizational control over the union membership of {196} approximately 50,000. But the weakness of the party lay in its dependence on these organizational measures. It could not appeal to the ranks for support on ideological grounds, and once a break in the party's command structure appeared, it became possible (though still with considerable effort) to oust it from the leadership.

Among the maneuvers which characterized the struggle between Curran and the party for control of the NMU was an interesting variant of "unity" tactics. The party's recognition of the impending split was apparently the basis for the formation of a Committee on Maritime Unity, which attempted to bind the NMU into a coalition with other unions in the industry under communist control. If the authority of the committee could be established, the NMLI would be outvoted and might be forced to make concessions that would weaken the Curran leadership. A long history of conflict among the maritime unions, always costly and often violent, gave the slogan of unity an appeal to the membership which could not be lightly ignored. This device was unsuccessful, however, although its failure did not inhibit Harry Bridges from proposing, in 1947, a merger of his longshoremen's union with the NMU. Since the break had already occurred, this proposal could have only a propaganda value, that of attempting to endow the communist elements with a halo as unity supporters.

Like other American workers, the seamen have not accepted communist ideology. This is the ultimate foundation of the party's weakness and results in the tendency for communist influence to be of an all-or-none variety. Since the party is completely dependent on the power it can generate through manipulation of its disciplined ranks, and the isolated positions which communists as individuals can gain are easily rendered untenable, the party must rely on the protection of its inroads by establishing monopoly control. Once that control is lost, it is likely to be swept out completely. Because the party must rely on organizational strategems, having no secure base in public opinion, it must bid for complete ascendancy or accept an insignificant role. {197}

The Paradox of Nonpolitical Unionism

The communist tacticians—and their opponents—must deal with a continuing dilemma. Their power rests on the exercise of nonpolitical functions. If they introduce overt political criteria into trade-union decisions, they are in danger of alienating the membership; if they fail to do so, their goals will be compromised.

---

[23] This tactic of using a person of prestige to establish control, and then isolating him organizationally, is common. Recent examples are the resignation of Harold Ickes from the predecessor of the Communist-Party-sponsored Wallace movement, and of Henry Wallace himself from the Progressive Party. These nominal leaders were surrounded by an entrenched communist fraction. Such leaders are often unaware of the party's rule until after its control has been established.

This difficulty is posed in an obvious way for the communists, whose very program calls for the politicalization of labor; it is important to the anticommunists as well, however, whenever the political initiative of the communists demands counter-measures which meet them on their own ground.

If the unions were completely manipulable, there would be no difficulty. But the difference between unions and "fronts" (peripheral groups) lies precisely in the more limited maneuverability of the former. Union members are not recruited primarily on ideological grounds, but on the basis of economic self-interest, al-though, of course, this has some ideological components. Hence there is strong pressure to justify decision on the needs of the union as a collective bargaining instrument. All the political elements in the labor movement must bow to this imperative, with the result that political contention takes place in an atmosphere of ambiguity, a shadowland of maneuver under the cover of simple trade-union activity.

The paradoxical position of the communists in relation to nonpolitical union-ism is emphasized by their *special* need to seek cover in a narrow emphasis on bread-and-butter issues. For tactical reasons, these most severe critics of trade-union neutrality[24] will be found advocating just that, or something close to it, when the exigencies {198} of the struggle for power in the unions require it. This has become increasingly true as the communists have learned to rely on covert organizational measures in the struggle for power rather than on a frontal ideo-logical appeal. The utility of this tactic is (1) to avoid self-exposure and (2) to place the struggle on an apparently nonpolitical basis so that the secret activity of the disciplined party members can gain its greatest relative weight.

The desire to avoid self-exposure is especially important to a communist lead-ership when it gains control of a union on the basis of organizational strategy but does not have firm ideological support among the membership. This is the typical case in the United States and is, as noted above, the basic source of communist weakness even in those unions over which they exercise a monopoly of power. For although they can assume command over all the sources of influence within the union, they cannot control—although they can often neutralize for long peri-ods—the pressure of the community at large on the minds of the membership. As a result, the communist leaders must present themselves as "simply good trade-unionists," insisting that their continued tenure depend on their effectiveness as unionists rather than on their political views.[25]

---

[24] "One of the bourgeois ideas, which the ruling classes have succeeded in inculcating among the working masses, is the idea of trade union neutrality, that is, the idea of the non-political and nonparty character of the trade-unions. . . . But in reality the trade-unions have never been and could never be neutral. Not only is neutrality harmful to the trade-unions, it cannot positively be maintained." "Theses and Resolutions," Third World Congress of the Communist International (1921). Reprinted in *Hearings,* Appendix, Pt. I. U.S. House Spe-cial Committee on Un-American Activities, 76th Cong., 1st sess., Washington, 1940, p. 279. This useful volume is a compilation of many basic communist documents.

[25] The shifting sands of communist policy, and the exploitative bent of the party, do not permit the communist leaders to follow a line entirely consistent with effective trade union-ism. During World War II, the communists advocated incentive wage schemes and the con-tinuation of the no-strike pledge into the postwar period, policies which no "bourgeois"

The importance of the ideological isolation of the communists, and the need to avoid exposure, was clearly demonstrated in the case of the Transport Workers Union, which was torn from the communist orbit in 1948. In this case, the ideological element was especially important because of the large Catholic membership, with its special alertness to communism. With the help of a strong leading personality, Michael J. Quill, the communists were able to maintain control for many years. But when a counterattack was launched in an organized way by Jesuit-trained elements within the union, and Quill {199} broke with the party, the communist fraction was unable to mobilize any significant rank-and-file support.

The communist leadership had always been more careful in the TWU than in many other unions to avoid confronting the membership with its own ideology, because it knew that its power rested on its ability to convince the membership of its devotion to them as simple union leaders. They were aided in this by the sensitivity of Catholics to the charge that they are dominated by priestly instruction in secular matters.[26]

This difficulty of the communists was exploited by Quill at a meeting of the executive board in September, 1948. The board was still dominated by the communists—this was the meeting just prior to the decisive convention—and had refused to endorse the candidates of either of the two major parties in the national election. A resolution was then introduced, by Quill supporters, endorsing Henry Wallace. This was done, Quill later explained, in order to "put the boys on the spot. They sang for Wallace for three days at Philadelphia and I wanted to see if they would vote for him. They're afraid to do so because they know the membership would cut their throats."[27] A board member from the communist-led faction explained that "we decided to table the endorsement of {200} Henry A. Wallace because we are in favor of leaving the question of whom to vote for in the national

---

unionist could accept. Moreover, unions are split, liquidated, reorganized, and otherwise manipulated in terms of the party's immediate needs rather than in the interests of the unions as such.

[26] See Jules Weinberg, "Priests, Workers, and Communists," *Harper's Magazine*, November, 1948. On the general question of tactical flexibility, the following comments by a CIO committee are pertinent: "The techniques used by the Communist Party in achieving control of a union and in then using the union for its purposes vary according to the nature of the industry, the tradition of the union, and the degree to which the union can be subjected to rigid control. As these factors change from time to time, the operation of the Party group within the union (i.e., the 'Party fraction') changes to meet the new situation. Although the Party fraction functions in a highly mechanical fashion on the theoretical level, accepting without question the line handed down from above, its tactical maneuvering may shift from day to day and even from meeting to meeting depending upon the particular needs of the moment. Thus, the operation of the Party fraction within one union may be completely different from that within another union. In all cases, however, the Party fraction in the union acts as a disciplined group and takes the orders of the day from the Party functionary assigned to or responsible for trade union work. "Report of the Executive Board Committee Appointed by President Murray to Investigate Charges against International Longshoremen's and Warehousemen's Union," Congress of Industrial Organizations, Washington, D.C., 1950, mimeo.

[27] *New York Times,* September 7, 1948.

election up to the membership."[28] Since the leaders openly criticized the other candidates, their neutrality was at best ambiguous, but it was still far greater than that called for by the communist theory of trade-union political action. Since the candidacy of Wallace was widely identified as a communist-inspired political enterprise, open support by the TWU leaders would have meant exposure before the membership.

This type of neutrality, of course, implies no doctrinal inconsistency. There is no abandonment of principle, but only a yielding to pressure. It may take many different forms, including the espousal of objectivity and the suspension of judgment. For example, one communist-dominated union, under pressure of the membership, hedged in its opposition to the "imperialist" war during the Stalin-Hitler pact with the formula: "It is not our purpose at the moment to discuss the character of the present war or the speed at which our country is being drawn into the maelstrom. . . . It may be that all the arguments are not on one side and there are many parts of the equation that don't add up."[29] Or, without actually supporting some Soviet act of terror (e.g., the Moscow Trials), the membership will be called on to "wait until all the facts are in," and to avoid stirring up hatred for Russia. As the communists understand very well, the withholding of judgment has itself political consequences. If they cannot gain support for their own views directly, they can at least exploit the possibilities of indirect aid through nonpartisanship. Passivity is especially useful when the immediate objective is to avoid criticism of the regime to which they are committed, or to weaken popular support for American policies abroad.

The flight to neutrality under threat of exposure is, however, of less importance than the deliberate exploitation of nonpolitical unionism in order to weaken an opposition which can only function openly, while the Bolsheviks themselves use conspiratorial methods. An important instance is the postwar struggle for power in the {201} Berlin trade-union movement. The communists gained and held control of the central labor organization[30] on the basis of complicated election procedures plus an insistence (with the support of Allied authorities) on nonpolitical candidacies. One report, based on social-democratic sources, reported on the election procedures as follows:

> According to this system, unions in each city district (Bezirk) send delegates to the Bezirk Conference of the FDGB. The Bezirk Conference then elects delegates to the Greater Berlin Conference, and the Greater Berlin Conference in turn elects the Berlin Central Committee. Since present rules forbid any party labels in the union elections, and the elections proceed so rapidly as to prevent information of the affiliations of candidates being disseminated, the large mass of non-party union members split their votes in the Bezirk Conferences, while the well disciplined SED minority always votes as a unit. Consequently, in every "unpolitical" election to the

---

[28]   *Ibid.*

[29]   *CIO News,* FAECT (Federation of Architects, Engineers, Chemists, and Technicians) Edition, April 7, 1941.

[30]   Freier Deutscher Gewerkschafts Bund (FDGB) (Free German Trade Union League).

Greater Berlin Conference, union members find that they have elected an overwhelming majority of SED adherents.[31]

Nor was this nonpolitical tactic forced on the communists; critics of the system urged revision to permit political designations, but the FDGB leadership insisted on the principle of nonpartisanship. In a situation characterized by two opposing elites (social democrats and communists) bidding for the support of an unstructured public, the communists refused to contend openly on an ideological basis, relying on organizational weapons to overcome their weakness in public opinion.

Neutrality in the unions offers the same kind of cover as that supplied by another generality, "unity." In each case, attention is focused on practical objectives, so that only those who operate conspiratorially are able to continue the pursuit of ultimate power objectives. The enemy is disarmed, his open, conventional weapons of political controversy rendered useless, while the secret communist apparatus continues to function. A whole army may march through the escape clauses in these bolshevik bargains. The difficulty is that {202} often only the communists possess the requisite political regiments.

Despite their ultimate program of politicalization, the communists have gained much from the very tradition of trade-union neutrality which they have so scornfully attacked. The atmosphere of political neutrality affords immunity from open attack by anticommunists, as well as a freedom of movement which permits the party fractions to exploit *incidental* opportunities for political advancement. This is especially significant where a union carries on activities beyond practical bread-and-butter issues. As we have seen above, in the case of the maritime industry, the communists quickly move to take over educational and political work, creating these functions where they do not exist. These tend to be areas of secondary interest to the practical-minded leadership, and the communists are quick to take advantage of this indifference.

Similarly, the communists have been especially active in such auxiliary groupings as the state and city CIO councils. These bodies have primarily a civic function, do not engage in collective bargaining or make policy on urgent trade-union matters, and hence are of relatively little interest to the ordinary union leader. For the communists, however, these are additional weapons that can be added to the party's arsenal in the labor movement. In important centers like New York and Los Angeles, communist control (now removed) of these councils made it possible to use them as sounding boards for the current party line, to help raise funds for party causes, to lend dignity and a semblance of community support to statements actually representing the opinions of only a small minority in labor. To the citizen unversed in the intricacies of union politics, the pronouncements of these councils would seem to be the official views of the CIO as a whole. Control of such a central body, moreover, even if it has few formal powers, can help the communists gain and hold control of local unions. In addition, the work of affiliated unions can be coordinated in ways that maximize the influence of the party.

---

[31] W. P. Davidson, "The Organization of Power in the Soviet Zone of Germany," unpublished MS, 1947.

The difficulties of functioning in an ideologically unyielding environment have driven the communists to full use of conspiratorial {203} methods. These have required that a new twist of meaning be given to the original demand that the unions be brought under the banner of communism. The party fractions have often found it advisable to avoid open political identification of the unions under their control, through a bid for the ideological support of the membership, and have contented themselves with the exploitation of whatever incidental advantages may be gained for advancing the party's influence. Unable to base their strength on direct influence among the members, they have had to rest on covert devices for the establishment and maintenance of minority control. As a result, they have had to act on the basis of legitimate trade-union aspirations. This is sufficiently obvious in the case of a communist fraction that agitates for more insistent pressure on employers, but it is less clearly understood as a factor in controversies within the labor movement itself.

The general consequence of this half-hidden contention is to give a political color to decisions in the labor movement. Not only do the communists decide ordinary trade-union matters on the basis of political criteria, but their opponents are forced to do so as well. The very existence of the communists as a political force in the CIO has increased the difficulty of maintaining a nonpolitical orientation for the organization as a whole. This means that controversies over apparently simple union matters, e.g., jurisdictional disputes, must be inspected for their political implications.

An instructive example of internal controversy in which a political struggle is presented as a conflict over purely trade-union matters (incidentally also a variant of communist unity tactics) occurred in the course of the fight for leadership in the automobile workers' union. In 1946, the union convention elected the anticommunist Walter Reuther as president by a slim margin, leaving the procommunist faction in control of the executive board. The following year was one of preparation for a showdown at the 1947 convention. As Reuther gained strength, and the national CIO leadership reaffirmed its anticommunist stand, the entire position of the communists in the labor movement seemed to depend on the outcome of the struggle in the United Automobile Workers Union, the largest constituent {204} of the CIO. In order to help meet this crisis, the communists characteristically relied on organizational tactics.

Overlapping jurisdiction had long been a source of dispute between the UAW and another CIO union, the Farm Equipment Workers. The latter was within the communist orbit and hence was deployable. It was decided to use this union as a weapon against the Reuther faction in the UAW by proposing a merger of the two organizations. Since such a merger would eliminate the jurisdictional disputes, and had already been under negotiation, the proposal was a source of acute embarrassment and threatened to upset the possibilities of an anticommunist victory at the 1947 convention. For by joining its two available forces—the FE leadership and the anti-Reuther majority of the UAW executive—the communists engineered an agreement to bring over 400 delegates into the UAW convention, with full voting rights. It also called for the establishment of a virtually autonomous unit in the UAW which would have meant the maintenance of the communists' control of the

FE even if they were not able to win the UAW leadership by means of this tactic. Since Reuther had won the presidency by a majority of only 124 votes at the 1946 convention, the addition of a procommunist delegation with immediate voting rights could readily have been decisive. Thus by effectively deploying its forces under the cover of simple trade-union objectives, the communists could hope to recoup losses suffered since their postwar reversion to open Marxist-Leninist aims.

What is especially interesting in connection with this tactic is that it forced the noncommunist opposition to conduct its fight on the basis of trade-union, rather than political, issues. The following account, written by a member of the Reuther forces, indicates the lines along which the debate was conducted:

> The chips were down and the battle was on.[32] In the following six weeks, officers and staff members on both sides rushed around {205} the country, debating the issue before local membership meetings. All of the odds were on the side of the Addes group and its Commie bird dogs, who were beating the bushes to flush votes for the merger proposal. The Commies had shrewdly picked a time of the year when membership meetings were poorly attended, many workers being away on vacations. To make our arguments against the merger stick, we had to beat down the charge that we were opposing admission to the UAW of thousands of workers whom we had always claimed as potential members.
>
> Our only hope was to stick to the facts, expose the completely undemocratic character of the merger proposal, and put our trust in the good sense of the UAW-CIO membership. Shooting from the hip, as it were, we plunked away at the merger on the following points:
>
> 1. It would undermine the industrial (as opposed to craft) union principles in the UAW constitution by setting up an autonomous FE Division inside the UAW-CIO.
>
> 2. It would also violate our constitution by giving the FE Division power to elect an International Executive Board member on a craft basis.
>
> 3. It specifically proposed to guarantee the jobs of all the officers and staff members of the FE-CIO.
>
> 4. It would have committed the UAW-CIO to assuming all the financial obligations of the FE-CIO (which neither Addes nor FE President Grant Oakes could document with a CPA audit until the fight was practically over).
>
> 5. It was designed to give the FE-CIO local unions full voting power at the coming convention of the UAW-CIO, as if they had always been members of our union. . . . And, with customary Commie thoroughness, it would have given the FE-CIO locals a chance to vote twice on the issue—once as FE-CIO locals voting to merge themselves with UAW-CIO, and again as UAW-CIO

---

[32] The anti-Reuther executive board majority voted to approve the merger, subject to a referendum vote by the local unions. Because of its uneasy tenure and the doubtful constitutionality of the agreement, it would have been suicidal for the board majority to attempt to carry through the merger without such a referendum and also to have the FE delegates vote at the coming convention.

locals voting to seat themselves in the UAW-CIO 1947 convention. We esti-
mated that the adoption of the merger on these terms would give Addes an
additional block of 450 solid anti-Reuther votes at the November convention of the UAW-CIO.

6. There was no provision whatsoever in the UAW-CIO constitution for
the kind of referendum vote dreamed up by the {206} "mechanical majority" to cloak its coup with a spurious membership sanction.[33]

The Reuther faction, by putting a strong countermachine into action, won the referendum battle. But it will be noticed that the arguments presented kept strictly to
the trade-union issues—Is the merger as presented good for the union?—without
raising the question of communism. These tactics were deliberate. "We knew,"
wrote Reuther in 1948,[34] "that the FE merger maneuver was communist-inspired.
But to base our opposition to it on that ground would have confused the membership by involving them in a vague debate on the merits of communism. . . . We had
beaten the Stalinists on the merits of the issue—but the issues were rescued from
the fog of double-talk and presented to the membership by hard work. That is the
way to beat the Communists." It is not to be supposed from this that in fact the
communist issue was never raised. "Cold turkey" talks among union leaders and
key rank-and-file elements must certainly have put the matter sharply, in terms of
the ultimate character of the union. But the leadership was apparently convinced
that the mass membership would be impatient with, and could not understand, a
controversy which struck at the underlying question: Shall the Communist Party
add our union to its deployable forces in America?

This estimate of the situation is shared by other anticommunist tacticians. For
example, a brochure issued by the U.S. Chamber of Commerce poses the problem
as follows:

> Union elections do not precisely parallel civic elections. In the latter
> case, a sound attack upon the "ins" often brings a large protest vote to the
> polls. With labor, the attacking of officers as Communists is more likely
> to produce confusion and lethargy. The Communists themselves will not
> normally admit the charge. They will smear and discredit the opposition.
> The average worker becomes so puzzled that his reaction is "A plague on
> both your houses." Of course if, in an exceptional case, it can be proved that
> most of the officers are really Communists, such an attack will be effective.
> But it is one thing to be certain of a fact, and another and {207} different
> thing to be prepared to prove it in public controversy and to an untrained
> audience. Ordinarily Communist charges are best reserved for the inner
> caucus and for word-of-mouth reports spread throughout the plant by the
> anti-Communist opposition.[35]

---

[33] C. W. Fountain, *Union Guy,* The Viking Press, Inc., 1949, pp. 206*ff.*

[34] W. P. Reuther, "How To Beat the Communists," *Colliers,* February 28, 1948.

[35] "Communists within the Labor Movement," U.S. Chamber of Commerce, Washington,
1947.

This policy is based on the assumption, for which there is some warrant, that the communists are unable to be good labor leaders because of their consistent effort to make political capital out of their positions in the unions. However, with the basic role of a union in the community at stake, it is likely that political considerations will effectively control the actions of the anticommunists as well. They cannot consistently choose to support policies which, good in themselves, have the consequence of perpetuating communist power. Until the union membership becomes politically alert, it is likely that an emphasis on trade-union neutrality will be useful to the communists, and not the barrier it might superficially seem to be.

Dual-Power Tactics

It has been said that revolutionists in modern society do not so much "seize" power as destroy and re-create it.[36] We shall explore this insight further in considering bolshevik tactics in the coup d'état. At this point, however, it is desirable to indicate how the communists apply the principle of dual power within mass organizations.

The bolshevik tacticians are keenly sensitive to the value of undermining existing leadership in ways that result not in chaos, but in the emergence of new organs of control. Contrary to popular impression, the communists never rely on the simple creation of disorder, for they know that power will not come automatically into their hands but may go to other emerging elites. The fomenting of confusion and chaos, therefore, must always be controlled, always accompanied by the careful construction of new instruments of order which can be prepared to fill the power vacuum. This involves an effort to divest the existing leadership (or government) of the basis {208} of its power by approaching from below to capture the institutional supports on which governance rests. The formal leadership, reduced to an "empty shell," can then be disposed of with ease.

The communist apparatus differs from the ordinary political machine in a number of important respects, among which is the ability of the party fraction in a union or other association to function on a rank-and-file basis. The party membership, including large numbers who are scarcely of cadre caliber, plus the periphery, can be deployed to attack an organization from below. The party may then avoid dependence on top-level maneuvers. Ideally, the party's key people do not work alone, relying on their individual capacities and the shifting sands of bureaucratic influence, but rather are supported by a mass base. This base need not be large to be effective; it is necessary only to create small forces well placed which participate diligently and follow a uniform policy. The attack can then be launched on the ultimate sources of power, the local branches. The compliance of the latter is sufficiently reliable in most organizations, so that factionalism tends to be of the courtier variety, largely confined to the struggle among cliques at headquarters. But it is precisely this reliability which the communists seek to dissolve. They are prepared to do so because the weapon they have constructed is adapted to political

---

[36] George S. Pettee, *The Process of Revolution,* Harper & Brothers, New York, 1938, p. 5.

combat at the grass roots.[37]

The activities of the party fraction in an organization create power where it did not exist before. At the same time, they undermine the established lines of authority. As this new power becomes available, it may be found desirable to establish a focal point around which the scattered areas of influence may gather. This new center, counter-posed to the formal leadership, can become a steppingstone to total control, or a vehicle for splitting off and maintaining in another form the local influence which has been won. Armed with its own press and personnel, this competing center becomes an agency of dual power. Its objectives may be very limited—as to intimidate the {209} leadership into concessions—or it may seek itself to become the real center of authority in the organization. Normally, however, the use of this tactic is limited to situations in which the over-all organization is not really subject to capture, the problem being to consolidate whatever local power can be achieved.

An attempt to build such a power bloc for the purpose of isolating the established national leadership from a large segment of the membership took place in the United Retail, Wholesale, and Department Store Employees of America.[38] This union had a firm anticommunist leadership, but several New York locals under communist domination sought to establish a coordinating center which, in addition to normal nonpolitical activities, would help to undermine the authority of the right-wing leadership. It was reported that a group of department-store locals, in collaboration with a large shipping clerks' union, formed a power bloc that insulated itself from the international union:

> Within the past year or two these five department store locals have organized what they call the Department Store Joint Board, which is, you might say, an organization within an organization. The international union has a joint board in New York City, but the five department stores have now formed their own joint board, and more and more according to their publication they are working together as one group, rather than five different groups on all sorts of projects.[39]

The coalition published its own paper and was apparently able to exclude the International from collective-bargaining arrangements in its area. In addition, attempts were made to change the practice whereby employers remitted checkoff dues payments to the international, which then deducted its share and sent the rest to the local. The proposed change would permit the local to interpose difficulties in the payment of dues to the International, or even to withhold them altogether.

---

[37] This does not mean that the communists are above, or do not engage in, bargains or other practices of bureaucratic cliques. But the characteristic method of bolshevism is to rely on tactics which mobilize the party membership and other manipulable elements.

[38] See "Investigation of Communism in New York City Distributive Trades," *Hearings,* U.S. House Committee on Education and Labor, 80th Cong., 2d sess., Washington, 1948, pp. 33, 82.

[39] See testimony of T. C. Kirkpatrick, *ibid.,* p. 383.

The joint board established to implement this coalition had four {210} departments: research and negotiations, education and activities, organization, and administration. In effect, therefore, a separate administrative center had been established to perform functions normally undertaken by the International. In establishing this center, the leadership of the dissenting locals freed themselves from dependence on the staff services of the International and at the same time laid the groundwork for eliminating the latter from all influence in the area.[40]

Communist infiltration of the American Legion after World War II sought to use a similar device. Under the direction of the party's National Veterans Commission, the communist veterans and their sympathizers undertook

> . . . 1) to join established Legion Posts and by the perfected use of caucus to take over the leadership; 2) to form new posts wherever the Legion officialdom could be lured into granting a charter; 3) to push hard through unions in which the Communist Party was dominant and work through the Union Labor Legionnaires, making it a semiautonomous part of the parent body.[41]

According to this report, the Union Labor Legionnaires "began as a caucus of trade union Posts, developed into the National Conference of Union Labor Legionnaires, an organization within an organization. Its greatest support came from the *Daily Worker, In Fact,* and *PM,* which also supported its resolutions against the Legion leadership and against American foreign policy where it treads on Soviet toes. The NCULL [National Council of Union Labor Legionnaires] had its own executive board, held its own conventions. . . ." Here again we see the effort to establish a center of dual power, facilitating the isolation of the central leadership and the creation of an effective factional instrument. The bolshevik emphasis on full mobilization of available organizational resources should be recalled in this connection. This would make such a subgroup as the NCULL {211} much more meaningful in communist hands than it would be under another leadership. A less power-oriented group might form a labor tendency in the Legion, holding educational conferences and exerting some pressure on the national policy without, however, setting up a dual center, with its own staff services, as a power threat to the established leadership. It is one thing to have a committee that calls occasional meetings for education and liaison. It is something else again to use such a committee as a means of building a machine. To be sure, noncommunist factions may also use such tactics, but they are especially characteristic of bolshevik intervention.[42]

---

[40] With its representatives excluded from the collective bargaining process, it would be increasingly difficult for the International to maintain its prerogatives for long, including the automatic receipt of dues. Indeed, the International seems to have been dependent on the employers to administer the checkoff in its favor. See testimony of Louis Broido, Gimbel Brothers, *ibid.,* pp. 33, 82*f*, 101.

[41] Ralph de Toledano, *Plain Talk,* October, 1946.

[42] It is significant that the communists did not hesitate to make the Legion a target in the period just after World War II, despite its strong anticommunist leanings. This is consistent

Although such devices reflect the covert operation of a communist fraction, the rise of competing centers may be the result of real shifts in sentiment and interest, quite apart from communist influence. Such was the Committee for Industrial Organization in the American Federation of Labor. Likewise, in the general political arena, the emergence of the Soviets of Workers' Deputies in 1917 Russia was not engineered by the bolsheviks. But characteristically *the communists have taken a practice which develops spontaneously in great struggles and have made it into a tactic to be applied by the party as an act of organizational will.* Especially within organizations where power vacuum is normal and membership participation {212} minimal, the communists have seen the utility of creating alternative centers of power even if they must be maintained by organizational devices rather than by mass approval. The Soviets would have been meaningless as agencies of dual power without mass support, and the CIO itself reflected urgent problems of the labor movement. But a disciplined caucus of 200 men adequately deployed, gaining one local after another and then sustained by the creation of a coordinating center, can realistically hope to win control over an organization of many thousands.[43]

The communist fraction itself is a covert agency of dual power. It functions as an alternative leadership, ready to man the organization once power is won. Never at a loss for reliable personnel, it can draw upon the party's resources for auxiliary support or, when in office, to fill appointive posts. It has its own lines of communication and chain of command; it stands ready to take advantage of any temporary breakdown of official controls, or upsurge of membership participation, which will in effect create a vacuum or a need for leadership. In all organizations, spontaneous nuclei of power emerge at every level. These are usually well dispersed and

---

with the Leninist injunction that the party should not fail to penetrate an organization just because it is "reactionary." The tactical orientation to the Legion was modified, however, as the American Veterans Committee gained strength. The latter was much more congenial a target since the liberal veterans were more likely to be associated with the AVC. While party members could be deployed into the Legion, the ideologically most vulnerable elements were not attracted to it. Hence, in effect, the party sacrificed a labor orientation for an easier propaganda field. The veterans organizations base themselves more on civic functions and fraternal sentiments than on community of interest; therefore ideologies and social attitudes are far more important as bases for participation than in the unions. Since, as has been suggested above, the party's propaganda in the United States appeals more to the middle class than to the workers, the tactical shift is not surprising. The party pays a price for its propaganda effectiveness among middle-class groups in the need to follow them organizationally. Of course, "going with the masses" does not imply any change in bolshevik principles: it has consequences only for organizational maneuver and for flexibility in propaganda.

[43] This depends a great deal on the structure of the organization, such as the size of the locals. It might not take much more strength to gain control of a local of 10,000 members than of one of 2,000. The communists sought to gain control of the United Automobile Workers Union, 1,000,000 strong, and were serious contenders. It is reported, however, that "the actual CP 'fraction' has always been quite small, not more than 500 nationally at any time during the past fifteen years. But the size of such a fraction is inconsequential in comparison with its strategic location, mobile discipline, and ability to influence non-party union leaders." See I. Howe and B. J. Widick, *The UAW and Walter Reuther,* Random House, New York, 1949, p. 150.

torn by conflicting interests, whereas the communist fraction strives to become a parallel organization, bidding for power at all levels but guided by its own center and having independent sources of support.

Like a predatory army, the communist fraction within an organization must attempt to sustain itself, to support its own leaders and functionaries. The best way to do this is to win power in a portion of the organization, thus permitting the use of official positions for factional purposes. Hence *concentration* is an important tactical principle even if the area selected is not especially valuable for itself, {213} i.e., as a source of social power. Often enough, of course, strategic value and tactical utility coincide. Thus we find the communists calling for concentration not only in key industries, but on a tactical basis as well. In 1946, one party leader called for concentration in the automobile plants in Flint, Michigan, and in the Ford Motor Company, adding: "Of course this does not mean that the only concentration in the auto industry is to be Flint and Ford, but a base here would influence the work elsewhere."[44] The control of large locals in these sectors of the industry would make possible the mobilization of their organizers, offices, press, and prestige for extending the power of the fraction.

A strong local dominated by the party may become the fraction's base of operations, its officers assuming a guiding role in relation to other party-led groups in the union. This seems to have been the function of the Wholesale and Warehouse Workers Union Local 65 in New York in relation to the group of department-store locals referred to above.[45] All were affiliated with the same international union, but according to the testimony, the department-store locals looked to "65" rather than to the International for leadership. The informal coalition was symbolized and strengthened when the department-store locals abandoned their own newspaper and accepted that of Local 65 as their organ. This paper served to bind together the communist-led elements in the union.

Dual-power tactics are, therefore, inherent in communist penetration of mass organizations. The communists seek to create power by building their own machine (fraction); by seeking allies (to form a faction controlled by the fraction); by winning local centers of power which may then be used as bases for further operations; and, when expedient, by establishing a formal center to isolate the captured areas from the official leadership, as the basis for a split if that should become necessary. Such a coordinating center may take many forms and may not exist at all in any overt form. It is in any {214} case only a penultimate step in the process of dismemberment which is basic to communist tactics, for it is the basic aim of communist activity to create blocs of power that can be detached from community ties. The subversion of institutional loyalties and creation of new allegiances is part of the stock-in-trade of bolshevism, and this is applied within mass organizations as well as in the community at large. Dual power is a name for potential

---

[44] John Williamson, "For a Mass Marxist Party of the Working Class," *Political Affairs,* March, 1946.

[45] See "Investigation of Communism in New York City Distributive Trades," *op. cit.,* pp. 32, 96.

split. Its organs are always subversive,[46] undermining old forms of authority and creating new ones. The objective is not simply to displace existing leaders, but to destroy them. In this process of destruction, physical liquidation of opponents is of minor importance compared with the corrosion of the institutional foundations upon which their authority rests.

Communism and Machine Tactics

Before leaving the discussion of communist tactics in voluntary associations, it is necessary to introduce a brief note of caution against the simple identification of communism with normal political "machines." To be sure, the use of disciplined forces for the achievement and maintenance of minority control in large organizations is hardly unique to bolshevism. Indeed, all political forces employ devices which at many points resemble those of the political boss and the bureaucratic clique. The communists, moreover, are especially prone to use patently undemocratic tactics because of their inability to depend on winning victories in a free political arena. They have come more and more to rely on their apparatus, and hence to adopt the characteristic methods of machine politicians. Reliance on membership apathy, arbitrary expulsions, milked treasuries, and centralized control is the hallmark of the communist just as it is of racketeering leadership in trade-unions and other voluntary associations. The racketeers look to their own personal advantage, the communists to the political advancement of the party.

But it would be a serious error to think of communist tactics as {215} simply machine tactics. There are major differences, both of structure and of method. In the first place, spontaneously developed power groupings are *local,* each tending to form a quasi-feudal domain in which a group of retainers becomes dependent on some leader and serves him in a disciplined way. Where alliances are made, these are always loose, being subject to dissolution when the interests of the local machine are no longer served by them, or are based on threats of violence. But in the bolshevik movement, the local party machine is nothing; the party center, everything. Hence predictions, based on criteria of survival, as to what would happen to ordinary machines in given situations might not be applicable to the communists. Not only can the party center manipulate the local apparatus (say a union fraction) to suit its over-all purposes, but it can also reinforce it and otherwise deploy a network of organizations. The organizational weapon, although it has its own strategic and tactical problems, is always ultimately subordinated in communism to political ends.

Secondly, communist organizational tactics are always qualified by a keen awareness of leadership as a political process. In a way that is foreign to the ordinary political machine, the communists display a high sensitivity to the role of the mass in society as a whole and in specialized organizations. Although they are quite prepared to assume the classic bureaucratic role when that seems expedient—as in minimizing participation in decisions—the bolsheviks are equally prepared to mobilize mass participation when that can be effectively controlled.

---

[46] This term as used here is nonevaluative; subversion may or may not be a good thing, depending on the institutions at stake and the forces at work.

Like other machine bosses, the communists depend on apathy. But they are also willing to appeal to the membership for support. A narrow machine hesitates to assume mass leadership and restricts itself to clique maneuvers.

Government Infiltration

In the revolutionary politics of classical Leninism, communism is related to the "bourgeois state" as a bomb to its target. A major training document, Lenin's *State and Revolution,* is devoted to the {216} thesis that the capitalist state apparatus must be smashed, that there can be no question of simply taking over the existing institutions of government. Whereas trade-unions are to be *captured.* the state is to be *destroyed.* A new and reliable officialdom, and new instruments of coercion, are to replace the shattered organs of the class enemy.

The essence of this strategic perspective has been maintained, but with important tactical modifications, in that era of Leninist maturity which is referred to as Stalinism. Post-Leninist bolshevism has learned how to exploit more fully the tactical flexibility which the use of organizational weapons allows. As these potentialities have been grasped, the image of the state has changed, although the ultimate objective of total subversion has remained. Lenin saw his movement only in its narrow revolutionary dimension; for him, the party and the working-class organizations were outside the pale of capitalist society); their mission was to destroy that society and to do nothing which would blur class lines or give a new lease of life to existing institutions.

Lenin relied heavily on the organizational integrity of the combat party to maintain the political purity of the movement in the course of conspiratorial work, including penetration of the unions. But he insisted that political criteria, dictated by a class struggle involving forces greater than the party itself, must place restrictions upon the deployment of communist cadres. His successors, however, have operated on the assumption that Lenin actually built better than he knew, in that the organizational methods which he taught could permit the movement to detach itself from its class commitments. The new leadership, now bound to the Soviet Union as the primary and indispensable instrument of world revolution, could exploit this flexibility by altering tactics as expediency might dictate, without sacrificing the distinctively bolshevik character of world communism.

The emancipation of bolshevism from its earlier political commitments has been especially useful for concentration upon democratic institutions as targets. Mature Leninism, operating in an environment of political democracy, could not long abstain from penetrating {217} governmental institutions, not for the purpose of blowing them up, but to gain incidental benefits for the party. To adhere to Lenin's image of the state as simply organized class violence would be to ignore these opportunities. It was necessary to recognize that the state has many functions, some of which have an intimate relation to the interplay of social forces in the community. Any pressure group having special access to government agencies can use this privilege to bolster its own political strength. Hence penetration of such agencies, using the discipline and deployability of the combat party, as well as the tactical support of auxiliary organizations, can be a means of gaining added influence. Like all power based on organizational weapons, this is contrived and tenuous, but it is important as a way of bridging the gap between what is often meager ideological support and the influence necessary for significant political intervention.

This orientation to democratic governments is, however, only a supplement to and not necessarily a contradiction of Lenin's formula. Taking advantage of present opportunities to gain special influence for the party by working within the government does not preclude "smashing the state apparatus" at a time of revolution. For a nonconspiratorial group, it would be very difficult to hold on to this long-run perspective; but so long as the insulation of the combat party is maintained, the short-run tactics will not be self-defeating. The firmly laid down character of the movement as a "world within a world" makes possible a tactical flexibility which would not be available to more loosely defined groupings.

Stalinism has made Leninism more flexible, so that all opportunities for power aggrandizement may be seized, even if this means working for the "bourgeois state." But this has represented not so much a transformation of the movement (as would have been the case if the Comintern had turned legalist and reformist) as it has a natural evolution of communist tactics.

An overemphasis on communist revolutionary goals, real as they are, can readily lead to a misreading of the aims of the party in its infiltration of government. Although the ultimate rationale of infiltration {218} may be revolutionary, it is an error to suppose that the communists always conspire to overthrow the government tomorrow. If we look for evidences of revolutionary activity, we may not find them, and yet we may miss the important functions which such penetration can perform. In communist parlance, "revolutionary activity" means anything that serves the party, from espionage to the distribution of leaflets. The stereotype of the bolshevik as a revolutionary fanatic and spy has, like most stereotypes, some element of truth; like others, however, this one should not guide objective analysis.[47]

In communist doctrine, the state has only one significant function: to protect the class interests of the bourgeoisie. This emphasis is still basic, and must be, in order to justify the revolutionary aims of the party. But tactically the government is viewed not as an integral unit, but as a loose network of agencies related to special publics, such as labor, agriculture, and the unemployed. With characteristic realism, government bureaus are looked upon as institutions which for many purposes can be treated as distinct from the state as an instrument of authority. Decentralization, bureaucratic prerogative, dependence on organized constituencies, and similar characteristics of administrative agencies combine to create areas of vulnerability that can be exploited for immediate political advantage.

---

[47] The problem of espionage is relevant, but at this point we are concerned only with the utility of government infiltration for political purposes. The role of the stereotype in serving to misread communist aims is also important in connection with the overemphasis on the communist as a propagandist. For example, investigations of communism in the motion picture industry, which see the role of the party agents as attempting to get anticapitalist ideas on the screen, are largely beside the point. The propaganda aspect is not unimportant, but it is more a matter of neutralizing anticommunist sentiment than of actively propagating the party's ideology.

It is important to bear in mind in this connection a key assumption of the communist tacticians. This is the recognition that governmental administration is susceptible to direct pressure. Especially in the United States, public agencies are not part of a tight and self-contained hierarchy. These bodies, although formally responsible only to established legislative, executive, and judicial authority, in fact tend to reflect the alignment of political forces in the community. {219} Such forces, however, are not necessarily identical with public opinion as expressed through the ballot. Rather, they reflect the weight of organizational and financial resources as these are brought to bear through pressure-group tactics. Minorities that can muster such resources in a degree disproportionate to their strength in public opinion can exercise influence covertly, beyond their capacity to win support at the polls. Recognizing the relevance of this situation to their own special problem, the communists have entered the arena, relying on the party and its solar system of auxiliary organizations to compete among the traditional pressure groups of business, agriculture, and labor.

These remarks carry forward our search for the bolshevik "operational code." This code identifies desired objectives and useful patterns of action to advance communist aims. We cannot automatically reach conclusions as to the *success* with which these strategic and tactical aims have been pursued. Indeed, although the communist *effort* to infiltrate government is well proven, and is consistent with everything else we know about the party's methods, *there is no convincing evidence that communists anywhere have been able to exercise decisive influence upon any major government policy as a result of such infiltration.* This assertion is not meant to include the infiltration that parallels open political control of key government offices, as in the case of the Spanish Republican government during the civil war or of the coalitions established in France, Italy, and eastern Europe immediately following World War II.[48] It does refer to the evidence regarding the deployment of communist forces, the party being a minority and wholly divorced from official participation in the government.

Bearing in mind our interest in the bolshevik operational code, it is possible to indicate what the communists *would like* to accomplish as a result of government infiltration. No conclusions are to be drawn regarding their actual achievements. We shall be concerned here with nonrevolutionary situations, when the direct {220} political influence of the communists is relatively slight and there is no question of a bid for state power.

Espionage apart, the political utility of government infiltration is twofold: (1) to influence the actions of such special-public agencies as can, through the exercise of administrative discretion, give auxiliary support to the communist struggle for power among labor, youth, and similar publics; and (2) to influence specific decisions, especially on matters of less than central interest to the target government, which may help a communist faction abroad or may increase vulnerability to Soviet diplomacy. It is noteworthy that neither of these functions requires that communist agents in government act as propagandists. In the first area, the issues are always related to some specialized subject matter, such as labor relations. In

---

[48]   See below, pp. 261-274, regarding communist tactics in relation to government in pre-seizure situations.

the second, the issues are equally far removed from communism as such, having to do with immediate questions such as the recognition of alternative opposition groups in Spain or the honoring of a labor leader in Mexico. On the other hand, conspiracy is essential to the fulfillment of these political functions. The agents who assume these tasks must not resemble the communist stereotype, yet they must be dedicated to the party and subject to its discipline. Hence, although the overt acts of communist agents in government are not directly related to communism, they are indirectly so, and the exploitation of these incidental opportunities for furthering the cause is probably the primary rationale for infiltrating government offices.[49]

In exercising discretionary power, administrative officials often have the opportunity to choose from among alternative courses of action those having desired consequences for favored elements in the community. Every administrator qualifies his decisions, to some extent, by taking account of the incidental consequences of his acts for matters outside his formal responsibility but in which he has some special stake. Much of this bureaucratic deviation from the straight and narrow path of duty is trivial, but sometimes it is of grave consequence for the power structure. This is especially {221} true where there are contending forces bidding for leadership of a public (agriculture, labor) and where recognition by a government agency may influence the contest. If bias is systematic, the full potentialities of using government posts as organizational weapons may be realized.

It follows that the job of communist agents is not necessarily to foment "revolutionary action" as that is popularly conceived—and as it was understood by Lenin—but to use their positions in order to serve the immediate interests of the party and the USSR. For example, the main work of American communist soldiers during World War II was not to foment discontent but to gain positions useful to the international movement. In the army, communists gravitate to posts which have incidental political utility: they become, if they can, editors, political intelligence officers, and members of education units. In such posts, they may be more interested in foreign civilian populations than in influencing the troops. Propaganda efforts in these posts may have little to do with subversion of morale, as in the last war, when these efforts centered mainly on emphasizing friendship with the Soviet Union and implementing party-line goals, such as neutralizing sentiment against the Chinese communists. In this task, they were aided by the general sentiment expressing friendly feeling for a wartime ally. Similarly, communist infiltration of military government sought to influence policy affecting the fortunes of local communist parties. Although this influence was probably significant temporarily in isolated cases, these statements are not meant to suggest that any widespread success was achieved. Nor do they deny that communists may at times be interested in adversely affecting troop morale, as in the calls for quick demobilization in late 1945 and 1946.

We see, therefore, that a major utility of infiltrating government is to control the effect of its agencies on power alignments in the community. Such activity is by no means peculiar to communism, since the goal of much informal pressure

---

[49] In the United States, the most heavily infiltrated agencies have been those which could have but little espionage utility, some of the more important being in local government.

is to have discretionary power exercised in favor of special interests. But where most lobbies are primarily interested in short-run gains for a constituency, the {222} communist lobby is primarily interested in preparing the way for ultimate political advancement. Thus, if the communists should gain strength in the staff of a local relief agency, the strategy might well be to prepare the way for favoring a communist-led unemployed organization which would arise in case of a depression. In the meantime, apart from bolstering the position of the party in the agency, little activity directly related to the over-all aims of the party might be observable.

An illustration of the incidental value of infiltration is afforded by former Senator Robert M. La Follette, Jr.'s exposure of the work of procommunist elements in the staffs of congressional committees.[50] The utility of this penetration is twofold: (1) to gain access to confidential information and (2) to manipulate the committee hearings so as to favor the friends of the party and deprecate its enemies:

> In general, committee staffs participate in executive sessions and have access to committee files, which frequently include private documents which the committee has obtained under subpoena on recommendation of the staff. Unscrupulous employees can give out this information to friends, as a private spying system against their enemies, as an advance tip-off of committee thinking, or as a means of bringing pressure to bear where it might affect a desired course of action. . . .
>
> With regard to minimum wage and FEPC legislation, it is my personal conviction that the Communists and fellow travelers who lobbied on these bills preferred to get no bills at all. I learned after the completion of the Senate hearings on the minimum wage bill that hearing schedules had been rigged to the end that testimony from anti-communist sources on the bill was not taken, or else received merely as a statement for the record rather than as testimony before the committee.

Since normally only personal appearances at committee hearings receive attention in the press, the manipulation referred to is a means of undermining the influence of anticommunist groups in the community, whether or not such groups support the specific legislation {223} in question. It is a reliable symptom of the operation of a communist fraction that opportunities to neutralize anticommunist elements in the labor and liberal movements are fully exploited. If the bias of the staff members in question had been simply and innocently liberal, there would have been no reason for them to discriminate against anticommunist organizations seeking to testify in support of measures generally regarded as liberal.

Senator La Follette also reported on the technique of infiltrating these committee staffs. Given a base in some executive department, the procommunist individuals could have themselves "loaned out" to the committee, "without any direct lines of responsibility to either the Senate or to the government agency on whose payroll they are carried." This practice was later curbed by changes in the

---

[50] R. M. La Follette, Jr., "Turn the Light on Communism," *Colliers,* February 8, 1947.

Senate rules to require that committee personnel be on the congressional payroll. It indicates, however, the possibilities available in the systematic use of administrative loopholes for the effective deployment of party agents, both those over whom direct discipline can be maintained and those who can be counted on to "go along" with advice from party circles.

Whenever the government reaches out to organize the population, as for civilian defense activities, it must necessarily depend to a large extent on volunteer participation and local leadership. It may be expected that the communists, always sensitive to the opportunities mass mobilization presents, will seek to inject themselves into the system. Thus, during the war, the party attempted to gain access to the civilian defense organization by creating volunteer committees and then seeking recognition of these committees by the Office of Civilian Defense. If the administration of such an agency were politically unalert, these volunteer activities might be viewed as meritorious displays of civic virtue, with the result that communist-led groups might be appointed to act as plant guards in vital industries. Indeed, in one area, the communists proposed to create armed plant-protection squads under union control, with the avowed purpose of combating sabotage in the oil and steel industries.

A similar tactic, of absorbing local groups into government bodies, {224} was more vigorously applied in France where, in the Marseilles area (as reported in October, 1947), the state police reserves were rendered unreliable. This was the result of an agreement that 50 per cent of the new force would be recruited from former members of communist-dominated resistance groups and the other half from former members of the Mobile Guard. Of course, this is a phase of the attack on government with a view to its destruction. The attempt to penetrate civil defense organizations in the United States during World War II should be viewed as an effort to strengthen communist influence in the community. The point is that these functions are not mutually exclusive. When the party is weak, its goal in penetrating the government is to gain vantage points from which its influence can be extended. But the very same process of penetration, given party discipline, is useful for ultimate revolutionary objectives and for sabotage.

It is only when we perceive the utility of government infiltration for day-to-day political objectives of the party that the penetration of institutions which have little sabotage utility, by a group which has no hope of revolutionary action in the foreseeable future, can be understood. Pressure-group activities, aimed at building communist strength among specific publics served by government agencies, do not preclude direct efforts at espionage, sabotage, or ultimate disruption of government itself. But undue attention to the latter may lead to an unnecessarily distorted emphasis. Matters of immediate importance may be ignored in the search for evidences of dramatic "revolutionary" activity.

CHAPTER 5
DEFENSIVE STRATEGIES

{225}
We shall now consider two patterns of action designed to increase the utility of organizational weapons by (1) warding off threats to the immediate source of power and (2) providing acceptable covers to conceal the use of organizations as subversive weapons. These patterns may be referred to as the strategies of neutralization and of legitimacy.

Neutralization of Threats to the Social Base

The Marxian theory of the class struggle, with its broad historical perspective, its vision of the unfolding of objective social forces, would seem to lend a sense of community to the various anticapitalist proletarian movements. This was indeed the case, before the full meaning of Leninism was writ large in history. It was, as we have seen, the basis for early versions of the united-front tactic. Marxism fostered a dedication to class aims, a radical split in the national communities, which sought to focus loyalty on workers' institutions and withdraw it from established governments. In fact, however, and especially since the Russian revolution, factional strife among the working-class parties has been bitter and violent. The reasons for the struggle are not difficult to see, and they provide a rationale for the bolshevik tactics to be considered here.

Controversy among left-wing groups is often thought of as fratricidal, but the use of this term is more deceptive than discerning. To speak of a conflict among brothers may suggest that however bitter the internal battle there exists a basic unity against the outside world. But between the communists and the social democrats there is a division so marked that, as the pattern is emerging today, they represent sharply opposed political conceptions. The basic characters {226} of these movements, as laid down in effective goals and established methods, are radically divergent. The modern social democrat—as represented in the United States by a Norman Thomas—chooses the capitalist rather than the communist when the alternatives are, for him, harshly posed. The most serious errors may result from a failure to take note of this divergence, e.g., in supposing that the social-democratic program of the British Labor Party would lead it into the communist political orbit.

Nevertheless, this *caveat* being accepted, it is certainly true that the struggle among the communists and their left-wing opponents has a special meaning. In the first place, there is the matter of origin; they share a common history, and surely some of the bitterness is due to the wish of each to safeguard this history from desecration. This is not merely a matter of words—even Hitler attempted to capture the term "socialist"—but of concrete traditions, of the quest to be a legitimate offspring of an honored father. Secondly, there are common targets and an overlapping of goals, as in the nationalization of industry, as well as undeniable convergences in ideology. These convergences have become decreasingly important as the noncommunist left has underlined its allegiance to political democracy and explicitly repudiated bolshevik totalitarianism. But they remain as sources of confusion and vulnerability, producing recurrent crises in the socialist parties.

But common origin and superficially similar aims do not of themselves constitute a serious threat to the communists. Indeed, it is probably the socialists who suffer most from this historical identification, for the communists have been very successful in kidnapping and subverting prestigeful symbols. What is really urgent is that the other left-wing movements *compete for the same social base* as do the communists. This base has in recent years been broadened to include middle-class liberals, but it does not encompass the whole of society. A political movement seeks out sources of power that can give it an indispensable leverage and thus permit it to intervene in the arena where great events are decided. To protect its relation to this social lever, to find a hold and tighten its grasp upon it, {227} becomes for the communists a primary task. It is here that the party is most vulnerable, for without its base it is nothing. He who can expose the party before the *relevant* public—the labor movement and liberal opinion—is therefore its main and intolerable enemy.

This is not a matter of emotional response but of the hard coin of politics. Programmatically, the communists may declare that the "bankers and bosses" or the "imperialists" are the enemy. But these forces do not challenge the communists at the source of power; they do not compete for the leadership of unions, they do not make appeals for the goodwill of liberal intellectuals, and above all they are not equipped to expose the communists as corrupters of the very ideals they claim to represent. The communists can compromise with the "class enemy," they can even support him, but they dare not tolerate the political existence of those who may offer the target groups an alternative ideological leadership or who can effectively expose the totalitarian practices of bolshevism in power. To be able to expose is not merely to know but to speak with authority, and only those who can appeal to workers and liberals in their own terms can gain a hearing.

The communists in power after their coup in Russia had little to fear from procapitalist propaganda, but they were much afraid of those who spoke with authority in the name of the ideals of the revolution. When the opposition at Kronstadt demanded revitalization of the Soviets, this was not a call for return to capitalism, but it was a far more potent subversion, It challenged the bolsheviks to put into practice what they themselves had demanded; so too with the anarchists, social revolutionaries, and mensheviks whose parties were liquidated; so also with the Workers Opposition and other inner-party groups which criticized the party regime. These elements were intolerable because they threatened the basis of communist power; they appealed to the same public, in the name of the same ideals.

Similarly, noncommunist leftists in a union are a far more urgent threat than the employers; the worker may discount the latter's accusations but heed those of fellow unionists. Moreover, the employer {228} does not usually offer an alternative leadership, whereas the inner-union opposition will do so. So too, frontal attacks by procapitalists on socialism as it exists in Russia are of little concern to the communists. They do not spend much time refuting such arguments. But when the social system in the USSR is attacked in *the name of* socialism or of labor or of "progressive" ideals, then there is a threat indeed. Those who are unfriendly to all labor organizations will not be effective, among unionists, in criticizing the Soviet trade-unions. But when a man identified with sacrifice to labor's cause returns from the USSR to record his disillusions, then every effort must be made to discredit the attacker. For he may reach and influence precisely those groups whom the communists hope to manipulate.

The elite that competes with the communists for control of a social base will naturally have something in common with them. The nature of the target group itself must determine that. This would be true regardless of such convergences as common origin or collectivist ideology. Catholics functioning in the Labor movement must make their bid for leadership in working-class terms and must be careful to avoid identifications that will compromise them in the eyes of the membership. All contenders for power molded by the same arena will have many things in common despite fundamental divergences in outlook and aim. A communist labor leader is still a labor leader. In a union, the battlefield itself enforces convergences, as when all contenders work together in a strike; but in the struggle for control of the spirit of the organization—its fundamental loyalties and aspirations and the community with which it will be identified—the fundamental cleavages emerge.

A common interpretation of left-wing conflict is expressed in such comments as the following: "The political enemies most feared by the SED are . . . the recalcitrant Social Democrats, who have been forbidden to reorganize their party in the Soviet Zone. As always, heresy is more hated and feared than opposition." This poses the problem as one of emotional response, implying that the communists would be more rational if they concentrated their fire on the conservative parties. In fact, however, "hatred of heresy" plays only a {229} minimal role in the attitude of communists toward social democrats. That emotional components are involved is not to be doubted, but the real issue is practical, and there is nothing irrational about communist concentration upon social democrats as the main target. The communist editors do not have to convince their readers that the conservatives are bad, but they do have to steel their ranks and their periphery against the possible inroads of the social democrats. The conservatives do not challenge communist power in the Berlin trade-union federation, but the socialists do. The day-to-day task of political combat is, for the communists, one of gaining control of target groups in competition with the noncommunist left. It is this and not emotional response that determines the content of the communist press.

Neutralization strategy concentrates upon (1) those who can threaten the integrity of the combat party itself by winning over its cadres; this is part of the rationale underlying the great party purges, and helps to explain the virulence of attack upon Titoism and Trotskyism; (2) those who threaten the party in the arenas of action, who compete with it for control over target groups and institutions.

The tactics useful for fulfilling these strategic aims include: (1) destruction of rival organizations through infiltration and disruption; (2) suppression of left-wing anticommunism by means of bureaucratic infiltration of publishing houses, cinema studios, and similar vantage points which may not permit open procommunist activity but do allow the neutralization of effective anticommunist work; (3) the *informal veto,* which permits the canceling out of strong anticommunists by retiring open procommunists in target arenas; and (4) the use of terror.

The immediate source of power for a communist leadership is its own rank and file, its cadres. This explains why the most violent means, including assassination, have been used against the Trotskyists, and why Tito's defection is so urgent a problem for the Moscow regime. Trotskyists, especially during most of their early history, and Titoists, gain recruits from the ranks of the communists themselves. In doing so, they attack the leadership where it hurts the {230} most, the precious vanguard of the vanguard, the indispensable source of organizational power. The intensity of the bitterness, and the willingness to use extreme forms of terror, varies directly with the immediacy of the threat to the party's power base. This includes, in the first instance, its own cadres. The effectiveness of this threat is also directly related to the intimate personal and political knowledge of the party and its leadership possessed by these opponents. The Trotskyists have always been the most effective exposers of the official communists, although not of communism, since they adhere to bolshevik principles and have assiduously obscured the totalitarian aspects of the pre-Stalinist Soviet regime. Similarly, Tito's break, and the potentialities of opposition developing from within the Russian party, carry the same threat.

The communist image of their social-democratic opponents is highly specific, and is expressed in the terms of a technical doctrine. A recent definition, offered to students at a Socialist Unity Party training school in Germany, indicates the continuity of bolshevik views on this subject with Lenin's formulation of a generation ago:

> *Social Democracy*—A policy of compromise with the bourgeoisie and subordination of the interests of the working class to those of the bourgeoisie. Social democracy is the ideology of the agents of the bourgeoisie within the labor movement. It involves continuing and deepening the split in the working class, and the effort to spread doubt among the workers as to their own power and as to the possibility and inevitability of their victory. . . .[1]

The attitude of the communists toward social democrats harbors an animus which does not extend to liberals and others who presumably, in Marxist doctrine, support the status quo. The crucial point is that "social democracy is the ideology . . . of the bourgeoisie within the labor movement." The socialists offer an alternative

---

[1] From *Telegraf,* "a Berlin newspaper usually favoring the Social Democrats"; quoted in W. P. Davison, "The Organization of Power in the Soviet Zone of Germany," unpublished MS, 1947. The quality of "unity" represented in the SED—the product of a forced merger of the social-democratic and communist parties in the Soviet Zone—would be clear from this if from nothing else.

leadership to the workers; they are always enemies in political combat. The liberals, on the other hand, whatever their historic role, are not so {231} directly tied to a specific social base and hence are not directly in competition with the communists; they themselves can be manipulated if proper organizational controls are established. Therefore it is always necessary, in interpreting communism, to keep in mind the concrete conditions of political struggle and to avoid reliance on the logical implications of general Marxist principles. The principles are always applied selectively, depending on the needs of the immediate situation. Liberals in the mass will not be thought of as agents of the class enemy; but anticommunist liberals functioning as an elite group will always be so designated. The same thing is true for the social-democratic ranks as contrasted with their leaders. This process of applying principles selectively, qualified by the urgencies of combat, is known in the Marxist movement as "thinking dialectically."

In the neutralization of competing leadership groups—of whom, historically, the socialists have been the most important—the main strategic goal is their organizational and ideological annihilation. In his exceptionally frank discussion, Cannon makes the bolshevik position clear:

> Partly as a result of our experience in the Socialist Party and our fight in there, the SP was put on the sidelines. This was a great achievement, because it was an obstacle on the path of building a revolutionary party. The problem is not merely one of building a revolutionary party, but of clearing obstacles from its path. Every other party is a rival. Every other party is an obstacle.[2]

This is true, of course, for all rivals, regardless of their political complexion. Even an organization very close to the bolsheviks in program would be marked for destruction because, competing in the same arena, it would be bidding for the limited number of individuals who can become effective cadres. The bolshevik objective is power for a specific party, and this means that it is all-important under whose leadership the trade-union militants fall. The existence of rival organizations is only tolerable when the drive to power {232} is inhibited, when considerations of program are given priority over organizational aggrandizement.

The task of destroying a rival organization is one to which the organizational maneuverability of the cadre party is especially adapted. The target is penetrated and a communist fraction is established. This group then foments a factional struggle which ultimately leads to a split, the communist fraction leaving and taking with it a small number of individuals who have been won over. In the meantime, as a consequence of the internal conflict, a large number of members will have left, repelled by the atmosphere of bitter contention. In addition, the target organization will have had to turn its face inward for some time, will have become confused, disoriented, and divided. Unity tactics may also be employed, the communist fraction calling for a united front, pressing an issue which will further divide the socialist target. This is briefly the history of the Socialist Party

---

[2] J. P. Cannon, *History of American Trotskyism*, Pioneer Publications, Inc., New York, 1944, p. 252.

in the United States, which was attacked and decimated, first by the official communists and then by the Trotskyists. These attacks were, of course, not the only reason for the decline in the influence of this party, but they helped materially to effectuate splits, defections, and ideological confusion. The attacks were planned like military assaults, with disciplined agents, continuous leadership, and definite objectives. The latter were mainly two: to win over a few hundred politically trained individuals who could become bolshevik cadres, and to destroy an organizational rival. It is especially pertinent that neither the communists nor the Trotskyists (both bolshevik in method) sought to *capture* the socialist organization. They hoped only to salvage something from the wreckage and to remove an obstacle, an alternative center for the organization of radicals, a competing elite among labor and liberal publics.

The cynical willingness to annihilate organizational rivals was most dramatically revealed in the response of the Russians to the Warsaw rising of August-October, 1944. During that period, after calls by the Russians for revolt against the Germans, and upon the Red Army's penetration to within ten miles of the city's eastern {233} suburbs, supporters of the London Government-in-Exile under General Bor-Komorowski succeeded in capturing a large part of the city. But the Russians were opposed to this government, sponsoring their own Lublin Committee instead. They apparently decided to permit the extermination of Bor and his followers rather than to suffer the increased prestige which would have accrued to the London government had Bor been successful. The Red Army by-passed Warsaw and made no strong effort to help the underground forces or to capture the city; Bor was attacked as a "criminal"; and even efforts by the Allies to aid the besieged rebels from the air were forestalled by Soviet refusal to grant them permission to land in Russia. As a result, the Germans had ample time to destroy Bor's forces. The London Government's most important hope for legitimacy and strength—victorious forces inside Poland—was effectively removed.

Apart from direct political combat with competing elites for control of the social base, the communists must attempt to neutralize attacks upon the party from any source. Since deception has become the keynote of communist activity, a large amount of effort must be expended to avoid exposure. This too requires major concentration upon the left-wing opponents of the party, for they are in the best position to conduct the kind of exposure which is most harmful. Benjamin Gitlow's story of the role of the anarchist leader, Carlo Tresca, offers a striking example.[3]

Tresca was a leading antifascist and had some influence among Italian-Americans. After the communist attack upon the anarchist organizations in Spain during the civil war, he devoted himself to exposing the communist underground, including the OGPU, with which (according to Gitlow) he had earlier had some contacts. Tresca interested himself in the disappearance of Juliet Stuart Poyntz, reputed to have been an OGPU agent, and then found an opportunity to frustrate communist intervention in a specific {234} organizational arena, the government-sponsored Italian-American Victory Council:

---

[3] Benjamin Gitlow, *The Whole of Their Lives,* Charles Scribner's Sons, New York, 1948, p. 339*f.*

The Council, to the communists, was of such great importance that orders were transmitted to the Communist party to do everything possible to capture it. But Carlo Tresca stood in their way. The Mazzini Society, the leading organization of Italian antifascists, due to Tresca's pressure, had previously, in principle, adopted the policy of excluding all totalitarian and fascist elements from the society. Now Tresca, who successfully had excluded them from the Mazzini Society, took up the fight to exclude both the Italian ex-fascists in America and the communists from the OWI Italian-American Victory Council.

Officials of the Office of War Information fought for their inclusion, but in Tresca's opposition they had an obstacle which they found difficult to overcome, for Tresca hurled damaging accusations, backed up by facts, against the communists and the ex-fascists parading as the champions of democracy.

The communist world superstructure was determined to capture the Italian-American Victory Council, for not only Italy was involved but the European continent, and Stalin's ambitions for world expansion. Moscow rounded up Italian communist agents by the hundreds and shipped them to the United States. The Comintern Rep demanded that the American Communist party settle its score with Tresca on the Poyntz case and on all other matters. The OGPU claimed he had abused their confidence and had treacherously double-crossed them.[4]

Shortly thereafter, Tresca was mysteriously assassinated, possibly by fascist rather than communist agents. However that may be, in his activities of exposure and political opposition, Tresca was at the time a far more dangerous enemy of the communists than was the "capitalist" government of the United States.

The attempt to neutralize anticommunism explains much party activity that is otherwise of doubtful utility. Thus the propaganda role of the communists in the motion picture industry—other functions, such as fund-raising, have probably been more important—has {235} been not so much to get procommunist ideas on the screen as to keep anticommunist propaganda off. Dalton Trumbo's "defense" of Hollywood in the communist press is revealing in this connection:

> We have produced a few fine films in Hollywood, a great many of which were vulgar and opportunistic and a few downright vicious. If you tell me Hollywood, in contract with the novel and the theatre, has produced nothing so provocative or so progressive as *Freedom Road* or *Deep Are the Roots,* I will grant you the point, but I may also add that neither has Hollywood produced anything so untrue or so reactionary as *The Yogi and the Commissar, Out of the Night, Report on the Russians, There Shall Be No Night,* or *Adventures of a Young Man.* Nor does Hollywood's forthcoming

---

[4] *Ibid.,* p. 340. Gitlow does not cite the evidence for his statements, but his story is consistent with the known facts of communist practice. The importance to the communists of control of the organizations of European immigrants and their descendants was discussed above, pp. 116-117.

schedule include such tempting items as James T. Farrell's *Bernard Clare,*
Victor Kravchenko's *I Chose Freedom,* or the so-called biography of Stalin
by Leon Trotsky.[5]

These "reactionary" items are all anticommunist works, most of them by members or ex-members of radical organizations. The filming of these books would be
a blow to the party, especially among liberals. (Protection of the social base is still
central.) Similarly, the production of *Mission to Moscow,* with its apology for the
Moscow trials, was a great help to the party because it assisted in shielding a most
vulnerable spot, one to which the liberal public was especially sensitive.

One of the most important tactics in neutralization strategy is the *informal
veto.* The communists are primarily interested in creating an atmosphere per-
missive of their intervention in labor and liberal organizations. This does not
presume the open espousal of communism, but it does require the suppression
of explicitly anticommunist activity in those circles. The answer is simple, but effective. If a debate is to be arranged, the communists will avoid asking for open
procommunists and use this as a basis for protesting the invitation of explicit
anticommunists. This tactic is predicated on conspiracy and deception. The communists and sympathizers appear as reasonable and restrained men who merely
"call into question" certain basic notions, who ask that "judgment be suspended"
on the Moscow {236} trials or on the Lysenko affair, and who suggest that criticism of Soviet totalitarianism does not serve the interests of peace. In this way,
the intellectual and moral principles of the target audience are undermined, and
open anticommunists can be labeled as fanatics who see grave danger where only
mild criticism is apparent. This helps to neutralize the anticommunists, who must
themselves often restrain attack, or formulate it in oblique ways, in order to avoid
isolation from the group.

The informal veto is a useful by-product of unity, where the threat of withdrawal can be used to suppress anticommunist criticism and to isolate leading
opponents of the party and of the Soviet Union. Once communists are admitted
into broader organizations, it becomes necessary, as a condition of unity, to limit
forthright criticism of matters deemed crucial to the communists. Criticism of
communism as a theoretical social system is not a serious threat, but exposures of
the conspiratorial nature of the party, the Moscow trials, or Soviet foreign policy
must be restrained. Hence unity for specific objectives is made to result in a more
widespread capitulation.

The neutralization of opposition elements finds its ultimate expression in
the use of terror. This includes assassination, defamation of character, and violent denial of rights of assembly in addition, of course, to measures available to
communist-controlled governments. In this connection, we need emphasize only
two points here: the relation of communism to individual acts of terror, and the
role of nonviolent terror.

A superficial sophistication in relation to communism sometimes leads to the
assertion that the bolsheviks are opposed to acts of terror, such as assassination.
It is true that Lenin, Trotsky, and others were opposed to episodic and unplanned

---

[5]   Dalton Trumbo, "Getting Hollywood into Focus," *The Worker,* May 5, 1946.

use of these means and to reliance on them as a substitute for mass action. But they had no moral objections to them and were willing to use them if they were coordinated with the general strategy of the party. Trotsky's defense of the Red Terror is in point:

> *Intimidation* is a powerful weapon of policy, both internationally and internally. War, like revolution, is founded upon intimidation. {237} A victorious war, generally speaking, destroys only an insignificant part of the conquered army, intimidating the remainder and breaking their will. . . . The revolution works in the same way: it kills individuals and intimidates thousands. In this sense, the Red Terror is not distinguishable from the armed insurrection, the direct continuation of which it represents.[6]

And on the moral issue:

> If it is a question of seeking formal contradictions, then obviously we must do so on the side of the White Terror, which is the weapon of classes which consider themselves "Christians." As for us, we were never concerned with the Kantian-priestly and vegetarian-Quaker prattle about the "sacredness of human life." We were revolutionaries in opposition, and have remained revolutionaries in power. To make the individual sacred we must destroy the social order which crucifies him. And this problem can only be solved by blood and iron.[7]

Lenin himself is even more explicit:

> "Killing is no murder" our old "Iskra" [No. 20] said about terroristic acts. We *do not at all oppose* political killing (in this sense, the servile written statements of the Opportunists in "Vorwaerts" and the Vienna "Arbeiter Zeitung" are simply revolting), but as revolutionary tactics, individual attempts are both impractical and harmful. It is only a mass movement that can be considered a real political struggle. Individual terroristic acts can be, and must be, helpful, only when they are directly linked with the mass movement.[8] [Emphasis in original]

Thus it is only anarchic terrorism which is repudiated. Bolshevik acts of terror are, of course, always "linked to the mass movement" when conducted under the aegis of party discipline.

The communists have been willing to use contrived riots to deny the right of opposition groups to meet. This is not simply a matter of antifascist activity, but of attempts to intimidate other left-wing organizations. Thus in the early days of the Trotskyist movement in {238} the United States, the official communists

---

[6] L. Trotsky, *The Defense of Terrorism*, George Allen & Unwin, Ltd., London, 1935, p. 55.

[7] *Ibid.*, p. 60.

[8] E. Hill and D. Mudie (eds.), *The Leasers of Lenin*, Harcourt, Brace and Company, Inc., New York, 1937, p. 401.

attempted to break up the gatherings of this new and threatening tendency, long before Trotsky was denounced as a "fascist." A large socialist meeting at Madison Square Garden was turned into a riot by the communists in February, 1934. And as late as 1944 the communists attempted to disrupt a pacifist meeting, addressed by a socialist leader and held under Quaker auspices. Activities of this sort have been episodic, apart from direct bids for state power, but they indicate the willingness of the party to attempt to eliminate oppositionist elements by any means, including direct efforts to deny them the streets.

Of special interest here, because it is less obvious and more readily used in organizational tactics, is nonviolent terror. This is "intimidation of the word," often more effective than violence against psychologically vulnerable individuals. The importance of terms of opprobrium for terrorization is extraordinary. This is not only the case in political struggle prior to seizure of power, but also after the establishment of the terror regime itself. Individuals can be effectively isolated by attaching some of the key "public enemy" labels to them. Characterization by such labels is an effective means of outlawing selected persons and intimidating their potential co-thinkers.

Lenin understood the utility of conscious attempts to discredit competing leaders before the public to which they are committed, and he defended his use of political calumny with no apology. In 1907, while the bolsheviks and mensheviks were still wings of the Russian social democracy, Lenin was tried by a party tribunal for slander against a group of menshevik leaders. According to David Shub's account, "Lenin admitted that he had slandered the Menshevik leaders but claimed that he was right in resorting to calumny, in order to discredit the Menshevik policies before the masses."[9] His own analysis of the polemic reveals the high self-consciousness which guided his action:

> I purposely chose that tone calculated to evoke in the hearer hatred, disgust, and contempt for the people who carry on such tactics. That tone, that formulation is not designed to convince, {239} but to break the ranks, not to correct a mistake of the opponent but to annihilate him, to wipe him off the face of the earth. Indeed that approach evokes the worst thoughts and suspicions against the opponent, and, it is true, instead of convincing and correcting, introduces confusion into the ranks of the working class.
>
> It is not permissible to write about party comrades in a language that systematically sows hatred, repugnance, and contempt among the workers to those that think differently from us. It is *permissible* and it *is imperative* to write in such a language about an organization that splits off . . . I am told: "You introduced confusion in the ranks of the working class." My answer is: "I purposely and calculatingly introduced confusion in the ranks of a part of the St Petersburg proletariat that followed the splitting Mensheviks and I will always act the same way during a split."[10]

Here Lenin was discussing not strikebreakers or spies, but right-wing social-

---

[9] David Shub, *Lenin: A Biography,* Doubleday & Company, New York, 1948, p. 93.
[10] Quoted in Shub, *ibid.*

ists who wished to support liberal candidates in order to forestall the victory of elements they considered reactionary. For Lenin, there was no line to be drawn between the literal traitor and the political opponents who espoused policies he thought ruinous. This attitude has been the basis of bolshevik aggression against other left-wing parties ever since.

Since Lenin himself did not feel that his own policies were sacred, and often changed tactics as the situation demanded, it is unlikely that he really believed that incorrect policy, as such, was an adequate basis for the charge of treason. Rather, as he says in the passage quoted above, the criterion is organizational: He consciously stimulated hatred and repugnance against "an organization that splits off." In other words, the group that now becomes a competitor for power among the workers is a legitimate target for slanderous attack.

In fact, of course, Lenin's injunction about the use of "comradely language" within the party was not long sustained after the establishment of the independent communist organizations. Polemics among the bolsheviks have been infused with a tone of bitterness and calculated evocation of hatred and contempt which seems incredible to the outside observer. This is sometimes explained, not without foundation, {240} by the deep psychological commitment which characterizes the bolshevik relation to ideas, especially to strategic and tactical doctrine. However, a factor of at least equal importance is discernible from the analysis presented above of the extension of elite-mass relations into the party itself. A break in the ranks of the party leadership means (or meant before arbitrary control through expulsion and arrest was established) competition for influence among the party "masses." This brings into play all the established techniques for annihilating a leader and confusing his followers.

From the use of *political* calumny—"Ehrlich and Alter were agents of Hitler"— the transition to *personal* slander is not difficult. There have been many reports of calculated defamation used against opponents of the party and of attempts to intimidate individuals by bringing to bear the intense social pressure of his immediate circle. Many naive people believe that they are being courageous when they "stand up against the world" and incur the wrath of remote and impersonal enemies while accepting the warm sympathy and encouragement of their friends. In fact, of course, conformity is relative to the specific social environment of the individual: it may be entirely nonconformist to be procapitalist in a milieu, however deviant, which is peopled by radicals. By the same token, it is the anger and contempt of those individuals and groups who constitute the individual's effective community that are decisive in social control. This was formalized in the 1938 constitution of the American party, which forbade *personal* or political relationships with "Trotskyists, Lovestoneites, or other known enemies of the party and the working class." Since the Trotskyist label is used without much discrimination, this provision had the consequence of threatening those who would leave the party with social ostracism. To quit would mean to need a new personal as well as political existence. This, it will be noted, is not intended to prevent association with capitalists or other formal enemies as defined in the program of the party, but to insulate the membership against corrosive influences within the left-wing movement and to intimidate defectors.

This extreme case reflects the urgency of threats to the immediate {241} source of power, the party ranks. But defamation is more generally useful. In an affidavit published by the California un-American activities committee, a former party member testified regarding the use of slander against opponents in the unions:

> . . . I wish to cite an instance typical of the manner in which the Communist Party retains control of unions; [F.A.], a member of the publicity staff of the Federal Theatre Project, took an active part in the organization of this union, but she opposed the election of [F.F.] as president. Inasmuch as he was the Communist Party choice it was necessary for every Communist to put forth all effort to elect him and to elevate him in prestige with the project workers, therefore [F.A.'s] opposition was given serious consideration by the Communist Party's fraction, aforementioned; it was the fraction decision, and therefore binding upon every Communist Party member in that union, to utilize a process of discrediting her in the eyes of all project coworkers, and the community at large; the Communists announced, by decision of said fraction, that they would "isolate, expose and expel" [F.A.], as an "enemy of the working class"; a plan of malicious gossip was devised; we Communists were to tell everyone who would listen that [F.A.] was "mentally and emotionally unstable, that she was a sexual pervert, and that she was in the pay of the Merchants and Manufacturers' Association." As planned, our gossip brought her near the point of nervous collapse; other Communist forces caused her dismissal from her position on the project, and with each outbreak of hers against what she felt to be injustice, we derided her for "hysteria"; until at last few project workers would listen to her stories. . . .
>
> . . . this fiendish calculation to destroy the reputation, the mind and the ability of a person to make a living revolted me and preyed upon my mind, and I remonstrated privately with [L.M.] for instigating, sanctioning and even compelling other Communist Party members to indulge in that inhuman practice; [L.M.] merely laughed at me and stated, "We must destroy our enemies by whatever method we can; we must regard *a lie* as a tactical maneuver." She went on to state that, according to official teachings of the Communist Party, that Communist work was to be conducted as a war, and that "all was fair" in war.[11]

{242} The actual use of organized calumny against open enemies of the party is of course important, but the threat is perhaps equally effective. Defamation may affect a man's influence, as in the case cited above, but the fear of it may also restrain opposition where it might otherwise appear. Individuals who are vulnerable to such charges as "reactionary," "fascist," "Trotskyist," etc., will often remain silent, even though outside the party, for fear they will be forced to endure a long period of unpleasantness and the suspicion of their friends, to say nothing of the generally repugnant label, "informer." There are a number of ex-leaders of

---

[11]   "Affidavit of Rena M. Vale," *Report,* Joint Fact-Finding Committee on Un-American Activities in California, California Legislature, 55th sess., Sacramento, 1943, p. 136*f.*

the party who have remained silent, although there is no doubt of a basic shift in their political views. Many more, of lesser importance, have chosen to avoid the usually unfavorable publicity which comes to those who attack and expose the party. By a full and systematic exploitation of the social pressure which restrains these individuals, the party is able to neutralize many potential enemies. The party relies heavily on the tendency of people to believe that "where there's smoke there's fire." This practice is akin to the promulgation of the "big lie," a major tool of modern demagogy.

The Search for Legitimacy

The rule is: those who wield power must establish their right to do so. This is not a pious wish, or a peculiarly democratic canon, but a general political necessity. Every ruling group that presumes to gather prerogatives for itself, or to inflict deprivations on others, must identify itself with a principle acceptable to the community as justification for the exercise of power. Such doctrinal tenets are known as principles of legitimacy. Their function is to establish authority as distinct from naked power. A rule is based on authority when most of those who are supposed to obey do so willingly and need not be coerced. This implies that a principle is recognized which states why the rulers are *entitled* to rule. All rulers, whether traditional, democratic, or totalitarian, need such a principle of legitimacy in order to reduce their dependence on naked power. In {243} this sense, to speak of hereditary monarchy as legitimate rule (or illegitimate) implies no moral judgment. It is merely an assertion of fact which, given known theory, establishes an antecedent probability that certain types of power will be effectively maintained or easily overthrown.

Hereditary succession and majority rule are obvious examples of monarchical and democratic principles of legitimacy. Similarly, diplomatic recognition by key foreign powers helps to legitimize power won in a coup d' etat. Less obvious is the traditional (but now insecure) principle which asserts the right of a conqueror to demand the peaceful submission and minimal collaboration of civilian populations. When this principle is accepted, military occupation of enemy territory is peaceful, dependent only on the outcome of the war as decided on recognized fields of combat. When the principle is rejected. the result may be guerrilla warfare, sabotage, and the repudiation of collaboration as criminal. During World War II, the practice of mass treason (Quislingism) to facilitate enemy conquest, and the importance of ideology, did much to undermine the traditional rules which sanctioned the exercise of authority won by conquest. The revision of traditional concepts has culminated in the attempt, only partially successful, to stamp as illegitimate all gains won as a result of aggressive warfare. Although this effort is related to moral choice, its success depends on what people actually believe and hence also on the empirical consequences of relying on the new principle in action. The identification of what *ought to be* legitimate has scientific and moral components, but the question of what *is* legitimate can be settled on the basis of purely scientific conclusions.

The problem of legitimacy accompanies power wherever it is manifested; it is not associated with formal institutions of government only. Thus the leaders of great industrial corporations have traditionally justified the power accumulated in their hands on the theory that they represent individual stockholders who have the right to delegate the prerogatives of property ownership. But with the radical bifurcation of ownership and control, and the concomitant {244} rise of self-perpetuating financial-managerial oligarchies, the traditional justification has lost much of its respect in the community. As a result, it has been suggested, there is insecurity among the power-wielders and a need to base themselves on some new doctrine, such as public service.[12] Similarly authority exercised in church, trade-union, and family relations must look to its stability; in doing so, the selection and propagation of principles of legitimacy is vitally relevant.

The *striving* for power must also be justified, not less than power already held. Great social overturns must, in the end, rely on victory itself as a source of legitimacy; but the advocacy of revolutions may be aided if the right to revolt, as in the Jeffersonian formula, is accepted by the community. So too does the attempt to link present change-seekers to revered national heroes, and to brand existing rulers as betrayers or corrupters of tradition, assert the legitimacy of political assault.

Turning to our special subject matter, it will be noted that the following discussion of the strategy of legitimacy points to a combination of organizational and propaganda devices. Indeed, propaganda may play the major role. However, in this context propaganda serves the primary function of increasing the utility of conspiratorial organizational practices and hence is properly thought of as tactically related to an organizational strategy. The objective of such propaganda is not to spread communist symbols, but simply to create an atmosphere conducive to the free use of the combat party and its agencies. Similarly, we speak of the organizational relevance of ideology when it performs internally oriented morale functions.

In Lenin's time, communist doctrine made few concessions to the need for historic grace, with respect to the population at large, but it was very much concerned with establishing its legitimacy as the heir of Marxism. Lenin's writings are replete with efforts to identify his thought with that of the master and to claim for bolshevism the role of true spokesman for the Russian social democracy. At its {245} founding, the Communist International was proclaimed the "true successor" of Marx's First International. In building a new movement out of an old one, Lenin was primarily interested in the radical public: it was out of workers and intellectuals who had already been influenced by socialism that he planned to forge his party of revolutionary cadres. His struggle for power was carried on *within* the Marxist movement. Therefore he was interested in justifying that struggle in Marxist terms, by invoking symbols influential among radicalized elements of the population. This looking inward helps us to understand Lenin's disregard for the established sources of legitimacy in that great outer darkness which he thought of as "bourgeois society."[13]

---

[12]   See Peter F. Drucker, *The Failure of Industrial Man,* The John Day Company, New York, 1942.

[13]   In addition, of course, "bourgeois" principles of legitimacy were rejected as a sham, to which the *activist* principle was to be counterposed. The point here is that the conditions

It is important to bear in mind that there is no long history of struggle by the bolsheviks in the broad arena of Russian politics. Lenin's was a party recruited from the social democracy and catapulted out of obscurity to the heights of power by social crisis and political vacuum. Apart from the brief period which culminated in the October coup, the Russian bolsheviks waged political combat in a highly restricted arena. Even the coup itself was directed against the socialists and liberals. The bolsheviks, by single-minded dedication {246} to the pursuit of power for themselves, reaped the harvest which had actually been sown by the liberal-proletarian-agrarian coalition which overthrew the Tsar. The problem of legitimacy was therefore limited to the justification of attack upon the social democracy in the name of Marx, and, almost immediately, to the ideological defense of the regime which arose from the coup d'état and weathered the civil war.

For some years after the Russian overturn, the face of the communist movement abroad continued to be turned toward the socialists, with the victory of the Russians playing a large role in establishing the legitimacy of the communists within the radical movement. In addition, the very struggle to define the character of the new International, as against the reformist socialists, pressed the Leninists to emphasize their revolutionary slogans, even at the price of isolation. Thus for a long period international communism, like the Russian bolsheviks before World War I, ignored the problem of legitimizing its quest for power in the eyes of society as a whole; it could do so because in fact it was not an effective participant in the power struggles of that larger arena.

But the communists outside Russia were unable to find their way to a quick October. After fifteen years of fiery manifestoes and internal preoccupation, the movement began to give serious consideration to problems of legitimacy. The possibility of direct competition with the established "bourgeois" parties emphasized the usefulness of gaining acceptance as legitimate participants in the democratic process so that publicity, a place on the ballot, and other advantages might be gained. Even more important, problems of legitimacy became especially pressing as dependence on organizational weapons increased, for the latter required acceptance in the community as a primary condition for effectiveness. Whereas Lenin

---

of the arena affect the choice of those principles that are to be set forth in propaganda. In analyzing communism, a distinction should be made between (1) the principle of legitimacy which bolshevism hopes to have accepted in the community and (2) the principles of legitimacy which are now accepted in the arena and to which the party must give at least verbal adherence in order to gain its needed entree. One goal will be to corrupt presently held principles so that the target groups come in fact to accept the bolshevik conception of legitimacy. The characteristically *bolshevik* claim to rule is activist-terrorist: we were the ones who mobilized and led revolutionary (terrorist) action against a bad (usurping) leadership; we drove out the Germans; we were the best resisters, etc. Authority is claimed on the basis of action. This extends to the typical effort of the communist fraction in a mass organization to have all decisions made by those who attend meetings rather than by referenda, which would include the non-activist members in decision making. The usual argument (congenial to the communists but not theirs alone) is that these non-attenders abdicate their rights by not taking an active part in the organization. Similarly, Lenin's concept of a "majority" of workers was, in practice, one of an *effective* majority, based on an estimate of those who could affect the coup d'état. Lenin could not accept the idea that "mere counting" or "parliamentary mathematics" could play any decisive role, or be permitted to do so.

had developed conspiratorial methods to be used primarily (but not exclusively) under conditions of autocratic rule, his successors perfected his methods for use in democratic contexts. As reliance on conspiracy more and more supplanted open revolutionary propaganda, the need to appear respectable necessarily increased in urgency. Consequently, {247} it is a mistake to assume that communist conspiracy is a function of repression: the latter is one source, of course, but the effort to elude open bidding for popular support is equally significant.

Although all political contenders must heed the community's sense of propriety in the choice of candidates, the Bolsheviks are particularly sensitive on this score. The traditional parties choose the "right" man in order to win; the communists need a respectable name in order to protect the right of the party to function. Much activity otherwise inexplicable can be understood as part of the search for legitimacy. The influx of communists into the armed forces in World War II served, among other functions, to create a corps of party veterans who could be exhibited at appropriate times (as at the encampment in Washington in 1947) in order to spread the idea that communists "did their share" as good Americans. To think of communists in the armed forces as seeking primarily to undermine discipline or to get training for revolution is to miss the political import of this activity.[14]

Similarly, even brief participation in posts of influence or of public honor can increase the usefulness of a procommunist spokesman. And the "capture" of Henry Wallace by the communist movement was an important triumph, not only because of his immediate pro-Soviet propaganda potential, but because a former Vice-President accepted the right of party members to function in a liberal organization. This is the significant fact that is often overlooked in the flood of controversy over who controls whom. The mere *right to participate* is invaluable to an organization which depends on covert devices for the attainment of positions of influence. Indeed, the search for legitimacy may lead the communists to participate in organizations even when there is no possibility of control. If the entire group is referred to as "democratic," and it includes the communists, the latter will gain in respectability.

The question of legitimacy is posed in the following criticism of the American Civil Liberties Union:

> By including such a pro-Communist as Corliss Lamont on its {248} Board of directors, not to speak of others who are frequent sponsors of pro-Communist fronts, the Civil Liberties Union not only virtually commits itself against endorsing any effective anti-Communist legislation, but *it also excludes the only substitutes for legislation against Communism, that is, the private exposure and boycott of Communists.* The inclusion of Lamont would seem to imply the view that the Communist movement is bona fide and respectable, rather than a worldwide conspiracy in the service of an aggressive government. So it is not just a case of the Civil Liberties Union differing with the methods of the Mundt-Nixon bill in opposing Communism. The effect of the Union's attitude is more far-reaching.

---

[14] See also above, p. 221.

This conclusion is supported by the fact that the Civil Liberties Union is avowedly willing to co-ordinate its activities with the Communists in opposition to the Mundt-Nixon bill, or on other similar questions. This again implies recognition of the Communist Party as a respectable group, for if the Civil Liberties Union cooperates with them why shouldn't others?[15]

Although communists as such were long ago barred from the leadership of the ACLU, this criticism suggests that the role of the fellow-traveler participants is to uphold the legitimacy of the communist party by presenting it as another, if sometimes mistaken, tendency in the liberal movement.

In order to gain legitimacy, communist peripheral organizations may sometimes follow apparently inconsistent policies. Thus there may be an attempt to identify with persons of prestige even if the latter are known anticommunists. For example, one magazine, following a pro-Soviet international policy, offered to give an "award" to Secretary of State George Marshall. Such a device permits the awarding organization to exchange a temporary and readily forgotten inconsistency for publicity and acceptability. The same goal may lead to the avoidance of a definitive public break (as manifested in vigorous attack and, especially, defamation) with potential legitimizers who have strayed somewhat from the party line. This would be particularly relevant in the case of motion picture stars and other nonpolitical persons whose individual pronouncements may not {249} carry much weight but whose appearance at meetings and on letterheads may induce widespread participation.

When colonial and dependent countries are political targets, control of international organizations is useful to legitimize communist propaganda. In such areas, communication with the main centers of labor, student, and cultural activity is normally poor, and the prestige of these centers is high. Those who can speak in the name of "world labor" gain legitimacy as being representatives of more than a single factional interest. Thus a spokesman for the International Student's Union can easily have a Student Council in Shanghai arrange a large meeting to hear him; if he delivers an anti-American, pro-Soviet speech, he will appear to be speaking in the name of a great body of student opinion. Such actions might not be very effective where the character of the international organization is well understood, or where there is an alert opposition ready to expose it; but in more remote places a vacuum is likely to exist which can, as always, be fully exploited. As in the case of the World Federation of Trade Unions described above, the same organization that appears to be fully discredited in the United States may continue to be useful in legitimizing the intervention of communists in the affairs of emerging labor movements in industrially less advanced areas.

In general, when communists (and others) participate in international voluntary associations, they derive legitimacy from the sheer fact of being American and from the ease with which persons little known in America may function as "representatives" of the nation's youth, women, and other basically unorganized sectors of the population. This is also true of communists and procommunists who come to the United States. An Indian, rising in an American auditorium to

---

[15] *The Commonweal*, June 25, 1948, p. 255*f.*

speak in the name of the "peoples of Asia," may get a respectful hearing, although he may actually be committed to the views of only a small segment of his country's population. These opportunities are, of course, available to all foreigners, but their systematic exploitation is characteristic of modern bolshevism, and {250} a reflection of the conscious effort to find legitimate vehicles for propaganda.

One of the most important sources of legitimacy for communists is also one of the simplest: the moral authority of hard work.[16] In every organization which they seek to capture, the communists are the readiest volunteers, the most devoted committee workers, the most alert and active participants. In many groups, this is in itself sufficient to gain the leadership; it is almost always enough to justify candidacy. As skilled organizers, often with highly competent advice easily available, the members of the communist fraction can launch a campaign of criticism against an incumbent leadership, not on political grounds, but on matters of practical policy. By avoiding the role of critic who does not participate in day-to-day work, they can effectively assert their right to participate in the leadership. This source of legitimacy is especially congenial to the communists because hard work is a token of activism. The latter is a crucial component of the bolshevik's own principle of legitimacy, that which he would like to have accepted by the community.

An interesting variant of the normal tactic of concealing communist affiliation in target groups is to have a few party members appear openly as such. If these selected individuals are especially careful to appear as loyal members interested only in the welfare of the union or other association, it may be possible to dispel fears of the party. The mere existence of the communist stereotype (the fanatical propagandist and saboteur) is helpful, for the presentation of individuals who behave conventionally and are "nice people" can do much to destroy the effectiveness of anticommunist attacks. The party is therefore interested in having some of its members (in addition to key leaders) openly accept the communist label in order to legitimize the right of communists to participate in the mass organizations. Ultimately the best defense against attempts to identify various activities as communist is to create a "so what" attitude: if communist {251} participation is accepted as legitimate, then exposure will be effectively neutralized.

These open tactics are associated with another useful cover for infiltration. In many contexts, tolerance of the party may be won if the belief is held that it has little influence. For example, refusal to recognize the extent of communist penetration of the CIO and naïve equations of the party's strength with its vote in national elections have created a favorable environment for covert activities. This can be aided by the open appearance of a few communists, who lend weight to the impression that they represent only an insignificant minority having no power. The man who openly announces his affiliation does everything he can to offset the stereotype; at the same time, a larger group of concealed communists "independently" supports his policies. The open existence of the party, moreover, can absorb the frontal anticommunist attacks so that the more vital covert activ-

---

[16] See Cannon, *op. cit.*, p. 239, regarding penetration of the Socialist Party: "Our first prescription for our people was: Penetrate the organization, become integrated into the party, plunge into practical work and thus establish a certain moral authority with the rank and file of the party."

ity may continue undisturbed. In the United States, where conspiratorial activity to compensate for lack of popular support has been most essential, the apparent weakness of the communist party has been one of its important assets. In order to assert its right to function, therefore, it is in the party's interests to deprecate its own influence.

From a propaganda standpoint, probably the most effective principle of legitimacy promulgated by the communists is that based on the distinction between ultimate and immediate aims. The right to participate, to have access to centers where power is created and transferred, is decisive for organizational weapons. This is aided by a doctrine of apparent compromise, the communists claiming that, although their program is ultimately the best, they will go along with lesser achievements. Given honest and straightforward political relations, it is not easy to refuse the help of hard-working individuals who make your cause their own. The communists, however, subvert these relations by keeping the struggle for power on the agenda permanently, making programmatic compromises without sacrificing the capture of an organization or a state whenever possible.

Equally important is the consequence that the communists come {252} to be viewed as standing at one end of a political *continuum:* they come to be thought of as favoring the social ideals of the liberals, "only more so." This is an important psychological victory, for then the communists are accepted as being within the same basic community as all "progressives" and hence rightful participants in its work. Actually, of course, the communists aim to make labor unions tools of the state and to deny civil rights to all. But this simple truth, which should set the bolsheviks aside as among the worst enemies of liberalism, has been effectively obscured from large numbers of well-meaning persons by immersing the party in the struggles of less-privileged groups in society. From the bolshevik point of view, no inconsistency is involved; they are interested in these struggles only as means of gaining influence, of "possessing" the masses. The power thus gained is to be used, not for the immediate benefit of the grantors, but according to the dictates of History as reflected in the shifting interests of the international party. The inconsistency lies with the liberals, whose failure to understand the nature of bolshevism as a power-oriented movement leads them to accept the public pronouncements of the communists as good coin. The result is the absorption of the party into the community of democratic idealism—a strategic victory of the first importance.

If the confusion of communism with liberalism is, as we suggest, a way of legitimizing the party's activities, this confusion has often been considerably increased by the most articulate (though not the most effective) enemies of bolshevism. Indiscriminate attacks upon all left-wing movements, and even New Deal liberalism, as "communistic" is of great help to the party, reinforcing its contention that the fate of all progressives and radicals is bound up with that of the communists. Such an attack identifies where it should distinguish and divide, and may serve to increase rather than to diminish the influence of the party among those key groups whose leadership it seeks to command.

CHAPTER 6
DUAL POWER AND
THE COUP D'ÉTAT

The bolsheviks came to power in Russia by assuming the leadership of a great revolutionary upsurge among the urban and rural masses. They did not create this sentiment, but took control of it away from the reformist parties. In this sense, the Russian revolution of 1917 was, despite the transition from Kerensky to Lenin, a single historical event. When the bolsheviks took power in October, they were riding the crest of a wave, always aware that their opportunity might be lost if they failed to gauge the running of the tide. That the historical moment might not be sensed was, indeed, Lenin's greatest preoccupation and anxiety.

Because of his many written appeals to the bolshevik Central Committee, in the period just before October, Lenin's views on the relation of party and class in the insurrection are readily available. In September, 1917, in an essay addressed to the committee he wrote:

> To be successful, insurrection must rely not upon conspiracy and not upon a party, but upon the advanced class. . . . Insurrection must rely upon the rising revolutionary spirit of the people. . . . Insurrection must rely upon the *crucial moment* in the history of the growing revolution, when the activity of the advanced ranks of the people is at its height, and when the *vacillations* in the ranks of the enemies and *in the ranks of the weak, half-hearted and irresolute friends of the revolution* are strongest.. . . And these three conditions in the attitude towards insurrection distinguish Marxism from Blanquism.[1]

This doctrine stressed that the party should be ready to act at the crucial moment; it also resulted in direct appeals for spontaneous action among the masses. Lenin called on the peasants to exercise {254} initiative, to seize the land; he wanted the workers to arm themselves and to displace management in the factories. Although in a short time he would curb this initiative, in the interests of the new regime, at the time of the insurrection he felt that revolution must come from below or not at all. The party had, in this view, all it could do to keep pace with the masses, who had launched the struggle in their own way.

---

[1] "Marxism and Insurrection," September 26-27, 1917, in V. I. Lenin and J. Stalin, *The Russian Revolution*, International Publishers, New York, 1958, p. 191.

The Role of Mass Action

In order to comprehend Lenin's position, it should be recalled that to him the mass represented a vast reservoir of energy. The availability of this energy increased with the intensity of the class struggle; hence it was always desirable to stimulate the initiative of the mass, to set it in motion. The party would then proceed to tap its new revolutionary resources. Given such a perspective, there is no contradiction between the aim of seeking a background of general revolutionary upheaval and that of establishing specific channels through which mobilization may take place.

This was the classic bolshevik strategy: to grasp the opportunities of social turmoil and at the same time to build organs of control. The combination of spontaneous mass action and tight organizational leadership would, it was believed, carry the class to victory. The workers as the social vanguard would, in their turn, be subordinated to the party as the "vanguard of the vanguard." Lenin often talked like an anarchist in the pre-October days, but this was deceptive (possibly also self-deceptive), for he was interested in anarchist slogans only insofar as they summoned mass action. He was not in favor of permitting this energy to find its own means of expression, save as consistent with the party's struggle for a monopoly of power.

Bolshevism since Lenin has diminished its emphasis on stimulating mass energy and has increased its reliance on the party and its agencies. The role of the mass, still important, has become more {255} and more passive. Two important reasons for this change may be suggested:[2]

1. Communist rule has become more quickly and more obviously repressive, so that spontaneous mass action has an undesired subversive potential. It is better not to summon forces which may get out of hand. Lenin was not concerned with this because of his supreme confidence, which his successor could not share, that the masses would welcome a bolshevik government once it had a chance to show whose interests it served.

2. Lenin's heirs have been able to perfect the organizational strategy whose foundations he laid and thus to minimize dependence on spontaneous mass action. A new approach to revolution was made possible which relied heavily on manipulation from the top. The new technique has presumed that communists can gain control of important sectors of the mass through established institutions, and can attain strategic positions in government, education, the arts, the press, science, and industry. The going institutions of society can, it is assumed, be captured or seriously infiltrated prior to a revolution. This is consistent with Lenin's

---

[2] Additional hypotheses include: (1) Since gaining power in the Soviet Union, the bolshevik leaders may now have a keener appreciation of the strategic importance which attaches to certain parts of a government machinery than they had prior to the October Revolution, the result being a depreciation of the importance of mass action. (2) Soviet experience with the problem of controlling the masses may have led to an increased emphasis on control rather than on spontaneity in the image of the mass. (3) The abortive character of several mass revolutionary attempts in the period following World War 1 (Germany, Hungary) may have reinforced the aim of controlling mass action. (4) Technological development has increased the possibility of centralized action.

perspective, but in practice very different from it.

Lenin did not expect his followers to be prominent officials. He thought that they would be leaders among the rank and file, that they would be carried forward with the mass, as new waves of revolutionary action battered the status quo. The bolsheviks would remain a minority opposition in the unions, but the crisis would eliminate the existing leaders and their vacillating successors, leaving the road to leadership clear. So it was in the soviets: "First the compromisers, {256} then us." The mass in a revolutionary crisis is a great hammer to destroy the stable, regular leadership of all institutions. That is why the crisis, its turmoil setting the masses in motion, is so important; for only in that way can the bolsheviks emerge from obscurity to the commanding heights.

Modern bolshevism has seen, however, that the party need not rely solely on such upheavals to gain power, although any crisis creating a power vacuum is useful. The communists can become a direct threat simply by mobilizing the forces they presently control, a result not so much of spontaneous mass action as of the patient pursuit of influence by and for the cadre party. As a result, without the upsurge Lenin thought essential, the party may have in its hands all the tools necessary for the execution of a successful coup; it may not need, and may find inconvenient, spontaneous action on the part of the mass.

The fact is that the alternative to Blanquism which Lenin stressed was not the only variant consistent with Marxist theory and with, indeed, his own basic perspectives. Lenin repudiated the Blanquist idea that social revolutions could be made by the conspiratorial action of an elite corps; he stressed, as we have seen, the role of the masses, the need to prepare them, to organize them, to adapt the art of insurrection to their moods. This does not mean that he romanticized mass action or valued spontaneity for its own sake; on the contrary, the whole spirit of his doctrine is one of discipline, control, restraint. He did believe in the utility of the mass for bolshevik aims, and feared that unless the masses were deeply involved the revolution would stop short of eliminating capitalism. But the new technique, although relying heavily on conspiracy, is not Blanquist either. The Stalinists are not less concerned about a mass *base* or about preparing for the coup by establishing communist strength in the factories and in the social institutions. There is no question of a simple *coup de force,* no palace revolution unbuttressed by strength in the key centers of social power. The difference does not lie here, but in the role of the masses: Lenin saw them as an active force, preparing the way for a quick rise to power. The Stalinists see this role as passive, {257} always effectively controlled, summoned as occasion demands to strike, riot, or parade.[3]

The Meaning of Dual Power

The transition from popular upheaval to a more controlled type of overturn may be better understood if we study the changing nature of *dual power* in revo-

---

[3] The ends of Lenin and his successors are basically the same: all power to the Communist Party. This changing image of the mass, which is not really fundamental insofar as the nature of bolshevism is concerned, but has important tactical consequences, reflects the increasingly explicit totalitarianism of bolshevism.

lutionary situations. For the basic strategy of dual power, modified by changing organizational techniques, has remained the foundation of the bolshevik coup d'état. We shall briefly review the conception of dual power as it applied in the Russian revolution, and then consider the organizationally relevant changes which have occurred.

"The most indubitable feature of a revolution," wrote Trotsky, "is the direct interference of the masses in historic events." Despite the conspiratorial elements of bolshevism, this emphasis on mass involvement has been central in its image of the transfer of state power. Characteristically, however, even in 1917 there was no *reliance* (however much it may have been encouraged) on a spontaneous "interference of the masses," but rather on the summoning of them at appropriate times by the general staff of the revolution. The involvement of the mass in a revolutionary enterprise, given organizational form, leads to the creation of the classic agencies of dual power.

Lenin saw dual power as a means of bringing the weight of the masses to bear in a revolution:

> The highly remarkable feature of our revolution is that it has established a *dual power*. . . . In what does this dual power consist? In the fact that side by side with the Provisional Government, the government of the *bourgeoisie*, there has developed *another government* . . . —the Soviets of Workers' and Soldiers' Deputies. . . . {258} *This* power is of exactly *the same type* as the Paris Commune of 1871. The fundamental characteristics of this type are: (1) The source of power is not a law previously discussed and passed by parliament, but the direct initiative of the masses from below ; (2) the direct arming of the whole people in place of the police and the army, which are institutions separated from the people and opposed by the people; order in the state under such a power is maintained by the armed workers and peasants *themselves,* by the armed people *itself;* (3) officials and bureaucrats are either displaced by the direct rule of the people itself or at least placed under special control. . . .[4]

It remained for Trotsky, however, to attempt a systematic formulation, along Marxian lines:

> The political mechanism of revolution consists of the transfer of power from one class to another. The forcible overthrow is usually accomplished in a brief time. But no historic class lifts itself from a subject position to a position of rulership suddenly in one night, even though a night of revolution. It must already on the eve of the revolution have assumed a very independent attitude towards the official ruling class; moreover, it must have focussed upon itself the hopes of intermediate classes and layers, dissatisfied with the existing state of affairs, but not capable of playing an independent role. The historic preparation of a revolution brings about in the pre-revolutionary period a situation in which the class which is called

---

[4] "A Dual Power," April 22, 1917, in Lenin and Stalin, *op cit.,* p. 20*f.*

to realize the new social system, although not yet master of the country, has actually concentrated in its hands a significant share of the state power, while the official apparatus of the government is still in the hands of the old lords. That is the initial dual power in every revolution.[5]

To speak, as Trotsky does here, of the winning of a "share of the state power" by the revolutionary class, while the governmental structure is still in the hands of the old ruling class, is to identify a transitional split in sovereignty. This is consistent with the bolshevik view that the substance of power is not contained only in the formal institutions of government, that it can be generated in new ways and {259} assume many guises. A government that loses its legitimacy or its monopoly of organized violence may cease to speak with authority in the community; its commands will cease to be obeyed. At the same time, new organizations, however unconventional, which do command respect and force may assume the prerogatives of sovereignty. In dual-power situations, the locus of sovereignty shifts from one center to another prior to a definitive resolution of the crisis. Ideally, the insurrection itself only confirms and records, with a minimum of social convulsion, the de facto transfer which has already occurred.

The case of 1917 Russia is so explicit—the Provisional Government versus the Soviets—that it may obscure the general problem, and the subtle forms, of the fragmentation of sovereignty. In the United States, the powers of the federal government are limited, but the constitution attempts to spell out the minimum powers required by a sovereign government. Where the issue was unclear, in the right of the federal authority to maintain its territorial integrity, a civil war was fought to decide it. Since that conflict, the advocates of local sovereignty have not seriously challenged the supremacy of Washington on matters crucial to the exercise of sovereign power. The federal-state relation has *not* been one of dual power, for the basic allegiance of the major institutions of the society to the federal government is not in question. This tells us what dual power is not: it has nothing to do with a legitimized division of authority which is stabilized around a central focus of loyalty.

Where that central focus no longer exists, where the allegiance of groups and institutions is divided among polarized contenders for supreme authority, a condition of dual power emerges. If, for example, a church were to arise which believed in its right to review, challenge, and reject the laws of the federal government; if it were able to attract considerable support among the people; to conduct its own education; to establish a private army—then, until some over-all resolution of the conflict were achieved, a situation of dual power would exist. The question of sovereignty would suffuse all issues. Such a case would not necessarily be one of a few months charged with tension; it might characterize an entire political epoch.

{260} The strategy of dual power is an organizational reflection of the politics of class struggle. The aim of the Marxists has been to split the community, to undermine the principles of legitimacy upon which existing authority rests, to create new institutions to rally the total allegiance of the workers. In action, such a policy

---

[5]   L. Trotsky, *History of the Russian Revolution*, Vol. 1, Simon and Schuster, Inc., New York, 1932, p. 206*f*.

inevitably creates organs of dual power. If a union leadership believes that the "bosses' government" is not to be trusted, then in a strike the union will be prepared to assume the functions of government on a local scale. If the official police are believed to be biased, the union may prepare its own means of maintaining order. If it is felt that the hospitals are being used to isolate union militants, special first-aid stations may be established. Such manifestations of dual power are usually episodic. Nevertheless, even these indicate its basic nature: the assumption of governmental functions and prerogatives by private associations when the authority of the sovereign is in decline.

Although a breakdown of the monopoly of organized violence and of control over key economic and social institutions may lead to embryonic dual-power situations, the important point is not the collapse of practical control as such. That may occur in disasters, or as a result of external attack, without serious consequences for the locus of sovereignty. Ultimately, the issue turns on sentiment. The emergence of significant dual power depends on the *alienation* of sectors of the community, not simply on new upcroppings of powerful forces.

Dual Power and Subversion

It follows that dual power may be created *without the generation of new social forms*. It may result from new combinations of disaffected institutions. The capture of local governments, agencies of a central government, or of labor federations permits the construction of a new state apparatus prepared to displace the old. The force which binds these elements together is the revolutionary general staff, the combat party. The state is dissected rather than smashed. By purging and indoctrinating the captured organizations, the communists {261} change them in a fundamental way: they destroy the *role* and the *loyalties* of these institutions while keeping them organizationally intact. They then cease to be normal participants in a constitutional order but become, on the contrary, prepared bastions for a revolutionary coup.

Thus we see that dual power may be the result of organized subversion. Key institutional targets are detached from the formal sovereign and are attached to the effective sphere of influence of a countergovernment, the communist party. When this directing group decides to assume total power, it has only to formalize its relations to the captured institutions. This bureaucratic form of dual power has its propaganda dimension and cannot, of course, develop without considerable social turmoil. Nevertheless it is a very different thing from that type of dual power which is supposed to arise spontaneously out of the struggle of the masses for self-expression.

In discussing communist infiltration of government agencies, we noted that in its post-Leninist phase bolshevism has modified the injunction that the capitalist state apparatus must be smashed. An increasingly realistic attitude, recognizing the weakly coordinated character of government agencies in a democracy, has led to tactics which attempt to capture the incidental political utility of routine decisionmaking. Such tactics are especially relevant when the communist party is a small minority and there is no question of a direct approach to power. If communists in government acted as if they were in a revolutionary situation, they would easily be excluded and the possibility of using these strategic positions would be lost.

But the infiltration of government under such conditions is not inconsistent with grosser forms of subversion. On the contrary, infiltration for incidental purposes (e.g., aiding communist-supported groups in the community) prepares the party psychologically and organizationally for attempts to control the character of the agency itself. Such an objective is in effect a return to the Leninist injunction. For if we consider the sociological meaning of "smashing" the state, it is not difficult to see that alternative methods may be employed.

{262} On the one hand, there is the method envisioned by Lenin: the old organizations will disintegrate, their bureaucratic structures will be dissolved, and new agencies will be established by the revolutionary regime. These new organizations might re-employ some of the old personnel, but there would be no continuity which might permit sabotage of the directives issued by the new state power. As always, Lenin sought to rely on new devices, expressing a sharp break with the past, symbolizing the new order for the masses. This is consistent both with his emphasis on completely reliable instruments (to be built and controlled by the bolsheviks) and with his stress on relating political decisions to the revolutionary consciousness of the mass.

However, the state apparatus may also be "smashed" without organizational disintegration. The latter is the simplest method, the most obvious, but it assumes a context of upheaval and a wide base of support which may not always be available. The history of post-Leninist communism has been, indeed, one of attempts to gain power with minimal mass support. Hence the need to exploit the possibilities of subversion through the use of organizational weapons. The point of "smashing" the state is not to create chaos for its own sake, but to eliminate an apparatus having basic loyalties to the existing order. If these commitments can be altered without actually destroying the organizations, a valuable tactical flexibility may be gained. This can be accomplished by purges or, especially in transitional periods, by systematic intimidation and indoctrination, resulting in a basic reorientation of the officialdom. When the communists capture an organization, they are not content to replace the top leadership; they attempt to overhaul the entire apparatus so that it may become a pliable instrument. This will maximize access to the rank and file and create a homogeneous environment of opinion to which conformity is demanded. Even if the personnel is not adequately won over, the total reorganization of the officialdom will ensure the maintenance of control. This is standard practice in a controlled union where, for example, not only headquarters officials, but all organizers and even shop stewards are made part of an integrated machine.

{263} Once it is recognized that a radical transformation of the character of an agency can be accomplished by organizational measures instituted from the top, the utility of partial control of the government becomes apparent. The older bolshevik theory rejected coalitions partly because it was felt that the communists must always lose, always be made the prisoners of the least radical member of the bloc. But this theory did not adequately take into account the power of the combat party as against that of the normal parliamentary parties. If the communist party were of the same type as the others, then the theory would have merit. It was particularly effective, from the communist viewpoint, as a criticism of the coalitions made by the socialist parties. But since the socialists were indeed basically of the parliamentary type, no conclusions ought actually to have been drawn concerning the role of communist parties in coalitions. As in all unity maneuvers, the bolsheviks enter a coalition in order to gain access to group or institutional targets. If participation in a coalition government offers opportunity to subvert a government agency through extensive infiltration supported from the top, then the maneuver may be successful even if the formal political goals are not attained. Moreover, when the seizure of total power is a serious possibility, control of a portion of the government structure will permit the establishment of a system of dual power, the controlled portion being detached from allegiance to the constitutional locus of sovereignty to function as a base of operations and an alternative administrative apparatus.

As the communist technique for penetrating the nerve centers of society is perfected, as the target is extended from key industries and mass movements to government itself, the need for a background of mass upheaval diminishes. The party comes to rely increasingly on its devices of penetration and control, as guided by its own general staff. Spontaneous outbursts of mass action may then embarrass the delicate operations of a stage-managed coup. {264}

The Case of Czechoslovakia

This analysis may be developed concretely if we consider the pre-seizure tactics employed by the communists in Europe after World War II, especially in Czechoslovakia. This pattern shows balanced use of manipulated mass action and bureaucratic entrenchment, each reinforcing the other under the guidance of the party.

The coup d'état in Prague of February, 1948, was a communist revolution of the new type. It was not an insurrection, involving attacks upon a ruling group, but a seizure of total power by those who already held dominant influence in the government.[6] It was a revolution nonetheless, for it resulted in a fundamental shift in the locus of sovereignty from constitutionally restrained parliamentarism to a totalitarian state. What was overturned in Prague was an *institutional system,* not a regime. This was made possible by preparations which had already, before the February events, rendered the Czech parliamentary democracy only a weak and distorted reflection of its former self, and had created the organizational basis for totalitarian rule. *This is the ultimate meaning of dual power.* The counterposition of contending social forces and forms, each bidding for the status of sovereign, is the classic expression of a confrontation of institutional systems. It

---

[6] See "The Coup d'État in Prague," Supp. III, *The Strategy and Tactics of World Communism,* U.S. House Committee on Foreign Affairs, Washington, 1948; Sir Robert Bruce Lockhart, "The Czechoslovak Revolution," *Foreign Affairs,* July, 1948; Ivo Duchacek, "The Strategy of Communist Infiltration: The Case of Czechoslovakia," Memorandum of the Yale Institute of International Studies, July 1, 1949; and Hubert Ripka, *Czechoslovakia Enslaved: The Story of the Communist Coup d'État,* Victor Gollance, Ltd., London, 1950.

is the latter confrontation which is essential. however, not the dramatic, obvious parallelism so sharply delineated in 1917 Russia.

In this sense, the Marxist formulation, as in the quotation from Trotsky, above (page 258), has a certain rough accuracy. The view that dual power reflects a critical stage in a transition from the rule of one social class to that of another focuses attention not upon the external forms of dual power, but upon its social meaning. The {265} dubious merits of the class theory need not detain us; what is essential is that dual power in its most significant sense has a social content of this basic sort. To view the matter in these terms is to encourage a search for the less obvious ways in which institutional dual power can be expressed. At the same time, the very fact that the Marxists themselves have formulated the problem in a similar way must lead us to expect them to adopt varying methods, as opportunity and expediency may dictate, which can be adapted to the basic goal—displacement of the existing system of governance by the unrestrained organs of communist power.

One commentary on the Prague events includes the following statement:

> In January 1948, Czechoslovakia was a democracy. It had a national coalition government that represented all parties. It had a constitutional system, in the sense that arrests did not occur without charges and trial. It had free speech and a free press. It had been possible to print parts of the book of former Secretary of State James Byrnes, *Speaking Frankly,* in the *Svobodno Slovo,* Prague organ of the Nationalist Socialist Party. Outwardly, the country was prosperous, largely Socialist, but democratic in all essentials.[7]

"Outwardly" is a key word here, and obviously qualifies the assertion in the first sentence of this quotation. For in fact, as was proved in action, the coalition government was not like other coalitions and the constitutional system had been readied for a coup de grace. There was no background of mass upheaval, nor any question of such a slogan as "all power to the soviets," for there were no soviets; and yet, behind an apparently normal, even "improving,"[8] situation, a split in the system of sovereignty had taken place.

The pattern of postwar government in Czechoslovakia was a product of the general pro-Russian orientation of the leading politicians after Munich, and, more immediately, of the occupation of the country by the Red Army in 1945. Benes and Masaryk hoped to base {266} their foreign policy on friendship with Russia and at the same time to maintain parliamentary democracy. The one goal strained against the other, the foreign policy requiring internal political concessions. The wish to make these concessions flowed from the Slavic orientation, and the practical need to make them was determined by the immediate impact of Russian military power. Lockhart describes Benes at Kosice as "the prisoner of Russia's (military) progress . . . more or less forced to accept an agreement which gave great power to the Communists."[9] The Kosice agreement of April, 1945, set up a

---

[7] "The Coup d'État in Prague," *op. cit.,* p. 8.

[8] The commentary just quoted goes on to say: "In some ways democracy in Czechoslovakia looked stronger than at any time during the war."

[9] Lockhart, *op. cit.,* p. 634.

National Front of Czechs and Slovaks, a parliamentary coalition committed to a program of agrarian reform and nationalization of industry. Elections were held in May, 1946, giving the communists a plurality and with it even greater strength within the government. The peculiar nature of this government, headed by communists within a parliamentary framework, was revealed during the period up to the coup of February, 1948. It was, as it could only be, a government within which a communist revolution was being organized. A review of the pertinent facts will show how this process developed.

The communists promoted the view that the coalition formed at Kosice, and maintained after the 1946 elections, was *irreversible*. The pact was assigned a special sanctity, hardly consistent with the temporary and fragile nature of parliamentary coalitions. In effect, the communists wished to deny to their opponents the right to withdraw from the bloc. Hence the National Front was actually not a normal coalition in a multiple-party system at all; it was a means of eliminating opposition to the government by forcing participation, since all pliable "democratic" parties were represented in the Front. Other parties were banned by the communist-controlled Ministry of interior, which used a licensing power for this purpose. The ultimate meaning of this nonparliamentary interpretation of the Front became clear when, in February, the noncommunist ministers attempted to alter the government by the normal procedure of resignation. The communists responded by declaring that the ministers had thereby violated {267} the Kosice agreement and hence could be denied the right to participate in a reorganized government.

In fact, therefore, the National Front functioned as a means of destroying the parliamentary system while maintaining its formal continuity. It was the cover behind which the communists could consolidate such control over key government departments as would permit the easy emergence of a new system of sovereignty.

Following the election of May, 1946, in which the communists won 114 out of 300 seats in the House of Deputies (38 per cent of the votes cast), Klement Gottwald became premier. The party took six ministries: finance, information, agriculture, interior, internal trade, and social welfare. In addition, the Ministry of National Defense was given to General Ludvik Svoboda, known as a procommunist. The importance of controlling the Ministry of Interior, with its police functions, is now generally understood. But what may be overlooked is the fact that communist control of such an agency has a special quality. The communists did not simply take over the top leadership, leaving the organizational structure intact, but made strenuous efforts to reorganize and indoctrinate the Security Police. The result was to create a potent instrument of dual power: the character of the police was changed from one committed to a constitutional parliamentary order into one which repudiated that order and was prepared to function as the instrument of a totalitarian elite. According to a former Czech official's account:

> The Ministry of Interior, which had already proved its value in the pre-putsch period, became with labor and Communist Party headquarters one of the chief directing centers of the coup. The Minister of Interior ordered several police regiments to Prague. Before they reached the city, they had to

take a new oath of allegiance to Prime Minister Gottwald. Their concentration in Prague increased the tension and made it obvious that the police, the most important arm of civil power, had become an illegal force on the side of the Communists.[10]

In order to create an organization which could be used in this way during a crisis, it was necessary to change its basic character. This {268} was the task of the communist Minister of Interior in the preseizure period: to change the Ministry and, especially, its police arm, from one committed to constitutional processes into one which could be used to effect a basic change in the political order by unconstitutional means. This could not be done in a day or by a simple order from the top. It required extensive infiltration, supported from above, as well as purges, indoctrination, and intimidation.

The character of an organization is reflected in its self-image and in the tools with which it is identified. There is a great difference between the political police in a democracy (however great the authoritarian *potential* of such an institution may be) and in a totalitarian regime. Thus Bramstedt, speaking of Germany, identifies the distinction in the following way:

> The main difference between the functions of the Republican and the Nazi Political Police was two-fold: (a) During the Republic the Political Police confined itself mainly to the defensive, combating the actual threat from individual opponents of the state; in the Third Reich (it) is deliberately offensive and motivated in its actions by the idea of prevention. (b) In the Republic the political criminal was only held to account for his unlawful political excesses and a sharp distinction was drawn in the police practice between an ordinary criminal and a "political criminal."[11]

Changes in character of this sort do not of themselves create dual-power situations. But such changes do permit the organizations to be used as instruments of dual power when they are controlled by a revolutionary general staff.

The change in basic role of the political police was only the most dramatic instance of a process of alienation which went on wherever the party had control. The Ministry of Information became a typical propaganda and control agency, on the one hand acting as a mouthpiece for the party, on the other attempting to exercise control over private informational and cultural activities. In this dual-power context, it does not matter that, for example, direct censorship of the press was not instituted until the February coup. What is important {269} is that the communists created, within the government, their own weapon which could, without difficulty, make the transition to a completely totalitarian regime.

In other words: the communists were creating, within the framework of the parliamentary government, a dual state apparatus, one which could form the essential nucleus of an all-communist government. As a result, a coup would be able

[10] Duchacek, *op. cit.*, p. 41.

[11] E. K. Bramstedt, *Dictatorship and Political Police,* Oxford University Press, New York, 1945, p. 101.

to accomplish what might otherwise require a mass upheaval. The key government agencies, already subverted, would not have to be smashed; and yet the goal sought by Lenin in his injunction to do so would be won. The building of this dual-power apparatus within the government received tactical support from the mass organizations under communist control outside the government. And throughout, the Communist Party was the integrating cement of the complex and informal procommunist movement in the government, in the factories, and among the peasantry. Unlike any other political party, the Communist Party was in a position to prepare an entire system of social control which could be automatically instituted at the time of the coup.

It is this system of dual power which transforms a coup into a revolution. Organizational preparation can largely eliminate the element of mass upheaval without sacrificing a fundamental transformation of the social order. This is a major lesson of the February events in Czechoslovakia.

This interpretation of the coup helps place the dramatic emergence of "action committees" in its proper perspectives. These committees were apparently made up of elements from the communist solar system of peripheral and controlled mass organizations—"representing" labor, youth, agriculture, publicists, artists, Partisans, etc.—in addition to delegates from the procommunist wing of the social democracy. They were thus not different from the typical "united-front" committee set up for propaganda purposes. In this case, however, these committees became vehicles for the transfer of state power. They were not so much the source of power, however, as legitimizers of it; it was in their name that government agencies and private associations were reorganized, nationally and locally. The {270} committees were summoned and constituted almost overnight, at the bidding of the communists. They performed the tasks expected of them with dispatch and were readily integrated with the dual-power apparatus which had been built within the government. Unlike the 1917 soviets, the action committees did not reflect a mass upheaval. Their formation, however, did symbolize the revolutionary nature of the communist coup and the continued adherence to an activist conception of democracy. Because of this symbolic role, the attention focused by the world press upon the action committees, and the quick comparison of them with the soviets, has some justification; but it would be a mistake to attribute spontaneous initiative to them or to think of them as the repositories of dual power.

The role of formal control of the national police through the Ministry of Interior was dramatically highlighted in the Czech coup. It was indicated above that in order for this control to be used for revolutionary purposes, a change in the character of the police organization must be instituted. This suggests a further hypothesis. Given the possibility of subverting government institutions, so that normal functions and structure are transformed into revolutionary weapons, control of the Ministry of Interior may not be indispensable. In other ministries, a clandestine armed force can be mobilized and supplied, ostensibly to fulfill some departmental function, or existing semi-police organizations can be reorganized and alerted for political intervention. Thus, when the French communists participated in the government after World War II, control of the Ministry of Labor led to the creation of a special armed force which, it has been charged, was organized allegedly for combating espionage in the aviation industry but in fact was used to consolidate communist control.[12]

Similarly, it would not be difficult to find pretexts for the organization of clandestine armed forces in connection with agricultural {271} administration, or even as "inspection teams" for a ministry of social welfare. Assuming that the noncommunist sector of the government is operating under constitutional self-restraint, the creation of an effective dual-power apparatus without the Ministry of Interior is hardly excluded, although it would obviously be more difficult. If this is recognized, it will be less easy for the communists to "prove their good intentions" by sacrificing control of this agency, now well publicized as of key importance.

Although we have been concerned here with calling attention especially to the dual-power potentialities of preseizure participation in parliamentary governments, it should be understood that this strategy extends to the whole of society. Wherever a nucleus of power can be won, the alienation of it from the established sovereign is a primary objective. This accomplished, the potentialities of the organization as a political weapon can be fully exploited. The trade-unions are, of course, especially important in this respect, for not only can they be used to attack the existing regime, but they can themselves assume quasi-governmental functions and hence can be readied for integration with the communist-controlled government sector to give strength to the new regime. If the crisis in postwar Berlin had taken somewhat different form, the communist-controlled trade-union federation might readily have become a major center of dual power. This means that where the question of ultimate power remains unsettled, the struggle in the unions must be a key focus of strategy. Lack of awareness of this rule may have influenced the actions of American Military Government authorities in Berlin, reflecting a general insensitivity to the power potential of ostensibly nonpolitical mass organizations, and especially to the strategy of dual power.

The creation of centers of dual power is associated with moves to resolve the political crisis in nonparliamentary terms, as in demands for direct representation of labor in the government. The communists build up their centers of strength whenever that is possible and then seek to combine them and to give them legal status. It is interesting {272} that a similar tactic was used by the communists in their efforts to retain control over the French General Confederation of Labor:

> Because of an apparent weakening of their basis among the organized workers, the communists (1947) discovered their love for the unorganized. At the National Council meeting of the CGT in November, they decided, over the vain protests of the minority led by the Secretary-General, Leon Jouhaux, that votes on the launching of a general strike should be taken not by secret ballot of the union members but in 'democratic fashion,' namely

---

[12] According to the *New Leader,* New York, March 15, 1947. Also, Duchacek (*op. cit.,* p. 17) reports concerning the workers' militia formed in Czechoslovakia in the immediate postwar period: "Their official function was to protect the factories against possible Sudeten-German sabotage. Their real function was to supply the Communist Party with armed units until the Police and Army could be sufficiently infiltrated."

in open meetings by a show of hands of organized and unorganized workers alike."[13]

The constitutional basis of trade-union democracy is thus subverted in order to coalesce centers of party influence. This is a phase of the irreversibility of communist control in parliamentary systems; the party may win the leadership by means of normal appeals to the electorate, usually under crisis conditions, but the new regime refuses to be bound by constitutional restraints which may permit its ouster in due course.

In achieving this irreversibility, the totalitarian elite adds a new dimension, dual power, to the coup d'état. It does not rely on force alone (coups based on the army) or on force plus claims to a popular mandate (Bonapartism); to these is added the mobilization of prepared institutional bases, especially trade-unions and the mass party. This institutional preparation is necessary because the communist regime seeks *total* power in society. It is, in this, vastly different from the military clique which may seize state power but which does not penetrate deeply into the social fabric.

The nazis too prepared for their coup of March, 1933, with weapons new to the classic coup d'état. These were, essentially but not exclusively, the mass party and the *Sturmabteilung*. The nazi party, like the communist, was a party of revolutionary activism. It participated in the parliamentary process, but was forged for action on the streets and in the social institutions. It was prepared to root out opposition, to be the eyes, ears, and fists of a leadership to whom {273} total loyalty was vouchsafed. This meant that the new regime did not have to rely on the formal mechanisms of government, thinly overlaid upon the social structure; it had an apparatus which penetrated to the city block and to the smallest village, identifying not only the most prominent enemies, but obscure subleaders of the opposition as well. Such a party, radically different in structure and in spirit from normal parliamentary organizations, is a major foundation for totalitarian rule. Together with the storm troops, the nazi movement constituted a state within a state. When we note that Hermann Goering, as Prussian Minister of Interior, reorganized the police administration and legalized the storm troops as auxiliary police, the parallel to the February events in Czechoslovakia becomes apparent. The nazis, like the communists, challenged the parliamentary system of sovereignty and created an organizational basis for their coup, thus ensuring that there would result not merely a shift in power from one faction in the state to another, but a revolutionary overturn.

Ultimately, and most significantly, dual power is reflected in the counterposition of principles of legitimacy. The communists and the nazis challenged the constitutional authority of parliamentary government, embracing in its stead a new version of democracy. The latter prizes mass action, *Schlagwort,* and tommy gun above representative assemblies. Its ideal and its justification is activism. This "new democracy" becomes the central doctrine around which the challenging social force is organized.

---

[13] H. W. Ehrmann, "Political Forces in Present-Day France," *Social Research*, Vol. 25, June, 1948, p. 2.

In the last analysis, it is only when such an alternative principle of legitimacy infuses the struggle for power that we can speak of an emerging "double sovereignty." This means that the *external forms* of an apparent dual power may exist—e.g., as soviets—without, however, any real break in the continuity of the political order. The soviets of February to October, 1917, in Russia, although symbolizing and foreshadowing the new activist principle, were in fact committed to parliamentary methods and restraints, before the bolsheviks won their irreversible majority. By the same token, the absence of such {274} external forms may mean only that existing institutions have been subverted, forming a dual-power apparatus that will emerge only at the time of the coup itself.

CHAPTER 7

VULNERABILITY OF

INSTITUTIONAL TARGETS

The analysis of organizational weapons, strategy, and tactics presented in the preceding chapters is based on a detailed examination of the record of bolshevik political combat. As an empirical study of the implicit and explicit "operational code" of the communists, it may stand by itself and will, it is believed, find general confirmation among those who are familiar with the history of bolshevism.

Before ending this inquiry, however, it is necessary to explore, in a tentative and preliminary way, the problems of social vulnerability and of political counteroffense. Our knowledge in these areas is on the whole too limited to permit the drawing of definitive conclusions. But it is possible to present a suggestive analysis which may help to clarify thinking on these matters. In doing so, we shall draw upon whatever theoretical clues and empirical materials may be available, recognizing that these are often too crude to offer anything beyond useful insights to guide future research. At the same time, where the preceding analysis clearly calls for programmatic conclusions, these will be indicated.

Organizational weapons are directed against the institutional receptacles of social power. It is evident that the nature of these targets conditions the effectiveness of the attack; hence our inevitable preoccupation with the factors that affect the vulnerability and resilience of social institutions. Since the organizational weapon is designed to *manipulate* target groups and social structures, it may be suggested that variations in the inherent manipulability of such targets will reflect corresponding vulnerabilities. Manipulability is in turn dependent on a number of general conditions, among which the nature of the *mass*, as that is exhibited both in society generally and in specific organizations, is of primary importance. The following analysis, frankly preliminary, attempts to bring to bear upon the {276} problem of institutional vulnerability a reformulation of the idea of "mass society."[1] It is suggested that a close inspection of our institutions from this standpoint will illuminate relevant areas of weakness.

The approach taken here is clinical. We are necessarily interested in social pathology, in appraising the capacity of institutions to meet, within their own terms, the requirements of self-maintenance. Self-maintenance, of course, refers to the preservation of central values and purposes as well as to the bare continuity of organizational existence.

---

[1] "Mass society" is used here as the best available substitute for a more abstract term which would denote the quality of "massness."

We shall deal with this problem by considering (1) the role of creative and culture-sustaining elites; (2) the quality of participation in mass society and mass organization; and (3) a catalogue of diagnostic symptoms of mass behavior. We proceed on the assumption that the achievement of adequate definitions reflects the close of this phase of inquiry rather than its beginning.

The Mass and Creative Elites

Critics of egalitarianism have sometimes put forward the view that the mass, incompetent and vulgar, is unable by definition to uphold the standards which sustain a culture or to participate effectively in political decisionmaking.[2] The mass is, moreover, a dire threat because what was once a passive multitude, a neuter element in the body politic, has now become dynamic. In this view, the consequences of democratization are seen as the spread of incompetence into new areas, and, indeed, the emergence of a type of man who may be found in all sectors of social life—the mass-man.

The mass-man, runs the antiegalitarian complaint, exerts a heavy {277} influence upon all areas of social life but is unqualified to do so. Whereas earlier the mass accepted its proper station, now it arrogates to itself the right to upset ideals of attainment and behavior established by traditional culture-bearing elites. The result is a cultural vacuum in which no group is able to give moral direction to society; there is an absence of standards to which appeal can be made; and resort to violence becomes characteristic of the age. In the words of a nazi playwright: "When I hear the word 'culture,' I reach for my revolver." Bolshevik activism replaces "parliamentary mathematics." In the nontotalitarian countries, too, a leveling process in education, literature, and politics substitutes the standardless appetites of the mass market for the canons of refinement and sober restraint. The mass rejects tradition and in doing so avoids responsibility for the continuity of constitutional order and the arts. Hence the very souls of nations are placed in tragic jeopardy.

This critique is not limited to antiegalitarian ideologists. Even among those who favor the general process of democratization, and who lack any feeling of contempt for the nonelite, there is some acceptance of the notion that the mass is inherently unqualified. Thus Mannheim, in tracing the "fundamental democratization" of society, saw negative consequences of the widespread intervention of intellectually backward elements into new areas of social life:

> The crisis in culture in liberal-democratic society is due, in the first place, to the fact that the social processes, which previously favored the development of the creative elites, now have the opposite effect, i.e. have become obstacles to the forming of elites because wider sections of the population

---

[2] See José Ortega y Gasset, *The Revolt of the Masses*, W. W. Norton & Company, New York, 1932, p. 120: "By mass . . . is not to be specially understood the workers; it does not indicate a social class, but a kind of man to be found today in all social classes, who consequently represents our age, in which he is the predominant, ruling power."

under unfavorable social conditions take an active part in cultural activities.[3]

Specifically, according to Mannheim, this democratization results in such undesirable effects as (1) an increase in the number of elites to the point where "no group can succeed in deeply influencing the whole of society" and (2) a breakdown of the exclusiveness of elites—that insulation from day-to-day pressures which permits new ideas and skills to mature.

{278} The import of Mannheim's critique is that creative elites are objectively necessary for the maintenance and development of culture. The mass is implicitly defined in contrast to these elites and hence it is conceived of as being essentially unqualified. This is not to say that such elites are necessarily identical with traditional aristocracies. And regardless of what one may think of a specific elite, it is, in this view, sociologically demonstrable that the creation and protection of elites is essential to a healthy society. A mass society is one which does not permit elites to carry out their cultural functions; thus it results in the sovereignty of the unqualified. Of course, "sovereignty" here does not refer to government, but to the locus of decisive cultural influence. The rule of the masses is not inconsistent with elite control of the state, for that rule is expressed in the fact that the governing elite is itself formed in the image of the mass.

If we examine this conception of the mass as unfit, we see that judgments as to the inherent competence of various strata of society are in fact irrelevant. *What is really identified is a social system in which the indispensable functions of creative elites cannot be performed.* It is not the quality of the individuals which is at issue, but their roles; it is not so much that the mass is unfit in any literal sense as that the nature of the system prevents the emergence of an effective social leadership. In a sense, a mass society is one in which *no one* is qualified. This is so because the relationships involve a radical cultural leveling, not because superior individuals do not exist.

If mass characteristics appear in a university, for example, this does not necessarily mean that the student body or the faculty is inherently incompetent. The large achievements in technical fields would be testimony to the contrary. What is at issue is cultural competence. Where the disease of "massness" has taken hold, we find the following symptoms: (1) the faculty is unable to reach the students as persons but merely trains them as experts; (2) conditions for the emergence and sustenance of intellectual elites on the campus are poor; (3) the faculty adapts itself to the mass character of the institution; (4) standards of conduct and of nontechnical achievement deteriorate; and (5) the meaning of the university as a culture-bearing {279} institution is increasingly attenuated. This says nothing about the inherent competence or incompetence of the participants, but it does say something about the nature and the consequences of a type of institutional participation. The latter is consistent with the literary-philosophical critique of the mass society as the "sovereignty of the unqualified."

---

[3] Karl Mannheim, *Man and Society in an Age of Reconstruction,* Kegan Paul, Trench, Trubner & Co., London, 1940, p. 85.

These remarks emphasize the difficulty of attempting to say that some given society, taken as a whole, is a "mass society." But if we understand that what we are asserting is a *relation between abstract characters*—"massness" and the quality of elites—this problem can be avoided. As in the case of any universal proposition, the statement "In mass society the creative and culture-sustaining elites are debilitated" merely tells us what can be expected, in the absence of counteracting forces, when social disintegration thrusts undifferentiated sectors of a population into direct contact with the areas of cultural incubation and development. Education, leisure, and politics have been most obviously affected by this process. Among its consequences is that political and educational agencies must adapt themselves to the intervention of the mass by permitting participation on the basis of low standards of knowledge and conduct.

But this adaptation is costly. Elites find it difficult to sustain their own standards and hence ultimately their special identity and function. This is most clearly evident in the institutions of higher learning: mass society threatens to transform them into institutions of specialized training. As higher education falls a prey to the mass, research as well as teaching is affected. The student no longer feels his relatedness to a community of scholarship; he is not concerned about, indeed is impatient with, the traditional values of university life. He does not look forward to becoming a new kind of man; he expects to retain his commonness, distinguished from the multitude only by a certain technical competence. Like his highly specialized professor, his participation is segmental, it does not commit him as a whole man to becoming the bearer and protector of the society's aspirations. In the faculties two new types will become more prominent: the technician and the demagogue. Only these will maintain {280} and increase enrollments; more important, only these will earn the plaudits of the student body. The student will become his teacher's judge, sometimes even explicitly so. The result will be a decline in the university's ability to affect deeply the life of the student and, concomitantly, an increase in the vulnerability of both faculty and student to the stereotyped blandishments of the marketplace.[4]

Similar tendencies threaten all the highly sensitive institutions which protect existing standards and are the sources of cultural development. Even the church is not immune to this danger. Impatient of theological subtlety (not merely ignorant and deferent, as in the past, but *impatient*), feeling uncertain and inadequate, the preacher as social worker is in full flight from his distinctive cultural role. He

---

[4] It may be suggested, in the light of the foregoing analysis, that a relation to the "community of scholarship" can be core participation (see p. 287) only through the mediation of the person-to-person relation of "disciple" to "master." It should also be noted that although mass behavior in education is most obvious in the great state universities, it arises as well in many colleges sustained by and for the moneyed elites. Here, too, the students are leveled by their common impatience with intellectual pursuits, and the faculty capitulates to the pressure for highly specialized training—and entertainment. The distinction between training and education perhaps sums up the impact of the mass. The best-known response to the pressures discussed here is found in the efforts of Chancellor Hutchins and his associates at the University of Chicago. For a recent statement, see *The State of the University, 1929-1949: A Report by Robert M. Hutchins Covering the Twenty Years of His Administration*, September 21, 1949.

becomes defensive about propagating religious values; he does not sustain the image of charitable or other activities as primarily spiritual missions. He finds new security in a feeling of oneness with the common man, but as a result he may fail as a moral and spiritual leader. Even where religion flourishes, demagogy may become the characteristic product of the times, the leader reflecting the mind and the fluctuating mood of the mass.

The strength of cultural values depends on the ability of key agencies to transmit them without serious attenuation and distortion. But this in turn requires that these institutions be secure, that the elites which man them be able to maintain their distinctive identities. This becomes increasingly difficult as powerful solvents—science, technology, industrialization, urbanization—warp the self-confidence {281} of the culture-bearers and, at the same time, expose them to the pressures of an emergent mass.

From a research standpoint, this analysis suggests that inquiry into institutional vulnerability should focus attention upon the conditions that affect the ability of elites to maintain those standards and self-images which invest the institution as a whole with its cultural meaning.

It should be emphasized that no commitment to established values and institutions follows from what has been said here. The problem is strictly clinical: *if* we wish to preserve the integrity of certain institutions, these are among the conditions we must investigate and control. Whether in any specific case the institution is worth preserving must be determined on other grounds.

The Quality of Participation

In the preceding discussion of elites in relations to the mass, we drew upon an older insight and reformulated it in clinical terms. We refer now to that idea of "mass" which associates it with such terms as "homogeneous," "amorphous," and "undifferentiated."[5] This {282} view in effect represents the mass-man as a

---

[5] The dissolution of group structure into a formless and manipulable mass is stressed in Emil Lederer's *State of the Masses,* W. W. Norton & Company, New York, 1940. Taking "society" as designating the system of social relationships which binds together groups and individuals, Lederer maintained that the present crisis consists in the substitution for society of the "institutionalized" (organizationally mobilized) masses. The mass-state is "built upon the eradication of groups, replaces reason by propaganda and enslaves man by delivering him to his emotions." It is a state where public opinion is "not the result of the slowly working interplay of interests and ideas, but where constant action and excitement are the order of the day." For Lederer, "mass" denotes an amorphous, structureless population, subject to crowdlike responses. He also saw the consequences of the emergence of the mass for the quality of culture, for he rejects the prospect of the classless society on the ground that stratification is indispensable to the existence of society. See also Sigmund Neumann, *Permanent Revolution,* Harper & Brothers, New York, 1942, p. 115: "Mob psychology, when it seizes a whole nation, destroys the web of its complex social structure. Like the individual differentiation of its members, so the innumerable associations of the living community are melted into one gray mass. This process of 'massification'—the dissolution of free organizations, the flattening of the social pyramid—in a way preceded the rise of modern dictators. They were the product of this disintegration of society which in turn *became* the basis of their established rule."

product of social disintegration.[6]

Consider a polar case, the transformation of the unemployed into a mass. The unemployed become a mass as their normal ties to community institutions and codes are broken down, as they are freed to reunite again in artificial ways. In other words, as family, church, and traditional political ties weaken, as the individual loses the sense that he has a secure status and accepted function in society, as alienation develops, a psychological atomization takes place. This process is not completed overnight; nor does unemployment as such automatically create a mass. What is crucial is the change in the quality of social participation consequential upon the loss of employment in a society that values work.

Among the effects of unemployment is, it appears, a general decline in social participation.[7] The individual's ties to friendship and to recreational and church associations seem to weaken with prolonged unemployment. Family life suffers and cannot easily be used as a refuge. This may begin as a result of the loss of funds necessary to maintain these relationships, especially in cities, where money income is so important. But ultimately the loss of self-respect and its accompanying insecurity must weaken the adherence of the unemployed man to the codes and symbols that have sustained his earlier motivations. This loss of faith in traditional values, combined with the breakdown of older patterns of family activity, of meeting friends, of going to church, casts him loose. He is on his own; but he finds this new freedom less than desirable. Many escapes are possible. He may take to drink, sleep more, seek out day-to-day satisfactions in gambling or sensual pleasure; he may retreat to extreme apathy; and he may search out new social and symbolic arrangements {283} as substitutes for his lost community. He has lost the moorings provided by the articulated social structure to which he belonged. He has become part of the mass. This process of withdrawal may take a long time; it is not easy to lose established modes of behavior. But the general direction has often been noted: the creation of a proletariat, in the strict sense of an alienated mass.

When the normal inhibitions enforced by tradition and social structure are loosened—and this, of course, occurs as a product of far more general and diverse conditions than unemployment—the undifferentiated mass emerges. It is because of this quality of the mass that the term has been associated with the idea of a crowd, most explicitly by Lederer. In the crowd, we find a *temporary* lack of differentiation, reinforced by circular response and high emotional pitch, with concomitant loosening of inhibitions. The amorphousness of the mass is similar but is the result of a general and persistent mode of life. It does not rest on psychological rapport but on the atrophy of meaningful human relations, the

---

[6] Other products of social disintegration include extreme forms of apathy and withdrawal. It may be that "massness" is an early, by no means final, stage in a process leading ultimately to the denial of meaning rather than to a search for it.

[7] The studies of E. Wight Bakke and his associates support this conclusion, although, of course, among the American workers observed, only the beginnings of the process could be discerned. See *Citizens without Work: A Study of the Effects of Unemployment upon the Workers' Social Relations and Practices*, Yale University Press, New Haven, 1940.

disintegration of traditional institutional systems, the rejection of old loyalties.[8] Moreover, the readiness for manipulation by symbols, especially those permitting sadomasochistic releases, is characteristic of the mass as of the crowd.

The alienated mass-man is in society but not of it. He does not accept responsibility for the preservation of value systems and hence may be easily moved to new adherence. Here the insights developed by Fromm in his *Escape from Freedom*[9] are applicable. The emergent mass is not stable. The freedom thrust upon it by the decay of social {284} ties has significant psychological consequences. The need for belongingness is unfulfilled; insecurity follows, and with it anxiety-laden efforts to find a way back to a sense of status and function, to a feeling of meaningful relatedness to society.

But these efforts are compulsive: enforced by urgent psychological pressures, they result in distorted, pathological responses. There arises the phenomenon of the *Ersatzgemeinschaft,* the substitute community, in which essentially unsatisfying types of community integration, most explicitly revealed in totalitarianism, are leaned upon for sustenance. This commitment is, however, suffused with tension and requires continuous renewal, resulting ultimately in a radical dependence of the individual on his substitute symbols, a vain effort to escape anxiety by blotting out his own identity. This process, as Fromm describes it, is conducive to submission to totalitarian control, aggression against the weak, nihilism, and compulsive conformity. These are the symptoms of "massness" when the disease is well developed.[10]

It follows that "mass" need not denote large numbers, although, of course, numbers are important, especially in urban areas. Indeed, it is theoretically possible to have mass phenomena associated with relatively small populations and conversely to have very large and densely settled populations which are not mass in nature. When we refer to a population as a mass, we are thinking of its members as undifferentiated, as forming an unstructured collectivity withdrawn from the normal, spontaneous commitments of social life. We are also thinking of the consequences which flow from this situation. Mass connotes a "glob of humanity," as

---

[8] "Meaningful" human relations atrophy as individuals are involved in experiences that cannot satisfy the need for healthy relatedness to other persons and to objects. Such relatedness, to be healthy and satisfying, must not threaten the integrity of the personality. Depersonalizing threats arise (1) when the individual becomes subordinate to the object, and is himself turned into a "thing," as in characteristic work situations in modern industry; (2) when social relations increasingly become transactions on an impersonal level, as in the spread of urban modes of life and bureaucratic involvement; and (3) when a split occurs between the life-experience of the individual and the forces that command his life, as evidenced in a loss of "social understanding," in the decreasing comprehensibility, the opaqueness, of social processes. On the latter point, see T. W. Adorno, *et al., The Authoritarian Personality,* Harper & Brothers, New York, 1950, pp. 665, 671. This work touches the analysis made here at many points. The decline of meaningful relations is often referred to as "alienation."

[9] Erich Fromm, *Escape from Freedom,* Farrar & Rinehart, Inc., New York, 1941.

[10] We have here reinterpreted Fromm somewhat, although not radically; he was primarily interested in the consequences of the isolation of the individual induced by modern capitalism and its supporting codes. His analysis may be generalized, however, so that his conclusions apply to social disintegration.

against the intricately related institutionally bound groupings that form a healthy social organism.[11]

{285} Prolonged unemployment, it is clear, offers only the most congenial, most easily recognizable, conditions for the emergence of a mass. In fact, *wherever culture impinges upon the individual only superficially*, the emergence of mass phenomena may be anticipated. By "culture," of course, we mean not simply the arts or manners, but the basic patterns of motivation and inhibition—the aspirations and the discipline—which are transmitted from one generation to another. When the culture is transmitted only weakly, as in the case of certain second-generation immigrant groups, and primitive peoples under the impact of white culture, inhibitions are poorly developed and motivation for social purposes is weak. In extreme cases, we find criminality, alcoholism, and loss of initiative and self-respect. These phenomena are well known. It is necessary to recognize, however, the continuity between these consequences of cultural attenuation and earlier stages in the same process which may have different, and less obvious, roots.

Precisely this cultural attenuation results from the attempt to adapt the character-defining institutions of a society—the schools, the churches, the political order—to the multitude. That this should be attempted is, of course, not a matter of choice. Industrialization and urbanization tend to weaken traditional value systems by confusing the distinction between means and ends and by depersonalizing the individual; at the same time, they corrode the older social structure and thrust ever greater numbers into direct contact with the centers of cultural development. As the family, the neighborhood, the work place, and the local community lose their near-monopoly over the life of the individual, new burdens are placed upon those centralized institutions which have historically been far removed from the common man. As a result, these institutions can only poorly perform, in their segmental way, functions that require intimate contact with the total individual; and, equally important, they become themselves incompetent to perform their essential creative tasks.

{286} The general consequence of such conditions is the weakening of social participation, and especially a superficiality in the relation of individuals to the ethos and social structure. To be sure, the breakdown of culture is never complete, and the mass may emerge even before an advanced stage of decay has been reached. It would be idle to look for some definite point at which society may be called "mass"; but the symptoms are identifiable: widespread alienation, a general cultural leveling, the compulsive search for substitute sources of security, and susceptibility to propagandistic and organizational manipulation. More important, these characteristics are reflected in varying degrees in specific institutional areas: education, religion, literature, communication, politics, and industry. Even

---

[11] The relation of the mass to the disintegration of personality is discussed by Bruno Bettelheim in a study of the consequences of internment in concentration camps administered by the Gestapo. See "Individual and Mass Behavior in Extreme Situations," *Journal of Abnormal and Social Psychology*, Vol. 38, No. 4, October, 1943, pp. 417-452. Of special interest are his remarks on the breakdown of values and regression into infantile behavior. The characteristics of this regression (including the incapacity to establish durable object-relations) cast additional light on the nature of the mass. See also Adorno, *op. cit.*

if mass phenomena are only partially characteristic of society as a whole, they may be strikingly so of specific sectors, e.g., among the youth or in some great industry. Especially in considering relative vulnerabilities within a society, it is important to conceive of mass phenomena in terms of a set of relevant predicates which may be useful in illuminating some *particular* group situation without necessarily being characteristic of society as a whole.

This emphasis on the quality of participation will permit us to gain some insight into the nature of mass *organization*. It is evident, from the discussion above, that there is more to the mass character of an organization than sheer numbers. We may say that a mass organization is one in which participation is segmental, mobilization is high, and the membership is relatively unstructured save by the formal devices of managerial control and by unmediated emotional attachments to a centralized elite.

Segmental Participation. In its most obvious sense, segmental participation refers to the partial commitment a man may give to organizations in which he has a limited interest and which do not affect him deeply. In extreme but not unusual cases, membership is of the "paper" variety, and the members themselves are easily manipulated by a small core of leaders and their supporting cliques. The mobilizability of the membership is usually low, however, and in order to create a mass organization the leaders must attempt to "activate" {287} the ranks. Thus, to take an extreme case, it makes little sense sociologically to speak of a large "book club" as a mass organization. And those trade-unions whose members' relations to the organization are limited to the checkoff payment of dues are not mass organizations.

A more significant meaning of segmental participation invites attention not to the *extent* of participation, but to its *quality*. Participation is segmental when individuals interact not as whole personalities, but according to the roles they play in the situation at hand. This is characteristic of urban life and of formal organizations where only the functional relevance of participants is prized. The personalities of individuals are leveled; men deal with themselves and with each other as abstractions and as manipulable commodities.[12]

The underlying distinction is sufficiently familiar: it is that between primary and secondary groups. Participation which provides needed emotional satisfactions is possible only in or through primary groups. We may have this "core participation"[13] in the person-to-person group and also in the secondary group, but in the latter by mediation through primary person-to-person groups only. Without the interposition of person-to-person interaction, participation in the secondary group can only be segmental. Fully evolved mass organizations resist such primary-group ties because these prevent free manipulation of the members; loyalties to subleaders can only be conditional, and only loyalty to the top leader is unconditional. But the latter, although involving primary *symbols*, is not a

---

[12] A recent work that explores this problem in many dimensions is David Riesman's *The Lonely Crowd,* Yale University Press, New Haven, 1950.

[13] A term proposed by Paul Kecskemeti.

person-to-person relationship.[14]

Segmental relations in a mass organization may be contrasted with those in large nonmass organizations, such as a church. To the extent that a church bases itself on primary-group relations at the grass roots and builds upon the incorporation of whole families into its communion, it may become very large without being a mass organization. {288} It is precisely this foundation, however, which the modern totalitarian party, and similar organizations, does not permit. It does not build upon, but on the contrary destroys, family and friendship ties.[15]

Mobilization. Mass behavior connotes weakened social participation; and yet "mass organization" is associated with a high degree of involvement. This apparent inconsistency is soon resolved, however, if we consider the meaning of mobilization. High participation in nonmass contexts is not mobilization; it is the spontaneous product of social relations that create an integrated life-pattern for the individual. Mobilization takes place when an unstructured population is set into motion by a controlling elite. When it is also understood, as we shall suggest below, that the very character of the mass-man predisposes him to be mobilizable through managerial and symbolic devices, then the bridge between the amorphousness of the mass and intense organizational activity can be readily discerned.

When the community structure and its supporting codes are viable, it may be expected that individuals will adhere only partially, with limited commitment, to organizations that are only weakly related {289} to the family-friendship core of community life. Such participants may be manipulated but not mobilized; they may constitute a source of power for some organizational leadership, but this power will be only a fraction of what it might be if the individuals could be

---

[14] On primary and secondary symbols, see E. Shils and M.J. Janowitz, "Cohesion and Disintegration in the *Wehrmacht,*" *Public Opinion Quarterly,* Vol. 12, No. 2, Summer, 1948, pp. 280-315.

[15] Correlatively, Max Weber noted: "Bureaucratic organization has usually come into power on the basis of a leveling of economic and social differences. . . . Bureaucracy inevitably accompanies modern *mass democracy* in contrast to the democratic self-government of small homogeneous units. . . . This not only applies to the structure of the state. For it is not accidental that in their own organizations, the democratic mass parties have completely broken with traditional notable rule based upon personal relationships and personal esteem. . . . Democratic mass parties are bureaucratically organized under the leadership of party officials, professional party and trade union secretaries, etc. . . . Of course one must always remember that the term 'democratization' can be misleading. The *demos* itself, in the sense of an inarticulate mass, never 'governs' larger associations; rather it is governed, and its existence only changes the way in which the executive leaders are selected and the measure of influence which the *demos,* or better, which social circles from its midst are able to exert upon the content and the direction of administrative activities by supplementing what is called 'public opinion.' Democratization,' in the sense here intended, does not necessarily mean an increasingly active share of the governed in the authority of the social structure. This may be the result of democratization, but is not necessarily the case. . . . The most decisive thing here—and indeed it is rather exclusively so—is the *leveling of the governed* in opposition to the ruling and bureaucratically articulated groups, which in its turn may occupy a quite autocratic position, both in fact 'and in form.' *From Max Weber: Essays in Sociology,* H. H. Gerth and C. Wright Mills (eds.), Oxford University Press, New York, 1946, pp. 224-226.

withdrawn from their institutional attachments and more fully absorbed into the organization. It is only with general alienation that the population—where and to the extent that it does not retreat into apathy—will turn for sustenance to what are usually impersonal structures. When this occurs, our analysis entails the prediction that participation remains segmental (in the sense of leveled, depersonalized relationships), but it is combined with a greater psychological commitment to the organization. The result is a group which may be manipulated *and* mobilized—hallmarks of the modern mass organization.

Symbolic and Organizational Manipulation. Mass behavior in organizations, as in society generally, is associated with a decline of primary-group bonds and a weakening of traditional symbols. This situation leads to new types of control, both symbolic and organizational. On the one hand, alienation from older loyalties creates a need for new social symbols, new "sacred" objects with which the individual can identify and to which he can defer. But these new man-symbol relations are *unmediated*: they contrast sharply with traditional symbolic controls. The latter are filtered through multiple agencies of social control, especially primary groups, where the ideas symbolized can be lived and acted out. These socially mediated values and symbols express themselves in the way personalities are molded and in the implicit understanding, the capacity to distinguish between the genuine and the fraudulent, which characterize an effectively transmitted cultural system. The impact of traditional symbol systems is softened by long and matter-of-fact adherence; it does not necessarily interfere with rational judgment and the accommodation of interests. But when social disintegration has loosened the older bonds, and has substituted shadow for substance in the transmission of values, then the individual's communion with the social symbols becomes artificial and forced. He is no longer {290} their legitimate offspring, and yet his compelling need may enforce an even more intense (but still segmental) attachment to the husks of social meaning.

The new unmediated man-symbol relationships have a manipulative directness. The individual becomes susceptible to extreme types of behavior, called for in the name of abstractions which have little to do with his daily life and which he has had no opportunity to test and reshape. Alienated from other objects of deference and devotion, the individual may focus all of his deference strivings on the new symbols; but since this is ultimately unsatisfactory, tension is not alleviated and an ever new expenditure of emotional energy is required. At the same time, the individual's stake in his new attachments is very great in the absence of other sources of satisfaction. All of this results in a measure of need which permits extensive manipulation.

An example of this process may be seen in alterations of the meaning of patriotism. Sentiments of this sort in a well-structured community provide a background of ideological unity that shapes the character of specific institutions. Attachments are mediated, not direct. They do not normally involve marked irrationalities (as opposed to being based on *non*rational, custom-bound elements) or hasty aggressions against deviants. And they are consistent with a common-sense understanding of the nature of the traditional political order. But a symptom of the emergence of the mass is the direct, emotionalized adherence to patriotic stereotypes, associated with a loss of intuitive understanding and a willingness to sacrifice the traditional content of the belief in exchange for emotional release. "Americanism" as a symbol can be dangerous because it is sometimes used to arouse mass responses in ways that affront the very foundations of our constitutional order; if it were simply a name for general sentiments reflected in the core attitudes of participants in a healthy community, it would not be dangerous and, indeed, would not be a *slogan* at all.[16]

{291} Another consequence of the absence of bonds in mass groups is organizational. The susceptibility to symbolic manipulation just discussed has often been noted. Less well understood, however, is the consequence of the breakdown of institutional ties for the freedom of the mass to reunite, not only symbolically, but under the control of managerial leaders. Symbolic identifications are reflected in and supported by the day-to-day associational behavior of individuals and groups. Again it is normal and healthy for the spontaneously evolving family and community relations to mold such behavior. But where segmentalized relations have destroyed the old, given pattern and are unable to create a new one, the resulting vacuum will not be filled by symbolic attachments. This vacuum will be occupied by a secular, power-oriented manipulable machine which provides new (though inherently less satisfying) means of social participation. That is why the mass party, in which emotion-invoking symbols are combined with techniques of mobilization, is the characteristic political vehicle in a mass society.

When these characteristics of "massness" become localized in specific organizations, the keynote of the latter becomes control, manipulability. The same conditions increase the vulnerability of institutions to penetration and manipulation by elites which may be, from the standpoint of the integrity of the institution, alien and irresponsible.

Diagnostic Symptoms of Mass Behavior

The utility of this analysis is not that it permits us to say of some population, "this is a mass." Rather, it may help us to be forewarned concerning the emergence of mass qualities among widely disparate groups which are subject, nonetheless, to certain common pressures. These qualities may weaken without destroying, may significantly characterize yet not wholly dominate, the specific areas in which we may be interested. To analyze mass behavior is to identify a disease. It will be best observed when its symptoms are well developed; yet {292} we wish to know its most general nature so that we may recognize its symptoms as early as possible.

We may now restate the major characteristics of mass behavior and their implications for institutional vulnerability. It should be borne in mind that these statements are meant to begin rather than to close an inquiry. At the same time, they are based on the conclusions of perceptive observers and seem to illuminate the specific area which concerns us here.

1. *Mass behavior results in the debilitation of creative and culture-sustaining elites.* At this point, it need only be emphasized that a statement of this sort is to be

---

[16] Compare the above with the discussion of "pseudo-conservatism" in Adorno, *op. cit.*, pp. 676-682*ff.* See below, pp. 301-304 on "Stalinoid" stereotyping.

used in investigating specific institutions and segments of society, not necessarily society as a whole.

2. *Mass behavior results in superficial adherence to stereotyped clues.* Foundation for this element of the syndrome was laid in the discussion, above, of segmental participation and unmediated symbol attachments. A few additional remarks here will be in point.

The cultural attenuation associated with the mass manifests itself in a peculiar relation of the individual to major cultural symbols. On the one hand, he is only weakly affected by them; he does not reflect their pervasive influence in his habitual conduct. At the same time, however, he develops a compulsive attachment to the symbols as such—not to their meaning—and to their institutional embodiments, especially if these attachments offer leverage for aggression. Thus it is characteristic of the mass-man to be only poorly influenced by the complex meaning of democracy, to be unable to make the necessary discriminations, and to have little conception of how to fulfill the value in his daily life; yet he may be easily susceptible to manipulation by wielders of this symbol, will swear allegiance to it, and will be prepared to use any means (including those ordinarily interdicted by democratic principles) against its purported enemies. Similarly, mass elements in a church may have little understanding of basic religious principles and reflect nothing of them in their own conduct; nevertheless they characteristically respond with special fervor to the symbols of the church and are its most aggressive defenders. {293} This ambiguous participation, both in symbolic and institutional experience, is fundamental in mass behavior.

These responses are not a matter of ignorance, of a simple "lack of understanding" among untutored elements. Values (and their behavioral correlates) are not transmitted intellectually; they are the standards of right conduct, of proper aspiration, that are taken for granted in a healthy society. Unmediated transmission, in the sense discussed above, results in a cultural impoverishment that has significant psychological consequences.

The political import of this condition is readily apparent. When values are stereotyped, symbol and meaning become divorced. Their content can then be manipulated with impunity; acts taken in the name of the values may in fact violate their spirit. The established political order can no longer be taken for granted. It must be defended explicitly and hence held open to attack as a secular, debatable thing. In the course of the struggle the embattled system becomes overrigid, identified with specific forces in the status quo, and thus even more vulnerable. At the same time, a pervasive need for new and more satisfactory relations is created, which is, in turn, transformed into disposable energy by demagogic managerial elites.

3. *Mass behavior is associated with activist interpretations of democracy and with increasing reliance on force to resolve social conflict.* Social disintegration entails the breakdown of normal restraints, including internalized standards of right conduct, and established channels of action.[17] This frees the mass to

---

[17]   The hold of traditional techniques of political participation—balloting rather than pressure tactics—must be broken before the activist tendencies come to the fore. Bakke (*op. cit.*, pp. 54*ff*) discusses the continued hold of custom as restraining the unemployed from

engage in direct, unmediated efforts to achieve its goals and to lay hands upon the most readily accessible instruments of action. Ordinarily, even {294} in countries having democratic constitutional systems, the population is so structured as to inhibit direct access to the agencies of decision. The electorate participates at specified times and in defined ways; it is not free to create *ad hoc* methods of pressure. The citizen, even when organized in a pressure group supporting, say, a farm lobby, can vote, write letters, visit his congressman, withhold funds, and engage in similar respectable actions. Other forms of activity are strange to him. But when this code has lost its power over him, he will become available for activist modes of intervention.[18]

It is the mass-oriented elite, fascist and communist alike, which is the advocate and engineer of activism. The mobilization of the mass takes place in the streets on a day-to-day basis. And it is characteristic of the communist-led mass organization that it will engage in unorthodox pressure tactics, e.g., the "invasion" of a state legislature. The meaning of such tactics, especially when they are used before any significant degree of mass character has emerged in the target population, is precisely to break down feelings of deference for the lawmaking body and to prepare for extralegal methods of intimidation. Communists attempt to *create* a mass, as well as to use it, although, of course, their long-term strategy is based on the assumption that deployable mass energies will be made available as a result of more general historical forces.[19] Like other aspects of mass behavior, activism is thus a result of the withdrawal of deference to established institutions. Its extreme versions are well known, as when mass elements, impatient with the niceties of legal procedure, set up their own tribunals. These may retain the external forms of juridical administration while transforming {295} its spirit. Such extreme measures, however, often taken in the heat of crisis, represent only the conclusion of a process which begins with the surrender to popular pressure of the values entrusted to a culture-sustaining elite.

4. *Mass behavior devalues social institutions and therewith subverts their character-defining functions.* Institutions are defended, often at great cost of life and resources, because they come to reflect society's self-image. They define its

---

engaging in types of political action advocated by radicals. Increased mass behavior would be expected if unemployment were indefinitely prolonged. Bakke also suggests that radical political action "requires a greater degree of hope and confidence in the future than many unemployed can muster." However, the characteristic activist responses of mass elements do not center upon utopian visions, but upon direct efforts to gain short-term release from intolerable situations: the need for immediate solutions to such problems as mass unemployment, the suffering of war, hunger, etc., and the ideological need for "some sort of answer."

[18] See Neumann (*op. cit.*, p. 111): "These dispossessed taken together composed the material of the amorphous masses of modern totalitarianism. They had lost or never possessed real group life. They now were ready to merge into a great stream of political activism giving them direction and fulfillment in a life which was no longer of their own making. 'To believe, to obey, to fight' became the motto promulgated by *Il Duce*. It was the chief political function of the new masses."

[19] This does not mean that other groups, neither fascist nor communist, will not be forced in the direction of activism. On the contrary, it is characteristic of the emergence of the mass that pressures are generated which force reluctant leaders to engage in activist ventures.

aspirations and its moral commitments; they are the source and receptacle of self-respect, of unique identity. No enemy is so dangerous as one who threatens these valued principles and structures. Like the Tenno in Japan, they are the haloed, reverenced symbols of public weal, the last bastions which dare not be surrendered, without which life itself seems worthless, cast down to a melancholy level of hopelessness and despair. This is in no essential different from an individual's attempt to protect the extensions of his own personality. Books, a house, signs of status, manner, clothing—any component of a "way of life"—may come to be valued for themselves because they define for the individual his essential nature. These are *his:* they have symbolic meaning for him, a meaning which sustains him against the depersonalizing pressures of the outside world.

Thus as particular modes of action become infused with value, i.e., institutionalized, they add to their direct functions that of defining the character of the group. The institutionalized modes of holding property, defining responsibility, transferring power, rearing children, and directing traffic are developed in order to satisfy specific needs. But, like habits in the individual, they have the indirect consequence of committing the society to an integrated system of values. Taken together, these valued institutions reflect the ethos of the culture, its peculiar way of self-fulfillment.

We may take it as axiomatic that a society becomes confused and uncertain, hence vulnerable to alien doctrine, to the extent that it loses this consciousness of a unique and valued identity. This does not mean, as many too quickly conclude, that a tight doctrinal unity is a necessary condition for cultural resilience. No more than {296} fanaticism in the individual, is general subservience to dogma a sign of strength. Nevertheless, it is essential that individuals feel they are living in a world of valued modes of life, all ultimately integrated by a sense of kinship. This does not require that men should all believe the same thing. It does require that (1) they should believe something and that (2) there should be a core of shared assumptions as to the ultimate distinction between good and evil.

In this context, however, we are concerned not with the problem of homogeneity, but with that of devaluation. Splits in the community, even those leading to civil war, do not necessarily imply a general weakening of values; splits polarize values and intensify adherence, sometimes resulting in a general strengthening of overall community.[20] The debilitation which comes from the secularization of social institutions is of another sort. The machinery of social life becomes just that—machinery, shorn of its valued, sacred quality. As culture decays, attention shifts from ends to means, from values to things.

The mass is at once a symptom of this atrophy and a contributor to it. Population sectors take on a mass quality as they are alienated from symbolic and institutional loyalties. But the movement is reciprocal. The pressure of the mass

---

[20] A community is not necessarily defined by the locus of sovereignty or by organizational boundaries, although these are often convenient indices. A community may break into segments because the common framework of decisionmaking is not adequate to deal with differences; yet these differences, although requiring organizational independence, are not necessarily such as to establish separate communions. A commonwealth of nations, a social movement, a council of churches, are examples of this ambivalent unity.

upon key social agencies, especially in education and science, results in demands for a short-term payoff. The cultural elites are insecure and do not feel that their special (but indispensable) prerogatives are justified. It is not only the general pressure of a factory system, but the capitulation to the demands for commonness which leads them to accept the standards which the mass-man insists must be applied to all alike. This leveling pressure, indifferent to long-run cultural meaning, combines with the demand for efficiency and service to deny {297} to institutions any intrinsic value. The mass thus joins with other forces in industrial society to transform institutions into organizations. They become technical (and expendable) instruments for the achievement of proximate goals.

The general effect of this process is to attenuate and confuse society's self-image; to increase the likelihood of severe shifts in behavior under the pressure of immediate exigency; and to make possible the capture of key institutions, no longer well-defined in character, by organizational manipulators.

The "Stalinoid" as Mass-Man

The mass-man is found not only in the streets, but in positions of institutional leadership. Here he lacks the competence to perform an essential chore—the defense of institutional integrity. In this way, the enfeeblement of cultural elites leaves key social agencies exposed to political assault.[21]

In order to study how mass behavior can influence the educated middle classes, we shall briefly analyze a social type that has received increasing attention in recent years. This is the "Stalinoid liberal"—a product of middle-class alienation. He is, of course, not the only such product. We choose him for analysis because of our special interest in vulnerability to communism; at the same time, we wish to discern how "massness" can shape the thinking of those who may assume leading roles in the formation of public opinion.

The term "Stalinoid" is usually employed as a rough synonym for "fellow traveler," but it is especially useful as a psychological category. Not every individual drawn into the communist orbit is Stalinoid, although this type may predominate. Moreover, the {298} Stalinoid may be a party member, although he will be no true bolshevik. However, the importance of identifying this type of individual lies not so much in the fact that he is recruited into the communist party, although this occurs, as in the fact that he is molded in crucial ways by party ideology *without being severed from his institutional environment and function.* He and others like him make up the hard core of the fellow-traveler circles that are manipulated by communist peripheral organizations and offer the party access to universities, churches, newspapers, political parties, and government agencies.

As a *political* type, the Stalinoid is identified by his adherence to the main line of the communist party, to the defense of its organizations, and above all to the

---

[21] This is by no means a matter of vulnerability to communism alone, although, of course, that is our preoccupation here. On the contrary, one very important example of such vulnerability is the way some universities, weakened by mass characteristics, have been unable to withstand attacks by anticommunist forces. The latter have subverted academic values in the interests of political orthodoxy.

defense of the Soviet Union. But such a position may be reached in many different ways. It is not the simple fact of political adherence which defines the Stalinoid; what is peculiar is the *quality* of his participation and support. We speak not so much of persons who hold a particular position, but of a type of mind, a pattern of predisposition and response. If we analyze the components of the Stalinoid mode of political participation, and the sources of his conduct, we shall see that these converge with the general characteristics of mass behavior. It should also be said that as a psychopolitical type the Stalinoid may just as readily be attracted to some other totalitarian movement. In what follows, consequently, we shall be interested in the general characteristics of the Stalinoid political personality rather than in specific political content, for the latter is only symptomatic of an underlying vulnerability to totalitarian manipulation.

The key components of Stalinoid political participation are (1) participation motivated by alienation from existing values rather than by positive belief; (2) the lack of a deep personal commitment to ideals and institutions, resulting in superficial and vacillating involvement; (3) participation on the basis of stereotyped political codes and symbols; (4) *Reapolitik,* including a radical bifurcation of means and ends; (5) a search for security substitutes {299} in political action. We shall briefly consider each of these symptoms in turn.[22]

1. A major element of the Stalinoid syndrome is the feeling of isolation, of anxiety, of the need to find some substitute for older rejected values. At the same time, this anxiety is not relieved by complete acceptance of the bolshevik way. There is a persistent feeling of insecurity that can find some relief through participation in party causes but which is always accompanied by incomplete acceptance. The Stalinoid enters politics not out of a strong sense of mission, but as a result of feelings of cynicism, frustration, and an unfulfilled need for social solidarity. This emotional basis accounts for the vacillation, the intellectual corruption, and the subordination to power that has characterized many communist fellow travelers. Alienation has made *superficiality* the mark of the Stalinoid, both in relation to his

---

[22] As in this whole area of vulnerability, little in the way of reliable data is available. The following analysis, meant only to be suggestive, is based on the record of middle-class participation in communist politics during, especially, the nineteen-thirties. A number of accounts have appeared which have attempted to identify the Stalinoid syndrome. Although these were written by anticommunists, partisan bias does not explain the agreement on the main characteristics of the Stalinoid which emerges. These accounts do not simply state that certain middle-class elements were in fact seduced by communism: they go further to indicate that certain repetitive symptoms of vulnerability are observable. In addition, as will be noted in the text, the image of the Stalinoid as drawn by these anticommunists is in major outline the same as that held by the communists themselves. See Arthur M. Schlesinger, Jr., *The Vital Center,* Houghton Mifflin Company, Boston, 1949; Eugene Lyons, *The Red Decade,* Bobbs-Merrill Company, Indianapolis, 1941; and Dwight MacDonald, *Henry Wallace, The Man and the Myth*, Vanguard Press, New York, 1948. See also the "confessions" of such well-known former fellow travelers as André Gide, Louis Fischer, and Stephen Spender in *The God That Failed,* Richard Crossman (ed.), Harper & Brothers, New York, 1949. It may be well to re-emphasize here the point made above that the "Stalinoid type" is not the only kind of individual who has been influenced by communism. In addition, on a more general level, David Riesman's analysis of the "other-directed" political style is illuminating. *Op. cit.*, Pt. II.

new loyalties and to traditional values. And this superficiality, under the pressure of anxiety, is not innocent: it results in compulsive responses with sadomasochistic overtones and in easy manipulation by symbolic and organizational devices.

It is significant that the communist image of the petty-bourgeois {300} participant in the movement, either as fellow traveler or as party member, also includes this stress on alienation. "Fellow traveler" is not a term coined by the anticommunists; it was first used by the bolsheviks themselves to characterize precisely the kind of person described here. To be sure, "petty-bourgeois" and similar class-angled terms are often used by bolsheviks as simple epithets. But it is not difficult to show that here they have attempted to identify a significant psychological category.

According to bolshevik doctrine, the petty-bourgeois individual is fundamentally subjectivist in his approach to politics, moved by fleeting fears and egotistic concerns. He is attracted to the movement not by "the logic of his social position," but rather by a personal sense of alienation. "Intellectual soul-sickness" is thought of as the petty-bourgeois malady, sometimes evidenced in more unreliable sectors of the party itself. The bolshevik does not think of *himself* as alienated, for he finds security in his devotion to the party and the revolution. He believes very deeply in something, whereas the petty-bourgeois is incapable of doing so. The latter is unreliable because he suffers a general alienation, not simply disaffection from capitalism. This alienation, with its corollary subjectivism, is the source of the petty-bourgeois participant's inability to take a firm stand for the party and to remove himself from his ordinary pursuits. He is not so much interested in the revolution as in his own ego needs, and these can often be satisfied, or mitigated, without a full dedication to the bolshevik way of life. Hence even when he joins the party, he is suspect until he takes such measures toward integration as will permit no turning back.

2. The Stalinoid is typically involved in the movement only through peripheral organizations. He may talk about the "revolution," may feel guilty and inferior to the true bolshevik, but he will not be able to take the final step. His is a revolt that provides emotional support but is relatively inexpensive. Above all, he is not withdrawn from the satisfactions he can get from continued participation in his middle-class world. This is not inconsistent {301} with strong political feelings. Indeed, the Stalinoid (or petty-bourgeois) is typically more emotional about his politics than the bolshevik. He "hates" capitalism and "loves" the Russians, and finds it difficult to take the matter-of-fact view of events which is natural to the hardened bolshevik. The latter is shored up by his Marxist and Leninist tutelage and may, indeed, be able to face the realities of the Soviet Union without losing his faith in the ultimate worth of revolutionary aspirations. But the utopian illusions of the Stalinoid must function in the present, for he is a man of the here-and-now, demanding current satisfactions for immediately pressing emotional needs. But precisely because his attachment to the movement and to the Soviet Union is a product of these emotional strivings, without the introduction of any reorganization of the personality, new symbols and attachments may readily be substituted. The alienated man moves from one fad to another. His actions are often accom-

panied by a high emotional pitch, but he never really commits himself as a whole person, always leaves an avenue of retreat.

All of this makes the Stalinoid suspect in the eyes of the party. At the same time, however, he can be very useful. Precisely because he is not withdrawn from his institutional environment—because he looks, dresses, talks like a conventional middle-class individual, because he has not compromised himself legally—he can serve the party well in gaining access to areas of influence so long as effective organizational controls are maintained in the hands of reliable personnel.

3. One of the symptoms of the corrosion of values is that they become stereo-typed, sloganized, hence incapable of deeply influencing thought and behavior. When political values are stereotyped, the abstractions in which they are ex-pressed—"the people," "democracy," etc.—become divorced from the traditional context of "understood" meanings; they become free-floating ideological symbols that can absorb any expedient content. Ideas once softened by a shared tradition, so that extreme and overliteral renderings were avoided, are now given a life and impact of their own apart from {302} that tradition. Ordinarily the relation between individual and symbol is mediated by a fundamental loyalty to existing institutions that avoids too harsh a contrast between the abstractions and the reality, always recognizing the distinction between an aspiration and a judgment. Adherence to stereotyped values is unmediated, permitting ready manipulation of those who are unrestrained by the common-sense nexus of loyalty and faith.[23]

Stereotyping is an inevitable hazard when ideas are used as weapons. In combat, as articles for export, they lose their essential cultural function, which

---

[23] After this was written, the recent study of *The Authoritarian Personality* became avail-able. This is an attempt, based on materials gathered in the United States, to assess vulner-ability to fascism. Although this work suffers from an apparent commitment to the view that fascism represents the only significant totalitarian threat, nevertheless the data reveal an especially pertinent, although tentative, conclusion. Questionnaires were designed to test vulnerability to fascism, and an effort was made to identify syndromes associated with those who exhibited high vulnerability, as indicated by high scores, as well as with those who had low scores. It was found that low-scorers exhibited weaknesses similar to those of the high-scorers, despite differences in ideology. Among these weaknesses is the tendency to "stereotypical" thinking — ". . . configurations in which the absence of prejudice, instead of being based on concrete experience and integrated within the personality, is derived from some general external, ideological pattern. Here we find those subjects whose lack of preju-dice, however consistent in terms of surface ideology, has to be regarded as accidental in terms of personality, but we also find people whose rigidity is hardly less related to person-ality than is the case with certain syndromes of high scorers. The latter kind of low scorers are definitely disposed towards totalitarianism in their thinking; what is accidental up to a certain degree is the particular brand of ideological world formula that they chance to come into contact with. We encountered a few subjects who had been identified ideologically with some progressive movement, such as the struggle for minority rights, for a long time, but with whom such ideas contained features of compulsiveness, even of paranoid obsession, and who, with respect to many of our variables, especially rigidity and 'total' thinking, could hardly be distinguished from some of our high extremes. All the representatives of this syn-drome can in one way or another be regarded as counterparts of the 'Surface Resentment' type of high scorer. The accidentalness in their total outlook makes them liable to change fronts in critical situations, as was the case with certain kinds of radicals under the Nazi regime. . . ." Adorno, *op. cit.*, pp. 771-772.

is to shape the outlook and the decisions of those who hold them. Agitation for tolerance, for example, may leave as a casualty the advocates themselves, who lose tolerance as a quality of the spirit while propagandizing for its stereotyped manifestations. Thus it is characteristic of the Stalinoid liberal that he makes of attitudes toward the Negro and {303} the Jew shibboleths of cultural and political judgment, losing in himself that quality of measured understanding and sympathy which is at the heart of tolerance as an effective value. His stereotyped approach makes it difficult for him to distinguish between professional anti-Semites or Negro-haters and those who are moved in less venal ways by received cultural predispositions.

The same process leads the Stalinoid liberal to violate the personalities of those whom he seeks to protect, since he emphasizes the label society has hung around their necks and fails to make distinctions among individuals within the minority groups. The human being, presumably the ultimate object of respect, is lost in the welter of ideological contention. When the liberal becomes a propagandist, when he substitutes for his spontaneous critical role that of the strident advocate, he disqualifies himself from the role of culture bearer. He becomes available for manipulation by those who know how to use sloganized, emptied-out values for their own political ends.

Here again we find a convergence with the Leninist image of the petty-bourgeois participant. According to this view, the petty-bourgeois party member or sympathizer is unable to "think dialectically." He holds to rigid doctrinal formulations because they are emotionally satisfying, and is unable to give them their proper flexible interpretations in action. This charge is lodged not only against those who show right-wing deviations (e.g., taking party support of an immediate program too literally, becoming emotionally involved in it, unable to see it in strategic and tactical perspective), but also against ultra-left elements. The latter, according to this view, are equally petty-bourgeois because they attach themselves to stereotyped Marxist formulae, as substitutes for action, and are unable to make the necessary adaptations to the realities of day-to-day combat. Just as the liberal petty-bourgeois attaches himself to stereotyped symbols because of a fundamental anxiety about his own values, so the petty-bourgeois ultra-leftist is too insecure in his commitment to Leninist doctrine to permit himself freedom of action. In each case, stereotyping is the result of a partial, anxiety-laden {304} adherence. The well-integrated Marxist, on the other hand, may take his fundamental commitments for granted and need not continually reassure himself by ritualistic restatements of orthodox belief.

4. Another symptom of alienation, further identifying the mass character of the Stalinoid liberal, is the devaluation of means and ends in action. The Stalinoid is a *Realpolitiker,* but his political realism is not that of the statesman bent on wedding expedience to his own sense of right; his is the realism of one who has no sure goals of his own, nor the intellectual tools for distinguishing between concessions to expediency and realized values. He is not so much a wielder of power as a worshiper of it; hence he is inevitably drawn into the orbit of those who know what they are after. Hence also he adapts his political behavior to the "irresistible trends of history": what matters is to be on the winning side.

The Stalinoid "progressive"[24] takes what he supposes is a "tough" attitude toward politics. He emphasizes the technical and the expedient. He is, characteristically, very much impressed by efficiency and effectiveness. Thus planning becomes valued for its own sake, shorn of humanistic content. The non-Stalinoid liberal rejects planning when it is not adequately shaped by democratic ideals. The Stalinoid is typically impatient of these restraints; consequently he is easily moved to admire the communists in China and Europe who "get things done" and to accept criticisms of the social democrats as simple vacillators. He is insensitive to the fact that the latter may undergo political travail precisely because they attempt to undertake social change without abandoning established values.[25] This devaluation of means is accompanied by a similar emptying-out of moral ends. When values decay, the goals of action tend to be reduced to technical terms. This is most obvious in the case of {305} attitudes toward socialism. It is typical of the Stalinoid to accept nationalization of industry as an end in itself, without considering the cultural, political, and economic context in which it takes place. This makes it easy for him to become attached to and defend the Soviet Union. In this way, the Stalinoids come to accept a major premise of communist politics: that there is an irreducible good in the Soviet Union which makes it ultimately superior to the capitalist countries. This is not the only reason for attachment to the Soviet Union, but, for our purpose, the point is that this attachment is aided by the loss of value perspective.

A similar devaluation is reflected in the Stalinoid application of a double standard when appraising, say, imperialism as practiced by Russia or by a western power. There is applied a doctrinaire interpretation of imperialism that loses sight of the human factor, the actual consequences for human life and dignity in the dominated countries. Imperialism becomes a matter of technical definition, and the older liberal focus upon the human consequences of exploitative expansion is lost.

5. The Stalinoid is distinguished from the traditional liberal by his search for release from anxiety. Emotional needs color his political participation. He does not have the moral courage that is usually assigned, by friends and enemies alike, to the old-fashioned liberal—the man who knew what his ideals were and how to stand by them. Rather, the Stalinoid is viewed, by those who use him as well as by those who oppose him, as being essentially weak and dependent, ultimately unreliable, capitulating easily to power, and subject to irrational moods and fantasies.

This irrationality and hunger for psychological ersatz comes out most clearly in the relation of the Stalinoids to the Soviet Union. They attach themselves to an emotionally useful image, the word become flesh, the vision of a "progressive" future revealed in the here-and-now. Because Russia is far away, it is possible for

---

[24] As MacDonald (*op. cit.*, p. 36) suggests: "The modern liberal generally calls himself a 'progressive,' a semantically interesting shift from a term which implies *values* to a term which implies *process*."

[25] This tendency of the Stalinoid to defend the communists and to attack the social democrats abroad is a major identifying symptom. They call themselves simple liberals and are therefore presumably less radical than the socialists; but in fact they ally themselves with the communists.

the Stalinoids to clothe it with self-serving illusions, to accept as good coin the propaganda of the bolshevik elite, to ally themselves with something that represents the union of power and perfection. They {306} can find a double release in attacking the evils manifest around them at home and at the same time by entering the communion of the Russian City of God. This adventure would be more or less innocent did it not entail an alliance with the unbridled power of a totalitarian regime.

It is extremely significant in this connection that the Stalinoid support for the USSR came rather late in the day. They did not rally to the Russian revolution until its totalitarian potential had been thoroughly revealed. The Stalinoid support, coming after the consolidation of the "proletarian dictatorship," and defending the instruments of terror and oppression, has always been *in favor of* tyranny.[26] This was the basic symptom of moral decay—that liberals and humanists should find themselves on the side of a police regime and yet believe they were following democratic precepts. They had not even the saving device, available to the true bolshevik, of refusing to consider anything immoral that aided the international party. The Stalinoids did not have this escape and therefore had to corrupt their own ideals by adapting them to the exigencies of Soviet politics.

The most dramatic, and most revealing, example of Stalinoid capitulation to power, enforcing a flight from the traditional liberal role, is found in their defense of the Moscow Trials. In these demonstrations of totalitarian method, which shook the liberal and labor public during the mid-thirties, the fundamental nature of the Soviet regime was brutally revealed. Those who had not {307} understood bolshevism before could have little excuse, if their ideals were meaningful, for failing to understand it now. Yet the Stalinoids flocked to the defense of the dictatorship. As Eugene Lyons put it: "The same editors and writers who once spoke up for Mooney, for Sacco and Vanzetti, who presumably cherished the memory of world response to a Dreyfus or Mendel Baylis case, now gave every benefit of doubt to an omnipotent state and its firing squads rather than to its victims." It was this response to the Moscow Trials which marked the turn to a totalitarianism espoused in the name of liberalism.

The Stalinoids are men who seek to salvage their psychological commitments even if this costs them the corruption of ideals with which they are normally identified. This presumes that these ideals have already been largely attenuated.

---

[26] Of course, most Stalinoids do not overtly defend terror and oppression as such. They excuse it as necessary to defend the regime against some dire alternative. They typically insist that the ordinary people under Russian communism are happier than citizens elsewhere (perhaps more secure because they are in a "noncompetitive" culture), that they are becoming happier all the time, and that they are thankful for being so much better off than their fathers were under the Tsarist regime. Excuses are made on the basis of a presumptive future good and in terms of supposed or real past evils. The Stalinoid recognizes "progress" as defined by industrialization and increased diffusion of urban skills as the basic good. This is a fact in the Soviet Union. For the Stalinoid, therefore, it is ungenerous to ask the two questions: At what cost? And were there no better alternatives? Such questions are raised only by those who wish to use their values as judgments upon events. Stalinoidism reflects an uneasy and disorderly retreat from those values.

In sum, we may say that the crucial difference between the Stalinoid and the Stalinist is that the latter has made the fateful leap to a new set of values. However ultimately indefensible these are, they do provide the individual bolshevik with a source of spiritual strength by placing him in a "world within a world." But the Stalinoid, alienated, fearful, and alone, seeks to attach himself to the communist "wave of the future" without severing his connections with the world in which he lives.

Two conclusions should be evident from the description above:

1. The most pervasive characteristic of the Stalinoid political personality is the weakening of values. And this, as we have suggested earlier, is the fundamental meaning of "massness." If this is so, the lesson is that mass responses are discernible among elite elements on which the most fragile, but culturally decisive, institutions must depend for the maintenance of their integrity.

2. Stalinoidism as a *political* category is only one among a number of alternative paths which alienated intellectuals and professionals may follow. The Stalinoid as we have described him is essentially a man who thinks in a certain way. The focus upon communism is in part arbitrary. *Many anticommunists have Stalinoid characters.* Stalinoidism creates a disposition to manipulation by totalitarian {308} political forces, if these forces don the outward insignia of accepted values. The communist-oriented intellectuals and professionals have no monopoly on alienation, with its attendant stereotyping and emptying-out of social ideals. The communists have been successful exploiters of this malady, but their success is only symptomatic of the underlying vulnerability of a society that permits its culture-sustaining elites to abandon their distinctive functions.

Vulnerability and Opportunism

The import of the above analysis may be restated as follows: where values weaken, manipulability rises. This weakening of values may characterize significant *segments* of society before a radical decay is observable in the entire social body. The intellectuals in particular are highly sensitive to the pressures which produce alienation and are likely to respond earlier and more acutely to them; at the same time, their response is especially important because they play a large role in the maintenance of institutional integrity.

In effect, then, we have discussed areas of cultural attenuation and have drawn the conclusion that where these exist they affect the distribution of power in society. Put as a general rule we may say: *Under conditions of political combat, those who have no firm values of their own become the instruments of the values of others.* This is the underlying reality which is reflected in the manipulability of "massified" elements of the population.

Cultural attenuation is consequential for organizational decision. It strengthens ordinary opportunism by robbing leaders and ranks alike of their moorings in traditional patterns of thought and action. It heightens the tendency for attention to be focused upon proximate goals, while ultimate (in the sense of character-defining) values are ignored. Opportunism is a readiness to adapt to situations that offer immediate rewards without weighing the consequences of such adaptation for the ultimate character of the group. Sometimes opportunism is forced upon a leadership by the exigencies {309} of action; its spread is also a symptom of general devaluation. In each case vulnerability to bolshevik attack is increased, although the circumstances may differ radically.

Decisionmakers in organizations do not always enjoy the luxury of completely controlling the consequences of action for the moral ideals they profess. This is due in part to the fact that responsible leaders are usually committed to more than one goal, including the survival of the organization. Action in one direction may lead to unwanted consequences in another; the result is continuous compromise and an emphasis on moderate, gradualist methods. The membership, however, especially if it has been schooled in stereotyped reactions, may not appreciate the difficulties faced by the leaders. As a result, an opposition may make political capital by calling for more radical implementation of the organization's professed ideals.

This process is normal, for the "outs" can be in varying degrees irresponsible with impunity, calling for measures which they themselves might not be able to fulfill if they were in office. The further away from power the opposition is, the easier such a challenge can be. The systematic exploitation of this tension is especially characteristic of the communists in labor and liberal circles, where mass-membership organizations have strong ideological commitments. The communists can be counted on to make the most of any situation in which labor leaders are caught between their own speeches, framed in class-struggle terms, and their wish to come to responsible arrangements with management. So too with liberal organizations which seek political reforms but which are committed to methods of moderation and compromise. The leaders of such groups are continuously faced with the danger that the membership will be provoked into adventures, or won over to the support of irresponsible propagandists. As a result, the leaders may be forced into extreme positions which they do not wish to hold, or even lose control of the organization.

The communists are in a better position to exploit this type of opportunism—generated by responsible action rather than by loss of {310} values—than are ordinary minorities because they are unrestrained by any considerations save those affecting their own power. They are in no sense a "loyal opposition." Moreover, having a single-minded approach to politics, they can, if they gain authority, institute much of the program they have espoused uninhibited by its consequences for other values. Those who admire the communists' ability to "get things done" are not usually sensitive to the high cost of this effectiveness.

Of greater importance than this type of opportunism—although its political consequences are not so easily observable—is that which reflects a weakening of values in social institutions. When institutions lose a value-based self-image, they are disarmed before those who may wish to promote alien modes of thought and practice, or to penetrate the institution for limited practical objectives. The communists (and other power cliques) can fully exploit their flexibility, adapting themselves to the immediate needs and moods of the target in order to facilitate access and subsequent manipulation.

This sort of opportunism, in which proximate aims are emphasized in the absence of a firm sense of ultimate values, is familiar enough: a foreign ministry which chooses personnel in terms of current policy rather than of long-term interests; a trade-union which ignores the social responsibilities of labor leadership; a university which becomes a conglomeration of specialists and administrators harboring few spokesmen for the basic values of education in a democracy; a political machine ready to deal with any group which will permit it to retain its hold on patronage; an idealistic political movement which, in its dedication to specific measures, loses sight of its spiritual foundations. *In each of these situations, the target is vulnerable because it applies to potential collaborators and participants only the most superficial tests—those having to do with criteria of technical competence and of agreement on immediate issues.*

An undue stress on proximate aims may be discernible even when institutional leaders have a great deal to say about ultimate moral ideals. The point is that these ideals must be made relevant {311} to concrete action. If they are merely vague honorifics which grace formal speeches and programs, but do not effectively guide decision, opportunism will result—often worse than in the case of those who do not profess to be moralists, because unrecognized opportunistic adaptations are more difficult to control.

This problem of embodying morals in action does not arise significantly in well-integrated societies; there the leaders follow a received code which serves the purpose fairly well. This, of course, still goes on in modern society. But as the areas of disintegration widen, and new threats to established values emerge, a high degree of self-consciousness is required. When the basic aspirations and commitments of an organization are in jeopardy, decisions must be made with a conscious view to their character-defining consequences. This requires attention both to the threat and to the methods used against it. For when there is no firm sense of what is to be defended, panic may result, leading to actions which, although designed to meet a threat to values, are in themselves subversive. Thus the defense itself is opportunistic, and no sure connection between institutional behavior and professed ideals is established.

An example of vulnerability to communist attack because of fixation on proximate aims is the socialist movement. This case is especially instructive because the socialists would not ordinarily be characterized as a proximate-aim group. They obviously associate themselves with long-term goals and with a set of "socialist principles." In fact, however, modern socialism has at times been acutely vulnerable to communist attack, especially to the unity tactics of bolshevik organizational strategy. This vulnerability has increased whenever the socialists have lost sight of their relation to the values of the liberal-democratic tradition and have given priority to certain immediate political and economic aims in such a way as to permit collaboration with anyone who supported those aims. This has sometimes led to united action with the communists—a process which has uniformly resulted in subversion of the socialist organizations. {312} So long as the socialists were not self-conscious about the basis of their differences with the communists, and were unwilling to reckon the consequences of such collaboration for the character of the socialist movement, a vacuum was created into which the communists moved quickly and aggressively. By the same token, however, once this self-consciousness is achieved—as it was in the United States following the civil war in Spain—the socialists become the most vigorous anticommunists. For they are on the front line of attack, among the primary targets for bolshevik subversion and annihilation. The fight against communism has forced the socialists to review their basic values and crucial policy decisions. It is this self-consciousness which is the first requirement for all institutions subject to similar threats.

Ultimate moral aims are not operationally relevant unless they modify the *present* character of an institution. The institution must reflect in its day-to-day behavior the ideals to which it claims commitment. Only then will it be able to judge the consequences of decision for moral ideals as well as for technical effectiveness. Indeed, only then will there be any significant moral conduct at all. It is in the character of an institution that we find the locus of restraint which continuously modifies technical decisions so as to make them conform to moral aspirations. Unless this process of modification exists, decisionmaking is reduced to its technical components, with the result that the indirect consequences for character are uncontrolled. In the case of the socialists, this was revealed in the necessity to avoid bolshevik methods of work, organizational practices, and defining symbols, if they were to preserve their integrity as a radical group within the liberal-democratic tradition. In effect it was recognized implicitly that socialists could not make political decisions in technical, power-oriented terms without at the same time weighing the consequences for the *kind of person* selected and molded by the socialist movement. This type of individual, as reflected in his basic attitudes and practices, must embody in himself the moral ideals to which {313} he claims adherence. He cannot be part of the democratic tradition and yet subordinate himself completely to a party leadership: he cannot yield to the sadomasochistic tendencies which are the mark of participation in totalitarian movements; he must refuse to accept the dissolution of the community which turns political opponents into "criminals" and mortal enemies; in short, he must reflect the values of moderation and respect which lie at the heart of the democratic ethos. It was precisely the embodiment of these values in day-to-day political life which was threatened when the socialists undertook to accept the help of the communists. For this acceptance reflected a willingness to make political decisions without weighing the consequences for character. Vulnerability declined markedly as soon as this was understood.[27]

The case of the socialists only poses in sharpened form the issue which faces all institutions. Vulnerability can be controlled only by the affirmation in practice of the moral ideals which define the character of an organization. This affirmation requires, above all, the shaping of individuals so that they become competent to

---

[27] It is obvious—given the existence of "Nenni socialists" in Italy and elsewhere—that the vulnerability of socialism has not been eliminated. However, it is a striking fact that where understanding of the characterological issue is achieved, the socialists become among the firmest opponents of communism. In assessing the resilience of any given sector of the socialist movement, it is necessary to consider the extent to which differences with communism are interpreted as fundamental cleavages. This will be reflected in a willingness to collaborate with "capitalist" parties and institutions rather than with the bolsheviks, who will be labeled as "red fascists."

apprehend those threats, from within and without, which endanger the institution's self-image. It is the failure to do this that leaves the door open to *effective* penetration. The mere fact of penetration, except where military security is at stake, is not important; it is what can be achieved by penetration that counts. Unions, universities, and other agencies which embody values have most to fear when they become bound to the moment, to the technical job at hand, to limited views of their social function. They are then softened for ideological and organizational manipulation: they will {314} become unable to distinguish between those who defend treasured aspirations and those who corrupt them.[28]

---

[28] It should perhaps be stated once more that this analysis presumes a conservative orientation, since it deals with the defense of the integrity of institutions. Whether any given institution is worth defending is a separate question. Moreover, it is clear that the defense of institutional character is not inconsistent with change: on the contrary, various changes may be indispensable if adequate adaptations, permitting the retention of basic modes of action under new social conditions, are to be made.

CHAPTER 8
PROBLEMS OF COUNTEROFFENSE

{315}

A complete program of anticommunist action must be based on a study of the conditions producing equilibrium in democratic societies. Such a study has not been undertaken here. Consequently, it must be emphasized that in this final chapter we are concerned with such conclusions regarding counteroffensive action as may be inferred from this report. It is believed that the foregoing analysis of communist strategy does suggest certain principles which are necessary for the intelligent formulation of policy. These principles, however, are not offered as a full "answer" to the problem of communism. They are relevant primarily to the context of political combat; and this context is only a part of that broad area—including measures enhancing the emotional and economic security of target groups—within which decisions affecting totalitarian threats to democracy are made.

The more we understand about the nature of communism, the more readily can we avoid (1) the failure to recognize its true aims and subversive methods and (2) those excessive reactions which threaten themselves to undermine the foundations of democratic society. Increased knowledge helps us to think concretely, to specify the problem in situational terms, to direct countermeasures to those areas where they are relevant and useful, and to avoid unsought consequences for the integrity of our institutions.

The problem of subversion has two aspects which are often confused. On the one hand, a group is considered subversive when it seeks to overthrow established authority by forcible means. It is here that the doctrine of "clear and present danger" most readily applies, the assumption being that governments ought to punish acts and not thoughts, and that measures of restraint ought to be consistent with the seriousness of the acts committed. However, {316} the problem is complicated when, as in the case of communism, subversion refers not only to a revolutionary program, but also to the manipulation of social institutions for alien ends, this manipulation being conducted covertly in the name of the institution's own values. It is this type of subversion which is meant when fear is expressed of the effect of communism in the schools, in the labor movement, and in liberal organizations. Such activities, and ultimate overthrow of the government, are of course related, but concern for the integrity of the institutions themselves leads us to seek modes of self-defense long before any clear and present danger to established authority is demonstrable.

We assume that institutional leaders, including those in government, have the right and the duty to defend the principles upon which their organizations are built. An inescapable corollary of this assumption is that the methods of action available to these leaders are limited. Since the goal is the defense of certain *values* (not simply of the power of an elite), the weapons used against subversion must be so fashioned as to preserve these values in the course of their defense.

These considerations, therefore, call for subtle and discriminating judgments, and can be given effect in policy formation only on the basis of detailed knowledge. This study has sought to contribute to our understanding of bolshevism in the hope that we may then be in a better position to make such decisions as would defeat the enemy without destroying ourselves. Given this perspective, the following conclusions deserve emphasis:

1. Each institution should be defended in its own terms. The appraisal of subversive threats to the integrity of institutions must take account of the differing conditions that affect the preservation of that integrity.

2. Anticommunist strategy should orient to the "intervening elites" through whom access to the mass is gained and who have the capacity to direct resentment into constitutional channels.

3. The denial of legitimacy is a key to the denial of access; {317} but measures which seek to influence legitimacy must be adapted to the nature of the arena.

4. In the denial of access, the aim is to isolate the communists; but this counterstrategy has to do with *political* isolation and cannot be equated with formal exclusion from membership in unions or other organizations.

5. Reliance on organizational weapons is, for communists and anticommunists alike, a sign of strategic weakness rather than of strength. Hence countermeasures taken within the context of organizational combat are, from the standpoint of the over-all defense of democracy against communism, of only tactical importance. Ultimately, only measures which contribute to long-term economic and political stability will be decisive.

The Need for Situational Thinking

Although the *problem* of subversion concerns the entire society, effective countermeasures require that attention be focused upon specific arenas and targets. This seems scarcely more than a truism. Yet many proposals for anticommunist action ignore the fundamental principle that political combat, like other planned struggles, requires situational judgment; i.e., the nature of the arena must be taken into account when tactical decisions are made. Communist strategy is selective and elite-oriented. Effective counteroffense must take account of this strategy, recognizing the sources of weakness and strength in bolshevism, adapting itself to the conditions of combat in particular arenas.

The problem of denying to the communists such strategic objectives as legitimacy, access, and the neutralization of opponents *may* be considered from the point of view of the total society. But when this is done, there is a twofold danger: measures of intimidation and coercion may be introduced at many points where they are not justified by the actual subversive potential of the communists, resulting in a needless weakening of basic civil rights and in the strengthening of arbitrary methods; at the same time, such measures may {318} be ineffective because they contribute to rather than weaken the strength of the communists among key elements in the community.

This general point will be clarified if we consider a few specific conclusions:

1. *Reliance on organizational weapons is a sign of strategic weakness rather than of strength.* In the general political struggle, organizational weapons provide the communists with important tactical advantages. But it must be remembered that these weapons have been developed precisely in order to overcome communism's fundamental weakness with respect to what is ultimately basic to political power—control over loyalties. Indeed, one of the general functions of organizational weapons is that of *eluding the need to win consent* as a condition for attaining or wielding power. When a power-oriented elite wishes to exercise authority beyond its ability to mobilize favorable opinion in its own right, organizational manipulation may be one method of doing so without the use of violence. The Leninists rely on organizational devices to gain power for a minority; and, indeed, any totalitarian government depends on such devices to control and mobilize the community.

In the United States, communist strength in the unions is dependent almost completely on the effective use of disciplined units of the combat party. This penetration and manipulation is abetted, to be sure, by the special circumstances of union organization, particularly (1) the ease with which one-party regimes are established within them and (2) the atmosphere of labor-management conflict, which binds the ranks to leaders under fire from the "enemy." Yet it is clear that the ideology of communism—either the traditional class-struggle variety or more modern stereotypes associated with Soviet patriotism—has with very few exceptions taken no hold upon the minds of labor's rank and file.

The situation among certain middle-class sectors is quite different, however. It is among these—especially professional and other groups who try to think for themselves and hence are accessible to ideological manipulation—that we find the fellow travelers of communism. Not necessarily accepting the doctrines of Marxism, {319} these groups are seduced by Leninist activism and are drawn to the Soviet Union for the easy symbolic gratifications it offers. The party's peripheral organizations operating among these groups are more and more becoming devices for the mobilization of latent support rather than for winning power by the covert manipulation of groups basically unsympathetic to the movement.

Where communist strength is based exclusively on the effective use of organizational techniques, the problem of counteroffense is relatively simple, once the need to oust the party agents from positions of influence has been recognized. The need is to create and encourage devices to mobilize latent anticommunist sentiment. The strategic advantages are on the side of the anticommunists, and there need be little anxiety concerning the ultimate outcome.

2. *Effective anticommunist opposition is that which is relevant to the specific arena of combat.* The Bolsheviks, in penetrating an organization, always seek to identify themselves with its aims—they become the "best workers" for whatever goals the organization seeks to attain. Occasionally, as in the case of their superpatriotism during World War II, affecting trade-union policies, the goals of the organization may be directly subverted. This is not ordinarily the case: what is usually at stake is the indirect consequence of communist control for the long-

range character of the organization and for its role in the community. The struggle for the "soul" of an organization—its evolving commitments to modes of action and its basic loyalties—can be carried on only by participants. Efforts to intervene from the outside are usually self-defeating. This means that opposition to the communists in any given arena must come from within, led by men whose loyalty to the institution is unquestionable. Even this criterion, however, is not enough. Not only must the opposition come from within the arena, but to be most effective it should be able to appeal to the same sources of support as do the communists, to meet them on their own ground.

3. *Defense against communism requires positive measures for the protection of institutional integrity, each in its own terms.* Institutions embody values, but they do not all do so in the same {320} way. Therefore no uniform program can be devised, or is needed, which will protect all institutions with the same devices for, say, the denial of access or of legitimacy. Simple formulae, such as those calling for the formal exclusion of communists from all organizations and institutions, reflect a failure to think in concrete strategic and tactical terms.

There is no sure way of gauging the point at which communism becomes a clear and present danger to the integrity of an institution. This requires an estimate of the total situation, taking account of many symptoms. But it is at least possible to say that such estimates should be based on evidence available for each case rather than solely on inferences drawn from the general threat to society as a whole. Given a world situation in which democracy is under attack, institutional leaders will naturally wish to be on guard—in the sense of *alert to*—the sources and methods of totalitarian attack. But repressive measures, themselves consequential for institutional integrity, should be taken only when evidence shows that the particular institution is in danger.

This localization of the clear-and-present-danger doctrine will avoid the twin pitfalls of innocence and hysteria. On the one hand, the existence of a general communist threat is recognized; on the other, the faulty process of leaping from a general threat to repressive measures in specific cases is rejected. Innocence in this context fails to recognize the potentialities of communism and hence is blind when the threat is real; hysteria sees concrete manifestations of the threat everywhere, is unable to distinguish the possible from the actual. Both responses inhibit the application of intelligence to the formulation of policy.

The need for application of countermeasures according to the varying needs of particular situations will be evident if we compare a university, a government agency, and a trade-union. These institutions vary in function, hence also in relative vulnerability. Few ideas are too dangerous to be afforded a place in a university. Given proper safeguards, even the espousal of totalitarian doctrine—if done openly and not secretly or deviously—can be permitted, if only {321} to function as a challenge within the intellectual community. Such participation can be controlled if the universities take account of the whole man, his entire background and prospective role on the faculty,

Administrative agencies, however, which must rely on the discretion of officials in action, face a different problem. Here there is no question of creating an environment most conducive to effective teaching and to the pursuit of truth, but of responsible and controlled decisionmaking. Therefore there can be no question of conscious toleration of elements inherently disloyal.

Labor unions face still other problems and have different opportunities for the elimination of communism. As voluntary associations organized democratically, the unions are political arenas; the existence of anticommunist power groupings is the most effective way of dealing with the problem. At the same time, the special role of the labor movement as a target of communist penetration calls for the cooperation of such power groupings on a national basis in order to pool resources and concentrate forces at crucial points.

In other words, apart from general alertness, the methods proper in one institutional context are not necessarily justifiable (or effective) in another. Each must be dealt with in its own terms, due consideration being given to the intensity of the threat and to the special needs of each in defending its integrity.

The Role of Intervening Elites

Apart from the state power of the Soviet Union, the most secure source of communist influence is not its own agitation, or its organizational effectiveness, but the unrest generated by stresses within society. This unrest calls forth its own leadership to create and man the machinery of social action—unions, pressure groups, political parties, newspapers. These heterogeneous and fluctuating leaders occupy a strategic role, for *the relation between the communists and the mass is mediated and largely determined by the prior relation of the communists to reformist organizational and {322} ideological elites.* This, as we have seen, is very well understood by the bolsheviks themselves and effectively shapes their choice of targets and methods of action. Their use of "unity" tactics and of peripheral organizations is based on the assumption that leaders of mass organizations and those who mold public opinion are susceptible to manipulation. Through such activity, oriented to elites, the communists seek to gain access to the major sources of power in the society. In general, the *direct* relation of the communists to the masses comes only after considerable preparatory work among the "natural" leaders of workers, farmers, and middle-class groups. While these leaders give expression to rank-and-file resentment and to the desire for change, they also reflect the basic loyalty of their followers to the established institutional order.

Such intervening elites, standing between the communists and the masses, have always been regarded as the "main enemy" in bolshevik political strategy. Although this basic perspective has not changed, latter-day communism has adopted a more flexible and sophisticated approach to the "petty-bourgeois" leaders and publicists. Lenin stressed the need for a frontal attack upon these elites to isolate them from the masses. In this, however, he displayed too much faith in the potentialities of open communist agitation; his successors have relied more on deception, using the techniques he himself developed. This has required an attempt to gauge the differential vulnerability and potential utility of elite members for the movement, instead of writing them off as simple collaborators and defenders of the "class enemy."

The importance to the communists of neutralizing threats to the social base has been discussed. The greatest animus is generally directed against those who challenge the communists in specific organizational arenas. These threats come primarily from socialists and others who share certain strategic perspectives and modes of action with the communists. Some reformists, however, especially unattached labor leaders, professors, and publicists, do not threaten the communists directly or in any relevant organizational way. They do constitute an ultimate political threat as a group which can, in {323} a time of crisis, help to divert the masses from revolutionary goals. Yet if approached "with patience and caution," these leaders can themselves be manipulated, hence treated as mass elements rather than as self-conscious elites.

Although it is true that socialists are among the "natural enemies" of the communists in the organizational battle, the socialists themselves are not invulnerable. This weakness has two important sources. First, the socialist organizations are themselves vulnerable to bolshevik penetration when they have failed to take a clear stand (as reflected in the indoctrination and selection of the membership) against the idea that capitalism is the main enemy, overlooking the threat to political democracy from sources not accounted for in the Marxian view of history.

When a socialist organization or a significant portion of its leadership is uncertain about its own character, it is possible for the communists to build a "left wing" within the organization. This left wing, composed of revolutionary socialists and secret communists, can then carry on a factional fight for control of the organization, either ousting the old leadership or itself leaving and thus weakening the party. Such activities are usually associated with strong feelings for "unity" with the communists. This process, which occurred in the United States during the mid-thirties, was evident in a number of European countries after World War II. As a result, the socialists have been weakened politically, although in many cases their antibolshevik stand has been clarified and firmly established.

It follows that socialist education, largely an elite-oriented operation, should be aided wherever possible.[1] The emphasis should be on strengthening the differences between socialism and communism. Any propaganda which slurs over these real and potential differences, with the purpose of identifying communists and socialists, will subvert this task. This is one area where mass communication techniques are not necessarily relevant. The need is for educational work, {324} through select-audience journals, books, and schools, which will strengthen antibolshevik understanding among the socialists and will lend assistance to those positive tendencies (including the Christian Socialists) which seek to ground the socialist movement upon a non-Marxian ideology.

The second source of socialist vulnerability is shared by any other reformist elite which champions social change while mobilizing mass resentment in the struggle for power. The socialists (and other reformist elites) must reflect, even while attempting to restrain, the sentiments of those who constitute their mass base. To the extent that this sentiment is congenial to (although not necessarily created by) communist programs, the reformist leaders may be forced into un-

---

[1] Rules of this kind do not imply advocacy of socialism or other reformist movements. To the extent, however, that they do exist as significant political forces, their capacity to fight communism should be enhanced.

desired positions. For example, pressure for "unity" with the communists may come from below, and the reformists may be forced into extremist positions which threaten social stability when general distress stirs the rank and file.

The political function of the intervening elites is to direct mass resentment into constitutional channels. The Leninists understand this very well, although, being interested only in the power relevance of group behavior, they identify this function of the reformists as their *only* role in society. It is precisely because the natural function of the intervening elites operates to sustain the established political order—while heading off the forces which may threaten it—that the communists devote so much strategic and tactical attention to them. This attention is divided between efforts to neutralize those who are direct organizational competitors and to win over those who, because of inadequate self-consciousness, can be treated as mass elements. An effective anticommunist program must also take account of these potentialities, strengthening the capacity of the reformists to enhance social stability.

The radicalism of the intervening elites, when it is manifest, reflects not so much a firmly held doctrine as it does the depth of the crisis. An upheaval within the labor movement, such as produced the CIO, will emphasize radicalism; so too will the problems of leading the unemployed. But as social conditions stabilize, the agencies of {325} reformism become institutionalized, and the leadership, being more secure, reasserts its fundamental commitment to the established order.

This normal process is best exemplified in the labor movement. Indeed, of all the reformist elites, it is the labor leadership which is least vulnerable to the blandishments of communism. That is because an established union leadership has a stake in a going concern, seeks to minimize risks to the survival of its organizations, and readily adapts itself to what seems a viable, even if limited, mode of social action. In the United States, communist strength in the labor movement is not significantly due to the weakness of the labor elite; such strength as they have (apart from the penetrative powers of the combat party) is largely a residue of their capacity to fill a vacuum during the days of the great labor upswing of the mid-thirties. As the strength and stability of the labor leadership has grown, its ability to defend itself from—and indeed to take the offensive against—communist inroads has markedly increased. This was understood by Lenin, who counted the leaders of the "yellow" trade-unions among his primary targets.

Although modern communism has revised early Leninist doctrine to the extent of softening its verbal attack in order to take advantage of vulnerabilities as they arise, the basic orientation has not changed, nor has the validity of Lenin's insight. When trade-unions are strong, they are a bulwark against communism; but when they are weak, they are communism's opportunity. Lenin's heirs have understood better than he that elites become vulnerable to seduction when their institutions are weak. But this understanding, permitting greater tactical flexibility, does not alter the fundamental fact that the natural course of labor leadership is toward acceptance of the established order rather than rebellion against it. The labor leaders, Lenin would have said, seize upon social unrest and direct it into channels which are consistent with the continued existence of the constitutional order. This, as we have suggested, is an accurate judgment. We need not follow

Lenin in his conclusion that this constitutes "betrayal of the masses."

Apart from the trade-union movement, reformism in the United States {326} has had few strong institutional centering points. Its leadership has therefore been unstable, easily influenced by the shifting winds of doctrine, not bound by any strong ideological loyalties. This condition of chronic weakness has made the "progressive" movement an easy target for the communists, who have preyed upon its sentimental attachment to vague ideas, putting themselves forward as "the most vigorous fighters" for the values of democratic idealism.

As in the case of the socialists, a key problem for these institutionally unattached reformist elements is that of character-definition. The need is to sharpen their own self-image so that the basic difference between reformist liberals and communists cannot be obscured. This heightened self-consciousness in turn requires an appreciation of bolshevism's challenge to democratic constitutionalism on a world scale, as well as education in and reaffirmation of the democratic values themselves. Of course, everyone needs education along these lines. But where education is part of an anticommunist *strategy*, it must be designed to strengthen those who are "on the line," not only because of their own vulnerability, but because, newly armed, they are in a position to carry on the struggle where it can do the most good.

In mustering the intervening elites, it is wise not to abandon those who have a "communist element." We do not write off a military position when the enemy has penetrated with a patrol; yet in anticommunist tactics this error is often encountered. It must be granted, understood in advance, that the communists will attempt to gain strength among the reformists; to identify the communist element is to *set* a problem, not to solve it. Just when a particular organization is to be written off as being hopelessly under communist control depends on the concrete circumstances, *including the possibility of competing for power within the organization*. In any case, the yielding of a particular organization should not be confused with the tarnishing of an entire social group as inherently subversive.

The essential point is that these intervening elites arise spontaneously under conditions of social stress and that they can perform the indispensable function of directing mass resentment into self-preserving {327} channels. They are therefore both obstacle and target for the communists; it behooves an anticommunist strategy to maximize the size of the obstacle and the impenetrability of the target.

The Denial of Legitimacy

We have seen that bolshevism is sensitive to the need to legitimize its striving for power. Further, our analysis has shown that the bolshevik approach to legitimacy is situational, always adapted to the contest for a specific political arena. Thus Lenin tried to show that his ideas represented the true Marxist heritage, and to appropriate the symbols and heroes of Marxism for his movement. Similarly, the bolsheviks attempt to guard their role as participants in the general community of democratic idealism so that they will be thought of as simply one tendency among others within the liberal-labor movement. In doing so, they establish their right to participate in the organizations of labor and liberalism, an indispensable condition for the deployment of organizational weapons against key targets.

The opponents of communism are, in general, aware of the problem of legitimacy. Thus legitimacy is at stake in proposals to outlaw the communists as a legal party, and in efforts to treat them as pariahs, outside the pale of the community. Such efforts, however, are inadequate when they fail to take account of the special areas within which legitimacy is sought. The communists have been political pariahs with respect to this nation as a whole during their entire history; yet this has not kept them from extending their influence among disaffected elements seeking change, where communist activity is most effective. These elements, when access to them is won, offer the communists a base from which ultimately to attack the community as a whole. *The problem is to deny them this base*, to see to it that the groups to whom they appeal (not the society as a whole) do not accept them as legitimate participants in the movement for social reform.

As we have seen, the targets of communist penetration are vulnerable to the extent that they lose sight of ultimate character-defining {328} values and consequently lose the capacity to apply any save superficial criteria to potential collaborators and participants. When liberals focus their attention exclusively upon goals, ignoring methods, they tend to accept the help of any proffered hand. Since, in specific areas, the strength of the communists may not be insignificant, this help may result in commitments which decisively alter the character of the reformist movements. But this process is not inevitable. Once the subversive potential of the communists is understood, it is quite possible for reformist organizations to eschew collaboration with communists and to become effective and self-conscious enemies of bolshevism.

If legitimacy in these key areas is to be denied the communists—for it is here, not in society at large, that they have been able to make significant inroads—then tactics must be adopted which will achieve that end. During certain periods, general legislation outlawing communism may be superfluous for the community as a whole; and precisely such legislation may have the consequence of strengthening rather than weakening the legitimacy of communists among those elements which provide them with an indispensable leverage in the body politic.

Legislative measures aimed at purging the labor movement of communist influence, but which actually operate to weaken noncommunist unions, serve to bolster the strength of the communists. Such action lends credence to their assertion that "what hurts us hurts labor." It follows that the communist issue should be clearly separated from general labor legislation. The rule is that nothing should be done tending to confuse communism with bona fide labor leadership, for it is precisely this confusion which the communists earnestly seek. The same holds for other reformist organizations and leaders.

These strictures as to the *misapplication* of the strategic principle of denying legitimacy do not, of course, impugn the principle itself. Indeed, one of the conclusions suggested by our analysis of communist organizational strategy may be formulated as follows: *Effective counteroffense calls for the denial to communists of legitimate participation in labor and reformist organizations*. This requires that {329} educational activities on the communist issue be *elite-oriented*. The history of communist manipulation of target groups must be made available to such elites in specific terms relevant to their own problems and aims. In addition, these groups must be brought to see the general threat of communism to democratic values so that (1) the urgency of clarifying their own positions will be recognized and (2) the image of communism as a "left-wing" of democratic idealist tendencies will be destroyed. Such a program of reorientation cannot take place in an atmosphere which confuses the distinction between the vulnerable target and the aggressor.

The orientation to elites helps to refine a policy which is, indeed, already widely accepted. Anticommunist strategy does take account of the possibility that acute social distress may thrust large masses "into the arms of the communists." It is therefore generally recognized that effective strategy—whatever one's feelings regarding the moral status of the participants—clearly requires that a distinction be made between the seducer and the seduced. This principle should be extended to include the relation of communism to reformist ideological and organizational elites.

It is in this area, far more than in relation to the population at large, that educational activity can be extremely useful. The problem is not one of mass propaganda, but of training opinion-leaders within those centers that mobilize masses in times of crisis. It has been amply demonstrated in practice that such leaders become strong barriers to the power drive of the party when they come to a full understanding of the meaning of communism. Not only is vulnerability reduced by the anticommunist self-consciousness of these elements, but, more important, new weapons relevant to the arenas of action can be forged for use in offensive action against the communists and the areas they control. A good example is the effective work of the International Confederation of Free Trade Unions on such issues as forced labor in the Soviet Union.

A primary objective of this educational activity, thus directed, would be to deny to the communists their role as legitimate participants in the movements of democratic idealism. For it is the belief {330} that the communists are only "more radical, perhaps even a little fanatical, but still part of the general community of those committed to democracy" which opens the door to their subversive operations. It must be recognized that this subversion is in the first instance directed against the reformist movements themselves, as a means of access to the society as a whole. To deny legitimacy is to deny access and hence to isolate and render politically impotent the bolshevik organizational weapons.

Historically, the labor movement has been associated with reformism; and the organization of labor has been a road to influence, not only for the communists, but for other political groupings as well. These other tendencies have for the most part been loyal to the basic interests of labor and have accepted, with many variations, its responsibilities to the entire community. At the same time, partly because of firsthand knowledge of bolshevism, partly because of the exigencies of seeking power for themselves, they have been the most consistent and effective barriers to communist expansion in the labor movement. These anticommunist resources should be broadened and exploited in the general counteroffensive. In order to do so, the common source from which these elements are drawn—the general radical and reformist tendencies in the country—should be made aware of the basic threat of communism, *not only to the status quo, but to the ideals of the reformers themselves.*

Such a program does not necessarily call for partisan support of the non-communist-left; it does suggest that where such forces exist their anticommunist potentialities should be recognized and aided. Such aid is not so much positive as negative: it is a matter of avoiding actions which would undermine the anticommunist leadership by insisting on politically irrelevant concessions. For example, employers who attempt to establish a docile union leadership will subvert the capacity of that leadership to sustain itself against communist-led pressure from below. In other words, the problem of legitimacy is faced by the anticommunists as well as by the communists: they too must retain their status as legitimate contenders for the ideals or interests of their followers.

{331} We have emphasized the role of reformist elites, because the denial of legitimacy in the arenas they control is crucial in anticommunist strategy. The need for situational thinking on the question of legitimacy is more general, however. Particular institutions frame their own bases for legitimate participation, and any effort to deny legitimacy to the communists must take these variations into account. Thus the legal, scientific, and teaching professions, being especially sensitive to moral issues, must be permitted to approach the problem of legitimacy in their own way.

The Denial of Access

The denial of legitimacy, when adapted to the needs of specific arenas, is a key to the denial of access. This is the point of much anticommunist activity. But it may be suggested that too much attention is devoted to the simple fact of whether communists do or do not exist within some organization. Of far greater importance is a question which does not raise such disturbing issues for democratic policy: Are there elements which accept the desirability of *political collaboration* with the communists? At first glance, this may seem to be much the same thing. But it is not necessarily so. The important point about unions, and other institutions accepting membership on nonpolitical grounds, is not that communists can become members. It is rather that noncommunist elements within these institutions can be used to conceal conspiratorial activity.

We have seen that the key tactic in the bolshevik strategy of access has been "unity." The communists have not gained very much from the simple ability to join other organizations, to have the narrow and literal access such a right affords. Their successes have depended on the capacity to induce other groups, through united action, to expose themselves politically as well as organizationally. It may be said indeed that organizational successes, in unity ventures, are empty unless they are accompanied by political victories, i.e., an actual gain in influence over the minds of the target elements. The most important such gain, a prelude to many others, is that which asserts the {332} continuity of communist aims with those of noncommunist groups.

The acceptance of communists on this basis affords them significant access to the ranks and to politically naive elements in the leadership. This is quite different from accepting the right of communists to belong to an organization when this right can be declared a derivative from the simple fact of citizenship. To debar communists from unions, or from the schools, is to raise questions of basic importance to the character of the constitutional order. But it may be suggested that formal exclusion solves nothing: it is not very useful when relevant, and it is unnecessary when irrelevant. If it is understood that the problem is not one of simple access, but of political collaboration, then we may conclude that the whole question of communist exclusion, with its constitutional implications, can be set aside. For then the problem becomes one of educating those who accept the "united-front" psychology—a task which may well be hindered rather than aided by repressive measures.

It follows that in the general attempt to deny access to the communists, the group to be given most attention is *not the communists themselves, but their collaborators*. This simply reverses the Leninist insight that given their objectives, the "main enemy" is not the capitalists, but those who sustain social order while seeking reform. At the same time, the anticommunists ought not to recapitulate the early Leninist experience, in which isolation and annihilation of reformists was conceived to be the appropriate strategic objective. Rather, an attempt should be made to discriminate among these groups, winning over some and isolating others, with particular emphasis on the organizational roles they play.

Conclusion

Our final point will serve to re-emphasize the *subordinate* role of organizational activity in the struggle against totalitarianism. Early in this study organizational strategy was defined as a derivative political strategy designed to maximize the utility of organizational weapons. To speak of organizational strategy and tactics is to define a special {333} sphere of interest and action. It must not be forgotten that this sphere is limited, providing special increments of power to political elites whose fundamental sources of weakness and strength must be looked for elsewhere.

From the general political perspective, rather than the narrowly organizational one which has primarily concerned us here, the strategic advantages of communism include (1) its historic plausibility, as that is bolstered by its relation to the Soviet Union, and (2) the instability of democratic society. In its quest for a monopoly of power, bolshevik political strategy links a revolutionary elite to whatever social forces are set in motion against existing authority. We have been concerned to show the organizational dimension of this linkage, but ultimately success or failure depends on the ability of the movement to provide "answers" to felt needs within the body politic.

The historic plausibility of communism stems in part from its capacity to bring order out of confusion, to master (without destroying) the industrial system, to provide new (if false) hope of security to an anxiety-laden population. These advantages are real and not illusory. They must be faced, for it is clear that the cost in tyranny, war, and moral decay will be paid by the masses, if the alternative is continued and acute anxiety. This price, however, is paid with reluctance. When there is another solution, retaining traditional political and moral values, it will be preferred to the communist answer. The reluctance of the masses to embrace communism is a strategic advantage for democracy, but it can be exploited only if social stability is maintained.

We must conclude, therefore, that in the long view political combat plays only a tactical role. Great social issues, such as those which divide communism and democracy, are not decided by political combat, perhaps not even by military clashes. They are decided by the relative ability of the contending systems to win and to maintain enduring loyalties. Consequently, no amount of power and cunning, in the realm of political combat, can avail in the absence of measures which rise to the height of the times.

INDEX

Page numbers reference the pagination used in the original editions. They are retained for purposes of continuity and referencing. The page numbers are embedded into the text by the use of brackets.

ABOUT THE AUTHOR

PHILIP SELZNICK (1919–2010) was Professor of Law and Sociology at the University of California, Berkeley. He was the founding chair of the Center for the Study of Law and Society and of the Jurisprudence and Social Policy Program in the School of Law. His other acclaimed books include *TVA and the Grass Roots*; *Leadership in Administration*; *Law, Society and Industrial Justice*; *Law and Society in Transition* (with Philippe Nonet); *The Moral Commonwealth*; *The Communitarian Persuasion*; and, in 2008, *A Humanist Science*.

qp

Visit us at *www.quidprobooks.com.*

www.ingramcontent.com/pod-product-compliance
Lightning Source LLC
Chambersburg PA
CBHW051953270326
41929CB00015B/2641